Patrick T. McWilliams

EXPOSITORY HERMENEUTICS: AN INTRODUCTION

ELLIOTT E. JOHNSON

Academie
Books   Grand Rapids,
Michigan
Zondervan Publishing House

Expository Hermeneutics: An Introduction
Copyright © 1990 by Elliott E. Johnson

Requests for information should be addressed to:
Zondervan Publishing House
Academic and Professional Books
Grand Rapids, Michigan 49530

The quotations from *The Validity of Interpretation* by E. D. Hirsch, Jr., are used with the permission of the publisher, Yale University Press, New Haven, Connecticut. Copyright © 1967 by the Yale University Press.

All Scripture quotations, unless otherwise noted, are taken from the HOLY BIBLE: NEW INTERNATIONAL VERSION (North American Edition). Copyright © 1973, 1978, 1984, by the International Bible Society. Used by permission of Zondervan Bible Publishers.

Library of Congress Cataloging in Publication Data

Johnson, Elliott E.
    Expository hermeneutics : an introduction / Elliott E. Johnson.
        p.   cm.
    Bibliography: p.
    Includes index.
    ISBN 0-310-34160-4
    1. Bible—Hermeneutics. I. Title.
BS476.J64   1989   89-15143
220.6'01—dc20   CIP

Edited by James E. Ruark

Printed in the United States of America

92 93 94 95 96 / DH / 10 9 8 7 6 5 4 3 2

This edition is printed on acid-free paper and meets the American National Standards Institute Z39.48 standard.

To my family
My wife Inge and children
Glenda, James, Phillip, Cristie,
Karis, and Jonathan
as we grow together toward Christlikeness

CONTENTS

Preface

A professor of mine once said, "Careful thinking is difficult, but clear thinking about thinking is even more difficult." This thought relates very well to the intriguing subject matter in *Expository Hermeneutics*. Thoughtful consideration in the reading of the Bible is our first step. Then hermeneutics reflects upon the reading, the interpretations, and exposition of the Bible. In addition, it considers the "Babel of Interpretations" and thh problem of judging which interpretation is valid among the various options.

The difficulty of the task is only matched by the reward of working through the maze of uncertainty and specifying a complex of reasoned answers. There is a clarity to be gained in not only stating what the passage means, but in specifying why these judgments are made. This clarity lends its weight to a strengthened sense of conviction ultimately based on the test of the relevant evidence judged to support the valid interpretation.

From the time I first worked my way through these questions, there have been many who have contributed to my understanding and the development of this book. I want to thank many of my professors and colleagues, who challenged my thinking about the biblical text while at the same time encouraging me to live and minister in response to biblical authority. This is where my journey began. Students have also challenged my thinking—and receive my gratitude. Among the many, Michael Green has served as a friend and contributor in the composition of draft editions. The administration and staff of Dallas Theological Seminary have also provided help in the production of these draft editions. As the book has finally taken shape, I wish to thank Jim Ruark of Zondervan Publishing House, whose editorial work both sharpened the focus of what was said and also clarified the way in which it was expressed.

Introduction

Let's recite a familiar nursery rhyme:

Little Jack Horner sat in a corner
Eating his Christmas pie.
He stuck in his thumb
And pulled out a plum
And said, "What a good boy am I!"

We all probably recited this rhyme often as children without ever once thinking about what it *really* means. *Means?* Like many nursery rhymes it seems to be mostly nonsense and fun.

Yet it is claimed by some that a number of nursery rhymes trace their origins to historical events and come down to us as veiled parables because of the political intrigues of those times. "Jack Horner" was supposedly the steward of the Abbot of Glastonbury during the time of the dissolution of the monasteries in England. By subterfuge "Jack" came into possession of the deeds to the nearby Manor of Mells and was commissioned to bear the documents, concealed in a pastry, to King Henry VIII for safety. On the way, however, he lifted the crust and extracted the "plum," presumably motivated to do so by bribe or other personal gain. A fanciful explanation, to be sure, but it has persisted for lo these many centuries.[1]

How about a psychological interpretation? We surmise that ill-mannered little Jack has been sent away from the table and consigned to a corner—a typical punishment in childhood. But his compassionate—or perhaps over-permissive—parents let him have dessert anyway. And the ill-mannered boy, not having learned his lesson, eats the dessert with his fingers, demonstrating the same bad manners that he did during the festive holiday meal when all the relatives were there. But Jack has the last laugh. "Good" may mean "clever" or "smart," for Jack has figured out that even if he misbehaves he will be able to get what he wants next time.

There may be still another meaning. Perhaps the nursery rhyme originated in an undeveloped country where the customs are radically different from those in the West. Jack sits in front of a family shrine in a crude, dirt-floored hut bereft of table and chairs. He is enjoying a special treat that even the poorest families go to great lengths to provide for this special holiday celebration because of its symbolic connection to the exalted God of the Plum Harvest. Little Jack, amid all the trappings of Third World poverty, nevertheless feels happy and contented because he knows that the spirits have smiled providentially and perserved all his family for another year.

Of course, these interpretations also

---

[1]Ivor H. Evans, ed., *Brewer's Dictionary of Phrase and Fable* (New York: Harper & Row, 1981), 600–601.

raise many questions: Who wrote the nursery rhyme, and what were the circumstances at the time of writing? What meaning did the author intend to convey in writing what he did? Did the words have the same sense for him as they have for us? What did the nursery rhyme mean to those who first heard it, and what by distinction does it mean to us?

And there we have hermeneutics in a nutshell. We thought childish rhymes were—well, childish rhymes. Yet this innocent-sounding nursery rhyme captures all the complexities of interpretation—not that far different from the kinds of hermeneutical problems Christians encounter when they confront a writing of far greater significance, the Bible.

TO KNOW THE BIBLE

Lay Bible study is so commonplace today, we easily forget that a mere five hundred years ago few people even had a Bible. The Bible was accessible only to the privileged professionals who had learned the dead classical languages in which the Scriptures were written. Today Bible study takes so many forms— personal devotions, small groups, television teachings—that we sometimes forget what a risky business it can be. Even the various and somewhat sophisticated Bible study methods available to us don't eliminate the pitfalls. These risks, whether or not we are conscious of them as we pull up our chairs for a small-group study, involve our understanding of the biblical text at hand. This problem of meaning can be reduced to two basic questions: *How do I know?* and *How do I know that I know?*

The thoughtful student is not only aware of these issues, but also recognizes that some kind of control or guidance is necessary to overcome the subjective influences each person brings to the reading of the Bible,

namely, premises, assumptions, and theological biases. This control is the business of hermeneutics. This book is about hermeneutics and its contribution to Bible study.

Hermeneutics is frequently defined as the science of textual interpretation of the Bible. As such it forms a natural complement to Bible study methods that seek to encourage the skill of biblical interpretation. But beginning with the work of the German theologian and philosopher F. E. D. Schleiermacher (1768–1834), the field of general hermeneutics developed, a scientific discipline that seeks to set out rules of interpretation to apply to all kinds of writing. It is not possible today to study biblical hermeneutics without considering the influence and concepts of general hermeneutics. So while this text is particularly concerned with biblical interpretation, the concerns and questions of general hermeneutics will intrude frequently into the discussion.

A wide range of disciplines contributes to the science of hermeneutics today. *Philosophy* enters the discussion through theories in communication of *verbal meaning,* in *epistemology* (theories of knowledge), and in the analysis of *language* and its expression of meaning.

Linguistics impinges on hermeneutics in terms of the scientific study of language. This includes *phonology* (speech sounds), *morphology* (the form and structure of language), *syntax* (the order of words in a sentence), and *semantics* (the nature and structure of meanings).

As a science, hermeneutics has not enjoyed the respect of the natural sciences because so little is understood about human cognition and verbal communication. Yet it is science, because it uses empirical processes to answer those two big, basic questions: How do I know, and how do I know that I know? From those processes have developed two broadly different but complementary strategies for biblical interpretation—one seeking to guide and control the legitimate practice of interpretation, the other seeking to test the relative merits of varying interpretive conclusions.

THE STRATEGY OF "LITERAL INTERPRETATION"

The first strategy, legitimate practice, recurs in church history as "literal interpretation." The term *literal* has been understood in at least two ways: (1) the clear, plain sense of a word or phrase as over against a figurative use, and (2) a system that views the text as providing the basis of the true interpretation. This twofold use of "literal" has resulted in a great deal of confusion. Removed from its proper context of hermeneutical discourse, the phrase "literal interpretation of the Bible" is often and erroneously taken (as by secular media) in the first sense and is construed as devaluing any figurative understanding of biblical language.

Our attention will be focused on the second sense of "literal," a system which, as conceived in the Protestant Reformation, promotes two important values:

1. A literal hermeneutic rests in the *right and responsibility* of the priesthood of the individual believer. The prerogatives of the priest as set forth in the Scriptures included his hearing the voice of God in the interpretation of divine revelation. This necessarily involved some means of testing the validity of that interpretation;

2. A literal hermeneutic places primary importance on the *historical* realm within which God's original revelation was expressed. The historical realm provides both the context of the original expression and the particular stage in the progress of biblical revelation when the message was expressed.

When it comes to biblical hermeneutics, therefore, we are concerned not only with rules of interpretation, but also with the matter of progressive revelation. The doctrine of inspiration is vitally important. In chapter 3 we will discuss how the premises, or principles, of general hermeneutics apply to Scripture and whether the Bible can be interpreted the same way as other writings such as a Shakespearean play or a sonnet by Milton or a novel by Kurt Vonnegut.

Given the differences of opinion regarding inspiration, it is understandable that some biblical scholars hold that modern advances in linguistics, literary studies, and the philosophy of language have made the literal system obsolete and out of date. But this book takes the view that these advances enhance our understanding of the hermeneutical premises and therefore the practice of interpretation as well.

These hermeneutical premises are to Bible study what a rule book is to a game. It is obvious that we can't just make up our own rules as we go along. To develop a set of rules that are fair, consistent, useful, and able to cover all contingencies requires much thought and hard work. But without such rules no one would be able to play the game a second time. Similarly, much thought and hard work are needed to understand the hermeneutical premises, but there is no substitute for this. Our understanding of the words that communicate God's revelation, the Bible, are influenced by the direction and control established in the hermeneutical premises.

When we speak of verbal communication, we have in mind not simply the transmission of information through the symbols of language, but especially the sharing of meaning between an author and a reader. Biblical hermeneutics involves studying the way that information is conveyed from the author (in *what* he says, *how* he chooses to say it, and *why*) so that the reader (who brings his own background and assumptions and biases to the situation) will understand what the author intended to communicate.

Author's intent considers all the relevant factors of the context to narrow the possible meanings down to one intended in the composition. The basic unit of meaning communicated is *an author's unit of text*. There is a widespread—and naïve—assumption in biblical exegesis that the *word* is the basic unit of meaning. This assumption is called into question by practitioners in various fields of linguistic and literary study. Each interpreter sets out to identify according to his particular discipline what are the boundaries of the meaningful unit, whether they embrace a sentence or a paragraph or even a book as a whole. It is emphasized in linguistic analysis that the textual unit does not commonly correspond to the semantic unit (a word or phrase). Literary analysis focuses attention on genre units (the forms of literary composition, such as story, poetry, or drama) to determine whether they characterize a whole book or only themes and motifs contained in the book.

A whole series of mistaken conclusions results from the faulty attention given to individual words. If words are the basic carrier of meaning, then a sentence conveys merely the sum of the meaning values of its components, the words. Therefore exhaustive interpretation must proceed by way of analysis—word by word, morpheme by morpheme—that divides a sentence into smaller and smaller units before they are all added together into the sentence once again. Such an approach may seem to be supported by a theory of verbal, plenary inspiration, but it is actually based on ignorance about the nature of language, literature, and communication in general. The meaning of a word depends not only on the textual sign itself, but also on its relation to other words and sentences that form the context of the author's literary composition. The consideration of all these contextual factors determines the type of meaning the author expresses. Thus the basic unit of meaning as regards the author's intent is not the word; rather, it is the author's text considered at first as a whole. The process legitimately goes, not from the smallest unit to larger ones, but from the largest context to smaller ones.

In this model of communication (and epistemology), the author's intended meaning is expressed in the text, but the understanding comes from the *construction* given the meaning by the reader. Because the aim in the task of interpretation is to reconstruct the limits of the text's meaning, the reader is obliged to *share in* what the author expresses, and the author is obliged to *communicate within* the realm of what the reader can share. Obviously it is possible that the Author/author[2] intends to say more than the original audience would recognize based on what they share at that moment in history. In the progress of revelation, more may become known about what was said, and subsequent audiences may understand the full intent better than the original audience.

Do you see what is happening here? Whereas lay Bible study is often concerned with words as the primary carrier of meaning, we are no longer talking about words. We have encountered literary form, linguistic analysis, and even the historical situation of the Au-

---

[2] "Author/author" refers to both the divine Author and the human writer. The construct does not assume a method of providential revelation or superintendence in writing, but it builds on the fact of both.

thor/author and their original audience. We have not just a text, but a context.

One semanticist writes:

Any meaningful linguistic unit, up to and including the complete utterance, has meaning in *context*. The context of the utterance is the situation in which it occurs. . . . Situation must be given *equal weight* with linguistic form in semantic theory.[3]

We are not going to concern ourselves greatly with semantics in our study of hermeneutics. While we will incorporate some aspects of semantic theory, with its emphasis on context and linguistic form, we will devote much more attention to literary analysis, which emphasizes literary composition and the author's intended meaning. The point is that whatever the particular discipline, we must deal with more than individual words or phrases in the science of interpretation.

This is entirely in keeping with the literal system of interpretation that came into prominence during the Reformation. The Reformers sought to promote direction and control in the interpretive process by applying four premises, or maxims, under the umbrella of the literal system: grammatical, historical, literary, and theological. All these maxims apply generally in the practice of interpretation, but we will find that each applies with greater or lesser probability to a particular passage of Scripture. The better an interpreter understands these premises, the more skillful he will be in applying them in a legitimate fashion.

In brief, therefore, we can say that we begin the task of interpretation by recognizing a *synopsis,* or summary, of the type of meaning of the whole book. This is commonly the perspective of literary analysis (see Mortimer Adler and Charles Van Doren, *How to Read a Book*). From the synopsis we go to an analysis of the type of meaning in the context, from which word and phrase units are then *exegeted.*

THE STRATEGY OF VALIDATION

The second strategy of hermeneutics that originated in the Reformation is to devise a means of testing the relative merit of an interpretive conclusion. While the Roman Catholic Church advocates a hierarchy of authoritative interpreters and tradition, Protestant churches have usually looked to doctrinal confessions as the means of testing interpretations. But confessions provide little help toward interpreting a particular passage of Scripture.

Given the importance of validation to textual interpretation, we need more than the test of a general maxim. Some standard is needed so that any particular interpretation can be judged for accuracy. How easy it would be if we had an answer section at the end of every Bible to provide a universal statement of meaning! Alas! We are left instead to find the standard in the *goal* of interpretation stated in a *prescriptive norm* of what must be interpreted if the interpretation is to accurately correspond to the text's meaning. This is to be distinguished from a *descriptive norm,* which would describe the meaning in some respect. The goal of interpretation proposed in this book is the Author/author's intended meaning as expressed in the text.

This system of literal interpretation further rests on two assumptions that set the framework for the task of hermeneutics: (1) evangelical belief (including the content of the gospel, the inerrant character of Scripture, and the necessity of Spirit-guided revelation), and (2) expository ministry (meaning to be unfolded from the biblical text).

---

[3]John Lyons, *Semantics* (New York: Cambridge University Press, 1977), 2:572.

These assumptions do not prescribe the meaning of any text in question, but do provide the framework within which the text's meaning is expressed and outside of which no meaning can be validated.

The reader will do well to refer as needed to the glossary of technical terms related to the tasks of hermeneutics and validation, as found at the back of this textbook.

PART ONE

BIBLE STUDY AND HERMENEUTICS

Introduction

There is an old saying that all young hunters learn: "If you don't know what you're trying to hit, unless you are a terrible shot you probably will miss." The same principle holds true for the work of attempting to interpret the Bible. The first question that any interpreter must answer is "What am I trying to do?" or "What is the goal of interpretation?" Part 1 proposes a goal of interpretation that is compatible with an evangelical commitment and an expository ministry.

For some students of the Bible the goal of interpretation is assumed and is not open to question. Thus, devoting four chapters of a book to the determination and defense of a goal for interpretation may seem unnecessary. However, there are two reasons why it is needed: (1) all Christians should be able not only to state what they believe but also to make a defense for what they believe, and (2) the choice of a goal in interpretation has such far-reaching effects on the interpretation of a text that even when interpreters with different goals use the same methods of Bible study, they might well arrive at different and often incompatible conclusions.

Chapter 1 will compare inductive Bible Study and hermeneutics with a view to demonstrating the need to go beyond inductive Bible study to the kinds of questions raised and answered by hermeneutics. In a word, hermeneutics provides the reader of a text with premises for interpretation and with strategies for applying these premises in a consistent manner. Because valid hermeneutical premises must be based on consistent thinking in epistemology, this subject will be discussed. It will be shown that a conservative or evangelical hermeneutical system uses five premises to recognize viable interpretations (literal, grammatical, historical, literary, theological). These premises will be developed more fully in chapter 3.

Chapter 2 will focus on defining the goal of interpretation as clearly as possible. The goal of interpretation proposed in this book is "to know the Author's/author's intended meaning as it is expressed in the text." Since the key idea to define in this statement of the goal is "intended" (or "intention" or "intend"), this concept will be shown to be ancient, widespread in use, and essential to the nature of communication. The difficulty with the term "intention" is that what it refers to is not to be equated with psychological experiences or thoughts of the author unless expressed in the text. In addition, it should not be thought of as indicating that the interpreter is searching for meanings which the author only desired or attempted to communicate. "Intention" is restricted to ideas actually expressed in the text.

Chapter 3 will examine the goal of interpretation in light of the five premises of an evangelical hermeneutical system introduced in chapter 1. As a result, the evangelical interpreter should become confident that an evangelical hermeneutic is reasonable, explainable, and consistent with the nature of the Bible.

Chapter 4 will give a response to eight significant and frequently stated objections to the proposed goal of interpretation.

CHAPTER 1

Inductive Bible Study and Hermeneutics

The two disciplines of inductive Bible study[1] and hermeneutics[2] are quite distinct from each other, but they are complementary and can be profitably examined together. The prominence of these two disciplines in the contemporary study of the Bible is in part the result of an epistemological crisis. People are asking two related but different questions, as we have already seen:

How do I know?

How do I know that I know?

Evangelicals propose that inductive Bible study is the answer to how we may know the Bible. They propose hermeneutics as the answer to how we may know that we know the Bible and know what it says in the modern world. There are some clear differences between the two disciplines.

---

[1] Inductive Bible study became a primary focus at Biblical Seminary in New York under its founder, Wilbert W. White. This tradition was developed by: Howard T. Kuist, *These Words Upon Thy Heart* (Richmond: John Knox Press, 1947); Charles R. Eberhardt, *The Bible in the Making of Ministers* (New York: Association Press, 1949); Robert Traina, *Methodical Bible Study* (1952; reprint, Grand Rapids: Zondervan, 1985). The work at Biblical Seminary was further developed at Wheaton College by Merrill C. Tenney, *Galatians* (Grand Rapids: Eerdmans, 1950), and at Dallas Theological Seminary by Howard Hendricks.

[2] Milton S. Terry's *Biblical Hermeneutics: A Treatise on the Interpretation of the Old and New Testaments* has been *the* American textbook in the field. It was first published in 1833 and republished in a revised edition in 1890 with a further revision in 1911 that was republished in 1952 (Grand Rapids: Zondervan) for use as a textbook and resource. Continuing interest in conservative interpretation prompted a series of texts: David Robert Dungars, *Hermeneutics: A Textbook* (Cincinnati: Standard Publishing, 1888); Sylvester Burnham, *The Elements of Biblical Hermeneutics* (Hamilton, N.Y.: Republic Press, 1916); George H Schodde, *Outlines of Biblical Hermeneutics: A Handbook for Students of the Word* (Columbus: Lutheran Book Concern, 1917); J. Edwin Hartill, *Biblical Hermeneutics* (Grand Rapids: Zondervan, 1947, reprint 1960); Rollin Thomas Chafer, *The Science of Biblical Hermeneutics: An Outline Study of Its Laws* (Dallas: Bibliotheca Sacra, 1939).

More recently the term *hermeneutics* has been relegated to a subtitle in favor of the more popular term *interpretation*: Louis Berkhof, *Principles of Biblical Interpretation* (Grand Rapids: Baker, 2d ed. 1952); Bernard Ramm, *Protestant Biblical Interpretation: A Textbook of Hermeneutics for Conservative Protestants* (Boston: W. A. Wilde, 1950, rev. ed. 1956); and A. Berkeley Mickelsen, *Interpreting the Bible* (Grand Rapids: Eerdmans, 1963).

Inductive Bible Study	Hermeneutics
Establishes the priority of the study of the biblical text itself.	Provides the balancing focus on normative premises that both guide toward viable interpretive practice and guard against illegitimate interpretive conclusions.
Presents methods and procedures in the study of the text.	Considers strategies leading toward understanding the text and emphasizes goals to be pursued in the study of it.
Requires that certain steps be followed in a specific order with a view to considering all the textual data with an open mind toward the meaning being expressed.	Brings alongside this the necessary extra textual data and broadened contextual considerations also needed to understand the meaning expressed.

Study methods are limited to the task of interpretation, while hermeneutics addresses the validation of accurate interpretation.

INDUCTIVE BIBLE STUDY

Inductive study sets a necessary goal because we want to know the Bible. An inductive process of learning is one in which we use the particulars of a passage to draw out a general meaning. This is the opposite of a deductive process, in which we begin with a premise or a universal statement and follow it to its logical conclusions according to the evidence offered in the text.

The sermons we hear on Sunday may use either approach. We could say more about sermons, because preaching is part of a continuum that leads back to exegesis, which in turn traces back to hermeneutics. But our concern is with Bible study. More relevant is the form of inductive study, using a threefold procedure, that is used widely in various Bible study manuals: observation (what does the text say?) leads to

interpretation (what does the text mean?), which leads to application (what does the text mean to me?). The quality of this or any other kind of Bible study, whether highly structured or casual, is only as good as the interpretive process employed with it.

Robert Traina writes, "The genius of an inductive approach to Scripture is its open-ended, experimental nature."[3] If we want to know the Bible, we must avoid bringing our preconceived conclusions to the text. We must study the text and allow the text to speak to us.

The open-ended character of inductive study must influence both our attitude and our practice. In attitude we need to be open-minded and let the text speak for itself. In practice, we must give priority to direct and independent study of the biblical text in sequence and in focus. By "sequence" we mean that our interpretation must rest on textual data and must be limited by textual meanings. By "focus" is meant that our study must be biblical if we are to be biblicists in our thinking, living, and preaching.

It is easy to see that, for all its

[3] Robert Traina, "Inductive Bible Study Reexamined in the Light of Contemporary Hermeneutics" in *Interpreting God's Word for Today,* ed. Wayne McCown and James Earl Massey (Anderson, Ind.: Warner, 1982), 53.

virtues, inductive Bible study provides an inadequate model for a complete and sufficient study of Scripture.

It is inadequate first of all because there is no such thing as "pure" inductive study. We all necessarily bring premises or presuppositions to the study of the text. Those premises affect the way we comprehend the meaning, the way we understand—that is, they have epistemological influence. This influence in the interpreter has been at the center of hermeneutical concerns since the time of Immanuel Kant (1724–1804).

Second, along with the interpreter's epistemological influence, hermeneutics must also deal with the writer's premises. It was Schleiermacher who first turned the attention of the interpreters away from the textual materials themselves toward the premises of the writer. This concern for the epistemological influence of the writer's premises led to a critical reassessment of the historicity and truthfulness of the biblical text (higher criticism) and more recently to development of "the new hermeneutic" (à la Bultmann), which focuses on the relevance of the ancient subject matter to the modern reader.

In either case, some way of dealing with a writer's and an interpreter's premises must be dealt with in the study of the Bible. Some premises are legitimate, such as a knowledge of the language and the historical occasion, and these are necessary in developing an accurate and precise understanding of textual meanings. Other premises in

inductive study are illegitimate because they either distort the meanings expressed or mislead the student to consider indeterminate or inconsequential issues. Human induction has inherent weaknesses. As a result, some discipline is needed that can distinguish between legitimate and illegitimate premises and guide the inductive study toward the most profitable issues. This discipline is called "hermeneutics," a word derived from the name of Hermes, the Greek messenger god. Hermeneutics helps us to know the Bible.

HERMENEUTICS

As we begin to investigate hermeneutics we quickly become aware of the wide range of issues involved. It may be an oversimplification, but we can see two primary issues reappearing throughout the history of interpretation concerning "how I can know that I know."

1. How can I know that what I know is true? (The critical issue).

2. How can I know that what I know is meaningful even in the modern world? (The relevance issue).

These two questions have been handled in quite different ways in the history of interpretation, leading to different conclusions and one or the other being given higher priority at a particular time[4] These answers and emphases

---

[4]Perhaps the most influential single factor in the history of interpretation has been the historical-critical method emerging late in the Enlightenment and being controlled by a scientific worldview. Before that point, interpreters largely accepted the biblical worldview in literal interpretation, which gave greater priority to the textual statements as spoken by God. Allegorical interpretation gave greater priority to the divine origin of the meanings that were not as closely tied to the text. The text provided a critical control in literal interpretation, and the divine Author brought a focus on the relevance for the allegorical interpretation. During the period of the historical-critical method, critical issues were judged, not by the text, but by a scientific worldview that held prominence. In the

were the foundational elements in the various hermeneutical systems. Each system has two elements in common: a faith position and a reasoned system.

A Faith Position

A *faith position* is the foundation of any system and begins with a response to what the Bible claims to be true of itself; the Bible is the Word of God.[5] Conservative, evangelical scholars have taken the Word of God at face value, in a direct way.[6] That is, the simple words of Scripture as written in the original manuscripts are the very words of God. Others, while taking the term "Word of God" seriously, set it in a broader context; so Karl Barth viewed the Word of God as event (Christ), as witness (Scripture), and as proclamation (apostolic preaching).

In either case, the faith position focuses on the question "has God said?" On the conservative side, faith rests in the received text as given in the original manuscripts as the very word of God. In regard to interpretation, the text that is handled after all the textual criticism has been done is still treated as the word of God.

B. B. Warfield formulated the position that has become the mainstay of thought for most evangelicals in the twentieth century. The doctrine of inspiration assures us that the Bible is God's Word. The doctrine as it is taught is *methodologically indispensable* for achieving a true interpretation of the text, but it is *logically dispensable* insofar as defense of the doctrine and the teaching of individual passages are concerned. Warfield argued as follows:

> Let it not be said that thus we found the whole Christian system upon the doctrine of plenary inspiration. We found the whole Christian system on the doctrine of plenary inspiration as little as we found it upon the doctrine of angelic existences. Were there no such thing as inspiration, Christianity would be true, and all its essential doctrines would be credibly witnessed to us in the general trustworthy reports of the teaching of our Lord and of his authoritative agents in founding the Church, preserved in the writings of the apostles and their first followers.[7]

Therefore, according to Warfield's reasoning, accepting this faith position in hermeneutics as methodologically indispensable does not violate objectivity. It is simply taking what the Scriptures say at face value in what they claim about God's authorship. An interpretation that is judged to be valid is still subject to a defense of its truthfulness. So the faith position forms the methodological base for the hermeneutical tasks, but the conclusions of interpretation are themselves subject to verification. In making this distinction, the conclusions that we reach based on the faith position are subject to testing; thus the faith position is not an assumption of what we seek to prove. We do

---

postcritical period, relevance has become the focus, and that judged largely by the values of the culture of modern man.

[5] David H. Kelsey, *The Uses of Scripture in Recent Theology* (Philadelphia: Fortress, 1975). Kelsey organizes three faith positions: (1) the Word of God is the very words of the text as expressed in the original manuscripts, (2) the Word of God is the human witness and recital to the events of God in history, and (3) the word of God is the human, imaginative literary expression of the events of God.

[6] Wayne Grudem, "Scripture's Self-Attestation and the Problem of Formulating a Doctrine of Scripture" in *Scripture and Truth,* ed. D. A. Carson and John D. Woodbridge (Grand Rapids: Zondervan, 1983), 19–59.

[7] Benjamin B. Warfield, *The Inspiration and Authority of the Bible* (reprint, Philadelphia: Presbyterian and Reformed, 1948), 210.

not get caught in a casuistic vicious circle.

On the critical side, faith resides either in reason or in contemporary values to answer the question "has God said?" A Jewish commentary offers an example of this approach: "the view that the Bible contains God's message to man has led to ever new interpretations, since it constantly forced believing readers to reconcile the words of the sacred text with whatever they held to be true on the basis of their own experience, the canons of logic, contemporary science, and their moral insights."[8] Another example of critical faith is the Protestant scholar Rudolf Bultmann, who seeks a canon within the canon based on what he regards as "ruthless honesty and absolute clarity" of historical criticism aimed to discover "what really happened."

A Reasoned System

Based on these faith positions, *reasoned systems* are constructed to comprehend "what God has said." Such systems seek to discern reasons in support of the most accurate or probable interpretation. It is in these tasks of reasoning that hermeneutics is concerned with recognizing viable interpretations and testing for their validity. As in the conservative faith position, a reasoned system finds a sense of relevance in an accurate interpretation of what God has said—that is, the word of God makes sense to us here and now.

Despite the distinctions between the faith position and a reasoned system, faith and reason have mutual influence in any epistemology. Neither element is completely absent. In the view of many evangelicals, faith not only establishes "God has said" but is also involved in comprehending "what God has said."

Yet by reason we consider the sense in which "God has said" should be taken and by reason we repel objections to our conclusions that "God has said" lest faith have an inadequate basis. It is consistent with the evangelical commitment to hold that while the faith position and a reasoned system can be distinguished methodologically, we can also recognize their logical mutual contribution. The model is established in the ministry of Christ. Christ offered himself as God's provision to be accepted by faith, yet the offer was always accompanied by evidences that demonstrated the reasonableness of the offer.

In this book we will develop a system of evangelical hermeneutics that rests upon an evangelical view of Scripture, a position ultimately received in faith but developed through a system of consistent, reasoned principles. As a reasoned system, it is a science of viable and valid interpretation. And as a science it seeks to analyze the tasks involved in textual interpretation that are consistent with the inductive study of the Bible. In addition, the science seeks to discern principles of viable interpretation that help us to recognize possible textual meanings in inductive study.

BASIC PREMISES OF INTERPRETATION

There are five premises, which have already been mentioned in connection with the Reformation.

1. Literal affirms that the meanings to be interpreted are textually based. This premise sets the framework for the system. All the other premises are derived from and developed within the scope of what literal affirms.

---

[8]Fritz A. Rothschild, "Truth and Metaphor in the Bible," *Conservative Judaism* 25 (1971): 4.

2. Grammatical affirms that these textually based meanings are expressed within the limits of common language usage. Language is polysemic, which means that any word or phrase or even any sentence is capable of multiple senses. These limits may be difficult to discern, but they still exist in theory and remain a legitimate aspect of hermeneutical study and interpretive goals.

3. Historical affirms that these textually based meanings refer, depending on their textual usage, to either historical or heavenly realities, to either natural or spiritual subjects. Moreover, we can look for allusions and references to situational meanings of the time when the piece was written.

4. Literary affirms that these textually based meanings are in part determined within the context of textual design considered in the composition as a whole. The textual composition incorporates such literary characteristics as coherent unity and prominence. In addition, the textual design incorporates the conventional norms of the literary genre.

5. Theological affirms that the textually based meanings are ultimately expressed by God through human agency. As such, the historical realm is not the source nor even the primary influence of the human author's knowledge and textual message. Therefore, textually expressed meanings that have their source in God are necessarily true and must be understood in a sense consistent with the theological context and the theological meanings. In addition, the message must be understood as progressively revealed in the historical progress of the canon.

A viable interpretation must consider all these premises. Note that these premises do not guarantee accurate interpretation; rather, they guard us against thoughtless errors and unrelated presuppositions. The question of the validity of an interpretation is judged on its merits according to the weight of the evidence. So again, as we have stated, the work of hermeneutics has two primary aspects. One is a theory of interpretation, which is associated with the task of viable interpretation (how do I know?); the other is a theory of validation, which is concerned with the task of valid interpretation (how do I know that I know?).

The premises of viable interpretation are designed to guide and direct inductive Bible study. This task and the consideration of these premises will be considered in the remainder of part 1 and in parts 2, 3, and 4. Our goal will be to clarify the hermeneutical basis and the inductive means of "coming to know the Bible."

Part 5 will consider the separate task of validation. It begins with the products of inductive Bible studies that are viable. In validation, the goal is to weigh and judge the relative merits of the various viable interpretations.

CHAPTER 2

The Goal of Interpretation

In one sense, an evangelical who has chosen to do inductive Bible study has already chosen a goal for interpretation. That goal is simply to know the Bible. The discipline of hermeneutics does not change the goal, but it can provide a clearer perspective on what we must know to claim to know the Bible. It also helps us to express that goal with greater awareness.

The initial problem an interpreter faces is that different hermeneutical approaches frame the goal in widely different terms. These approaches can be sorted into two categories: critical and relevant. *Critical* approaches develop a goal in which they may (1) emphasize demythologizing the biblical message, (2) critically reconstruct the literary form and content of the message, or (3) attempt to turn the critical focus on the textual traditions incorporated into the canonical manuscripts. *Relevant* approaches define the goal as a pertinent message for a modern audience—as the expression of an existential worldview, for example, or perhaps as a liberation message for a modern social struggle.

Our approach will incorporate both aspects. It will be *critical* in that an interpretation must be subject to a rational defense; it will be *relevant* in that a biblical message of God can be related to our day in some canonical sense. Our goal of interpretation—to know the Author's/author's intended meaning as expressed in the biblical text—satisfies both criteria: the critical criterion, because the Author's/author's textual usage provides a rational basis for judging what is claimed to be the meanings of the text; and the relevance criterion, because the Author, being God, continues to speak in some sense (2 Tim. 3:16) that makes his Word profitable and applicable.

This goal incorporates the five premises of viable interpretation defined in chapter 1, orders them within a strategy, and apportions to them an appropriate and related emphasis. In this chapter we will define the goal of interpretation. In chapter 3 the goal will be related to the five hermeneutical premises of viable interpretation. In chapter 4 this goal will be defended against criticism from proponents of other goals.

THE TERM *INTENDED*

The key word in our statement of the goal of interpretation is the word *in-*

tended. Several propositions will help to define and clarify the term.

1. The term "intend" in hermeneutics has enjoyed ancient, widespread usage among interpreters. An ancient and respected tradition bases biblical interpretation on both the textual expression (the specific phrase or passage in view) and a consideration of authorial composition. That is, this hermeneutical tradition asserts that the author sets the limits on the meaning communicated by a passage.

Various means have been used to discover where the author sets these limits. Some interpreters have looked for the key in the author's biography, or in other writings by the same author, or in the historical setting of the author's writing, or in the historical issues of the author's times. While the knowledge gained from this scholarly research is helpful, I contend that it does not determine what limits the author set on meaning in that particular textual expression. Rather, the limits of meaning are set by what the author wrote in the text while writing the book as a whole.

Early biblical interpreters prescribed these limits in the conflict that existed between the Antiochene and the Alexandrian methods of interpretation. The former was decidedly more rational, historical, literal, and Aristotelian; the latter, mystical, allegorical, and Platonic. In the Antiochene school, Theodore of Mopsuestia commented on Paul's use of Genesis in Galatians 4:22–23 by saying that Paul "attempts to prove his assertion from actual events as well as from their written record, which the Jews acknowledged as factual account. This certainly was his *intention* from the start."[1] Thus this leading figure of the Antiochene school stressed the interpretation of an *author's* meaning as expressed *in* the text. Furthermore, this meaning was seen as determined by the author's intention, or intended use of the language in the text.

Other writings reflect this perspective. Discussing James 2, John Calvin wrote, "It is not possible to understand what is being said, or to make any discerning judgment on the terms, unless one keeps an eye on the *intention* of the author."[2] Francis Turretin, another Reformed scholar, said, " 'Literal meaning' describes not only that which is based on the strict, not figurative, meaning of the words, by which it is distinguished from 'figurative meaning.' as was often done by the Fathers, but it also describes the meaning *intended* by the Holy Spirit and expressed either strictly or in figurative language."[3] Thomas Aquinas acknowledged the necessity of the literal meaning as "what the Holy Spirit or author *intends.*"[4]

Later on, B. B. Warfield recognized the importance of considering intention in interpretation of the life of Jesus:

The incidents which the narrators record, again, are not recorded with a biographical *intent,* and are not selected for their biographical significance, or ordered so as to present a biographical result: in the case of each evangelist they serve a particular purpose which may employ

---

[1]Theodore of Mopsuestia, *Commentary on Galatians 4:22–31,* trans. Karlfried Froehlich, 95–96 (emphasis added).

[2]John Calvin, *Calvin's Commentaries,* trans. A. W. Morrison, ed. David W. Torrance and Thomas F. Torrance, vol. 3 (Grand Rapids: Eerdmans, 1972), 285.

[3]Francis Turretin, *The Doctrine of Scripture,* trans. and ed. John W. Beardslee III (Grand Rapids: Baker, 1981), 200.

[4]Thomas Aquinas, *Summa Theologica,* 1.1.10C and 1.1.9.

biographical details, but it is not itself a biographical end.[5]

Milton S. Terry, in his highly regarded work *Biblical Hermeneutics,* recognized the role of intention. Discussing the single sense of the text, he wrote, "A fundamental principle in grammatical-historical exposition is that words and sentences can have but one signification in one and the same connection. The moment we neglect this principle we drift out upon a sea of uncertainty and conjecture." In the case of the book of Daniel, Terry wrote, "The writer *intended* to inform his readers in a particular way."[6]

In this century, Bernard Ramm has sought to present a system that would characterize conservative Protestantism. "This is the primary and basic need of hermeneutics: to ascertain what God has said in Sacred Scripture."[7] I. Howard Marshall has defined the goal of interpretation this way: "Our aim is to discover what the text meant in the mind of its original author for his *intended* audience. Exegesis seeks for an interpretation of a passage which will account satisfactorily for all the features of that passage, both on its own and in its context."[8]

All this shows that there is consistent testimony within the conservative Reformation tradition that the Author's/author's intended meaning is related to the goal of interpretation. The viewpoint of this textbook is that this intended meaning *is* the goal. This concept determines the limits of the possible textual meanings.

The goal of interpretation has been debated, not only in regard to the Bible, but in the field of general hermeneutics also. There has been a common line of thought in literary criticism in this century that contends that the meaning of a work is independent of its author. In this view, which E. D. Hirsch calls "authorial irrelevance," a piece of writing may have as many meanings as there are critics. Hirsch casts a skeptical eye on this viewpoint and argues forcefully that the meaning of a work lies in the intent of the author.

Almost any word sequence can, under the conventions of language, legitimately represent more than one complex of meaning. A word sequence means nothing in particular until somebody either means something by it or understands something from it. There is no magic land of meanings outside human consciousness. . . . Whenever meaning is attached to a sequence of words it is impossible to escape an author.

To banish the original author as the determiner of meaning was to reject the only compelling normative principle that could lend validity to an interpretation.[9]

P. D. Juhl goes a step further, for he is more dogmatic than Hirsch on the importance of the author's intention.

Whereas Hirsch is more or less explicitly offering a recommendation as to what critics ought to do in interpreting a text—namely, try to ascertain the author's intention—my view is that they are necessarily doing so already, in virtue of what it is for a literary work to have a certain meaning. . . .

[5] B. B. Warfield, *The Person and Work of Christ* (reprint, Grand Rapids: Baker, n.d.), 25.
[6] Milton S. Terry, *Biblical Hermeneutics* (1884; reprint, Grand Rapids: Zondervan, 1974), 205.
[7] Bernard Ramm, *Protestant Biblical Interpretation* (Boston: W. A. Wilde, 1956), ix and 89–96.
[8] I. Howard Marshall, ed., *New Testament Interpretation* (Grand Rapids: Eerdmans, 1977), 15.
[9] E. D. Hirsch, Jr., *Validity in Interpretation* (New Haven: Yale University Press, 1967), 4–5.

I shall attempt to uphold the view that there is a logical connection between statements about the meaning of a literary work and statements about the author's intention, such that a statement about the meaning of a work is a statement about the author's intention.[10]

Juhl is saying, therefore, that a statement about one is a statement about the other. But that says more than we want to say. While Hirsch regards the author's intention as a goal by choice in interpretation, Juhl sees it as a goal by necessity. It is only necessary in the broader model due to the nature of personal verbal communication. Verbal communication is the expression of a message by an author to a reader; to banish the author is to redefine communication.

There are valid questions about how appropriate Juhl's model is for biblical communication, since it was developed in the field of literary criticism to deal with a range of meanings in literature. The model is strained if the author is unknown or if the text is the product of an editor—or of multiple editors, as some critical scholars propose for certain books of the Bible. Therefore evangelicals must confine themselves to the textual data. Moreover, the Bible adds a factor that no human literature contains: God spoke through human prophets and through the words written by human authors. These human authors were responsible for the form of the text. Yet the Author, not the authors, ultimately determined what was to be communicated. So even with the complex questions that surround the identity of the human authors of the Bible, the intended meaning as expressed in the text is still the logically necessary goal of the interpreter who wants to hear God and communicate with him.

Alonso Schokel, writing in the Roman Catholic tradition, recognized the absence of this model of communication:

> The whole theory of the four senses was not applied by the Middle Ages to the authors of Scripture, but to the books, to the works themselves: the allegorical sense, and the tropological and anagogic senses, were there in the text, visible to the Christian who read with faith. They never asked whether or not the author of this or that book of the Old Testament perceived these senses with the same precision that they did.[11]

This situation, however, still leaves us with the task of defining "intended meaning." This is the function of proposition 2.

2. "Intended meaning" is that meaning which the Author/author has expressed in the written text. The difficulty raised by this proposition is that the word "intend" incorporates ambiguities because it refers to the author's role in the expression of meaning. It is clear that there are many aspects of the author's role in the writing of modern books, let alone ancient books, which are lost to interpreters. Thus certain definitions of "intent" must be rejected, as follows:

a. "Intention" is not to be identified with the psychological experience of the author. The proposed definition of "intention" excludes reference to any thoughts of the author, either before or during the time of writing, which are not expressed or implied in the text.

Some critics, however, would include the broader psychological experience of the author. Schleiermacher theorized that knowing the author is

---

[10] P. D. Juhl, *Interpretation* (Princeton, N.J.: Princeton University Press, 1980), 12.

[11] Luis Alonso Schokel, S. J., *The Inspired Word* (New York: Herder and Herder, 1965), 256.

essential. His early writings specify two tasks of hermeneutics, one grammatical and the other psychological. Consider this statement:

> An act of speaking cannot even be understood as a moment in a person's development unless it is also understood in relation to the language. . . . Nor can an act of speaking be understood as a modification of the language unless it is also understood as a moment in the development of the person.[12]

This statement by itself may be useful, but Schleiermacher's later refinements and emphases, especially as represented by Wilhelm Dilthey, gave an improper emphasis to the psychology of the author. That overemphasis is evident here:

> Before the art of hermeneutics can be practiced, the interpreter must put himself both objectively and subjectively in the position of the author. . . . On the subjective side this requires knowing the inner and the outer aspects of the author's life. . . . By a knowledge of the individuality of an author, grammatical interpretation can be brought to a level that it could not reach on its own. The goal is to reproduce the subjective bases for the combination of particular elements of a text in order to learn how to grasp the train of thought.[13]

The problem is that such individual mental acts are private and inaccessible to the interpreter. Yet later scholars who used and developed this approach emphasized similar psychological and private conceptions of intention. For example, Wimsatt and Beardsley's conception of intention is the "design or plan in the author's mind."[14]

At least three objections can be raised against this view of intention:

(1) Juhl has observed that there are numerous conscious activities which are intentional but not planned. For example, to talk to a friend I must first intend to visit him; however, my intention does not require that I plan out how I'm going to lift my legs and move my feet. I just do it.

(2) This view makes intention a separate event that precedes or accompanies the performance of an act of speech or writing. This especially holds true when my intention is to communicate meaning. Juhl has observed that "when we decide to speak to someone or to write something, we usually do not plan in advance precisely what we will say; rather, our specific intentions are formed in the process of formulating the sentences we use."[15] Thus, to make psychological experience the criterion leads us to draw lines arbitrarily where there are no actual distinctions.

(3) Most tellingly, Quentin Skinner notes that the personal motivations for an author to write have no necessary or logical relation to what he actually does write.

> To speak of a writer's motives seems invariably to me to speak of a condition antecedent to, and contingently connected with, the appearance of his works. . . . this distinction between motivation and intentions, with the isolation of the idea of an intention *in* speaking or writing with a particular force, lies, of course, in the implication that an agent's motives *for* writing (though not his intentions *in* writing) can be said to stand 'outside' his works, and in a contingent relationship to them, in such a way that their recovery does seem to be irrelevant

---

[12] F. D. E. Schleiermacher, *Hermeneutics,* ed. Heinz Kimmerle (Missoula, Mont.: Scholars Press, 1977), 99.

[13] Ibid., 113, 153.

[14] W. K. Wimsatt and Monroe Beardsley, "Intentional Fallacy," 1–13.

[15] Juhl, *Interpretation,* 134.

to the determination of the meaning of the works.[16]

Thus we conclude that intention is not to be identified with the psychological experience of the author.

b. Intention does not distinguish between the meanings expressed and meanings merely desired and unsuccessfully expressed. The most comprehensive discussion of the term "intention" for writing comes out of the field of linguistic philosophy. G. E. M. Anscombe, drawing on Wittgenstein's observations, which "came to have the status of a standard methodology device in linguistic philosophy," has analyzed the concept of intention in her book *Intention*.[17] She raises important questions in regard to intended meanings—namely, What questions are appropriate to ask of the text? and, What kinds of answers do we expect the text to provide?

> What distinguishes actions which are intentional from those which are not? The answer that I shall suggest is that they are the actions to which a certain sense to the question "why" is given application; the sense is of course that which the answer, if positive, gives a reason for action.[18]

As Anscombe asks the question why, she seeks to distinguish statements in the text that are intentional from any statements that may not be intentional. This assumes that the text or a reconstructed context will provide sufficient evidence to answer the question.

In seeking the answers Anscombe suggests that the interpreter desires to distinguish between actions that give a positive answer to the question why and actions that are unintentional "bungles" or "errors" and are therefore negative. However, Anscombe recognizes that the text at hand may not offer sufficient evidence to answer such a question positively and so the interpreter will need to incorporate additional data to find the answers. In the case of the Bible, this additional data may be found in a philosophical apriority such as Kant's distinction between the knowable and the unknowable, or D. F. Strauss's distinction between the reasonable, natural causation and the unreasonable, supernatural causation. Or the data may be sought in a critical structure of authorship and manuscript dependence as in the Gospels. But the scarcity of literary and historical evidence to support these answers leaves these conclusions less than convincing to many interpreters. In such cases the text really is an inadequate basis for distinguishing some statements as intended and other statements as not intended by a given author.

In response we argue that the fundamental interpretive question is, *What* is the author saying? or, What is the author's meaning? Every text gives primary evidence to answer this fundamental interpretive question. The meaning of a text involves what an author says and not directly *why* he writes or why he writes a certain way.

Nevertheless, the question of why an author writes is often related to determining what the author means. In fact, an interpreter's understanding of an author's reason for speaking may influence his perception of what an author means in the text. The problem is that while any text naturally provides primary evidence to disclose what an author means, it does not necessarily provide sufficient evidence as to why a statement is written. Yet in the broad context of the whole literary unit—that

---

[16]Quentin Skinner, "Motives, Intentions and the Interpretation of Text," in *On Literary Intention* (Edinburgh: Edinburgh University Press, 1976), 216.

[17]G. E. M. Anscombe, *Intention* (Ithaca, N.Y.: Cornell University Press, 1963).

[18]Ibid., 9.

is, the whole book—we would expect to find some answers why.

In the case of biblical literature, reasons why are found in the theological character and design of the canonical books. And these reasons do influence our perception of what the author means. In addition, reasons may be found in the literary form. A story may be narrated to establish a model or a prototype, or it may merely illustrate a truth already stated. If the narrative is a model, then all the elements of the story mean something for the reader. If the narrative is simply an illustration, then only those elements that support the truth are meaningful in the author's use of the story.

So while the text as a whole provides evidence to answer the question why an author writes, it does not necessarily provide sufficient evidence to distinguish intentional statements from unintentional errors. With biblical manuscripts, after the task of textual criticism has been applied, the perspective of the evangelical interpreter is that all the textual particulars and statements made in the text are viewed as intended by God—which is the doctrine of verbal plenary inspiration.

c. Intention does distinguish between what is meant based on what is written and what is not meant based on what is written. The term "intend" is used to make a distinction between what *is* meant from what *could possibly be* meant. It is absolutely essential to recognize that the Author's/author's intention does not separate what is meant from the text. Rather, intention highlights a distinction between meaning based on what is written in the text and context and meaning based only on the language or the historical considerations or some aspect other than the

text. What is meant must be understood from the words of the text. The term "intention" gives direction to this task of comprehension.

One aspect of comprehension concerns determining the sense of a textual construction.[19] On the one hand, since language is polysemic, a textual construction (a word, a phrase, or a sentence) understood according to general usage usually allows a number of possible senses. On the other hand, that same textual construction has limitations according to the author's total written context (e.g., a book). It is through his unified composition as a whole and its coherent, related parts that an author expresses his intended sense or senses. It is within the composition as a whole that an author narrows and specifies the related meanings from among the shared possible language senses.

In other words, the textual context in which a construction is used is the primary factor in determining its intended meaning. For example, we might encounter the word *form* in a manual on home remodeling today, in a biography of Winston Churchill tomorrow, and in a denominational book of church order the day after that. Because of the context we will readily understand that one expression refers to a builder's mold, another to Churchill's secondary education, and the third to the prescribed ceremony for a baptism.

The author's usage also includes a historical context, from which his meaning may be inferred and with which he may have shared an unstated but assumed meaning. However, what is written in the text supersedes the historical context in determining the meaning. The textual clues must control any shared but assumed meanings.

---

[19]Textual meaning includes, following Frege, both *sense*—the "what" is immanent in the sentence—and *reference*—the "about what" of discourse—where reference relates language back to both the speaker and the world.

If, however, the human author is an unknown person, the interpreter is obliged to work within the limits of knowledge found only in the text itself.

These limitations in historical knowledge have given rise to numerous critical theories of redactors or editors being involved in the historical composition of books of the Bible. Of course, any thorough discussion of the question of authorship must rest on the evidence available for each individual book. Still, some general considerations may be helpful to this discussion of the author's intended meaning.

(1) Any direct biblical witness to authorship must provide the framework within which an evangelical interpreter works. But biblical statements must be examined to discern whether they actually refer to authorship. For example, Paul's using an amanuensis on occasion does not detract from his authorship; whatever the role of the amanuensis was, it is not to be considered editorship or authorship. Moreover, referring to sections of canonical writings by the name of a prominent author (e.g., Isaiah) does not affirm authorship of that book.

(2) Numerous books of the Bible give little or no direct witness to authorship (such as Samuel, Kings, and Hebrews). While this fact limits the interpreter's historical knowledge, it does not invalidate an implied author who intends the textual senses.

(3) There is some reasonable evidence of editorial additions (such as Deuteronomy 34) and of editorial updating (as in Ezra), but this admission of reasonable evidence does not necessarily lead to the positions that critical scholars have taken. Despite the proliferation of critical theories of manuscript history, there remains limited evidence for a multiplicity of editors or redactors in biblical books. The evidence available independent of these critical theories is not sufficient to undermine a working unity within the canonical manuscripts of books—a premise with which some critical scholars agree.[20]

Thus "intention" is used to focus the interpreter's attention on the primary importance of an author's textual context in interpreting meaning. It also will have the effect of bringing restraint into interpretation, limiting our conclusions about meaning to those that can be demonstrated to be based on the text.

SUMMARY

In conclusion let us restate our propositions regarding the goal of interpretation:

1. The term "intend" in hermeneutics has enjoyed ancient and widespread usage among interpreters.
2. "Intended meaning" is that meaning which the Author/author has expressed in the written text.
   a. "Intention" is not to be identified with the psychological experience of the author.
   b. Intention does not distinguish between the meanings expressed and meanings merely desired or successfully and unsuccessfully expressed.
   c. Intention does distinguish between what is meant based on what is written and what is not meant based on what is written.

---

[20]Brevard S. Childs, *Introduction to the Old Testament as Scripture* (Philadelphia: Fortress, 1979).

CHAPTER 3

Hermeneutical Considerations of the Goal of Interpretation

Schleiermacher long ago posed a broad question that has affected the science of hermeneutics and the art of biblical interpretation ever since: "Can the biblical writings be interpreted subject to the same conditions that apply to all other kinds of literature?"

Our answer lies in the five hermeneutical premises introduced earlier.

We have asserted that the stated goal of inductive Bible study and of biblical interpretation is to ascertain the Author's/author's intended meaning as expressed in the text. Our goal is not different from that applied to literature generally. The Bible, however, does involve the unique authorship of God speaking through human authors. This will certainly influence the hermeneutical application of the premises, depending on one's faith position concerning God's Word. What that influence is will be developed in the following discussion. Basically we will show that the Bible is a fully human book yet without error (error not being necessary to humanness), and that it is a fully divine book yet without any mystical or magical sense independent of the textual expressions.

FIVE HERMENEUTICAL PREMISES

The first of the five hermeneutical premises is the most basic.

1. The Literal Premise

The literal premise affirms that the meanings to be interpreted are textually based.

This norm states that the meaning is based in the text that the Author/author wrote. It is consistent with our goal.

This concept of the literal norm was defined in a study in linguistics on literacy and reading comprehension and expression done by David R. Olson and Angela Hildyard.[1] In their study, the goal in reading was to know the speaker's meaning. Two aspects were considered to be variables: semantic structures (meaning) and possible worlds (of reference). Given these variables, there are three distinct ways to read a text: (a) a *casual* reading, in

---

[1]David R. Olson and Angela Hildyard, "Literacy and the Comprehension and Expression of Literal Meaning" (*Trends in Linguistics Studies and Monographs* 24), in *Writings in Focus,* ed. Florian Coulmas (New York: Moulton, 1981), 291–323.

which semantic structures are altered and one's perception of the world (context) is treated as invariant; (b) a *literal* reading, in which the semantic structures are invariant and the perception of the world (context) is altered by the textual sense; and (c) a *metaphorical, or indirect,* reading, which results from varying or altering the reading of both the semantic structures and the perception of possible worlds until they match.

The thoroughness of the Olson-Hildyard study provides a contemporary linguistic basis for distinguishing a literal reading from other readings. The literal reading is preferred because it holds to the textual expressions with the greatest integrity. Other readings more readily alter the textual meanings in view of the possible perceptions of the world.

The three distinct ways to read a text may be illustrated by the passage in James 2:14: "Can such faith save him?" In what sense do we understand the word "save"?

Casual reading: Since "save" always means deliverance from the eternal judgment of sin, it must mean that here. This meaning follows from my knowledge of the term in other passages in spite of no mention of eternal judgment in context.

Literal reading: Since the context (v. 15) mentions a problem from which deliverance is needed, in this usage "save" means deliverance from a brother having no food or clothing. In context, an active faith can save a brother from such need by the works it is willing to perform.

Metaphorical reading: Since "Christ alone saves from sin and its consequences," this usage of "faith saving" must be understood in a figurative sense. The question has the meaning "can such faith *help* him?" "Help," then, means something less than deliverance by divine intervention from the consequences of the trial.

As these instances illustrate, only the literal reading limits the interpretive process to the immediate context. This alone is a purely textually based meaning. A literal reading always seeks clues that are either stated in or related to the textual expression in some grammatical and historical sense.

Martin Luther lent support to this understanding of the literal norm in his principle of *sola scriptura.* At the Leipzig disputation (1519) he affirmed: "No believing Christian can be forced to recognize any authority beyond sacred scripture, which is exclusively invested with divine right."[2] At the Diet of Worms (1521) he replied to Johann von Eck's demand that he recant his alleged errors: "Unless I am convinced by the testimonies of the sacred scriptures or manifest reason, . . . I am bound by the Scriptures which I have adduced. My conscience has been taken captive by the Word of God."[3]

Luther's words referred specifically to the claim of the Roman church to

---

[2] Martin Luther, *Werke* Weimarer Ausgabe 2:279, trans. F. F. Bruce, in *New Testament Interpretation* (Grand Rapids: Eerdmans, 1977), 30.
[3] Ibid., 7:838.

have sole and infallible authority to interpret Scripture. But his principle applies generally to all attempts to set an authority above or along side the Bible. What Luther said is that the Scriptures are sufficient in themselves. No outside authority, such as historical, comparative, or critical studies or theological predispositions are warranted to alter or expand upon the biblical meanings. *Sola scriptura* implies that the text of a book is sufficient to express the message in an adequate form. Scriptural statements are all sufficiently clear in themselves so that no authority is needed to change, specify, or complete what the text says. A book of the Bible is sufficient to express its meaning as intended and also provides the information needed to be properly understood. This emphasis on the sufficiency of the text is intended not to rule out the realm of historical reference as a factor in interpretation, but rather to repudiate it as the basis of meaning.

Gerhard Ebeling formulated Luther's principles in these terms:

Holy Scripture is to be understood only through the Spirit through whom it was written and whom we encounter in no more contemporary, vital fashion than in the biblical text itself. The greater the danger of understanding the Scripture according to our own spirit, the more we must turn from all human writings to Holy Scripture alone. For there alone do we receive the Spirit who enables us to judge all Scripture, pagan or Christian.[4]

The "understanding . . . according to our own spirit" that disturbed Ebeling included a naturalistic view of the world that would transform many biblical statements into metaphorical expressions with moral force only. As if anticipating this idea, Luther stated that any biblical statement is understood as being consistent with other biblical statements rather than needing to be reinterpreted according to some modern worldview.

This conclusion rests on the logical premise of the unity and coherence of the sense found in the book. Louis Berkhof supports this premise of the unity of the sense of Scripture.

It is of greatest importance to understand at the outset that Scripture has but a single sense and is therefore susceptible to a scientific and logical investigation. This fundamental principle must be placed emphatically in the foreground, in opposition to the tendency . . . to accept a manifold sense—a tendency that makes any science of hermeneutics impossible.[5]

Ramm contends that "there can only be confusion of the meaning of the Word of God, and even obscuration, when under various pretexts the unity of the sense is abandoned."[6] Walter Kaiser goes further in concluding that "under the strong impetus of the Reformation there was a renewed emphasis that there is only *one sense* or meaning to be gleaned from every passage if the interpreter is true to his mission."[7]

One or Many Meanings?

The debate over one meaning or many originated in the vigorous discussion that took place between the Alexandrian school's support for *sensius plenior* (many senses) in allegorical in-

---

[4]Gerhard Ebeling, " 'Sola Scriptura' und das Problem der Tradition," in *Das Neue Testament as Kanon,* ed. Ernst Käsemann (Gottingen: Vandenhoech and Ruprecht, 1970), 315: in reference to Martin Luther's *Werke,* Kritische Gesamtausgabe (Weimar: 1883–), 7:97, 1–3, 11–13.
[5]Louis Berkhof, *Principles of Biblical Interpretation* (Grand Rapids: Baker, 1950), 57.
[6]Bernard Ramm, *Protestant Biblical Interpretation: A Textbook of Hermeneutics for Conservative Protestants* (Boston: W. A. Wilde, 1950, rev. ed. 1956), 125.
[7]Walter C.. Kaiser, Jr., *Toward an Exegetical Theology* (Grand Rapids: Baker, 1981), 44–45.

terpretation and the Antiochene support for a single sense in literal interpretation.

This difference has been perceived as a distinction in kind: Does the text have many meanings, or just one meaning with related submeanings?

Recent discussion has tended to reduce the difference to one merely of degree; consider this statement from Karlfried Froehlich: "The difference between Alexandria and Antioch seems to reflect more the methodological emphases and priorities of the schools."[8] However, the historical discussion makes it clear that the distinction is in fact one in kind.

A distinction in kind means that there is a basic difference in the perception of the type of textual meaning that the Bible expresses. On one side Clement of Alexandria wrote, "Almost the whole of Scripture is expressed in enigmas."[9] If that is the case, then it is the task of the interpreter who has received the deeper knowledge imparted by Christ to open the symbolic, enigmatic truth of biblical language. By contrast, Tertullian warned against seeing the scriptural message as basically enigmatic. "Even the prophets, he cautioned, said many things without allegory or figure; not everything in the Bible comes as image, shadow, or parable."[10]

It is clear that the biblical revelation is expressed in different styles and literary genres, yet the meaning expressed is not necessarily enigmatic or equivocal. If there were equivocal statements, then two incompatible interpretations could claim equal support. This was the problem with the Greek

oracle at Delphi; its statements were couched in ambiguous language that could be interpreted in opposite ways with equal validity. For example, the Greek oracle to Pyrrhus as he was on his way to invade Italy is said to have announced: "I say that Rome Pyrrhus shall overcome." When Pyrrhus failed to conquer Rome and complained that the oracle had deceived him, he was told that the oracle was not to blame for his mistaken interpretation. Of course, the oracle is equivocal.

If the meaning of the biblical text were truly equivocal, then the communication of meaning would be indeterminate and a truthful statement would consequently be impossible. An interpreter would never know if A or B is meant if A and B can claim equal support. Thus, if the textual meaning were equivocal, the Bible's claim to be revelation would be deceptive and false. So any claim to see multiple, textually unrelated senses in the biblical text must be rejected outright. The Bible communicates a single, textually determined meaning.

The difference between one meaning and many is also a distinction in kind because there is a basic disagreement on what relates the component meanings. The literal tradition, in affirming that there is a single meaning to be interpreted, does not deny that there are component or subordinate meanings expressed in the words and constructions of the text. However, it requires that all these component or subordinate meanings must be related through a unified and coherent textual meaning.[11]

---

[8] Karlfried Froehlich, *Biblical Interpretation in the Early Church* (Philadelphia: Fortress, 1984), 20.

[9] Clement of Alexandria, *Stromata* 6.124.5–6, trans. Karlfried Froehlich, in Froehlich, *Biblical Interpretation,* 16.

[10] Froehlich, *Biblical Interpretation,* 24: quoting *On the Resurrection,* 19–21.

[11] It is understood that a single meaning corresponds to a single unit of text. This unit of text may be a sentence or a paragraph or a chapter or, in particular, a book. A book is the

And that raises the fundamental question of what relates the component meanings.

The Alexandrian theologian Origen saw the multiple meanings of Scripture as being related by issues other than the text and context.

In the Proverbs of Solomon we find this kind of directive concerning divine doctrines in Scripture: "And you, write down those things threefold in your counsel and wisdom that you may reply with words of truth to those who ask you" [Prov. 22:20–21]. This means, one should inscribe on one's soul the intentions of the holy literature in a three fold manner.[12]

In a similar way Origen argued that *The Shepherd of Hermas* (Vision II.4.3) suggests a threefold sense of Scripture in analogy to the tripartite anthropology of the philosophers. Just as human beings consist of body, soul, and spirit, so Scripture edifies by a literal, a moral, and a spiritual sense.

One proponent of the Alexandrian school was the Augustinian tradition, of which John Cassian was a leading figure. Cassian, a contemporary of Augustine, formalized a fourfold hermeneutical principle.[13] The standard example is Jerusalem: literally, Jerusalem means the city of the Jews; allegorically, the church (Ps. 46:4–5); tropologically [metaphorically], the soul (Ps. 147:1–2, 12); anagogically [spiritually], our heavenly home (Gal. 4:26). These interpretations were related by the theological goal of interpretation, as stated by Froehlich: "Augustine's hermeneutics was a commentary on this Tyconian theme: The *goal* of all biblical interpretation must be the double love of God and neighbor, the ordering of the Christian life toward our heavenly home (*On Christian Doctrine* 1.35–36.39–40)."[14]

In both Origen's and Augustine's hermeneutics, the component meanings of a passage were related by some principle extrinsic to the textual expression, that is, by a philosophy or a theology. These broader contexts sponsor multiple meanings of a biblical text.

Relationship Between Meanings

The literal tradition, in contrast to the Alexandrian and Augustinian traditions, insists that component meanings must be textually based and textually related. Various scholars have tried to show how this works.

One approach affirms that the single meaning is textually based and related by the possible limits in the meanings of the language system. In other words, the interpreter's understanding of a construction is *restricted* to those meanings actually used in that language, in situations similar to the grammatical and historical context of the unknown construction (i.e., the text being studied).

Consider, for example, the sentence "On payday, I will get the trunks." Whatever I am going to get (a bathing suit, a storage container, a section of a tree, etc.), it must be something that we twentieth-century users of English call a trunk. In the year A.D. 2500, the meanings of "trunk" may include a type of computer, but that would not give someone living at that time the

---

only independent unit of the text with a single meaning determined exclusively by an author. Other smaller, component units of the text are more difficult to recognize. Independent, contextless units of the text, such as a sentence, may be justly construed as having more than one meaning. This matter is difficult to determine without any presuppositions, so it is theoretically wise to begin with the book as a whole.

[12] Origen, *On Principles: Book Four*, 2.4, trans. Karlfried Froehlich, in *Biblical Interpretation*, 57.

[13] *Confessions*, 14.8 (c. 420).

[14] Froehlich, *Biblical Interpretation*, 28.

right to interpret my sentence to mean that I was going to get a computer. Also, English grammar limits "trunk" to being a noun; it is not now used as a verb or a preposition. Thus the normal way a word or construction is used determines one set of limits on the meaning. This is what Bernard Ramm was affirming when he wrote, "The customary socially acknowledged designation of a word is the literal meaning of that word."[15]

This understanding of the single meaning as limited to the possible language meaning is important because we cannot exceed the meanings shared by the original speakers of the language. The concept seems self-evident to most of us, but historically it has not always been applied. Yet the idea of a single language meaning is inadequate because it does not explain the relationship between actual variant meanings of a word. Dictionaries and grammatical constructions often provide for different and even unrelated meanings for the same word or construction. This is not the same as a unified, coherent textual meaning.[16]

A second approach toward understanding the single, textual meaning is that the relationships are determined by the author's intended usage from among the possible language senses. Thus, while we confront a number of possible meanings, we narrow down the options by examining them in light of the author's intended meaning. This analysis will be developed in part 2, but two illustrations here will demonstrate the need to choose between several possible and legitimate meanings.

One kind of choice involves *conflicting senses*. We find an example of this in Job 19:26. One possible translation,

"without my flesh I shall see God," stands opposed to another possible translation, "in my flesh I shall see God." Since the logic of a single sense demands that component meanings cannot be conflicting, these two viable historical-grammatical senses cannot both be right. But the goal of a single meaning alone provides no guidance for us to decide which is valid. Thus the literal tradition looks to the author's intended meaning as expressed in the text as the basis for the decision.

A choice is also required when a text admits *multiple and unrelated component senses*. This happens often in Bible study. An illustration of this is the term *katalambanō* ("seize") found in John 1:5: "darkness did not *seize* the light." The translation is vague and ambiguous. Normal linguistic usage recognizes three legitimate lexical options:

a. To seize mentally, i.e., "darkness did not comprehend the light."

b. To seize physically, i.e., "darkness did not suppress or extinguish the light."

c. To master, i.e., "darkness did not master the light" (with the submeanings, [a] comprehend as a prelude and condition for [b] extinguish).

Options *a* and *b* at first sight appear to be unrelated senses. They are not contradictory, so we cannot exclude them on that account. But mental comprehension is not necessarily related to physical extinction, so it would appear that we need to choose between the two because of their unrelatedness. Yet it is also possible that the author used the term in a sense that combines *a* and *b* as submeanings of a broader unified sense (*c*). How do we determine which is the correct sense? M. Smith has suggested

---

[15] Ramm, *Protestant Biblical Interpretation*, 90.

[16] Eugene A. Nida, *Componential Analysis of Meaning* (The Hague: Moulton, 1979), 126.

that the clues of the context as expressed by the author indicate the third unified sense is the correct choice.[17]

The literal tradition allows for any of the three options as the single sense of the text. But the goal by itself of one meaning gives no discriminating direction for making the choice. Therefore J. I. Packer broadens the sense of "literal" as "the meaning which the human writer, inspired as he was, has actually expressed in the words that he has chosen to use."[18] Thus, as Smith recognized in John 1:5, the goal of interpretation is finally understood as *the unified meaning that the Author/author intended as expressed in the text.*

In conclusion, while it is common to think of a single, unified sense at the word level as illustrated above, it also follows that any textual unit could also be thought of as having a unified sense with the same methodological benefits. This textual unit could include anything up to the book as a whole. What we mean when we say that these larger textual units have a single sense is that all the component senses are related in a coherent (logical and orderly) unity. The constitutional qualities of coherence will vary from book to book, depending on the literary genre and the author's style. But it is always appropriate to seek out the unity and coherence of a book that is well written.

The Analogy of Faith

A corollary in the literal tradition implied in *sola scriptura* is *the analogy of faith*. When trying to extract meaning from a study of the text itself, the analogy of faith becomes very important. This principle, like the literal tradi-

tion generally, was given great emphasis during the Reformation. The Reformers used this principle in refuting the special place of authority the Roman Catholic Church had assumed in the interpretation of Scripture. "The Catholic Church had insisted that it had the power to interpret Scripture, and it could by this power make the obscure Scripture clear. The Reformers countered by stating that the guidance in understanding the obscure Scripture is to come *from the Scripture.*"[19]

The analogy of faith, simply stated, is that *Scripture interprets Scripture.* "The meaning of any single biblical statement is not contradictory to any teaching of other Scripture on the subject. God's Word, presumably, does not affirm and deny the same thing at the same time in the same respect. So a verse should be taken in accord with the broader theological context."[20]

The author of a text may well use terms and constructions that he does not define in context, and these terms may be critical to our understanding his thought. It would seem that the author assumes his audience shares with him the sense of these terms. *The analogy of faith leads us to expect that these terms and constructions are primarily informed from prior revelation.* This expectation is confirmed by the apostle Peter's description of Old Testament authors: "holy men of God spake" (KJV) or "men spoke from God" (2 Peter 1:21). While these were certainly men of their age, they are particularly characterized as "men of God." That implies that the senses they imparted were meanings God had given.

---

[17]M. Smith, "*Katalambano,*" *Journal of Biblical Literature* 64 (1945): 510f.

[18]J. I. Packer, "Biblical Authority, Hermeneutics and Inerrancy," in *Jerusalem and Athens,* ed. E. R. Geehan (Philadelphia: Presbyterian and Reformed, 1971).

[19]Ramm, *Protestant Biblical Interpretation,* 126.

[20]Gordon R. Lewis and Bruce A. Demarest, *Integrative Theology,* vol. 1 (Grand Rapids: Zondervan, 1986), 30–31.

This thought will be developed later in the book.

Accepting prior revelation does not exclude help that can come from contemporary literature of the Ancient Near East, but that literature is not the primary source of informing us about what the biblical authors said.

What the literal premise affirms is that the Author's/author's intended meaning is primarily based on and understood from the text spoken in the progress of revelation. The text is sufficient to determine the intended sense.

The primary objection to this statement of the literal premise arises from the process of communication. Can the meaning be textually determined when it must be construed by an interpreter? And is not an interpreter's preunderstanding (not textually based) necessary to construe the meaning correctly? Drawing on an illustration used earlier, I cannot construe "trunk" unless I have already thought about "a tree trunk," "a storage trunk," and "a pair of trunks." While it is true that communication does not occur unless the interpreter shares a sufficient preunderstanding, meaning to be communicated is determined by written textual expression.

Hermeneutical premises, however, not only affirm the textual basis of the meaning, but also qualify the *preunderstanding* of the interpreter. The next four premises set limits on the relevant understanding that an interpreter brings to the text and uses in interpretation.

2. The Grammatical Premise

The grammatical premise affirms that the textually based meanings are ex- *pressed within the limits of common language usage.*

The first consideration in preunderstanding is a knowledge of the language. We consider "the common use of language" the medium the Author/author uses to express the message and confront the question, Can biblical language be interpreted subject to conditions different from those applying to all other kinds of language?

Froehlich sees this question of distinction as one of the basic problems of biblical hermeneutics.

> God did not use a language of his own or the "language of angels" (1 Cor. 13:1) but made human language of particular times and places the vehicle of biblical revelation. . . . God has the same problem with human language we all have. This is the price of incarnation. Human language is contingent, open, ambiguous and therefore in need of interpretation.[21]

The common language medium used in the Bible will be assessed under this grammatical norm in two propositions.

a. Language is a public medium that is commonly used in an imprecise fashion. As a public medium of communication, the language chosen by God is potentially shared by both the initiated and the uninitiated in the things of God. Language is the basis for God's communication with the world and a necessary means for his revelation of himself and his works to mankind. Had God chosen to use a private Holy Spirit language, no one could have shared the meanings who was not initiated to a relationship with the Holy Spirit. Although the language used in revelation may be most familiar to the community who speak it and use its idioms and allusions,[22] by the analogy of faith its

---

[21] Karlfried Froehlich, "Biblical Hermeneutics on the Move," *Ex Auditre* 1 (1985): 4.
[22] This is the argument of Nigel Turner, "Syntax," in J. H. Moulton, *Grammar of New Testament Greek,* vol. 3 (Edinburgh: T. and T. Clark, 1963), 1–9.

meanings are not separated from the uninitiated who desire to know.

Human language is often ambiguous because language forms are polysemic, that is, the forms (words, constructions, sentences) are often capable of different senses. Thus the sentence "The door is open" could imply a command to shut it, express information about what is open, or be an indirect invitation to come in. More information is needed to resolve the ambiguity. Complicating the ambiguity, a given word may have innumerable potential references. "Door" could refer to a massive oak church door, the barred entrance to a prison cell, or even the opening on a doghouse. Additional clues are needed to resolve this ambiguity. Such clues may be provided through further communication—that is, the more that is said, the less ambiguous the words are likely to be. Because of this, a whole literary unit such as a book, which would contain many clues, is seldom capable of two unrelated senses.

Besides being polysemic, human language is contingent. By this is meant that language meanings are often dependent on more than issues within a language system. "Language always involves a speaker and a listener. The process of reception, language as it is *heard,* must be part of the investigation."[23] Situational and cultural factors may be unstated but assumed.

This complication may be reduced somewhat when it is the Author/author who determines the textually expressed meaning. We do not need to consider as viable all possible factors that may be present in a culture; we need only to consider those that the Author/author assumed and shared with his original audience. For example, an ancient biblical writer may have been aware of erroneous worldviews and cultural perceptions contemporary with him. He may even have shared some. But he was not controlled by his cultural worldview any more than modern believers are controlled by a current, secular worldview. In addition, the ancient writer's intention is based on what he expressed in the text and what this implies, and not on any other values and views he may have shared with his ancient culture. So although the contingency of human language is a problem, it is not an insurmountable one.

b. Language is a medium that can make accurate statements in spite of a lack of precision. At one point Wittgenstein argued that language is a picture-medium, but he later changed his mind.[24] It is clear that language is not so complete as a picture and that language syntax does not correspond to the world in every respect. In the simple sentence "The door is open," it is not clear whether the door is merely unlocked, is standing ajar, or has been thrown wide open. No precise mental picture has been given. But the statement may be accurate in corresponding to reality even though it remains ambiguous. Determining the correct sense of the statement involves selecting and giving value to certain facts that clearly distinguish that state of affairs from many other possible states of affairs. The author is not talking about windows or walls, and he is not uncertain or does not place qualifications on what he affirms. The door is open, even though at this moment we do not know exactly in what way that is meant.

Therefore language, in spite of its limitations for expressing what we may desire or expect, is a medium that can communicate with accuracy and express truth. The issue of truth spoken

---

[23] Froehlich, "Biblical Hermeneutics on the Move," 4.

[24] Ludwig Wittgenstein, *Tractus Logico–Philosophieus* (London: Routledge and Kegan Paul, 1971) and *Philosophical Investigations* (New York: Macmillan, 1968).

concerns primarily the Author/author who speaks and not the medium that is chosen. Of course the medium, as well as the condition and design of the communication, does affect the hearer's comprehension, but that issue will be considered in our discussion of the stages of inductive study. Thus the first valid area of preunderstanding that we bring to the text and use in the interpretation of the text is a knowledge of the language in which the text is written.

3. The Historical Premise

The historical premise affirms that the textually based meanings, when so indicated by textual usage, refer to historical realities and/or allude to situations or ideas.

The second aspect of preunderstanding, after the grammatical, involves a knowledge of the historical realm. The historical realm is legitimately related to the textual meanings in two ways. First, there is *that about which* the Author/author writes; second, there is *the historical occasion* as reconstructed from textual clues and a knowledge of the historical culture.

What the Author Writes About

Regarding the first, since the biblical authorship includes God, the realm of reference includes both natural and spiritual, earthly and heavenly realities. As we examine a text's historical reference, some probing questions arise in the biblical accounts.

What, for example, is the historical status of the temptations in the wilderness? Have the N.T. writers woven event and interpretation together in such a way that interpretation may appear in the guise of

historical event? Was the story of the tearing of the temple veil (Mark 15:38) intended to be a historical account and/or a piece of symbolism (to signify the opening up of the presence of God to all believers)?[25]

Discovering the answers to these questions has been the focus of major problems in recent hermeneutical debate. For example, Froehlich judged the relationship between biblical language and history to be a central question. "Its [biblical language] relation to a specific history and to historical reality in general" is the issue.[26] He developed three distinct approaches to address the issue of historical reference.

a. A conservative position is based on an understanding of *inspiration and divine authorship* which results in the conclusion that the biblical text speaks of historical realities in truth. "Biblical interpretation is needed, but the need arises more from the use of language than from problems with the reality of the history it points to. The Bible is a book *sui generis* precisely in terms of its unique historical reality."[27] In this position the historical references are based on the textual expression and are taken by convention to be direct references unless there are clues given in the text to indicate otherwise.

b. A second position rests on the presence of *fallible, human authorship* of the Bible in which the reality of the historical reference must be tested and verified through critical techniques. "This does not mean that the biblical work is not true. Rather, the historical truth in and behind the text, the history to which the text points, is part of the goal of interpretation, not its presupposition, and this goal must be reached by

---

[25] I. Howard Marshall, *New Testament Interpretation* (Grand Rapids: Eerdmans, 1977), 15.

[26] Froehlich, "Biblical Hermeneutics on the Move," 5.

[27] Ibid.

the same means that are applied to all literature.''[28] Thus the initial question reappears: Can the biblical writings be interpreted subject to conditions different from those applying to all other kinds of literature?

c. A third position is that *the written text is autonomous or dead.* Supporters of this position are found in both structuralism and the New Criticism in literature. From their perspective the autonomy of the written text dissociates it from its author and from reference to any limited historical realm. ''The historical reality to which the word of the Bible must be related is not only tied to then and there of ancient history (if it is at all). It is the history or, to use a more current term, the story of the hearer today and in all ages. My story participates in the general structure of reality communicated by the linguistic metaphor.''[29] This position also rests on the established conclusions of historical criticism. The questions raised by this position are the principle questions in the contemporary debate concerning the historicity of the Bible.

The first legitimate relation between the historical realm and the text would be a direct, straightforward correspondence between them based on textual developments. In our preunderstanding, the more comprehensive our general knowledge, the better our understanding is likely to be. But historical knowledge only enriches textual meanings; it does not create meanings based on the historical realm or specify meanings beyond the textual development.

A second relation would be the historical occasion for writing, as indicated primarily through allusions and less often through direct references. The issues involve the author, the original audience, and their relationship. There are questions about the time of writing and the time of events; questions about the location of writing and of the events written about; and questions about the cultural setting and about presuppositions that must be shared by the author and the interpreter. These historical questions need to be dealt with in the interpretive task.

Reconstructing the Historical Occasion

The second aspect of preunderstanding involves reconstructing the historical occasion based on the textual clues and a knowledge of the historical culture. The only concern arises when the construed historical occasion becomes the basis of particular meanings that are not shared by and based on the textual usage.

Our answers to the questions raised by historical allusions and references are influenced greatly by our use of the historical critical method. I. Howard Marshall defined the goals of historical criticism as the elucidation and testing of the historical accuracy. The goal of elucidation is unquestionably valid for removing a lack of clarity in regard to textual statements. In our simple illustration ''The door is open,'' if we knew the historical occasion of that statement and the door to which the speaker referred, the ambiguities mentioned earlier would be removed. Such elucidation, based on careful historical research, would be of inestimable value.

The major problem in using historical criticism turns on the test of historical accuracy. It is not that such historical examination is inappropriate. The Bible is a book of history with frequent references to historical events and some references to supernatural phenomena. The problem arises when a textual record does not provide sufficient evi-

---

[28] Ibid.
[29] Ibid.

dence to demonstrate with satisfaction its own historicity.

In the European debate over the use of historical criticism, both Gerhard Maier and Peter Stuhlmacher reject its legitimateness when it is based on presuppositions that preclude transcendence and divine intervention.[30] Bruce Waltke considers it "illegitimate to call into question the Bible's accuracy either because the events it relates are not otherwise well attested or because they are contradicted in nonbiblical sources."[31]

There are sufficient historical and theological reasons to acknowledge the Bible's claim for general historicity. A foremost reason focuses on the heart of the Christian message and its record of the empty tomb. This is a record of a historical event that is supported by the written testimony of at least three witnesses: Matthew, Peter (in the gospel of Mark), and John. G. B. Caird points out that the Jews were quite concerned about the rules of testimony. "It is well to recall that the ancient Israelite had in his legal system ample acquaintance with the notion of sufficient attestation."[32]

The tests of historical criticism cannot prove or disprove (except by presupposition) that a miracle took place. But it can demonstrate the consistency of the historical accounts bearing witness to an empty tomb and can reason to a historical probability in favor of the interpretation of the Resurrection. That provides no problem to a historical method in spite of the miraculous nature of the event.

The problems arise in other cases where the historical textual evidence is not sufficient to answer the interpreter's questions about historicity. In such instances a critic searches for additional evidence that may be generated from assumptions or theories. The problem is that these assumptions and theories are not accepted by all interpreters, so the additional evidence generated must be viewed in these cases as inconclusive. For example, redaction criticism rests on one of several theories of textual dependence among the gospel accounts. The redaction critic attempts to demonstrate the theological tendencies of a gospel writer based on the supposed priority of Matthew or Mark. The fundamental flaw in this methodology is that any conclusions about theological tendencies drawn from a gospel writer's use of his sources is no more conclusive than the validity of the theory of textual dependence.

Is there a "legitimate" realm for using historical criticism that questions and tests the historical references to events, persons, and objects found in Scripture? Waltke lists six conditions that make historical criticism legitimate:

a. We must deal with the use of conventional language in reference to historical authorship. Does the use of the name in relation to a piece of literature really mean authorship?

b. In determining what happened we must deal with belief in dual causality. We might say that "God tempted David, and Satan tempted David." These seemingly incompatible statements are not contradictory.

c. We must determine the actual historical occurrence referred to in different literary genres. In the reference

---

[30] Gerhard Maier, *The End of the Historical-Critical Method* (St. Louis: Concordia, 1977), and Peter Stuhlmacher, *Historical Criticism and Theological Interpretation of Scripture,* trans. and intro. Roy A. Harrisville (Philadelphia: Fortress, 1975).

[31] Bruce K. Waltke, "Grammatical Problems," in *Hermeneutics, Inerrancy and the Bible,* ed. Earl D. Radmacher and Robert D. Preus (Grand Rapids: Zondervan, 1984), 83.

[32] G. B. Caird, *The Language and Imagery of the Bible* (Philadelphia: Westminster, 1980), 201.

to Lazarus and Abraham's bosom in Luke 16, does the literary composition imply historical reference?

d. We must recognize the literary conventions associated with the use of numbers.

e. We must recognize that speeches in the text (as in the Gospels and the book of Acts) are abbreviated versions of what was actually said and to that extent are not reproducing the speech verbatim. This fact of composition may affirm a distinctive emphasis or point of view in one of the parallel accounts.

f. We must recognize that the chronological order of the historical events in narratives may be rearranged, but not at the expense of textual markers when they indicate chronological order. These textual markers must be carefully considered.[33]

In these situations the textual sense must be examined with great care in order to test whether the historical reference or allusion is in fact a direct reference. The historical critical method has the role of clarification and a measured role of testing the references where the textual sense is unclear.

4. The Premise of Textual Design

The premise of textual design (literary) affirms that the textually based sense of any subsection is determined within the limits of the textual design of the composition as a whole.

This premise is important because verbal communication requires our knowing more than the grammar and the historical realm of a text. The textually based sense of any part of a written work is determined in part by the textual design of the composition considered as a whole. Textual design contributes to the *way* something is said, which in turn contributes to *what*

is said. Thus this third premise of preunderstanding involves a knowledge of the literary genre of the text.

Rudolf Bultmann sought to change the interpretive form of biblical statements through "demythologization." He saw supernatural and nonscientific statements in Scripture as prescientific man's attempt to explain religious experiences in the form of historical events—the result being "myth." Responsible understanding, then, requires the reader to peel away this mythologic skin to get at the religious intention of what the Bible says.

Bultmann's ideas met resistance on two fronts. Literary formalists objected to his disregard for literary aspects of composition and literary genres. Evangelicals disputed his writings on historical grounds, questioning whether we can have a meaningful gospel statement without references to heaven, hell, and the supernatural (Bultmann's "myth").

The question is also raised whether a prose interpretive summary can adequately communicate the meanings of an original poetic statement. This introduces the matter of textual design into our hermeneutic as a way of considering the richness of the original expression. Literary norms or conventions help account for poetic or figurative meanings as well as directly expressed meanings. The conventions consider both the cognitive domain of reference but also emotive and volitional components of the textual sense. A propositional summary of the message comes close to accounting for the cognitive sense of an *expository* text, but it does not correspond as adequately to the fuller range of component senses in a *literary* text. Thus we need to consider carefully the textual design to account

---

[33] Waltke, "Grammatical Problems," 84–86.

for the full range of textual meanings, particularly in literary texts.[34]

Still another related question arises regarding the so-called multiple meanings of poetry as over against the single sense required by the literal premise. What is the literal sense of a poem? What is the literal reference of prophecy? In each case it is claimed that the norms of the literary genre imply multiple and possibly indeterminate meanings. So how do the literal premise and the multiple meanings of textual design relate?

Biblical Poetry

Biblical poetry has rich imagery, compact statements, and parallel structure, with plays on words—all of which seem to make multiple meanings inevitable. We will examine several biblical texts that interpreters have advanced as expressing multiple meanings, and in so doing we will seek to show that the multiple meanings when considered within the literary conventions express *related component meanings*. This relatedness is based on literary terms, not on grammatical or historical grounds.

We must lay the groundwork for this exercise by citing some vocabulary relating to component meanings. Gottlob Frege made the following distinction between the *sense* of a statement and the *reference* of the statement: *Sense* refers to the components of meaning that are expressed in the text (definition of terms, syntactical meanings between constructions and sentences, etc.) irrespective of a particular historical reference; *reference* refers to components that are concerned with the relationship of particular senses to the real world in a particular historical setting. The investigation of reference components of meaning is first of all a question of intended relationship and then a question of truth in correspondence to the real world.[35] That is, in dealing with reference, we first of all determine the sense and intended reference and then determine whether that meaning corresponds with historical reality.

There is another distinction to be made, namely, denotation versus connotation. *Denotation* refers to the defining components of meanings *specified* in the use of a word. Denotative components of a word may be considered either in relation to a particular referent (the way an author uses the word) or in relation to a general referent (general language use). *Connotation* refers to other components of meaning *implied* in a word that are associated with the use of the word. As with denotative components, connotative components may be considered in a particular authorial usage or in a general range of uses in a language. These components of language meanings may be cognitive, emotive, or volitional.

Consider a simple example. If I refer to an "old easy chair" that is in my living room, the denotation is that of a piece of upholstered furniture of some age; the connotation is that it provides comfort and is something important because I am fond of it.

As a biblical illustration of the problems presented by poetry, we need look no further than Psalm 23. The following interpretation by Leland Ryken suggests multiple levels of meaning:

> Because of its concentration, poetry often says several things at the same time. The

---

[34] The term "literary" is used in two senses in this text. It is used in a general way to refer to each book in the Bible as great literature. In its narrower sense it distinguishes the design of the text—literary rather than expository.

[35] Gottlob Frege, "On Sense and Reference," in P. Geach and M. Black, eds., *Translations From the Philosophical Writings of Gottlob Frege* (Oxford: Blackwell, 1960), 56–78.

result can be called ambiguity or multiple meaning. Sometimes a poem achieves this complexity and compression by being laminated (consisting of two or more levels of meaning). For example, Psalm 23 is on one level a description of the shepherd's relationship to his sheep, but throughout the poem there is a second, human set of meanings.[36]

Mortimer Adler and Charles Van Doren, in *How to Read a Book*, attribute this quality of "lamination" to the conventions of the literature to which the author submits himself. "The imaginative writer tries to maximize the latent ambiguities of words, in order thereby to gain all the richness and force that is inherent in their multiple meanings."[37] In the conventions of poetry, a single meaning may be ambiguous or general in language structure without being equivocal in composition. So "ambiguity" here does not imply uncertainty of meaning; rather, it refers to the possible presence of two or more meanings in the language use that may be related into a unified meaning in composition.

This is the case in Psalm 23, because the two levels, animal and human, are not unrelated or in conflict. The author obviously intended to speak of the human spiritual realm in terms of the animal natural realm. This general statement of the author's intended meaning is supported by many textual clues that make this abundantly clear (v. 1, "my," "I"; v. 2, "me," "me"; v. 3, "my soul," and so on). Thus Psalm 23 is simply a developed metaphor.[38] The author, David, uses the

richness and force of the image of a shepherd in referring to YHWH because such emotive richness and force is unattainable in direct statements about God.

Another example of multiple meanings suggested by Ryken is Psalm 46.[39] Ryken organizes the psalm as follows: God's presence in the midst of natural upheavals (vv. 1–3), God's presence in the midst of military threats (vv. 4–7), and God's assertion of his authority against warring nations (vv. 8–11). Ryken then proposes three interpretations of the psalm:

a. A song of Zion that focuses on confident worship due to God's presence amid threats in his temple;

b. A song of victory that celebrates God's intervening protection in times of military and political threats to his people; and

c. An apocalyptic vision that celebrates the ultimate conquest of God in behalf of his people.

These three interpretations are not incompatible with the goal of a single meaning if it can be shown that all three are simply components of a unified meaning of the psalm.

Two possible conflicts appear. The first conflict would arise from the differences among the interpretations. But it seems to me that the difference between interpretations *a* and *b* is simply a matter of different emphasis in interpretation. In the first, the reader's attention is focused primarily on worship; in the second, attention is given to the hymn as a whole. It is in this interpretation of the "sense as a whole" that the textual

---

[36]Quentin Skinner, "Motives, Intentions and the Interpretation of Text," in *On Literary Intention* (Edinburgh: Edinburgh University Press, 1976), 217.

[37]Mortimer J. Adler and Charles Van Doren, *How to Read a Book,* rev. ed. (New York: Simon & Schuster, 1972), 206.

[38]E. W. Bullinger, *Figures of Speech Used in the Bible* (reprint, Grand Rapids: Baker, 1968), 735. "A *metaphor* is confined to a distinct affirmation that *one thing* is *another thing,* owing to some association or connection in the uses or effects of anything expressed understood."

[39]Leland Ryken, *The Literature of the Bible* (Grand Rapids: Zondervan, 1974), 135.

statements about "natural upheavals" are recognized as figurative representations of the agitation of Israel's military foes.[40] Only if the early descriptions (vv. 1–3) are taken out of the context of verses 4–11 could the natural description be construed as simply nature rather than as military or political description. Thus the three interpretations may be simply distinguished as two interpretations: a historical reference in interpretations *a* and *b* and an apocalyptic reference in interpretation *c*.

Having considered the apparent conflict between interpretations *a* and *b,* can we resolve the apparent conflict between these two and interpretation *c?* We could say that the historical references communicate a sense that is limited in its degree of realization, while the apocalyptic reference communicates a sense that is completely realized. These meanings of limited and full reference are not conflicting; they are a typical example of biblical prophecy, which commonly has a single sense but a near and a far reference. Thus the three interpretations proposed by Ryken may be seen as simply partial interpretations of one comprehensive meaning of the whole psalm that may be summarized: "God's presence among Israel assures them of ultimate conquest over the nations in spite of the impending threat of the nations."

A second problem in considering a unified, comprehensive meaning of the whole psalm lies in the reference to a river in Psalm 46:4. Ryken suggests that the historical reference and the apocalyptic reference may be incompatible.

> To read the psalm in this way [historical reference] necessitates a symbolic reading of the landscape described in verse 4. Jerusalem had no river running through it, and the city's water was supplied by aqueducts (Isa. 7:3 . . .). The river that gladdens the city of God is symbolic of God's grace and presence.[41]

The problem is that in the apocalyptic view of Jerusalem, as described in Revelation 22:1–2, the city has "the river of the water of life." Does this view of the future Jerusalem mean that the apocalyptic interpretation of "river" has a direct, literal sense while the historical interpretation has a figurative sense? That would introduce different senses that are not based on the text, which could deny the goal of a single, unified meaning.[42]

This difference in semantics exists when "river" in a figurative sense ("God's presence and grace") is compared with "river" in a natural, literal sense ("a large stream of water flowing through a well-defined channel"). The associated component of meaning— namely, "blessing"—is not a defining, denotative component of "river." The connotative sense of "blessing" is not necessarily related to a stream of water flowing through a channel. A river at flood stage does not connote blessing.

---

[40] Ibid., 137.

[41] Ibid., 136–37.

[42] Eugene Nida has demonstrated the incompatible difference between a natural, literal sense and an extended, figurative sense in his illustration with the word *dog:* "Figurative extensions of meaning involve *totally different* semantic domains, with relations between the base and the figurative meanings established by means of some supplementary component or reinterpreted diagnostic component. When one says 'that guy's a dog,' the meaning of 'dog' obviously does not have a referent to a particular quadruped of the canine class. Rather, this meaning of 'dog' is roughly equivalent to the abstract 'contemptible,' and in the meaning 'dog' belongs to the semantic domain of such words as 'contemptible, worthless, and despicable,' with which it overlaps in meaning. The fact that 'dog' can be used in this sense results from the conventional association between dogs and this quality" (*Componential Analysis of Meaning,* 126 [emphasis added]).

The context of the psalm, "God's presence assures them of conquest," does not imply any natural sense of "river," but only the figurative sense of blessing flowing from God. The question of two senses only arises when a historical realm (with no actual river present) and an apocalyptic realm (with a river present, Rev. 22:1–2) are allowed to determine the meaning.

What difference does this make? The problem is that the two senses are textually undetermined and unrelated. In fact, the textual clues in no way suggest a literal river. Nor does an apocalyptic reading require a reference to a literal river. The fact that there will be a "river of life" in the apocalyptic Jerusalem does not mean that Psalm 46 refers to this river. Rather, the psalm refers in both the historical and the apocalyptic readings to the blessing issuing from God's presence that results in conquest over the nations (46:5–6). So a natural reading of the text recognizes one meaning intended in the use of the word "river" in Psalm 46.

Therefore, in this reflection upon the psalm, rather than undermining the goal of interpretation as a single, unified meaning, the psalm can be plausibly read to express a comprehensive sense implying both a historical and an apocalyptic ultimate fulfillment.

Biblical Prophecy

The second genre that at times seems to fly in the face of the goal of a single meaning is prophetic literature. Perhaps the most common contention surrounds a *change in meaning* from the natural, historical sense to a spiritual, prophetic sense. A term may have one meaning in its first usage and then appear to have another or changed meaning in subsequent Old Testament or New Testament quotations of or allusions to the passage. This contention appears in the

position held by Patrick Fairbairn, as may be evidenced in his interpretation of "Abraham's seed."

> The promises . . . were made to Abraham and his seed; but to his seed *only in the sense explained by the Apostle* (Rom. 4, 9; Gal. 3); that is, to those who might spring from Abraham's loins, in so far— but in so far only—as they stood also in his faith and walked in his footsteps; and along with these, to all who should possess the same spiritual standing, *whether they might belong or not to the number of his natural offspring*. The possession of the spiritual element was thus, in every age, stamped as the essential thing."[43]

The change in sense concerns his conclusion that "the spiritual element" was the essential thing in every age. As he develops his argument, the "essential element" becomes the "only element" because the natural element comes to experience God's judgment. From a reading of God's word to Abram, however (Gen. 15:1–5), it appears that God is saying that both physical descent and spiritual relation are essential. After the long delay in fulfillment of the promise, Abram suggested that a servant in his household be his heir (Gen. 15:3). Undoubtedly the trusted and respected servant shared in Abram's faith, but he obviously was not physically a seed of Abram. God promised specifically that the seed who would be Abram's heir would be "a son coming from your own body" (Gen. 15:4). Thus physical descent is an essential element in diagnosing the sense of seed and heir, along with a spiritual relation to God. Later, Abraham pleaded for his offspring Ishmael: "If only Ishmael might live under your blessing!" God replied, "Yes, but your wife Sarah will bear you a son, and you will call him Isaac. I will establish my covenant with him" (Gen. 17:18–19). Thus the meaning of "Abraham's

---

[43] Patrick Fairbairn, *Prophecy* (reprint, Grand Rapids: Baker, 1976), 46 (emphasis added).

seed" is defined contextually by both a physical relation to Abraham and a spiritual relation to the election of God.[44] These both must be considered essential in the original uses.

To an evangelical interpreter, the crucial question here is, Does the New Testament bring authority to interpret the Old Testament in a sense different than and changed from the sense of its original usage? In the case of "Abraham's seed," does Paul's added revelation that both Jew and gentile believers today are Abraham's seed (Gal. 3:26–29) justify changing the original sense into an essential, spiritual sense? In his later affirmation "not all who are descended from Israel are Israel" (Rom. 9:6), Paul emphasizes that "physical is not sufficient"—which is quite different from saying that "physical is not necessary or essential." Paul affirms that "all Israel will be saved" (Rom. 11:26) as a fulfillment of Old Testament prophecy (Isa. 59:20–21; 27:9), by which he distinguishes "all Israel" from the limited "remnant chosen by grace" (Rom. 11:5) in Paul's day. Thus Israel in both of Paul's uses is necessarily both physical and spiritual.

Again, in Romans 4:16, Paul recognizes Gentiles as the seed of Abraham in Christ along with the natural and spiritual seed under the law. This interpretation does not change or limit the sense of the Old Testament uses, nor does it change the promise; it merely recognizes that in Christ, Abraham's inheritance has been shared more broadly to include also a spiritual seed who are in Christ. This corresponds to God's promise to bless all families of the earth through Abraham (Gen. 12:3).

Therefore, in the epistles to the Galatians and the Romans, the word "seed"

has two distinct senses that can be distinguished by their diagnostic, denotative components in context. Isaac is Abraham's seed in a *physical and spiritual* sense. The Gentile Christian is Abraham's seed in a *spiritual* sense alone, being "in Christ." Being "in Christ" does not mean that one has a share in Christ's physical life or in Abraham's physical life. Therefore we conclude that Paul is using "seed" in two different but related senses. "Spiritual seed" has a broader semantic domain than "spiritual and physical seed." The semantic domain of *seed (spiritual)* includes Cornelius and Luke as well as David and Peter, while *seed (spiritual and physical)* includes only David and Peter. While David and Peter are included in the domain of *seed (spiritual),* Cornelius and Luke are excluded from the domain of *seed (spiritual and physical).*

It has been asked, "Is it a priori impossible that God would introduce such a 'surprise' factor [spiritual and physical seed to become only spiritual seed] in the manner of fulfillment? Can we deduce from first principles of interpretation, without any reference to the actual content of the Bible, that God cannot do such a thing?"

In response, one can only concede that God *could change* the terms of his promise. However, in view of who God is, *would he do so* in the sense of not keeping what he had originally promised? In a certain parable of Jesus, the landowner had the right to pay those who worked one hour the same amount as those who agreed to work all day (Matt. 20:1–16). But this does not constitute a change in or rejection of the landowner's original agreement. The question remains, *Did God change* the

---

[44]Ramm, *Protestant Biblical Interpretation,* 266. Ramm would generally agree with the "single sense" of the Old Testament usage. But he seems to concede this conclusion: "Therefore, interpret prophecy literally unless the implicit or explicit teaching of the New Testament suggests typological interpretation."

terms of his promise to Abram as reflected in the content of the Bible?

In the present age, Jewishness or physical descent is not a necessary component of relationship to be an heir to Abraham's blessing (Eph. 3:4–10; Acts 15:1–21). Yet Paul distinguished a future age and affirmed a hope for Israel of spiritual *and* physical blessing (Rom. 11:1–32). In this context, physical Israel is distinguished from those who are physically Gentiles (Rom. 11:25–26). Paul thus recognized that Israel as seed is distinct in sense from Jew/Gentile as seed. Therefore, since the Old Testament promise refers to Israel as seed, it remains valid to anticipate a future hope for Israel, since it has not yet been realized. And so it appears that the biblical usage supports an expanded sense of Abram's seed to include both natural/spiritual seed and only spiritual seed. But the expanded sense does not deny or change the original sense, in which God will save "all Israel" (natural and spiritual).

Other examples of prophetic genre that appear to communicate different meanings are developed from the ambiguity inherent in the genre. Herbert Wolf has argued for this position in his study of Haggai 2:7 called "The Desire of All Nations: Messianic or Not?"[45] Traditionally interpreters have taken the phrase "the desire of all nations" to refer to "the Desired One." More recently this phrase has been construed as referring to "desired or precious things" (NASB, JB, NEB). The grammatical difficulties within the verse are judged to be a part of the designed ambiguity. Wolf writes:

> I think the plural verb in Haggai 2:7 does leave the way open for this kind of ambiguity. The interpreter is free to include both the personal "desire" and the material "treasures. . . ." Probably he selected "treasure/desire" because it afforded the exact ambiguity he needed, while the other term for "wealth" (*hayil*) tended to exclude the personal reference. Ultimately it applies to the gathering of the treasures of the nations after the second coming of Christ and to "the glory and honor of the nations" brought into the New Jerusalem (Rev. 21:26), but it can also refer to that "treasure" or "desire of nations," "the messenger of the covenant in whom you delight" (Mal. 3:1).[46]

The question of interpretation becomes, Are the distinct and legitimate meanings which the ambiguity of the grammar permits intended by the author in the meaning of the whole text? The two grammatically possible and yet distinct meanings are "the desired *things* of all nations" (wealth) and "the Desired *One* of all nations" (the Messiah). The nations' desire for wealth is a "natural desire" for "material wealth." By contrast, the nations' desire for a Messiah is a "spiritual desire" for "divine deliverance and rule."

The Hebrew word translated as "desired things" or "Desired One" is a homograph—an instance of two or more words having the same spelling but different meanings.[47] Contextually, both meanings could be combined in the idea of the restoration of temple glory.

---

[45] Herbert Wolf, "The Desire of All Nations in Haggai 2:7: Messianic or Not?" *Journal of the Evangelical Theological Society* 19, no. 2 (June 1976): 97–102.

[46] Ibid., 100–101.

[47] There are several linguistic forms that prove interesting in translation. A homograph, such as we are dealing with here, is a word that is spelled like another but has a different meaning or derivation or pronunciation; an English example is *present* ("gift") as compared with to *present* ("offer"). Homophones are words that are pronounced alike but differ in meaning or derivation or spelling (*tare* and *tear*). Homonyms are words that are spelled and pronounced alike but have different meanings (*bear*, the animal; *bear*, carry).

This would involve a "spiritual desire" for "divine restoration of temple glory including material wealth of the nations." If the sense of the whole context does relate these two meanings, then the distinctive meanings become components of the single sense. If the sense of the whole context does not support both meanings, then the interpreter must choose the one that is most consistent with the meaning of the whole text.

One more argument has been advanced to support a change in sense from an Old Testament geopolitical form of the kingdom to a present, spiritual form. It has been argued that during the course of his ministry Jesus sought to open Israel's eyes to the spiritual intention of these prophecies. It is important to qualify what is asserted here. While Jesus does emphasize the spiritual dimension of the Old Testament, he does so because of Israel's blindness to the spiritual. This does not demand a change of the Old Testament sense of promises, but merely an emphasis on the spiritual component of the Old Testament. In one example it is asserted that Jesus "transferred the 'temple' from a physical building to His Body (John 2:19–21)." But Jesus' words "destroy this temple" may be merely a metaphorical use of "temple" to refer to the spiritual analogy between his body and the building, God's dwelling place. Nothing in the text supports the idea of "transfer" or supports an allusion to fulfillment.

In summary, through these several examples we have attempted to clarify the definition of the "single sense" expressed within the conventions of poetic and prophetic genre. This single sense is determined in the components of the Author's/author's intended usage. In Psalm 46, military conquest historically and apocalyptically involves the same sense in the denotative components. Connotative components of unique historical references do not change the sense of the text. In Paul's use of "seed," careful observation of his *distinct use of diagnostic components* can enable the interpreter to distinguish two senses in different contexts. However, *distinct diagnostic components* such as "wealth" and "Messiah" cannot be considered as one sense unless wealth is taken in a specific reference to temple adornment under Messiah. The author's usage must give evidence of combining these components in a related single sense before both can be affirmed as intended by the Author/author.

In our example, the shared connotative components that become the *figurative diagnostic sense* of "river" do involve a "single sense" in both historical and apocalyptic references. In Psalm 23, "shepherd" is not used by David in a limited, natural sense of a man who herds and takes care of sheep. Rather it is used in a figurative sense that is built on the diagnostic component of "taking care of." The figurative sense of God who takes care of David is thus the single meaning.

5. The Theological Premise

The theological premise affirms that the textually based sense is the revelation of God, which determines the truthfulness and the radically unique content that is progressively revealed.

Each of the hermeneutical premises considered so far is an appropriate issue for preunderstanding in general hermeneutics. In our discussion, however, the uniqueness of the biblical text has at times become evident, as in some of the corollaries to the literal and historical premises. But we address the matter of biblical uniqueness directly in the fifth premise of preunderstanding. This concerns reaching valid conclusions about the nature of the Bible and correct interpretation of broad and progressively revealed themes of biblical content.

The basic feature of the Bible that needs to be considered among the general principles is the divine and human authorship. Christian hermeneutics has long wrestled with the perplexing problem of the dual authorship of Scripture. The intended sense must be discovered in the shared divine and human expression of the text, a union that J. I. Packer views as a theological "mystery":

Evangelicals stress that Scriptural composition is a *mystery* in a sense parallel to that in which the incarnation is a *mystery*—that is, that the identifying of the human and the divine in the words of the text in the one case, like the taking of manhood into God in the person of Jesus in the other, was a unique divine act of which we cannot fully grasp the process of the event. Scripture is as genuinely and fully human as it is divine. It is more than Jewish-Christian religious literature but not less. There is a true analogy between the written Word and the incarnate Word. In both cases, the divine coincides with the form of the human, and the absolute appears in the form of the relative.[48]

Packer does not try to explain the mystery by making a distinction between divine and human components of meaning. Instead he deals with the dual authorship by seeing simultaneously both true humanity and true deity in the product of the text.

True human expression entails sharing the meaning that would enable the author to write in his language and in his personal style. It is impossible to explain exactly how God shared the meaning of the text with man, but that is not at issue in interpretation. What is at issue is *the intended meaning expressed in the text.* Error is not a necessary trait of human intention, even though it is a common trait of fallen man. Historical and cultural perspectives are not necessary traits of human intention, though they are common traits of historical man. Despite human limitations, the human author was enriched by divine providential guidance.[49]

True divine authorship affirms that the content was originated with God (2 Peter 1:20–21), resulting in Scripture's having a divine source. God then providentially shared the meaning with the human author. The human authors "spoke from God as they were carried along by the Holy Spirit." The product is a verbally inspired text that is shared as God's word and the human writer's word (2 Tim. 3:16).

The task of interpretation must take place within these limits of Authorship/authorship. If the goal of interpretation is to determine the author's intended meaning, the immediate question arises, Which author? Since intention involves both the chosen expressions of a text and the realm of reference, and since both authors share in the expression of the text, the overall "sense of the whole literary unit" is at least a shared meaning. This "sense of the whole," which is shared by both authors, is the single meaning of the whole text. So the ultimate goal is the single, unified meaning originating with the *divine Author,* as expressed by the human author.

Yet it seems clear in several passages that the human author did not consciously share in the full implications of all that he wrote. This seems evident in the apostle Peter's statement in 1 Peter 1:10–11:

---

[48] J. I. Packer, "Biblical Authority, Hermeneutics and Inerrancy," in *Jerusalem and Athens,* ed. E. R. Geehan (Philadelphia: Presbyterian and Reformed, 1971), 144–45.

[49] This does not necessarily imply dictation. Even today the believer is responsible to have his "mind renewed" through divine instruction (Rom. 12:1–2).

> Concerning this salvation, the prophets, who spoke of the grace that was to come to you, searched intently and with the greatest care, trying to find out the time and circumstances to which the Spirit of Christ in them was pointing when he predicted. . . .

The passage implies that human writers at times meant more than they knew or were aware of. But this raises questions: (a) Does the divine Author's intended meaning exceed the human author's intended meaning? (b) If they intend different meanings, are they unrelated or radically different even if they are not in conflict? (c) What control remains in the single meaning of the literal tradition if the divine and human authors intend different meanings?

Walter Kaiser discounts the first two questions on the grounds that there is a single intent and a single meaning shared consciously by the human and divine authors. But the third question requires some attention. In regard to 1 Peter 1:10–12, Kaiser asks:

> Does this text teach that the writers of Scripture "wrote better than they knew"? Indeed it does not. On the contrary, it decisively affirms that the prophets spoke knowingly on five rather precise topics: (1) the Messiah, (2) His suffering, (3) His glory, (4) the sequence of events, . . . and (5) that the salvation announced in those pre-Christian days was not limited to the prophets' audiences, but it also included the readers of Peter's day.[50]

What was it, then, that the prophets "searched intently" for? All the modern translations connect "time and circumstances." But Kaiser holds that although the prophets were searching, without success, about the time when these things would take place,

this passage does not teach that these men were curious and often ignorant of the exact meaning of what they wrote and predicted. Theirs was not a search for the *meaning* of what they wrote; it was an inquiry into the *temporal* aspects of the *subject,* which went beyond what they wrote.[51]

But even if Kaiser's model of shared meaning is right, aren't there passages like Daniel 9:24–27 that involve meanings of time? It seems clear that Daniel was ignorant of the date of "the decree to restore and rebuild Jerusalem," even though he wrote about it. So it must be that Daniel wrote more than he understood. But this ignorance on the part of Daniel does not imply a mindless writing of the text. Nor does the lack of knowledge necessarily imply a dictation of texts to the prophet, although that may be true in this instance. But the question remains, Does this ignorance undermine the literal goal of a single, unified meaning?

What the human and divine authors share is a knowledge of the unified sense of the whole text and a knowledge of the related senses of the textual expressions. This knowledge is the basis of the composition of the text. This unified, intended sense is expressed in the text and provides the control of the literal tradition. What unsaid components of sense there may be which are necessarily related to the textual sense and which are known to God and unknown to the human author, the interpreter has no way of knowing from the textual signs alone. What components of reference there may be, either historical or prophetic, which are known to God and unknown to the human author, again the interpreter has no way of knowing from the text alone. Yet all these components that are related to the

---

[50] Walter C. Kaiser, Jr., "The Single Intent of Scripture," in *Evangelical Roots,* ed. Kenneth Kantzer (Nashville: Nelson, 1978), 125.

[51] Ibid., 126.

textual meanings are necessarily intended by God. And these components of meaning are encompassed in the goal of interpretation of the Bible. In parts 2 and 3 we consider how to recognize and exegete related components of meanings that are not stated directly in the text but are necessary to its meaning.

In conclusion, while the divine Author's intended meaning may exceed the human author's conscious meanings, yet the shared single meaning of the text is the basis of and has control over any related fuller sense and reference.

But there is another aspect of the uniqueness of the Bible: its content. Bultmann attempted to deal with this issue in his concept of demythologization. To him, the essential uniqueness is cultural; the ancient view of spiritual health is uniquely different from a modern worldview of psychological health. The ancient view of justification by faith is myth that has no relevance to modern man; the ancient and outmoded myth must be replaced by a relevant idea. While modern man knows more thoroughly about many things about the world, truth stated in the *kerygma* sits in judgment on modern man.[52]

For Bultmann, the gospel has limited authority in the content of the *kerygma*. He denied the radical authority of the Bible to sit in judgment on the thoughts and intents of man's heart, even modern man with his supposedly superior knowledge.

By contrast, I believe the uniqueness of the Bible is not ancient culture as distinct from modern culture, but the gulf between a spiritual viewpoint and a natural viewpoint. Jesus' message received similar criticism from his contemporaries as it does from a modern critic. Yet those for and against him shared a similar worldview and common cultural presuppositions. The Jews of Jesus' time, both for and against him, were nearly all supernaturalists who acknowledged both God and Satan. So the uniqueness of the biblical message lies not in its cultural viewpoint, but in its spiritual viewpoint. This spiritual message sits in judgment on all natural men, ancient and modern, with the thoughts and intents of our hearts.

Faith is not required for initially hearing the biblical message, but a studied resistance and rejection of that message will prevent understanding. An openness of faith toward God and the spiritual impact of his Word is necessary if we are to increase in wisdom. A responsiveness to God and to the spiritual impact of his Word is necessary to becoming mature. This is an essential hermeneutical preunderstanding in the pursuit of the goal of interpreting the Author's/author's intended meaning.

SUMMARY

The hermeneutical premises that illumine the goal of interpretation provide the framework within which viable interpretation takes place. The five premises deal with the goal in different ways. The literal system affirms that the goal of the meaning to be interpreted must be *based* in the text, and the grammatical, historical, literary, and theological premises establish the range of *preunderstandings* that the interpreter shares with the author and draws upon in properly construing the meanings expressed in the text.

---

[52] Rudolf Bultmann, *Kerygma and Myth* (New York: Harper & Row, Harper Torchbooks, 1961), 210.

CHAPTER 4

Objections to the Proposed Goal of Interpretation

Nearly every book of the Bible contains passages that have been interpreted in completely different and in even incompatible ways. Disagreements over interpretation can often be traced, not to differences in exegetical and theological method, but to a more fundamental cause: the goal of interpretation. A goal has such far-reaching effects on the interpretation that even using a common method will not prevent interpreters from coming to different conclusions. Thus in part 1 we have given considerable attention to clearly distinguishing our goal of interpretation from other goals and to carefully considering the hermeneutical aspects of the goal. This chapter will deal with several objections to the goal of interpretation we have proposed.

By way of review, our proposed goal is to determine the single or unifying meaning of the text that the divine Author and human author intended to communicate. We have defined our terms and have dealt with hermeneutical questions relating to that goal. The final step will be to defend that goal against objections that can be and are often raised.

Our defense of the stated goal of interpretation centers on the answers to two fundamental questions. The first question:

1. Does the text communicate meaning?

Our goal asserts that there is a single, unifying meaning in each literary unit. This thought was derived from convictions emerging from the literal tradition. If an author is going to communicate meaning that can be understood and known to be true, then all the component meanings must be capable of textual relationship to a unifying and comprehensive meaning. An enigmatic or equivocal meaning in composition can not communicate truth. Textually unrelated meanings can never be known from textual clues alone. In biblical communication, one unified and coherent textual meaning is necessary for theological reasons, which we will identify. In the meantime we confront the second question:

2. What determines that meaning of the text?

The assertion that the divine Author's/human author's intention as expressed in the text determines the meanings has raised several objections. Some arise from theoretical discussion of the proposed goal; others arise from practical evaluation of the process of how readers attempt to reach their goal in the interpretive process. Eight objections in all will be considered.

OBJECTION NO. 1

The goal of interpreting a single, unified coherent textual meaning is unnecessary *because God is free to communicate as he chooses.*

The question has been raised whether God is bound by constraints of normal human communication. Is God governed by the constraints of human convention and human linguistic form? Does this not put an artificial constraint on God? Or, does his desire to communicate with mankind not subject God to the shared dimensions of human communication? It will be argued that God's character and God's ways with his creation necessarily limit him if he intends to communicate with mankind. There are at least four reasons for this:

a. This goal is necessary because of the condition of mankind. If God created mankind to know him, it is necessary that when God speaks, mankind can understand and know what his words mean. While there may be other aspects in man's knowing God, this knowledge is not less than verbal since God has spoken. For verbal communication to exist, verbal meanings must be shared between God and mankind. These meanings are distinct from intuitive or private kinds of meaning that are independent from what God and mankind share in the text. Shared knowledge must be based on and determined by the text they share. For man to be able to know the textual meanings, these meanings must be related to one another in a textually unified whole. If there were unrelated meanings, they would of necessity be determined by something unrelated to the text. Thus the text must communicate a unified

meaning composed of related meanings in order that humans can know what God has spoken to them.

b. The goal is necessary because of the veracity of God. If God speaks truth, then it is necessary that the meaning can be recognized as true. The primary meaning must be shared with component meanings that are unified, related, and *noncontradictory*. If the meaning is true, then a statement may mean *A* or non-*A*, but it cannot mean *A and* non-*A*. The same statement cannot mean contradictory meanings at the same time and in the same context. So the textual meaning must necessarily be unified and coherent in the sense of consisting of textually related and noncontradictory meanings.

c. The goal is necessary because of the righteous authority of God. If God judges mankind in righteous judgment—and he does—then he honors man's right to know what he is responsible for. While there may be varying terms of responsibility, for some it means an obligation toward verbal revelation (Rom. 2:17–29). This implies that man is not only capable of knowing, but also capable of knowing that he knows. This in turn requires the presence of a single meaning that is textually determined. Differences as to what the textual meaning is can be weighed according to textual support for a given construction. A meaning that can be textually validated then becomes a righteous basis for God's authoritative judgment.

d. The goal is necessary because of the condition of God's creation. Mankind's knowledge of God's creation consistently offers evidence for unity existing amid complexity. The world within creation is identified as a *uni*verse rather than a *multi*verse in spite of the complexity. Mankind's practice of classifying and categorizing the natural world evidences the generic unity of the "kinds of God's creation." The very character of human language witnesses to mankind's innate view of life as one-and-many, even as Adam named the creation and could speak about the creation with God and with other humans. Is it not then natural—in fact, necessary—to expect the creative revelation of God to be a unified arrangement of related components? This expectation is further supported in the practice of exegesis by those who treat the Bible's literary composition as a unity. Indeed, if God's creative work is a coherent unit involving diverse complexity, then of necessity his revelation to mankind must also be treated as a unity with related and noncontradictory components.

OBJECTION NO. 2

The author's intention is an unstable *goal because the meaning of the text changes in history and even in time may change for an author.*

In the first aspect of this two-pronged objection, a number of theories of textual meaning claim that the meaning of the text changes. Rene Wellek and Austin Warren declared this in their work *Theory of Literature.*[1] In the late eighteenth century, Johann Gottfried Herder challenged the previously accepted assumption that human nature is essentially the same in all times and places. The result of this challenge was a view of history called "historicism," which holds that a text's meaning changes in essence from era to era. While we recognize that there have been different interpretations of a text in different eras, we assert that a text must be read within the historical set-

ting in which it was written, and we do not accept the conclusion of the radical historicists that the meaning of a text is essentially different from era to era.

E. D. Hirsch has identified three fallacies inherent in the radical historicist view and relevant to biblical interpretation.[2]

a. The fallacy of assuming that the past is inscrutable. The radical historicist position maintains that the past is so different from our time that its texts can only be understood by an initiated few. Hans-Georg Gadamer was rightly critical of Schleiermacher for importing nineteenth-century rational ideals into interpretation while ignoring the concrete historical facts of the past.[3] But at the same time he conceded that "one is set within what various traditions mean really and primarily that one is subject to prejudices and limited in one's freedom."[4] Gadamer meant by this that an interpreter's "fore-conception" or prior knowledge of the subject informs and even distorts his understanding every time he reads about that subject in whatever historical tradition.[5] Thus limiting a reader to his own historical understanding implies that certain things in the past are innately inscrutable to modern man. The historicist remedy to this is to modernize the meaning.

An antidote to this historical fallacy, however, is to be found in Edmund Husserl's distinction between perception and the object perceived. He argued that historical objects do not change in time and that modern man needs to reconstruct his perceptions consistent with what is known of the ancient object.

---

[1] René Wellek and Austin Warren, *Theory of Literature* (New York: Harcourt, Brace, 1956).

[2] E. D. Hirsch, Jr., *The Aims of Interpretation* (Chicago: University of Chicago Press, 1976), 38–42.

[3] Hans-Georg Gadamer, *Truth and Method* (New York: Crossroad, 1975), 260.

[4] Ibid., 245.

[5] Ibid., 261–62.

b. The fallacy of assuming that the past is homogeneous. Another historical perspective argues that biblical interpretation often stresses the homogeneity of a historical period (the sameness between periods of history) without placing a corresponding stress on individuality within that period. The line of reasoning typically takes the form of a syllogism such as the following:

> The Stoics used *logos* to mean the mind of God, guiding, controlling, and directing all things.
>
> The apostle John uses *logos* to mean the source of creation.
>
> Therefore the apostle John built on Stoical thought.

The weakness of this type of argument is that it fails to examine the text for John's particular usage, which may be distinct from Stoic thought.

This weakness can also be seen in the works of scholars belonging to the "history of religion" (*religionsgeschichtlich*) school. This approach to the New Testament "endeavoured to set the religious presuppositions of primitive Christianity in their contemporary near Eastern and Greco-Roman context [and] promised at one time to provide powerful help towards its [primitive Christianity] interpretation."[6] It is evident here again that any assumed homogeneity must also be demonstrated by the historical usage of an author in the Bible's text.

Old Testament studies that employ cognate languages to increase modern man's knowledge of obscure Hebrew words must recognize that their investigations offer the interpreter only possible and potential meaning. The *actual* meaning must be established in the context of the author's usage. This limitation potentially applies to shared concepts used in Ugaritic or Arabic or Akkadian sources. Even studies of the meaning of phrases or clauses that share common constructions with cognate languages must discover actual meanings of the construction in biblical usage in the canonical context.

Hans Walter Wolff recognized this, for example, as he wrote:

> Israel showed itself to be concerned with the demythologizing of death, which (in view of the country's neighbors) appeared both different and essential for the believer in Yahweh . . . [and] usually talk about the descent into *še'ōl* as the world of the dead means no more than an indication of burial as the end of life (. . . Ps. 16:10).[7]

The translators of the New King James Version in Psalm 16:10 left open the possibility that more than "grave" was meant, and so they transliterated the Hebrew "Sheol," implying a technical term and revelatory content. The sense of "Sheol" may add to the culturally shared sense of "grave," and this added sense would be based on what had been revealed about death as the judgment of God (Gen. 2–5).

A major emphasis of hermeneutics in the nineteenth and twentieth centuries has been to define the historical setting of biblical literature as the context within which a term or construction is to be understood. This approach has demonstrated (1) the necessity of historical analogy to avoid modernizing, and (2) the danger of drawing parallels where similarity is very superficial.[8] Such historical investigation is valid

---

[6] F. F. Bruce, "The History of New Testament Study," in *New Testament Interpretation,* ed. I. Howard Marshall (Grand Rapids: Eerdmans, 1977), 48.

[7] Hans Walter Wolff, *Anthropology of the Old Testament* (Philadelphia: Fortress, 1974), 102–3.

[8] James M. Robinson, *New Frontiers in Theology,* vol 2: *The New Hermeneutic,* ed. James M. Robinson and John B. Cobbs, Jr. (New York: Harper & Row, 1964), 13.

and at times necessary, but it must avoid the assumption of a homogeneous past.

c. The fallacy of assuming that the present is homogeneous with the past. The assumption that our present perspective is homogeneous with the past is a construction as artificial as any "reconstruction" of the past. However, just such an assumption is frequently made. For example, Rudolf Bultmann constantly asserted that the essence of the biblical message is concerned with human existence and that human existence is the central issue with which contemporary man is essentially concerned.[9] Therefore, Bultmann argued, since existential concerns are the primary concern of *modern man,* "he will find the answer in the New Testament—provided all nonessential stumbling-blocks have been removed from the New Testament by the demythologizing programme."[10] Gadamer offers the basis for such an approach when he says:

> We see here again that understanding means, primarily, to understand the content of what is said, and only secondarily to isolate and understand another's meaning as such. Hence the first of all hermeneutic requirements remains one's own foreunderstanding, which proceeds from being concerned with the same subject.[11]

This contention that the author's meaning is unstable rests on certain assumptions about mankind's knowledge of the historical past. But these assumptions are by no means necessary. The fallacy of historicism rests in these erroneous views of the past. Historicism is in part a reaction against the danger of modernization of the biblical text and an attempt to deal with the limits of man's historical knowledge.

The ancient biblical text, although composed over a period of almost two thousand years, is itself not necessarily alien to us even though it is at times admittedly distant and foreign. The capacity of the human consciousness to imagine worlds and historical eras other than one's own enables the interpreter to overcome many problems of ancient communication. Such imagined shifts in thought are possible because there are fundamental and parallel experiences in human existence that are enhanced in biblical revelation by the presence of an unchanging God.

Note that this capacity of the human consciousness does not mean that there are *no* problems in historical understanding of the text. The absence of supporting historical data both inside and outside the biblical text, however, is not a sufficient basis on which to assume either an inscrutable past or homogeneity in the past. The principle of stable and knowable historical meaning is not overturned by difficulties in establishing particular historical meanings.

Now, having dealt with the first aspect of the objection—that is, that a text's meaning can change historically—we must consider the related statement that the meaning can change for an author over time. There are three points that refute this position.

First, there is an important distinction between revising a text and changing the textual meaning of what was originally said. Revision may be undertaken (1) to clarify the original statement, or (2) to repudiate the original statement and replace it by another. Such textual revisions by an author do not change the textual meaning, even for himself.

---

[9]Rudolf Bultmann, "The Problem of Hermeneutics," in *Essays Philosophical and Theological,* trans. J. C. G. Greig (London: n.p., 1955), 234ff.

[10]Bruce, "The History of New Testament Study," 51.

[11]Gadamer, *Truth and Method,* 262.

Second, there is an important distinction between textual meaning and an author's "response" to his text. Hirsch notes that "the phenomenon of changing authorial responses is important because it illustrates the difference between textual meaning and what is loosely termed a 'response' to the text."[12] An author may see what he once wrote in a new light and recognize it as being inadequate, wrong, or confusing; but to reject what one once said is not to say that the meaning of what was said has changed. Indeed, the very fact that we can make a distinction in meanings acknowledges that the original meaning is stable and has not changed.

Third, Hirsch distinguishes between the meaning of a text (which does not change) and the significance of a text (which may change).

> *Meaning* is that which is represented by a text; it is what the author meant by his use of a particular sign sequence; it is what the signs represent. *Significance,* on the other hand, names a relationship between that meaning and a person, or a conception, or a situation, or indeed anything imaginable. Authors, who like everyone else change their attitudes, feelings, opinions, and value criteria in the course of time, tend to view their own work in different contexts. Clearly what changes for them is not the meaning of the work, but rather their relationship to that meaning.[13]

Thus the arguments for a change in meaning over time can be eliminated by (1) clarifying the nature of apparent changes that occur, and (2) establishing that the author's intention expressed in the text does not change for the author. We may therefore conclude that since the author's intention is stable, the goal of interpreting that intention is also stable.

OBJECTION NO. 3

The author's intention is an irrelevant goal because the issue is not what an author means, but only what the text says.

This objection has been defended in two ways:

a. Semantic autonomy: T. S. Eliot propounded in "Tradition and the Individual Talent" the theory of semantic autonomy, which in essence states that the meaning of written language is impersonal, objective, and independent of the life of its author. Eliot based his theory on two grounds: (1) the author has no control over the words he has loosed upon the world, and (2) he has no special privileges as an interpreter of them.[14]

b. The author's success: Wimsatt and Beardsley wrote, "The author's desire to communicate a particular meaning is not necessarily the same as his success in doing so. Since his actual performance is presented in his text, any special attempt to divine his intention would falsely equate his private wish with his public accomplishment."[15]

These two arguments are formal defenses for the consideration of a text separated from its author and do not have a direct influence on biblical study. So let's "go around Robin Hood's barn" in responding to them.

Most exegetical commentaries and articles about biblical texts focus on verbal meaning and verbal forms. Generally absent from these discussions is

---

[12] E. D. Hirsch, Jr., *Validity in Interpretation* (New Haven: Yale University Press, 1967), 7.

[13] Ibid., 8.

[14] T. S. Eliot, "Tradition and the Individual Talent," in *The Sacred Wood* (London: Methuen, 1960).

[15] Wimsatt and Beardsley, "Intentional Fallacy," 1–13.

any consideration of the author's role in communication. Thus an extensive body of literature virtually ignores the author as having any determinative role in narrowing usage and meaning. James M. Robinson correctly observes that what is normally treated in the discipline called hermeneutics is a "discussion of the language of the text."[16] For example, Bauer asserted in his lexicon that "it is the purpose of this lexicon to facilitate the understanding of texts that were composed in the Late Greek described above."[17] In his fine introductory grammar, Eugene Goetchius wrote:

> *Grammar*—the system of formal structural devices or "rules" which a language uses to indicate the relationship between words and arrangements of words. . . . [it] enables us to understand what words mean in particular contexts and, hence, to understand at least to some extent what a word means *before* we look it up in a dictionary, and . . . to choose correctly from among the assorted meanings which a dictionary offers.[18]

Underlying this understanding of verbal meaning is the insistence that a close correlation must exist between form and meaning. The nature of this correlation is important. Many interpreters accept an unstated assumption that Hirsch has verbalized: "if the rules and canons of construction are made precise, and if the tools of linguistic analysis are sharpened and refined, the problems of interpretation will be resolved into operational procedures."[19] Further support for this perception that the task of interpretation is merely linguistic and textual is sometimes

found in the doctrine of verbal plenary inspiration. Since the very words of the biblical text are so critical, a simple consideration of them and their grammatical relation is sufficient to disclose their meaning. Thus, in practice the author's intention becomes irrelevant to the task of interpretation.

This unstated assumption can be easily shown to be invalid by considering the case of irony. The presence or absence of irony changes nothing in the text *except its fundamental meaning*. Many of the parables of Jesus are full of irony. He told them in order to make one audience understand a different meaning from another (Matt. 13:10–17). Therefore it is a fundamental error to assume that the particular meaning of a text is directly and completely revealed in the textual form and style apart from a consideration of the author's context.

Hirsch has argued against this unstated assumption in a discussion of "stylistics and synonymity."[20] His argument for *synonymity* does not rest on the criterion of universal substitutability proposed by the analytic philosophers, but on the criterion of occasional substitutability of common speech. Practical synonymity exists at several levels: (1) at the level of the morpheme, the various forms, in highly variable relations between form and meaning, are synonymous (*ou, ais, as* as alternate genitive forms in Greek, or *d, t, ed* as past tense markers in English); (2) at the level of stylistic choices or at the level of lexical choice, two words in particular uses may be completely synonymous (*legō* and *laleō* in Greek, or "jacket" and "coat" in English); (3) at

[16] Robinson, *New Frontiers in Theology,* 12.
[17] W. F. Arndt, and F. W. Gingrich, *A Greek-English Lexicon of the New Testament and Other Early Christian Literature,* trans. Walter Bauer (Chicago: University of Chicago Press, 1957), xviii.
[18] Eugene Van Ness Goetchius, *The Language of the New Testament* (New York: Scribner's, 1965), xv.
[19] Hirsch, *The Aims of Interpretation,* 22.
[20] Ibid., 50–73.

the syntactic level, although this is more complex, there are contexts where distinct forms are synonymous (present and aorist tenses, as in the gnomic present and the gnomic aorist in Greek,[21] or active and passive voice in English). In each case, the simple point is that the author's use of a text is not irrelevant. While the author's role in every particular case is not equally clear, that role is nonetheless essential.

And that brings us to the formal objections of T. S. Eliot on the one hand and Wimsatt and Beardsley on the other. The latter objection—that an author does not necessarily succeed in communicating his meaning—is not germane to biblical interpretation, because the biblical text is the expression of the Author's/author's intention by definition. What the divine Author intended to communicate, he succeeded in expressing in the text.

Eliot's objection—that the author's thoughts and feelings are irrelevant to the meaning—requires more careful consideration. It is unfortunate that Hirsch did not answer this objection, but merely proposed that if Eliot's account were true, no criterion of validity would be possible. It would lead, Hirsch said, to meaning based on public consensus, when no such consensus is possible (see Objection No. 7). "If a text means what it says, then it means nothing in particular. Its saying has no determinate existence but must be the saying of the author or a reader."[22] While what Hirsch says makes sense, his critics are generally agreed that he failed to establish that the meaning of a text must be the author's intended meaning.[23]

If by "intention" we mean the reasoned expression of the author's composition, then intention is logically related to the meaning of the text. The logical argument goes like this:

If the verbal sequence is a reasoned expression, and the reasoned expression is meaningful, then the verbal sequence is meaningful.

If the verbal sequence is not a reasoned expression, and the reasoned expression is meaningful, then the verbal sequence is meaningless.

P. D. Juhl has argued that in common practice we acknowledge the logic of meaning as the reasoned expression of an author.

Unless we regard the text of a literary work as the record of someone's use of the words in question to say something, it would make no sense to attempt to seriously interpret it. If, for example, a parrot utters a syntactically or semantically deviant sentence, then the question of interpreting it, of making sense of the parrot's "utterance," clearly could not arise. And surely the reason is that the parrot cannot (properly speaking) be said to have *said* anything.[24]

But if a child made the utterance, we would try to make sense of it—even if he or she violated the conventional rules of grammar.

If there is a logical connection between a text and the author's intention, then the text cannot be separated from the author. Thus, by definition the author's intention must not be separated from the text, because it guided the manner in which the text was expressed. There could be no message or meaning without the intended action of

---

[21]Nigel Turner, *A Grammar of New Testament Greek,* vol. 3: *Syntax,* ed. James H. Moulton (Edinburgh: T. & T. Clark, 1963), 63, 73.

[22]Hirsch, *Validity in Interpretation,* 13.

[23]Barrie A. Wilson, "Hirsch's Hermeneutics: A Critical Examination," *Philosophy Today* 22 (Spring 1978): 24, 32; and P. D. Juhl, *Interpretation: An Essay in the Philosophy of Literary Criticism* (Princeton, N.J.: Princeton University Press, 1980), 12.

[24]Juhl, *Interpretation,* 109.

the author speaking or writing, and thus what the text says and what the author means are necessarily related.

OBJECTION NO. 4

The author's intention is an inaccessible *goal and therefore a useless object of interpretation.*

This objection finds expression in what James Barr calls "cultural relativism." Whereas historical perspective makes the goal unstable, cultural perspective makes the goal inaccessible because of the constitutional nature of cultural categories. "By an extension of the great Kantian insight on which it is ultimately based, interpretive perspectivism argues for the constitutive nature of cultural categories."[25] The "great Kantian insight" is that "man's experience is preaccommodated to his categories of experience"—i.e., our mental organization of what we perceive constitutes our experience. Our perspective is limited by our own cultural experience, and so we cannot fully understand the author's perspective. Barr has summarized the effect of cultural relativism.

> The Bible, like all other literature, is *dependent* on the cultural milieu (in fact, a plurality of cultural milieus) in which it was written. Our modern culture is different, and it is *not possible* that the same work, the Bible, can have the same meaning as it had in its own cultural milieu. Any work or text composed in an ancient time and an ancient culture has its meaning in that time and that culture, and in our time or culture may have a different meaning or indeed may have no meaning at all.[26]

In addition, with this concept of cultural separation D. E. Nineham calls into question the original interpretation of historical events.

> We are still bound in integrity to ask whether if we, with our twentieth-century background, had been there, we should have felt the historical events in question to demand any explanation in supernatural terms; and we can be sure that if so, the terms we should have used would not have been the ones used by biblical writers.[27]

The biblical writers are understood to have been conditioned by their cultures to view death as an enemy, or by the idea of a chaos that threatens to engulf the world, or by the notion of man as a body-soul entity. Thus, since ancient assumptions are different from ours, perception and interpretation will also be different.

There are three arguments against the position that cultural relativism makes the author's meaning inaccessible. First, cultural perspective ultimately implies that verbal meaning exists *only* by virtue of the perspective that gives it existence.[28] It follows that it is impossible to distort a meaning that cannot exist in the modern world. If body-soul existence is conditioned on that culture and if these cultural values are no longer shared, then body-soul existence is meaningless. Barr is correct in casting such views as radical.

Second, from the viewpoint of biblical revelation, the authors and interpreters, despite cultural differences, have in common what is necessary to communicate. They are, by means of creation, made in the image of God.

---

[25] Hirsch, *The Aims of Interpretation,* 48. Kant postulated a universal structure in human subjectivity that constitutes experience and that thereby guarantees the possibility of scientific knowledge.

[26] James Barr, *The Bible in the Modern World* (New York: Harper & Row, 1973), 39 (emphasis added).

[27] D. E. Nineham, "The Use of the Bible in Modern Theology," BJRL 52 (1969): 188.

[28] Hirsch, *The Aims of Interpretation,* 48.

One aspect of God's image is the ability to communicate. Communication is by definition a sharing of meaning that occurs through public signs of language that have relationship to this meaning. This culturally public aspect of communication must be distinguished from the private—and culturally particular—experience of writing. Meaning can be reproduced, even if the cultural experience is inaccessible.

Third, ancient cultural writings merely represent a special case of communication with another person through writing. It is necessary to share facts of the language and assumptions in the culture so as not to miss allusions or to mistake the contemporary sense of words; but these are preliminary tasks that remain squarely in the public domain. While the task of interpretation is more difficult when dealing with ancient and culturally foreign writings, it is not impossible. Moreover, the nature of the Bible as divine revelation establishes the basis for a timeless character of its message rather than a time-bound message meaningful to one culture alone.

OBJECTION NO. 5

The author's intention is a trivial *goal because the construct of the author's intention is based on circular reasoning.*

Schleiermacher discussed the problems inherent in understanding by using the model of a hermeneutical circle. In essence, this concept states that the process of understanding is necessarily circular because we cannot know a whole without knowing some of its parts, yet we cannot know the parts as such without knowing the whole that determines their function. Simply put, this means, "The understanding of a particular is always conditioned by an understanding of the whole."[29]

Schleiermacher's discussion of the technical and grammatical tasks was consistent in his early writings. Grammatical interpretation is the art of finding the precise sense of a given statement from its language and with the help of the language. We should construe the meaning from the total pre-given value of the language and the heritage common to the author and his reader.[30]

In Schleiermacher's later writings, however, the technical became psychological. Psychological interpretation is given priority when one regards language exclusively as a means by which a person communicates his thoughts.[31] The interpreter seeks to put himself "inside" the author.[32] Nothing in a passage is self-evident. The focus is not on analysis of the passage, but on comprehension, the process of understanding.

The hermeneutical circle's function is summarized by Gadamer:

> According to this theory, the circular movement of understanding runs backwards and forwards along the text and disappears when it is perfectly understood. This view of understanding culminated logically in Schleiermacher's theory of the divinatory act, by means of which one places oneself entirely within the author's mind and from there resolves all that is strange and unusual about the text.[33]

Martin Heidegger enlarged this concept of the hermeneutical circle, and

---

[29] F. D. E. Schleiermacher, *Hermeneutics: The Handwritten Manuscripts,* ed. Heinz Kemmerle (Missoula, Mont.: Scholars Press, 1977), 59.

[30] Ibid., 70.

[31] Ibid., 99.

[32] Ibid., 64.

[33] Gadamer, *Truth and Method,* 261.

Gadamer sees this as a decisive turning point. Heidegger described the circle in such a way that the understanding of the text remains permanently determined by the anticipatory movement of foreunderstanding by the interpreter. "The circle of the whole and the part is not dissolved in perfect understanding but, on the contrary, is most fully realised."[34]

Heidegger described meaning in terms of horizons. He wrote, "Meaning is the 'upon-which' of a projection in terms of which something becomes intelligible as something, it gets structure from a fore-having, a fore-sight and a fore-conception."[35] Heidegger used the phrase "horizon of understanding," which is the fore-having *from* which or *upon* which something is understandable as the thing it is. Gadamer understood this feature to be the core of Heidegger's theory of hermeneutics.

> The circle, then, is not formal in nature, it is neither subjective nor objective, but describes understanding as the interplay of the movement of tradition and the movement of the interpreter. The anticipation of meaning that governs our understanding of a text is not an act of subjectivity, but proceeds from the communality that binds us to the tradition. But this is contained in our relation to tradition, in the constant process of tradition.[36]

So the hermeneutical circle begins in either the subjectivity of the private perspective of the psychological analysis of the author (Schleiermacher) or in the historicity of the perspective of horizon in the tradition of the interpreter's knowledge (Heidegger). The ultimate ground of knowing is thereby made trivial, whether based on subjective or historical grounds.

J. I. Packer suggests as an alternative

> the "exegetical circle"—a concept springing from recognition of the truth (for truth it is) that exegesis presupposes a hermeneutic which in its turn is drawn from an overall theology, which theology in its turn rests on exegesis. This circle is not, of course, logically vicious; it is not the circle of presupposing what you ought to prove, but the circle, or rather the ascending spiral, of successive approximation, a basic method of every science.[37]

Thus the ground for evangelical hermeneutics is biblical authority. It is evident in the clear statements of Scripture and in the words and resurrection of Jesus Christ. This is the starting point: the nature and truthfulness of biblical revelation and a general view of this Christian truth. The understanding of particular texts begins with a reading of the whole text, from which *corrigible schemata* (constructs of meaning subject to a textual determination) are developed, what Hirsch calls "this making-matching, constructive-corrective process."

> The model of corrigible schemata is . . . a more useful and accurate model than that of the so-called hermeneutical circle. Unlike one's unalterable and inescapable preunderstanding in Heidegger's account of the hermeneutic circle, a schema can be radically altered and corrected. A schema sets up a range of predictions or expectations, which if fulfilled confirms the schema, but if not fulfilled causes us to revise it.[38]

So the process of interpretation involves making a statement and then

---

[34] Ibid.

[35] Martin Heidegger, *Being and Time* (Oxford: Blackwell, 1962), 193.

[36] Gadamer, *Truth and Method,* 261.

[37] J. I. Packer, "Biblical Authority, Hermeneutics, Inerrancy," in *Jerusalem and Athens,* ed. E. R. Geehan (Phillipsburg, N.J.: Presbyterian and Reformed, 1971), 146.

[38] Hirsch, *The Aims of Interpretation,* 32.

attempting to match that statement against the details of the text. When the details do not match, the statement must be corrected until there is correspondence. This approach acknowledges that the *best* evidence for the author's intended meaning is found in the text, although it is not the *only* evidence. Moreover, there is the interpreter's overall understanding of the Bible, which provides broader textual data of the divine Author.

This appeal to the *text* as the best evidence is not an appeal to *interpretation* of the text. It is an appeal to certain *textual features* that provide evidence for the meaning of the text if and only if they are evidence of the author's intention. So the ultimate ground for authority is the textual particulars. The interpreter's understanding of the author's intention is a construct determined by the text and subject to correction dependent on matching with the textual particulars. Thus basic doctrinal conclusions do remain as settled convictions because they rest in the clear teaching of the text and the combined understanding of the text by generations of Spirit-led interpreters.

Still, the ultimate ground of interpretation is the test of Scripture, which is *revelation*. In this ultimate sense, the hermeneutical circle is wrestling with the creatureliness of man and his capacity to know. On what does a finite creature ground or found his knowledge? Schleiermacher grounded it in an intuitive and thus private identification with the author. Heidegger grounded it in the being and historical existence of the interpreter. Packer grounds human knowledge in the fact of God's self-revelation to mankind. Man's ground for knowing is God and the basic fact that he has spoken; or in Francis Schaeffer's phrase, "God is there and

he is not silent." Thus the goal of reaching the author's intention is based, not on circular reasoning, but on cumulative reasoning—a spiral rather than a circle (see chap. 5).

OBJECTION NO. 6

The author's intention is a meaningless goal because the author often does not know what he means.

Gadamer affirmed Schleiermacher's maxim of hermeneutics. "Schleiermacher asserts that the object is to understand a writer better than he understood himself. . . . this statement concerns the whole problem of hermeneutics."[39] In the history of interpretation this maxim has yielded two main types of authorial ignorance.

Schleiermacher understood authorial ignorance in relation to conscious and unconscious meanings of the author. This may be illustrated in the following conversation, as related by Hirsch:

> "Did you know that those last two sentences of yours had parallel constructions which emphasized their similarity of meaning?"
>
> "No! How clever of me! I suppose I really did want to emphasize the similarity, though I wasn't aware of that, and I had no idea I was using rhetorical devices to do it."
>
> What this illustrates is that there are usually components of an author's intended meaning that he is not conscious of.[40]

This kind of understanding of a text can be called "better" in that it is a more explicit, worked-out-to-a-greater-degree knowledge of the text. It commonly occurs in exegesis when the interpreter refers to rules of grammar or literary forms that the author may have used without noticing them because he lived in the language. What must be

---

[39] Gadamer, *Truth and Method,* 169.
[40] Hirsch, *Validity in Interpretation,* 21.

made clear is that this "better understanding" does not refer to defining components of meaning expressed in the text, an aspect crucial to our goal of interpretation. These defining components are the basis for the reasoned expression of the text that came into existence in writing. These are held in common by the human and divine authors.

The second kind of authorial ignorance is important because it provides the basic assumption of all higher criticism. This is authorial ignorance of subject matter due to a limitation in sources for historical issues or to limitations in perception because of cultural conditioning. It was in this sense that Kant and Fichte read Schleiermacher's maxim.

> In the spirit of rationalism, [Schleiermacher] claims solely through thought, through the development of implications of an author's ideas, to achieve insights that correspond to the real intention of the author—insights that he would have to share if his thinking had been clear enough.[41]

Gadamer also followed this approach. He stated, "The artist who creates something is not the ideal interpreter of it. As an interpreter he has no automatic priority as an authority over the man who is simply receiving his work."[42] Gadamer grounded his position, not in the rationalism of Kant, but in the historicism of Heidegger. Instead of accepting at the stage of understanding the objective validity of what an author is saying, the interpreter sees the content of the text in the horizon of one's own foreunderstanding, which proceeds from being concerned about the same subject matter.[43]

Fusing an author's textual horizon

with the reader's historical horizon thusly lends some concern to Anthony Thiselton's use of this model: "Understanding is not simply a matter of looking up individual words in a grammar and dictionary, but of communication between two sets of horizons."[44] While the scope of interpretation is more than grammars and dictionaries, does interpretation ever involve altering and correcting the author's horizon?

This form of authorial ignorance is inconsistent with biblical affirmations about the message expressed in the text. Although human authors share historical and cultural limitations, when they speak as prophets or apostles they are borne along by the Holy Spirit (2 Peter 1:20–21). The product of the text is inerrant in all that it affirms (2 Tim. 3:16). Thus, in biblical exegesis such Authorial/authorial ignorance is excluded by the nature of revelation.

Finally, discussion of such authorial ignorance moves from the task of understanding to the task of evaluation. In this regard, the pursuit of higher criticism is not a tool of understanding, but a tool of criticism. It is an evaluation or criticism of the perceived truthfulness or relevance of the textual meaning. Such evaluation has a place, but it is not a part of communication.

OBJECTION NO. 7

The author's intention is an arbitrary goal since it is not the only genuinely discriminating norm.

In this objection there is a division of opinion, even among allies of authorial intent, on the value of the author's intention in determining the textual meaning. Hirsch argues consistently

---

[41] Gadamer, *Truth and Method,* 171–72.
[42] Ibid., 170.
[43] Ibid., 269–72.
[44] Anthony C. Thiselton, *The Two Horizons* (Grand Rapids: Eerdmans, 1980), 168.

that the author's intended meaning is the only genuinely discriminating norm.

Strangely, Juhl challenges Hirsch's conception of the nature of the goal and posits that a group of distinguished literary critics would serve as an equally discriminating norm because they "could in practice undoubtedly resolve a larger number of interpretive controversies than an appeal to the author's intention."[45] This group would be appointed or elected to serve as arbiters in disputes about the meaning of literary works. Their majority vote would arbitrate the meaning.

Hirsch, by contrast, argues that the "myth of public consensus" is based on a fundamental error of observation and logic. It is an empirical fact that such a consensus or group of arbiters does not exist except in the Roman Catholic system. However, the great contention raised against this comes from the basis of their selection and the merit of their interpretations. It is a logical error to erect a stable normative concept (i.e., *the* public meaning) out of an unstable descriptive one.[46] The public meaning and the distinguished critics' meaning are nothing more or less than those meanings that they happen to construe from the text, and there is no necessity or compulsion for acceptance; either group could be wrong.

The issues involved in the selection of arbiters may be clarified by considering a series of questions. The first set of questions is: Who would choose the arbiters of interpretation? Would the mass of interpreters be expected to choose the arbiters? Would the mass of interpreters choose someone else because they are not expected to understand or they are not able to understand? What would be the special qualification of the arbiter?

Questions such as these make it clear that there is no necessary reason for who would be chosen, and if the choice of a certain individual is not necessary, but rather optional, then how could the group be considered a genuinely discriminating norm? In our legal system there is a necessary basis for a trial by jury—the inherent sense of fairness and morality found in common human beings in a society. But no such common sense of competence exists by which to necessarily choose a group of arbiters to judge textual meanings, unless we accept the doctrine of apostolic succession and infallibility in interpretation. Without a necessary competence in their interpretation, such a group would possess no compelling authority to justify their choice of meaning. So, instead of relying on interpretation by a group of experts, it is preferable that individuals accept a responsibility to interpret as part of their relationship to God.

More questions follow: How would these arbiters compel agreement with their interpretation? What intellectual or moral compulsion exists in the majority? While our society might settle for living according to the will of the majority, why must our thought be so directed, particularly in the case when the majority interpretation is perceived to be inadequate or in error?

By contrast, the author's intention compels agreement because he gave expression to the message and in that activity set limits on the textual medium. It is not that the author pronounced the meaning as a flat declaration, as Juhl implies.[47] Rather, at a certain time in history, the author spoke and disclosed his meaning through the textual clues. It is this discriminating and necessary norm that compels agreement in principle. To gain agreement in

---

[45] Juhl, *Interpretation,* 20.
[46] Hirsch, *Validity in Interpretation,* 13.
[47] Juhl, *Interpretation,* 20.

fact demands a humble discussion and careful articulation of the reasons for valid interpretations.

OBJECTION NO. 8

The single meaning as the author's intention is an inconsistent goal because literary genre demands multiple meanings and critical practice demonstrates multiple interpretations.

This criticism has arisen from the practice of structural exegesis. This position is expressed in Susan Wittig's "Theory of Multiple Meanings." Her central thesis is that the unstated signified in a parable is an invitation to the reader/hearer to supply the realm of reference.[48] Her initial premise assumes that "the text of the parable obviously *is* polyvalent. It *does* admit a variety of possible meanings."[49]

Wittig's premise has been sharply and repeatedly contested. For example, Joachim Jeremias concluded: "[Adolf] Jülicher not merely proved incontestably by hundreds of cases that allegorizing leads to error, but also maintained the fundamental position that it [allegorizing] is utterly alien to the parables of Jesus."[50] Jeremias himself sought to find a single meaning, "to recover the original meaning of the parables."[51] The unstated signified (to what does Jesus refer when he talks about farming?) in the parable of the soils (Matt. 13; Mark 4; Luke 8) was not an invitation to the hearer to supply his own realm of reference, but an invitation for the disciples to puzzle over the issue of reference and, if need be, to turn to the Author for his intended reference (Mark 4:10–13).

Thus there is no model to be found in the Lord's parables for Wittig's theory of polyvalence. In fact, Wittig herself demonstrates the interpretive practice found in Jesus' reference to "those who are outside." Those who are outside might well conclude that Jesus simply intended to talk about farming. This would clearly be irrelevant and confirm their prior rejection of the Christ. But this interpretation was not a viable alternative. Rather, Jesus provided the one interpretation of his intended meaning and was not giving sanction to the equal validity of multiple interpretations in the ambiguity of the parables reference.

An even more fundamental problem arises when Wittig attempts to apply conclusions reached in her study of parables to any and all literary genres. Any genre other than a "parable-like" genre will include the signified directly stated. In narrative, the historical characters or event are mentioned directly; or in prophetic literature, the future is talked about directly, albeit with some vagueness. But she counters, "It is likely that the signified owes as much to the meaning system in the mind of the perceiver as it does to the signifier itself."[52] Then she explains the idea of a meaning system as being sought within the mind of the perceiver:

> Equally probable, a powerful, well-organized, and stable analytic system may *generate* a particular kind of significance, even though the structure of the second-order signifier does not immediately suggest it—and even though the sender may not consciously intend the sign to be perceived as parabolic.[53]

[48] Susan W. Wittig, "A Theory of Multiple Meanings," *Semeia* 9 (1977): 84–85.
[49] Ibid., 84.
[50] Joachim Jeremias, *The Parables of Jesus* (New York: Scribner's, 1963), 18.
[51] Ibid., 19.
[52] Wittig, "A Theory of Multiple Meanings," 89.
[53] Ibid.

This idea that the signified resides in the mind of the hearer assumes that different readings of a text as seen through either Buddhist or Christian, Freudian or Marxist eyes are equally valid—in fact, encouraged. This particular application of the Heideggerian hermeneutical circle, preunderstanding, and the generative capacity of the reader as an author of meaning illustrates interpretation that is historically grounded.

Thus Wittig's conclusion is clearly inconsistent with Christ's interpretation of the parables, let alone other passages and the disciples' interpretation in context. In addition, since textual clues to the realm of reference are ignored, the realm of authority has been removed from the text to the interpreter and his preunderstanding.

CONCLUSION

Three fundamental questions have been raised in part 1. Two of the questions were addressed in the goal of interpretation: The biblical text communicates a single, unified textual meaning that is determined by the Author's/author's intention as expressed in the text.

One question has not been addressed: How is this textual meaning to be interpreted? With the goal of interpretation established, the question of the strategy for reaching that goal needs to be examined next. That will be the focus of parts 2 and 3.

PART TWO

RECOGNITION

Introduction

A little boy woke up in the middle of the night seeking the bathroom. As he got out of bed, he banged his leg on a piece of furniture, turned to open the door, and bumped into a wall. There he stood utterly confused. After a moment he recognized where he was and remembered that summer vacation was over and he was now back home in his own bed. The reason why his brother's bed was in the way and why a wall appeared where he didn't expect was perfectly clear: he wasn't where he thought he was. Therefore the particulars he encountered didn't make sense.

Not knowing where we are can lead to serious errors! That is why the task of recognition is the important first step in studying the Bible; it gives the interpreter the "big picture" of what a book is about. The overview kind of understanding of a book that is gained in the task of recognition is essential to correct exegesis of the particulars of the book. Unfortunately, biblical authors did not use the methods that most modern authors use to give their readers such an overview such as introductions, summaries on the dust jacket, tables of contents, and title pages. Therefore part 2 deals with the process an interpreter can use to gain such an overview.

Chapter 5 is concerned with defining the task of recognition. Recognition will first be described from the perspective of inductive Bible study, which uses a four-stage, spiraling process of preunderstanding, recognition, exegesis, and application. These stages form what is called *the hermeneutical spiral*.

The goal of the task or process of recognition is to develop, through a series of questions, several summary statements that constitute an *essential summary*. This series of statements is an expression of the Author's/author's intended meaning as expressed in the whole text or book. The statements are referred to as *the message statement, the theological themes statement, the textual design statement*, and *the goal statement*. Together they form the interpreter's recognition of the meaning of the text as a whole, and as such they provide the framework within which all interpretations of particulars in the text will fit.

Chapters 6 and 7 will introduce the two roles of hermeneutical criteria in the inductive, or discovery, stage of interpretation. First, the criteria describe the reader's *expectations* in approaching the text. These expectations result from the goal of interpretation—identifying the Author's/author's intended meaning—and from the legitimate range of preunderstanding shared with the original readers. Second, the criteria describe the *categories* of the reader's initial comprehension. That is, as we read, we move in thought from what we know in general about the subject to what the author communicates in particular. This is the stage of recognition, and this is the role of the hermeneutical criteria.

CHAPTER 5

The Task of Recognition

Inductive Bible study has been widely used by evangelicals because they desire to know the Bible. This desire has been honed and refined through hermeneutical considerations toward achieving the goal "to know the Author's/author's intended meaning as expressed in the biblical text as a whole."

In explaining exactly what this goal involves, an interpreter must deal first with the question of "how do I come to know?" Inductive Bible study has suggested that the answer is "I come to know by studying the biblical text itself." We accept this goal. The function of hermeneutics at this stage is to address the related question of "How can I know that what I know is true and relevant?" The answer should contribute to the strategy we use in inductive study to discern textual meanings.

In this regard, Schleiermacher focused more on the process of understanding than on analysis of the text itself. Because of this, he proposed that the Bible is understood in the same way as any other book. We saw in part 1 why this principle is skewed due to the divine authorship of the Bible; now we will see another reason why Schleiermacher's expectation falls short. His expectation is that understanding the written text of the Bible is as natural as reading any other book even though the reader brings the added resource of the Holy Spirit and the active presence of faith in what God says.

Despite this important difference, Schleiermacher's strategy for understanding is helpful. Two maxims explain his process:

(1) I am understanding until I encounter a contradiction or nonsense. (2) I do not understand anything that I cannot perceive and comprehend as necessary. In accordance with this second maxim, understanding is an unending task. . . . The understanding of a particular is always conditioned by an understanding of the whole.[1]

That is, understanding comes as I read the text. I understand what I am reading, word for word, sentence by sentence, as each new component fits "necessarily" in relation to what I understand the author to be saying in general. This understanding of what the author is saying is determined by the

[1]F. D. E. Schleiermacher, *Hermeneutics,* ed. Heinz Kimmerle (Missoula, Mont.: Scholars Press, 1977), 41, 59.

sense of a whole that "conditions" the meaning of each part. Whenever I come to a word or sentence that does not fit, it means I do not really understand. It does not fit either because it contradicts or because it is unrelated and so is nonsense—nonsense because I descry a meaning that does not fit in context with what the author says as a whole.

This process may appear to be circular and without closure—and thus we have the hermeneutic circle. That perception led Schleiermacher to find closure in the intuitive recognition of meanings from the author's personality. Thus the psychology of the author became, for Schleiermacher, the key to understanding, as we noted earlier.

J. I. Packer has more accurately perceived the process, not as a circle, but as a spiral.

> If we would understand the parts, our wisest course is to get to know the whole—or at any rate, those parts of the whole which tell us in plain prose the writer's central ideas. These give us the keys to all his work. Once we can see the main outlines of his thought and have grasped his general point of view, we are able to see the meaning of everything else—the point of his poems and the moral of his stories, and how the puzzling passages fit in with the rest.[2]

An illustration of this model of recognizing meaning was demonstrated in one woman's experience at a lecture entitled "Social Concern." It was advertised as a "date night," and the women in the class were to bring their husbands or boyfriends. This student attended, expecting to hear something about husbands and wives expanding their social friendships with other couples. When the lecture began, she became totally confused. The speaker began by reading from the Declaration of Independence. While the student understood the meaning of all the words in the reading, they made no sense whatever in regard to "social friendships." Eventually the woman realized what type of social concern the speaker was talking about: social in the sense of "national or community conscience." Thus she understood the words' particular meanings only when she understood the type of meaning as a whole; yet she only understood the type of meaning as a whole by hearing and understanding the particular words. She had experienced the spiral process of understanding.

This spiral process of inductive study involves at least four tasks:

1. Preunderstanding. This stage of understanding involves the broad and general understanding a reader brings to the Bible. This includes language skills and knowledge culled from his culture and life. To this he adds knowledge of the language, history, and culture of Bible times. He also brings important knowledge gained from repeated readings of the Bible itself and the faith involved in a personal relationship with God. In that personal relationship, the Holy Spirit is active in the reading and interpretation of the Bible.

2. Recognition. The task of recognition involves reading the text to comprehend the essential meaning of the whole text. The Author's/author's overall intended meaning is recognized in discerning the type of meaning expressed in the whole text, as stated in an essential summary. This is an inductive principle.

3. Exegesis. This involves reading the text to analyze the full range of meanings and implications necessarily intended. The full implications intended by the Author/author are analyzed and

---

[2]J. I. Packer, "Biblical Authority, Hermeneutics and Inerrancy," in *Jerusalem and Athens,* ed. E. R. Geehan (Philadelphia: Presbyterian and Reformed, 1971), 144–45.

exeged from the type of meaning expressed in the text as a whole, from the grammatical and historical hermeneutical premises, and from the constructions of the text. This is a deductive principle.

4. Application. This task involves relating the message of the text to situations and people of our day according to God's working in the present.

The strategy for defining the basic tasks of inductive Bible study is shown in figure 5.1. How these four tasks relate to each other can be depicted in the model of a spiral. Each application of the tasks has the potential of narrowing the gap between our interpretation and the actual, textual meaning.

Figure 5.1

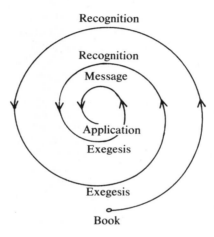

Recognition

Recognition

Message

Application

Exegesis

Exegesis

Book

PREUNDERSTANDING

The first step in the actual study of the Bible is summarized in the inductive principle of recognition. Since the purpose of this book is to consider the mutual contribution of inductive study and hermeneutics, we will seek to clarify the task of recognition and then consider it in the perspective of hermeneutics. Let us first state the definition of the task.

Task of Recognition: The Author's/author's overall intended meaning is recognized by comprehending the type of meaning expressed in the whole text, as stated in an essential summary.

This definition includes four elements which are essential to inductive Bible study and which in turn need to be defined: (1) meaning, (2) recognition, (3) comprehension, and (4) essential summary.

MEANING

Among all the elements of inductive Bible study, "meaning" is the most important and also the most difficult to define.[3] There are several theories of verbal meaning.

---

[3] A good summary and evaluation of various theories of meaning is found in John S. Feinberg's chapter "Theories of Truth," in *Hermeneutics, Inerrancy and the Bible,* ed. Earl D. Radmacher and Robert D. Preus, (Grand Rapids: Zondervan, 1984), 26–35.

Theories of Meaning

1. The referential theory. Bertrand Russell was a noteworthy proponent of the referential theory. In general, proponents of this theory identify the meaning of a word with (1) what it refers to (the referent), or (2) the relation between the words and its referent.

Several deficiencies exist if this is accepted as a complete theory defining verbal meaning. A classic example is "the morning star" and "the evening star," which both refer to the planet Venus yet do not have the same meaning. Another problem is the assumption that every meaningful expression does refer to something. For example, the word "to" as a marker of infinitive constructions is referentially meaningless. The same is true of "did" in a negative construction such as "I did not go." Although what is referred to does not define verbal meaning, it will be necessary in thinking about verbal meaning and its interpretation to consider the relation of the sense to the realm and object to which it refers.

2. The ideational theory. John Locke stated the classical ideational theory: "The use, then, of words is to be sensible marks of ideas; and the ideas they stand for are their proper and immediate signification."[4] That is,

The conception of language and speech that lies behind this statement is as follows: Language is essentially an instrument for the communication of thought. Thought consists of a succession of ideas in consciousness, these ideas being directly accessible only to their possessor. In order to make others cognizant of one's thoughts, one employs publicly observable sounds and marks as representations of these ideas. Communication is successful when my utterance arouses in you the same idea which led, in me, to its issuance.[5]

While Locke's theory seems to account generally for meaningful verbal communication, it lacks an explanation for the origin of thought and language. Thus this conception of thought has been criticized because it assumes that thought exists independent of language. "If we are to explain meaning in terms of word-idea association, we will have to bring in ideas which are identifiable apart from recognizing what the word means. Otherwise, the explanation will be circular."[6]

The theory also lacks a substantial articulation of a basis for truth in verbal ideas. This nominalist conception of the relation between thought and reality is less than convincing to most.[7]

At the same time, the role of the author and his thought as expressed verbally do have a place in defining verbal meaning. The problems of this theory must not obscure the obvious role of persons in communicating verbal meaning. Verbal meaning inseparably binds an author and his verbal text. It is just as erroneous to separate meaning from an author's verbal expression as it is to separate verbal ideas from that expression.

3. The stimulus-response theory. A third view of verbal meaning, the stimulus-response theory, arose in part as an answer to a perceived inadequacy in the ideational theory. This view proposes

---

[4]John Locke, *Essays Concerning Human Understanding,* 3.2.1.

[5]*Encyclopedia of Philosophy,* ed. Paul Edwards (New York: Macmillan and Free Press, 1967), 3:235.

[6]Ibid.

[7]Nominalism is a doctrine of the late Middle Ages holding that all universal or abstract terms (such as truth or beauty or the concept of circle) are mere necessities of thought or conveniences of language and therefore exist as names only and have no general realities corresponding to them. Only a particular and individual object or event has reality.

that aspects of meaning include the listener's response in the communication situation. Thus proponents search for meaning in regularities of connection between utterances and publicly observable features of the communication situation. Leonard Bloomfield explained the "meaning of a linguistic form" as "the situation in which the speaker utters it and the response which it calls forth in the hearer."[8]

The stimulus-response theory is saddled with the assumption that every meaningful linguistic unit is a "sign" of a discriminable extralinguistic thing, aspect, or state of affairs. This assumption does not account for, by way of example, the infinitive marker "to" in "he commanded him to go," which has no correspondence to any response but is meaningful.

John Austin has labeled this responsive aspect of verbal communication "the perlocutionary act." This act "is the *achieving of* certain *effects* by saying something."[9] Austin distinguishes this authorial activity from other activities involving verbal meaning. Activities involving verbal meaning are all conventional activities, but "perlocutionary acts are not conventional, though conventional acts may be made use of in order to bring off the perlocutionary acts."[10] Our reply to this is that achieving certain effects in the hearer is certainly a concern of communication and of hermeneutics, but that is not the basis for defining verbal meaning. Otherwise a statement would be meaningless until and unless it has an effective response in the audience.

4. *The meaning-as-a-function-of-use theory.* The fourth theory relates verbal meaning to usage and stems largely from the work of Ludwig Wittgenstein. Behind this theory is a pragmatic view of the nature of language—simply speaking, "meaning is use." Wittgenstein wrote, "Look at the sentence as an instrument, and at its sense as its employment."[11] While this theory incorporates some aspects of idea and stimulus-response theory, it stresses the behavior of the speaker as the focus in the use of language. The verbal action of the speaker is viewed more broadly than simply the stimulus that elicits his utterance, more broadly than the responses to which it gives rise. Underlying this concept of verbal action and verbal meaning is the commonsense notion that the sense in which a person employs words is a function of what he is using the words to do.

Austin has classified linguistic behavior into "locutionary," "illocutionary," and "perlocutionary" activities based on a distinction introduced by Ferdinand de Saussure between *la langue* (language) and *la parole* (speech). This distinction marked the birth of modern linguistics. By *language* de Saussure meant the whole stock of words, idioms, and syntax available, the potential and common property of all users of language. It is often called "the public meaning." By *speech* he meant any particular and actual use of a language by a speaker or writer. He proceeded to classify linguistic behavior in speech.

Austin began with a sentence, for the sentence is the smallest linguistic unit with which a complete action can be performed. The locutionary act consists simply of uttering the sentence with a certain sense and reference. In the perlocutionary act, as we have noted, the author produces certain effects such

[8]Leonard Bloomfield, *Language* (Chicago: University of Chicago Press, 1984), 139.
[9]John L. Austin, *How to Do Things With Words* (Oxford: Clarendon Press, 1962), 108.
[10]Ibid., 121.
[11]Ludwig Wittgenstein, *Philosophical Investigations* (New York: Macmillan, 1968), 1:421.

78

as convincing, persuading, or frightening someone. As stated, it is not involved in identifying the verbal meaning, since two different sentences can produce the same effect. For instance, "mankind is on the verge of extinction" and "boo!" can both be used to frighten people, but this does nothing to indicate even the slightest similarity in meaning. Yet perlocutionary effect does influence the way language is used by the speaker and applied by the hearer. It is important to applying the verbal meaning.

Still, it is the illocutionary act that identifies the author's use of the meaning. Two distinct locutionary acts— "Would you open the door?" and "Please open the door"—entail roughly synonymous illocutionary acts. Both are used to ask someone to open a certain door. But their distinct force sponsors different implications of meaning.

If all this seems a bit complicated, let's simply recognize that usage influences meaning.

While this theory makes some helpful contributions to understanding the verbal meaning of sentences, it encounters problems with individual words. How does one explain the meaning of a word in terms of what speakers do with the word? Also, besides an author's use of words, some notion of referential correspondence is needed to identify meaning. Furthermore, this strictly conventional basis of definition does not adequately account for the meaning of words or explain the nature of truth. A strictly conventional use of language considers only the functional meanings in communication and excludes any correspondence to a historical realm. Such usage could perpetuate erroneous cultural perceptions encoded by conventions in a language system. In this way a language system would undermine any divine use of human language to express truth. Therefore this theory has useful aspects, but is inadequate as a complete description of verbal meaning.

In summary, it is evident that no single theory of meaning is entirely satisfactory. It is not the purpose of a text on inductive study and hermeneutics to develop a theory of meaning, yet any system of interpretation assumes a concept of verbal meaning. For our purposes, therefore, the following aspects of meaning must be included: a notion of reference in history, use of language in its context, acts performed by an author expressing a sentence, and the conventional use of language and literature.[12]

These aspects of verbal meaning fit well into the goal already advanced. Verbal meaning is the Author's/author's (performative acts) intended (textual sense and extratextual reference) use of language (within the conventions of established usage) in the text as a whole (use in context).

Sentences as Meaning Bearers

Along with the meaning of words, it is important to recognize that sentences or propositions bear verbal meaning.[13] Sentences carry verbal meaning as a predicate of verbal communication. So we may say, " 'Procrastination' means to put things off" or "John means by 'procrastinate' to put things off." In these two examples verbal meaning includes authors, references ("procrastinate"), use of language, and a context.

---

[12] For a comparable conclusion see John Feinberg, "Theories of Truth," 35.

[13] Propositions will not be used because of the numerous technical questions that have arisen in philosophy concerning their nature and validity. The components of meaning in a proposition and a declarative sentence are identical (subject and a complement in which an affirmation is made about the subject).

The meaning expressed is found in the predication or affirmation of the sentence.

This view identifies a sentence as the meaning bearer as over against a word or phrase. According to Paul Ricoeur,

> The sentence as a whole is the bearer of the meaning. Here we mean to designate something other than and something more than the signified of the individual signs (i.e., words or phrases). It is a distinctive feature which may be identified as the predicative function. . . . The predicative constitution of the sentence provides it with a meaning. This meaning should be called the intended rather than the signified of the sentence, if we want to preserve the distinction between the semiotic (sign system) and the semantic (meaning system) order. This intended is what we seek to translate when we transpose a discourse from one language to another. The signified is untranslatable in principle (reproduction of equivalent signs). It cannot be transposed from one system to another since it characterizes one system in opposition to the other. The intended, on the contrary, is fundamentally translatable since it is the same intended unit of thought transposed from one semiotic system into another.[14]

So the verbal form in which meaning is expressed is a sentence. It states in the complement of the sentence what the author means about the subject.

RECOGNITION

The second term to be defined is "recognition."[15] Recognition occurs while we are reading. Every Christian, whether scholar or layperson, is responsible to read the Bible. This stage of the task of interpretation is therefore one that all share. The differences in what they recognize are due to their attentiveness to the text and to the preunderstanding or background knowledge of the Bible that they bring to their reading of the text. But these are differences of degree, not kind.[16]

The reading stage is *pretheoretical,* that is, it is a necessary task that precedes technical or critical discussions of the meanings of the text. Most technical studies of philology, grammar, or even semantics are preceded by

---

[14] Paul Ricoeur, "Creativity in Language," *Philosophy Today* 17 (Summer 1973): 99. Added comments are mine. Ricoeur is using "intended" in the sense of reference defined.

[15] Emilio Betti, *Teoria generale della interpretazione,* 2 vols. (Milan: Giuffre, 1955), 1:343–432; discussed by E. D. Hirsch, *Validity in Interpretation* (New Haven: Yale University Press, 1967), 24n., 25, 112, 121f., 245, and by Richard E. Palmer, *Hermeneutics: Interpretation Theory in Schleiermacher, Heidegger, Dilthey, and Gadamer* (Evanston, Ill.: Northwestern University, 1969), 54–60. Our use of the term "recognition" does not follow the limited application that the term had in the writings of Betti, the Italian historian of law. He used the term to distinguish between different kinds of interpretation: recognition of historical and literary texts, presentation of dramatic and musical texts, and normative application of legal and sacred texts. In this book, however, recognition is used of the initial reading stage of any text in which the goal is the recognition of the intended type of meaning as a whole.

[16] Mortimer J. Adler and Charles Van Doren, *How to Read a Book,* rev. ed. (New York: Simon and Schuster, 1972). The most useful element of preunderstanding is a knowledge of the original language. While skill in the use of Greek, Hebrew, or Aramaic is a valuable tool, it is not indispensable for recognition. A good translation or even a comparison of several translations can provide sufficient clues for a skilled reader to comprehend the type of meaning. The scholar will have access to greater data through knowledge of the language and culture. Such knowledge prepares him to explain and defend his recognition, but it does not separate him from the untrained believer who is willing to read with care. This conviction rests firmly at the heart of the work of Adler, who advocates reading the great works of literature in good translations.

this reading stage, although most authors writing at the technical stage in their discipline overlook the contribution that reading and rereading the text has had for their conclusions. This happens because the focus of their work is to analyze and categorize the meanings of a text at a level of examination that concerns words, syntactical constructions, or other units of meaning other than the text as a whole.

Besides technical works, the theoretical stage includes critical studies in which the scholar argues for his professional assessment of the appropriate context and meaning of a given written account. The reading stage should precede any such critical or extended technical study. It is this foundational and often overlooked task of reading that our discussion of the principle of recognition seeks to examine and define.

Royce Gruenler has written a refreshing word in his admonition to be *attentive* to the reading of the biblical text.[17] His basic idea is built on the earlier work of C. S. Lewis, who, like Gruenler, regarded the reading of the Bible as a precritical stage. Lewis wrote out of his love for reading:

> But who in his sense would not keep, if he could, that tireless curiosity, that intensity of imagination, that facility of suspending disbelief, that unspoiled appetite, that readiness to wonder, to pity, and to admire.[18]

Lewis pointed out the fallacy of an assumed sophistication (a posture that is all too common among scholars):

> This process or growing up is to be valued for what we gain, not for what we lose. Not to acquire a taste for the realistic is childish in the bad sense; to have lost the

taste for marvels and adventures is no more a matter for congratulation than losing our teeth, our hair, our palate and finally our hopes. Why do we hear so much about the defects of immaturity and so little about those of senility?[19]

In giving attention to the text we must *listen* before we respond. We must receive before we react. We should hear before we disapprove. Lewis condemns this harsh spirit of criticism: "The supreme objection to this is that which lies against the popular use of all the arts. We are so busy doing things with the work that we give it too little chance to work on us. Thus increasingly we meet only ourselves."[20]

The interpreter must, therefore, be involved in "active" reading, which is reading for information and understanding, not simply for pleasure or for its own sake.[21] The goal of active reading is *recognition* of the overall sense of the text. Active reading is a process of thinking, questioning, formulating, and reconsidering that leads to a dawning awareness of the sense of the whole text that fits all the parts of it. James M. Stalker testified to the process of recognition in his reading of the epistle to the Romans:

> As I proceeded I began to catch the drift of Paul's thought; or rather, I was caught by it and drawn in. The mighty argument opened out and arose like a great work of art above me until at last it enclosed me within its perfect proportions. It was a revolutionary experience. I saw for the first time that a book of Scripture is a complete discussion of a single subject; I felt the force of the book as a whole, and I understood the different parts in the light of the whole as I had never understood them when reading them by themselves.

---

[17] Royce Gordon Gruenler, *New Approaches to Jesus and the Gospels* (Grand Rapids: Baker, 1982), 146–52.
[18] C. S. Lewis, *An Experiment in Criticism* 62–63.
[19] Ibid.
[20] Ibid., 85.
[21] Adler and Van Doren, *How to Read a Book*, 3–15.

Thus to master book after book is to fill the mind with the great thoughts of God.[22]

Reading for recognition involves a rethinking or thinking through of the original composition. Questions raised in the dawning awareness stage must be answered from the text. Formulating these answers consists in following the author's pattern of thought, that is, retracing the structure of the book in its development of sense as a whole. This is precisely what Lewis admonished: "Find out what the author actually wrote and what the hard words meant and what the allusions were to, and you have done far more for me than a hundred new interpretations or assessments could ever do."[23]

To read a biblical text in the way Lewis prescribes seems to bear a close resemblance to the words of the Lord Jesus: "But the seed on good soil stands for those with a noble and good heart, who hear the word, retain it, and by persevering produce a good crop" (Luke 8:15).

COMPREHENSION

The third term to be defined is "comprehension." We all took "reading comprehension" tests in elementary school, and it is that same sense that is used here. It naturally follows the task of recognition, in which the interpreter reads the text to gain a dawning awareness of the overall sense. That dawning awareness reaches full development in comprehension. Thus comprehension involves settling on textually based answers to the essential questions that are raised during recognition. This does not include analysis of the text; we limit comprehension to the initial stages of interpretation.

In comprehension we seek to specify what set of meanings defines the sense of the whole biblical book. The interpretive tool or technique that reveals these meanings is the asking of questions. "The interpretive question is in reality the intermediate step between observation and interpretation," says Robert Traina.[24] Mortimer Adler maintains that the essence of an active reader is that he asks questions. His simple prescription for active reading is: "Ask questions while you read— questions that you yourself must try to answer in the course of reading." He explains: "Any questions? No. The art of reading on any level above the elementary consists in the habit of asking the right questions in the right order."[25]

So how do we do what Traina wants or what Adler wants? How do we identify and structure the questions?

The essential questions arise from our definition of verbal meaning and the actual bearer of verbal meaning. If verbal meaning is borne in a sentence, then the essential questions must focus on the predication that the author makes in the text as a whole. Therefore the two initial questions must be:

—What is the author talking about? (Subject)
—What does he say or predicate about that subject? (Predicate, or complement)

The answers to these questions combine to form a sentence—simple, compound, or complex—and this sentence summarizes the sense of the text as a whole. But in accordance with the

[22] Quoted by James M. Gray, *How to Master the English Bible* (1909; reprint, Chicago: Moody Press, 1951), 15–16.

[23] Lewis, *An Experiment in Criticism,* 121.

[24] Robert A. Traina, *Methodical Bible Study* (1952; reprint, Grand Rapids: Zondervan, 1985), 97.

[25] Adler and Van Doren, *How to Read a Book,* 46.

complexities of the sense of many texts, it would be wise to probe the predication further to comprehend better the full dimensions of what the author is saying. *What* an author means is necessarily influenced by *how* he expresses it and by *why* he expresses it. Moreover, *what* an author means is commonly influenced by *when and where* he expresses it. All these components of the author's predication are frequently expressed indirectly in the author's textual design. Thus another set of fundamental, interpretive questions must be:

— What does the author say about the subject in the textual design?

— As to how, when, and where he speaks, what does he say about the subject?

— As to why he speaks, what does he say about the subject?

Comprehension of the textual meaning as a whole involves the answers to these essential questions. We must know from every point of view what the author is saying about the subject, i.e., his predication.

ESSENTIAL SUMMARY

The answers that constitute the essential summary of the meaning are the product of carefully constructed questions. These questions have already been introduced, but now need to be refined and restated. The two initial questions

What is the author talking about? (Subject)

What does he say or predicate about that subject? (Predicate, or complement)

can be combined into one question:

1. What is the message?

This *what* question addresses the first and main focus of the essential summary. (Two other questions will deal with the *when, where, how,* and *why*.)

This message statement has two components, subject and complement, reflecting the two initial questions. These are the irreducible minimum for a summary of what the book is saying.

Subject

The subject is what the author writes about. The interpretive key is the question, What is the author talking about? As readers we are expecting the text to disclose the answer. But we immediately face the situation that few texts give direct or explicit clues about what the author wants to address in a central or comprehensive sense. Nevertheless, there are several things we can know about this subject.

a. The subject is the *organizing* or *unifying* topic within the literary unit. Considering the unit as a whole with a beginning and an end, there is one subject (broad or narrow) to which everything else may be related or by which all is unified.

b. The subject thus has *prominence* in order to tie together all the other subjects in subordination in some sense to the one subject.

c. This subject is commonly introduced at the *beginning* of the text or in some shared context with the original readers. For communication to take place, the reader must understand what the author is talking about. If the author fails to introduce his subject somehow, then what he says has no relation to any subject in particular. Communication of a message is thereby thwarted. (Remember the woman who was confused during the lecture on "Social Concern.") An alert and perceptive reader will look for the subject in the beginning of the book.

d. The subject involves unity in the world of *reference*. Because it names or denotes something in the historical realm, a subject is also recognized by (i) the denotation of textual terms, (ii) the

83

conventional clues within the literary genre specifying the kind of reference to the historical realm, and (iii) any unstated meanings known to and shared by the original readers and the author (say, for example, "baptism" and the ritual practices of Judaism). The subject of the literary unit may thus be recognized in the primary reference to the historical realm. All other references or allusions will be related to this primary reference.

The subject is recognized in answering the question, What is the book talking about? Other questions help to answer this main one.

—What subject dominates thought about the book?

—What is the title given to the book?

—What terms or synonyms are repeatedly used in the book?

—Is the subject appropriate to or commonly dealt with in this literary design?

—Where might this book be cataloged and its call number occur in the library?

The statement of the subject will involve either a simple noun phrase or a complex or compound noun phrase.

Complement

The complement is what the author wants to communicate in regard to his subject. The interpretive key here is the question, What is the author saying about the subject? The answer to this question is the most important feature of whatever book we happen to be dealing with. That is obviously the case because it expresses the author's contribution to the discussion about the subject. It is the feature that distinguishes the book from all others that address the same subject. Thus it is of major importance for the interpreter to know what an author's contribution might be.

To put it another way, the complement expresses the judgment or predication the author wants to make about his subject. This judgment may take different forms; it may affirm a truth or deny an error, explain the nature of an involved subject, expound unknown implications about some relevant subject, or explore the ramifications of the practical impact of some subject. Whatever form the complement may take— an affirmation, explanation, defense, exposition, or exploration—it represents an author's judgment on the subject appropriate for that occasion.

The judgments made can be either *theoretical* or *practical*. An affirmation of truth or error, or an analysis of the nature of the subject, expresses theoretical judgments. The application of the subject to habits and lifestyles invokes practical judgments. In the Bible many of these judgments are theological because they involve God and his actions on behalf of his people.

So the subject is developed through some kind of judgment that determines the type of message. The interpreter's statement of the complement expresses his comprehension of the coherence of the book by showing how the parts of the book bear a reasonable and purposeful relation in a unity with the whole.

Stating the complement completes the sentence that began with the subject phrase. The answer to the complementary question—what does the book say about the subject?—completes the subject statement in the form of a declarative sentence. A theoretical complement would include a verb in the indicative mood; a practical complement would include a verb in the subjunctive mood (using "should" or "ought").

In summary, the message answers the fundamental question of "what the author said in the text." It has two components: a subject that expresses the unifying topic the author talked about, and a complement that expresses what the author said about the subject. The subject is the unifying element in the whole composition. The complement expresses a coherent judgment that may be theoretical or practical.

Some additional questions may help in comprehending the answers that a book contributes.

—What are other themes in the book and how are they related to the unifying subject?

—What points does the author want to make in writing this book?

—How does this book compare with other books about the same subject?

—Is there a relationship between the theological themes and what the author is saying?

—Why does the author write this book?

These additional questions need to be refined to be included in our essential summary. The *why* question is often puzzling as we attempt to discern the wide range of possible reasons for writing. Some reasons may be relevant to the meaning, and others may not. There is a principal reason that relates to every book in the biblical canon: the overarching and compelling reason for writing the biblical books is theological. The author writes about a subject in order to reveal God, his will, and his purposes concerning that subject. This was precisely the role for which God raised up prophets and apostles. There are particular questions related to these, and they will be developed under the hermeneutical premise of theology. But the basic question (providing the

second feature of the essential summary) is:

2. What are the essential theological themes in the progress of revelation expressed in this book?

The third feature to be considered in the essential summary, namely, textual form. An author writes about his subject as occasioned by a historical audience (*when, where*), with certain aims for that audience (*why, how*) and by composing the text with a certain literary strategy (*how*) appropriate to communicate with that audience. The author's goal is to elicit a response from the reader. These are matters pertaining to the hermeneutical principle of textual form. Thus the basic question is:

3. What is the textual design?

SUMMARY

This chapter has introduced and defined the principle of recognition in the inductive study of a text. The Author's/author's intended meaning is recognized in discerning the answers to three essential questions of interpretation of the textual meaning:

1. What is the message (the subject and what the author says about the subject)?
2. What are the essential theological themes?
3. What is the textual design?

The answers to these questions are stated as three sentences formulated from the text, and these sentences comprise the pattern of an essential summary of the writing.

CHAPTER 6

Hermeneutical Considerations of the Task of Recognition—I

Hermeneutics affects Bible study first of all in the inductive stage by clarifying our expectations according to our preunderstanding. There is a danger that the criteria can be misused to *legislate* meanings and thus remove the discovery inherent in inductive study. Yet inductive study is limited by the nature of the material we read. We are not free to find just any meaning under the guise of inductive study. Thus hermeneutical criteria attempt to frame the task of textual interpretation, and they do so at two points:

1. The goal of the task of interpretation must be defined in terms appropriate to the interpreter's work with the text. This is in contrast to terms describing the author's writing of the text. This statement must incorporate all the characteristics that were defined in the consideration of the goal (part 1). *Literal* will describe how the interpretation is based on the text to satisfy the goal of interpretation of the author's intended meaning as expressed in the text.
2. The preunderstanding of the interpreter is framed by four premises that the modern reader must share with the original reader: *grammati-cal, historical, literary,* and *theological* knowledge. These shared preunderstandings allow the reader to expect and recognize meanings from which the author draws as he expresses the new message.

The four premises not only frame the interpreter's expectations but are also categories for the initial comprehension of the text. That is, as we read the text, we draw preliminary conclusions about the meaning of words and phrases and make tentative judgments about the historical references and allusions. In addition, clues and markers indicating the textual design contribute to an awareness of the composition as a whole. These initial conclusions and judgments apply to the parts that seem clear, and they become the basis for beginning to recognize the theological themes progressively revealed in the book as a whole. Within the context of our initial comprehension of the terms, the historical refererences, the textual design, and theological themes, the first recognition of the message will be construed. In this way, our reading and interpretation of a biblical book begins using the task of recognition and the hermeneutical principles.

In this chapter we will consider the literal premise and the complementary premises of grammatical and historical knowledge. Chapter 7 will be devoted to the textual design and theological themes.

LITERAL

The literal system affirms that the textually based meaning is recognized as a corresponding type of meaning.[1]

The literal system measures the accuracy of interpretation in terms of a textual base. The accuracy is determined by *correspondence to the text.* An accurate interpretation corresponds to the *type* of meaning expressed in the text. However, the distinction between accurate and inaccurate interpretation must be considered in terms of correspondence at different levels of generality. For instance, an accurate translation demands a type of correspondence judged at a specific level of the meaning of words or phrases expressed in a different language. But a synoptic or synthetic interpretation of a book as a whole corresponds to the type of meaning at a comprehensive, general level. Correspondence at this general level is obviously more difficult to judge; we have proposed a correspondence between the pattern of the essential summary statements and the meanings in the text.

This interpretation, then, is a pattern of summary statements that recognize the type of meaning expressed by the text. Such a summary must select from among the many meanings in the text some traits or components that express a corresponding type of meaning in general and as a whole. As such, the essential summary statements also imply (but do not state) in package form the range and content of textually expressed meanings. Two important questions emerge from this discussion of the recognition of the type of meaning:

—What components or traits are *necessary* for the statement of the type of meaning to correspond to the range of meanings expressed in the text?

—What set or pattern of components is *sufficient* to correspond in comprehensive yet the type of general terms of meaning expressed in the text?

These questions will be considered as we define the phrase *type of meaning.*

1. Definition of type: Type as a set or pattern of traits. Interpretation is a process of classifying the unknown in relation to what is known. This process has been applied to literature in terms of literary genres. Wellek and Warren

---

[1] Grant Osborne also acknowledges the close connections between the literal sense and the type of meaning. See his chapter "Genre Criticism—Sensus Literalis," in *Hermeneutics, Inerrancy and the Bible,* ed. Earl D. Radmacher and Robert D. Preus (Grand Rapids: Zondervan, 1984), 165–90. The term "type" is chosen because of its capacity to describe and share the textual condition of verbal meaning and to describe and share the relation between the textual unit and the referent nature of verbal meaning. To describe biblical literature as expressing a "type" of meaning is not to be confused with "typology." As described, the term "type" simply describes the fact that biblical literature can be classified in terms of shared textual senses, and based on these, the literature refers to the realm of reference.

"Typology" is a term coined to describe a particular and unique type of biblical literature. It is commonly an instance of historical narrative with the additional defining trait of prophecy in that historical instance. This additional trait is part of the textual sense. This "historical type" refers to a "historical antitype" that has the trait of fulfillment of the prophecy. So the traditional recognition of typology is simply a special case corresponding to the model of verbal meaning as being a type whole with trait components, a whole meaning, and component defining meanings.

define genres by classifying them according to traits: "Genre should be conceived, we think, as a grouping of literary works based, theoretically, upon both outer form (specific meter or structure) and also upon inner form (attitude, tone, purpose—more crudely, subject and audience)."[2] In a biblical perspective, John J. Collins defines genre this way: "By 'literary genre' we mean a group of written texts marked by distinctive recurring characteristics which constitute a recognizable and coherent type of writing."[3] In each case a set of traits (elements of form or distinctive, recurring characteristics) defines or sets the limits for a type of meaning or literary genre.

Recognition is the first stage of interpretation. In recognition, the reader begins with what is unknown, the text. If he is to reason from the known to the unknown, then what he knows, he must know about the text in general as preunderstanding. This is where the model of a type and a set of defining traits provides an appropriate framework for thinking about interpretation. The reader knows the traits in general as preunderstanding for textual composition and looks for them in the text in particular. He classifies the meaning of the text as having meanings of this type.

The etymology of the word *type* provides the elements of the model. "Type" is from the Greek *tupos,* which means "impression, cast, model." The stamp has an aggregate of features with a certain cachet or physiognomy that identifies the impression.[4] The type is known in general by the features of the stamp. Each individual impression of the stamp marks an individual impression with the general features in a unique imprint.

The model of thought about interpretation involves recognition of the unknown individual impression in terms of general knowledge of the features of the stamp. In other words, the type of meaning is known in a general knowledge of a set of traits and recognized in the new expression of the set of traits in the unknown text. This set of traits that defines the type of biblical meaning has already been introduced in the questions of the inductive study. The questions identify the traits in the most general terms. These traits form a pattern: theological themes, textual design, and unifying message.

2. Definition of type: Type as one text that is a member of a class of texts sharing at least one trait in common.
The process of reasoning about the world and literary texts does not begin with a known archetype that has stamped its set of traits on numerous individual imprints (deductive). Rather, an interpreter of the world or of literary texts begins with many individual imprints that appear to have components in common (inductive). The evidence of shared components invites a process of classification. When that evidence has involved the realms of natural creation, it has led to development of elaborate systems of classified life forms of biology or zoology. Similar systems have followed in the worlds of chemistry and physics. It is at this level of classification that the shared components of literary texts must initially be considered. A type of meaning involves "a grouping of literary works" or "a group of written texts."

But the process of classification of

---

[2] Rene Wellek and Austin Warren, *Theory of Literature* (New York: Harcourt, Brace and World, 1956), 221.

[3] John J. Collins, "Introduction: Towards the Morphology of a Genre," in *Apocalypse: The Morphology of a Genre (Semeia* 14 [1979]): 1

[4] *International Encyclopedia of Social Sciences,* vol. 16, "Typologies," 177–86.

literary texts has not enjoyed the kind of general agreement that has been reached in classifying our knowledge of the natural world. A handbook of modern literary criticism flatly states that "the concept that there are literary genres . . . has, since the early nineteenth century, been losing ground" and suggests that perhaps three "categories" of genres are all that is needed: fiction, drama, and lyric.[5] This difficulty in identifying a class of textual meanings with wide agreement was illustrated in the debate between Robert Gundry and the Evangelical Theological Society over the presence of Midrashic genre in Matthew.[6]

In spite of the lack of general agreement on the matter, the value of thinking of textual meaning as shared sets of traits among literary texts is indispensable to both recognition and exegesis. Although literary texts involve less consistent patterns of traits than those found in nature, yet the model of reasoning in which we recognize the unknown in terms of what is known does not change. Thus a literary text must be read to recognize a type of meaning known by a set of traits and known as a member of a class of texts sharing at least one trait in common.

This work of classification is commonly done in a library. Here books may be classified by "subject" or by an aspect of "textual design": fiction or nonfiction. Other evidences of classification are found in the Bible itself. The canon is a class of books sharing a common theological trait. In addition, the canon itself witnesses to classes of books that have a shared trait or traits: Torah, Prophets, Wisdom, Gospels, Epistles, Apocalypse, and so on.

3. Type-trait model: Interpretation of literary texts. The term "type-trait" is not widely used by specialists in hermeneutics, but neither is it unheard of. German writers used similar terms in form criticism: *Gattung,* referring to smaller literary units such as psalms of individual lament, miracle stories, or proverbs; and *Form,* used in a roughly similar sense. English-speaking authors tend to use the word "genre" to refer to whole works such as gospels, collections of oracles, or epic works, and "form" to designate smaller textual units. We want to replace this range of vocabulary with one term—"type"—that is applicable to any unit of textual meaning. I have chosen the term "type" to free the following discussion from many of the conflicts that have occurred in the past over technical issues associated with the terms "genre" or "form."

It is useful to make a brief and selective survey of varying literary viewpoints, and we will begin with Herman Gunkel (1862–1932), a prominent form critic. His work with *Gattungen* basically involved a method of classifying portions of a text that resulted in smaller and smaller sections being considered so that each section might be defined by an identical set of traits.[7] Austin Farrar, a biblical scholar, was highly critical of this approach because of its fragmentation of the text:

> Form criticism [as practiced by biblical scholars] is rather misleading so called, because the name suggests an attempt to appreciate the form of a complete literary unit, say St. Mark's Gospel. Whereas what form-criticism studies is the form of the small constituent parts of the Gospels; anecdotal paragraphs, for example, or even such small details as apparently self-

---

[5] Sylvan Barnet et al., *Study of Literature* (Boston: Little, Brown, 1960), 91.

[6] Robert H. Gundry, *Matthew: A Commentary on His Literary and Theological Art* (Grand Rapids: Eerdmans, 1982), 623–40.

[7] James Muilenburg, "Form Criticism and Beyond," *Journal of Biblical Literature* (1969): 1–18.

contained gnomic sentences. . . . [By contrast] in the literary realm, . . . the pattern of the whole comes first.[8]

Thus the form-critical method became counterproductive as an interpretive tool. In seeking an identity in traits, the interpreter moved to smaller and smaller units of the text, and as a result the technique became inconsequential for interpreting a book as a whole.

Furthermore, the meaning of these segments of text was related to the history of the formation of the text rather than the present shape of the text as a whole. The form of such segments was understood to be caused by the *Sitz im Leben*—the life-setting. J. P. Fokkelmann has challenged the preoccupation with such historical questions at the expense of an interpretation of the meaning of the text.

> For one or two centuries they [biblical scholars] have expended such "enormous efforts" in framing theories on the origin of biblical texts and on the history of their transmission that the study of the text itself, which is "only" the final shape of the tradition, but, for all that, the only one given, seems to have suffered somewhat.[9]

So Fokkelmann has proposed a different focus of attention in literary study. His goal is "to demonstrate especially a method of structural explication which starts from the principle that these texts belong to narrative art and which consistently takes this fact into account."[10]

Thus biblical scholars have become somewhat disillusioned with the form critics' emphasis on the smaller segments of the text and their preoccupation with the origin and transmission of these texts. James Muilenburg stated to the Society of Biblical Literature that he is above all concerned with

> understanding the nature of Hebrew-literary composition, in exhibiting the structural patterns that are employed for the fashioning of a literary unit, whether in poetry or in prose, and in discerning the many and various devices by which the predications are formulated and ordered into a unified whole.[11]

There are clear signs of a trend among biblical critics toward greater interest in and study of literary genres. Form criticism focused attention on smaller units of text recognized by a set of specific content and formal traits whose literary message was explained by specific historic occasions. Subsequent interpretation has given attention to larger textual units that share a set of literary traits, whose message is explained by the unity present in the final canonical composition. This change in focus among biblical scholars is a helpful corrective.

Some literary critics have also focused new concern on the role of the type-trait model in textual interpretation. The type, or genre, with its set of traits is not merely a descriptive classification along the scientific model, but it has an interpretive and even generative role. Northrop Frye, in *Anatomy of Criticism,* his encyclopedic treatment of literary interpretation, discusses "the theory of genres." He proposes to specify the role of genre as interpretive of a composition's organization; "if the direct union of grammar and logic is characteristic of non-literary verbal structures, literature may be described as the rhetorical organization of grammar and logic."[12] Thus the role of type

---

[8]Austin Farrar, *A Study in St. Mark* (London: Dacre, 1951), 21–22.
[9]J. P. Fokkelmann, *Narrative in Genesis* (Assen, the Netherlands: Van Gorcum, 1975), 1.
[10]Ibid., 5.
[11]Muilenburg, "Form Criticism and Beyond," 8.
[12]Northrop Frye, *Anatomy of Criticism* (Princeton: Princeton University Press, 1957), 245.

in our terminology is to recognize in a composition the principle of organization that is designed "to clarify, not to classify."[13]

In the same spirit, Leland Ryken writes:

> Literary genre is nothing less than a norm or *expectation* to guide the reader in his encounter with the text. An awareness of genre will program our reading of a work, giving it a familiar shape and arranging the details into an identifiable pattern.[14]

He distinguishes between the principle of organization in literary writing and that in expository writing.

> Through the centuries, people have agreed that certain genres (such as story, poetry, and drama) are literary in nature. Other genres, such as historical chronicles, theological treatises, and genealogies are expository (informational) in nature. Still others fall into one or the other category.[15]

The role of clarification that genre provides in literary interpretation is precisely the benefit that we seek to gain in using the type-trait model in biblical composition. When we first encounter a text, we immediately begin to make judgments as to the type of communication it is; in our preunderstanding we identify certain traits and because of them associate the writing with a certain type, or genre.

E. D. Hirsch has taken the discussion further by asserting that type or genre is a principle which not merely clarifies but ultimately specifies textual meanings. Mary Gerhart summarizes that idea very simply: "There is no meaning without genre; that is, verbal meaning is always 'genre-bound.'"[16]

This development in the conceived role of genre in Hirsch rests in his unique use of the term "genre." The common use of "genre" refers to the "kind" of work of art, from the French word meaning "kind" or "genus." It is used in this sense to specify the pattern of traits shared in general by a number of works of art. But Hirsch speaks in terms of "intrinsic genre," which changes the use of the term from traits shared in general to those traits expressed in particular terms corresponding to one text alone.[17] In this textbook we will use our term "type of meaning" in both senses. In the hermeneutical premises we will talk about the type of grammatical, historical, textual, and theological meanings in general. This will help us to clarify our appropriate preunderstandings. In addition, we will talk about the type of intrinsic meaning of a text in terms of the essential summary statements of that text.

This specifying of the intended meanings (see part 3) on the part of the interpreter is based on what happens when an author communicates. An author's communication of a verbal meaning is both a temporal and a conscious process. It is a temporal process in that the meanings are expressed in a temporal sequence; it is a conscious process in that at any moment of expression, the author is only conscious of his immediate word choices. Yet, since at no time in the process is he simultaneously conscious of all the particular meanings he is going to express, something must be present to guide the

---

[13] Frye quoted approvingly by Tzvetan Todorov, "Literary Genres," CTL 12 (1974): 962.

[14] Leland Ryken, *How to Read the Bible as Literature* (Grand Rapids: Zondervan, 1984), 25.

[15] Ibid.

[16] Mary Gerhart, "Generic Studies: Their Renewed Importance in Religions and Literary Interpretation," *Journal of the American Academy of Religion* (September 1977): 312.

[17] Hirsch uses "type" when discussing the role from the author's point of view and "genre" when discussing the role from the interpreter's point of view.

conscious expression in time. Hirsch wrote about that guiding mechanism:

> How does a speaker manage to put one word after another unless his choice and usages are governed by a controlling conception? There must be some kind of over-arching notion which controls the temporal sequence of speech, and this controlling notion of the speaker, like that of the interpreter, must embrace a system of expectations. . . .
>
> Even when the meaning which the speaker wishes to convey is unusual (and some aspects of his conveyed meaning will almost always be unique) he knows that in order to convey his meaning he must take into account his interpreter's probable understanding. If his interpreter's system of expectations and associations is to correspond to his own, he must adopt usages which will fulfill not only his own expectations but also those of his interpreter.[18]

Hirsch selected a portion from Augustine's *Confessions* to show how the process of a controlling conception works. In that passage, Augustine reflects on a psalm he memorized. As he expresses what he remembered, his knowledge of the psalm as a whole guides his temporal repeating of it line by line. This is a special case of the process of authorship in which the same temporal expression is guided by a conscious controlling sense of the whole.[19]

Then, from the point of view of the reader, the same temporal interpretation is specified by a conscious controlling conception that is present. Hirsch relates how a class of his students dealt with John Donne's poem "A Valediction Forbidding Mourning." Hirsch says that the students expected the poem to be about a dying man and interpreted the various elements in that light. The professor had a difficult time persuading them, because of their expectations at every point, that the poem instead concerns a temporary physical absence.[20]

The role of the type of meaning in influencing our expectations of textual meanings is more clearly seen when the reader is frustrated in his understanding. Ironically, Donne's poem proved not to be frustrating enough, we might say, or else the students would have caught on more quickly that their expectations were wrong. Other writers have affirmed this ironic aspect of the process suggested by Hirsch. Lars Hartman considered *Gulliver's Travels* by Jonathan Swift in this regard:

> On the surface, the book appears as a travel-book, not least by its matter-of-fact style. . . . A reader who has come little more of age recognizes that such a genre classification . . . does not fit, for he senses how much ironic criticism of mankind's follies is contained in the story.[21]

Gerhart makes the point with Swift's *Modest Proposal:* "Swift's essay is

---

[18] E. D. Hirsch, *Validity in Interpretation* (New Haven: Yale University Press, 1967), 78.

[19] *Confessions,* 11.28, quoted in Hirsch, *Validity in Interpretation,* 79. This passage appears in a discussion of Augustine comparing human consciousness and divine consciousness in foreknowledge. Out of his concern over foreknowledge Augustine illustrated the concept of intended meaning in a specialized system of expectations of a memorized psalm. But a less specific system of expectations accompanies any choice to speak. Even in very informal intentional speech, the speaker can claim, "I know what I want to say." Such expectations or knowledge arise from his choice of a type of meaning. It is his knowledge of a type of meaning that guides his choices in the particulars of the text expressing that type of meaning.

[20] Hirsch, *Validity in Interpretation,* 73–74.

[21] Lars Hartman, "Survey of the Problem of Apocalyptic Genre," in *Apocalypticism in the Mediterranean World and the Near East,* ed. David Hellholm (Tübingen: J. C. B. Mohr, 1983), 330.

designed to deceive all readers for a time and then require them to recognize and cope with their deception."[22]

Our model of type-trait will build on the work of Hirsch. "Type of meaning" in general refers to "the expectations which include range of vocabulary and syntax, the tone of the work, the extension or rejection of particular connotations, and the explications of relationship between the person and the reader."[23] These general characteristics are specified in an intrinsic summary statement of the type of meaning by the pattern of traits expressed in a certain text (the traits having defined or set limits on the verbal meaning, as we saw earlier).

4. Type-trait model: Interpretation of biblical books. One of the questions that remains open in our approach to literary interpretation of the Bible concerns the portion or construction of the text that the interpreter chooses to read in order to initially recognize the author's meaning. Ryken chooses to work with an artistic literary unit, whether it is also a textual unit (a paragraph or a chapter) or simply a portion of a textual unit (a theme or motif expressed in several chapters) that displays an artistic unity. Fokkelmann works with textual units that display thematic unity, such as 2 Samuel 9–20 and 1 Kings 1–2, which deal with King David.

The type-trait model of verbal meaning is flexible and capable of being applied to any section of the text. But the relationship between the construction of textual form and the semantic unit of type of meaning must be the determining factor in deciding where to begin. The relationships may be described as follows:

Form	*Meaning*
Morpheme:	The simplest form capable of a wide variety of unrelated meanings (such as *pin* or *s* in *pins*)
Word:	A lexical unit capable of a variety of meanings, some possibly being unrelated
Sentence:	A grammatical unit capable of several possible meanings
Paragraph:	A thought unit capable of supporting fewer possible meanings and essentially one message
Book:	An author's compositional unit corresponding to one unified message

Since the book form is a textual construction that alone corresponds to the message determined by the author, it will be the unit of the text with which the interpreter should logically begin his work. This work corresponds with the goal as an effort to recognize the intended type of meaning that the author expressed in a text form.

The basic unit of study is further suggested by the very name *Bible,* from the Latin *biblia,* meaning "books." Moreover, the biblical exegete works primarily with books of the Bible. These form the basis of an expository preaching and teaching ministry. So the unit of text with which the task of reading for recognition begins is the whole book, which expresses the unified message.

---

[22]Gerhart, "Generic Studies: Their Renewed Importance in Religions and Literary Interpretation," 313.

[23]Ibid.

It is advantageous that this point of initial reading provides an unbiased, evenhanded approach to the study of either literary genre or expository genre. That is important, because the Bible is an encyclopedia of various textual genres. Whatever set of traits defines the type of meaning in a book, it can naturally be applied to a variety of genres (expository and literary).

5. Type-trait model: The task of recognition. The type-trait model provides an appropriate guide for the task of reading and the goal of recognition.

If the reader will examine his own experience, he will recognize the role of the two aspects: the particulars of expression (traits), and the overall type of meaning in his *own* process of reading. The reader begins with the text as written. But when the reader is asked, "What does the text mean?" he must answer in his own words. His own words or selected words from the text construct his comprehension of the whole. They state his recognition of a type of meaning.

Should the reader respond, "Here, read it for yourself," others might well conclude that he may not have understood it. But if he answered in his own words or with a selected quotation from the text, we would conclude that this is what he comprehends the book to be about, or in our terminology, what he recognizes as the author's type of meaning. The answer does not repeat the exact form in which the meaning was written, but is a statement of the same type of meaning.

These two aspects of interpretive thought are simply the two aspects of communication: textual expression, and the author's intended meaning. They are reflected in the adage, "The text means what it says and it says what it means," which distinguishes the aspect of expression (saying) from the aspect of meaning. The two are necessarily bound together; meaning is communicated in saying, and without saying no verbal meaning is communicated.

The type-trait model of interpretation has some necessary benefits for the literal tradition. Historically, philosophical categories or types have held a very prominent place in philosophy. Manley Thompson writes, "Categories are classes, genres, or types supposed to mark necessary divisions within our conceptual scheme, divisions that we must recognize if we are to make *literal sense* in our discourse about the world."[24]

In a parallel fashion, we must seek in our exposition of the Bible to recognize the categorical limits and boundaries of the types of meanings that correspond to the textual expression if we are to know the literal sense. Thus the type-trait model is not simply widely recognized, but is also necessary to establish a literal system of interpretation.

The principal problem we face in the recognition of a book's type of meaning considered as a whole is to discern what is necessary and sufficient for it. While the message is necessary to recognize the meaning of a book, is it sufficient in itself? Or would some pattern of statements be broader to comprehend the richness of the book's meaning?

In the semantic analysis of a language system, the more we know of the language, the easier the task. The limits of meaning of a word or construction can be more readily determined by comparing and contrasting related words. In analyzing literature, such comprehensive knowledge is difficult to gain. Moreover, it is difficult to grasp the complexity and richness of mean-

---

[24]Manley Thompson, "Categories," *Encyclopedia of Philosophy,* ed. Paul Edwards (New York: Macmillan and Free Press, 1967), 2:46.

ings within the meaning of the book as a whole.

Given the lack of a clear tradition to explore the range of what is sufficient, we propose a pattern of three statements as sufficient to consider the uniquely expressed biblical meaning. The most evident component is the *message* of what is said in the book. But it is insufficient in and of itself because it gives little attention to what is meant on the basis of the way it is expressed and the distinctive content expressed.

Thus the pattern would do well to also consider these two other aspects. The first is the *textual design,* which takes into account the range of meanings intended in everything from, say, the poetical Song of Songs to the directly reasoned argument of Romans. Both books express a cognitive message, but the extent of affective meanings is much richer in a song than in a reasoned discourse. The second aspect directly expresses the *theological* content involved in progressive revelation. This theological content distinguishes the books that are included in the canon from those that are not.

This threefold pattern attempts to frame in direct statements the content that limits what a book says in its intended richness. Although there may be some overlap between the three statements, yet in what they distinctly affirm they set the limits of the range of textual meanings. The pattern corresponds to biblical books expressing meanings of this type.

6. Type-trait model: Conclusion. In concluding our definition of type in literary analysis, we can appropriately cite certain guidelines and warnings, as suggested by Edward Tiryakian.[25]

a. The methodological function and meaningfulness of the type classification are basically twofold: *codification* and *predication.*[26] In codification, a type subsumes and relates traits that are defining or associated components to that type. In predication, a known type anticipates defining and associated traits that may not be known or presently recognized. These two characteristics explain the conscious and temporal nature of human communication and knowledge. The predication function is active at the stage of recognition; the codification function is active at the stage of exegesis.

b. "Much of the methodological usefulness of typologies lies in their being synthetic constructions from the data so that no specific actual instance or element would be taken for the type itself."[27] This feature of human knowledge and communication reflects the distinction between expression and type. The type of meaning of a text comprises the set of traits or components that are able to match the sense or define the meaning as a whole in a literal correspondence between type and textual meaning. The recognition of these defining traits comes through a process called *pattern-recognition.*[28]

This means that as the interpreter reads, he is alerted to see a pattern of traits that is known from the expectations of the type in general. What this pattern of traits is generally has been introduced in the essential questions of inductive study. The process of pattern-recognition is different from a process of abstraction, however.[29] Abstracting is

---

[25] *International Encyclopedia of Social Sciences,* vol. 16, "Typologies," 177–86.

[26] Ibid., 178.

[27] Ibid., 179.

[28] Lyons, *Semantics* (New York: Cambridge University Press, 1977), 1:16.

[29] Peter Geach, *Mental Acts* (New York: Humanities Press, 1957).

the doctrine that a concept is acquired by a process of singling out in attention some one feature given in direct experience—*abstracting it*—and ignoring the other features simultaneously given—*abstracting from* them.[30]

The process of abstraction of a theme or principle that is frequently used in interpretation holds the great danger of misrepresenting the controlling and limiting function of context.

In summary, type is the pattern of defining traits matching, yet distinct from, particular expressions in the text.

c. "The more explicitly stated the typology, including the relation between types, the more the typology functions as a theoretical model."[31] This observation provides direction for discussing the type character of literary meaning in the Bible. Our purpose in this book is to begin discussing the types of meaning in biblical literature. It is an invitation to make explicit this method for making essential summaries defining the type of meaning found in every book in the canon.

d. "Classification in general by structuring the manifold dimensions of concrete experience, also distorts it, i.e., it emphasizes discontinuities."[32] This is a danger inherent in the classification of any body of knowledge. We are warned about our attitude toward the recognition and codification of types. It can "freeze" the discussion of meaning at the level of typological classification; it can introduce stereotyping as a mode of interpretation unless we as the interpreters are willing to change the type recognized when the matching textual data demand such a change. Thus the warning focuses on the controlling reality of the author's textual expression; all recognized types of meaning must be measured by their correspondence to

the actual text. This warning gains in importance in part 3.

GRAMMATICAL

The grammatical system affirms that the textually based type of meaning is expressed by an author within the limits of common language usage.

This premise addresses the choice of vocabulary within the common lexical stock and grammatical conventions of that original language usage. The fact that the reading of the text should be within the conventions of shared grammatical usage highlights a number of expectations. The interpreter needs to be alerted to the range of possible meanings that can be communicated in verbal forms. Three issues will be addressed regarding our expectations in reading.

1. Reading in translation or in the original language. It is almost self-evident that the most knowledgeable reader is one who reads the text in the original language. In this reading he has access to the greatest number of textual clues shared directly with the author. As he becomes a skillful reader he can also gain a sensitivity to and awareness of stylistic and conventional usage.

These facts have been acknowledged by interpreters since the Reformation. Yet, can a translation truthfully communicate the Word of God? As stated earlier, in the doctrine of verbal plenary inspiration the very words of the text are understood as the words of God as stated in the original manuscript. While this is true in its most precise sense, can we limit "Word" to the linguistic symbols of the original manuscript, or can the sense of "Word" be accurately taken to refer to the Author's/author's

---

[30] Ibid., 18.
[31] *IESS*, vol. 16, "Typologies," 179.
[32] Ibid., 179.

96

intended sense? If we grant the latter, then to the extent that it faithfully translates that sense, the translation could be called the Word of God. J. I. Packer has taken this position, saying that verbal plenary inspiration

> does not imply a Koranic view of inspiration, whereby translations of the original are precisely *not* the Holy Book. As reformed theology used to say, it is the sense of Scripture that is Scripture, and all translations are in truth the Bible, at least to the extent that they are accurate.[33]

This understanding of the term "Word" is implicitly agreed to by the eminent advocate of a liberal education, Mortimer Adler. In *How to Read a Book* he advocates reading the classics in good English translations. In this way common people can gain a liberal education. This is possible because the words of a Greek or Latin manuscript are not necessarily limited to the original signs, but can be translated in the shared sense of the author in another language. This premise is equally true where accurate translations of the Bible are available.

2. Problems with language. Common language usage introduces a number of problems for clarity of expression that the reader must deal with.

> Changes in meaning, polysemy or multiple meanings, bivocals and the use of different words for the same referent belong to the conventions of a language and present problems for the exegete, along with the well-known problem of deciding the meaning of hapax legomena.[34]

a. Polysemy: This is a basic element of genius in human language that at the same time may cause uncertainty in verbal communication. By polysemy we mean that any component of language (word, construction, sentence, etc.) is capable of a range of senses and is capable of unlimited references to appropriate objects. It is therefore serviceable for innumerable speaking occasions and repeatedly useful without having the meaning exhausted in one historical situation or reference. A reader must be sensitive to this potential range of usage. Consider, for example, King David's speaking of building God's "house" (2 Sam. 7:5) and God's responding by promising to build David's "house" (v. 11).

b. Changes in sense: With the passage of time, a word that originally meant one thing by constant repetition may change its sense and referent. Hebrew expresses psychological states by words indicating the organs of the body, such as "kidney" or "heart."[35] This same phenomenon occurs in more important cases. "Language appropriate for tangible expressions of the Canaanite religion came to be filled with new meaning when referred to the LORD, who did not have physical form."[36] So Canaanite expressions such as "food of God" or "to see the face of God" meant, in the Hebrew usage, "offering" and "to be received into God's audience." G. B. Caird comments that "to 'see the face of' a person was a regular Hebrew idiom for being received in audience by someone of consequence (e.g., Gen. 43:3, 5; 2 Sam. 14:24)."

---

[33] J. I. Packer, "The Adequacy of Human Language," in *Inerrancy,* ed. Norman L. Geisler (Grand Rapids: Zondervan, 1979), 211.

[34] Bruce K. Waltke, "Grammatical Problems," in *Hermeneutics, Inerrancy and the Bible,* ed. Earl D. Radmacher and Robert D. Preus, (Grand Rapids: Zondervan, 1984), 100.

[35] G. B. Caird, *The Language and Imagery of the Bible* (Philadelphia: Westminster, 1980), 66–68. Compare the renderings of Psalm 73:21 in the King James and New International versions.

[36] Waltke, "Grammatical Problems," 100.

c. Double reference: A metaphor is the transference of a word from its normal referent to a second referent in order that the second referent might be illuminated by the first. Jesus often used metaphors, as when he told his disciples, "I am the vine; you are the branches" (John 15:5). Or consider Revelation 3:20: "Here I am! I stand at the door and knock."

> A problem that arises in the case of metaphor is that of deciding when one is dealing with a dead metaphor. . . . As long as the speaker and his audience are aware of the double reference it is a living metaphor, but when, through overuse, the first referent is lost sight of, it fades and eventually dies.[37]

As a consequence, a dead metaphor has lost all of the comparative sense and is simply a direct reference with the comparative elements assumed in a new sense of the word.

There is another aspect of multiple reference that complicates the biblical use of language. One aspect of language that facilitates communication is the capacity of words to be used with multiple references. Any word can be used in various contexts to refer to different objects of the same type of sense. The word "tree" may be used to speak of the great sequoia reaching hundreds of feet into the air and having a diameter of many feet, or to refer to a tiny sapling. They appear different, yet both are trees. In human communication, where consciousness is limited by time and space, a reader has little difficulty discerning the referent or different referents, as with the trees. But in divine communication, where a prophet may speak with a near referent and one or more distant referents intended, the interpretation becomes complicated. So when God promised Eve a "seed," she thought it was Cain (Gen. 4:1) and really had no idea that the ultimate reference would be found to be Jesus Christ (Luke 3:23, 38). Yet such multiple reference does not admit double meanings of unrelated or incompatible referents (double entendre).

d. Bivocals: Bivocals pose a problem primarily for one working with an original language, but it is important enough to be considered here. Caird writes:

> It is one of the curiosities of language that many of the words expressive of feeling are bivocal, i.e., capable of signifying both stimulus and response, while some words which are their partial synonyms can signify only the one or the other.[38]

He illustrates the phenomenon with a few English examples (fig. 6.1).

Figure 6.1

Stimulus and Response	Stimulus Only	Response Only
Love	Darling	Affection
Honor	Worth	Esteem
Wonder	Prodigy	Awe
Curiosity	Oddity	Inquisitiveness
Delight	Treat	Zest

[37] Ibid., 116.
[38] Caird, *The Language and Imagery of the Bible,* 27.

Words that are bivocal in the original must be bivocal in either translation or exposition.

e. Hapax legomenon: This problem—the occurrence of a word or expression only once in a text—is dealt with primarily in lexicography, and an English reader does not address it directly. However, it is an important matter that requires a knowledge of cognate language usage as well as clues within the context of biblical usage. To a great extent, the student of biblical language is dependent on the expert in judging the influence of cognate usage. Yet in the final analysis it is the textual context and usage that determines the authorial sense of the terms.

3. Range of language usage and possible meanings. Any reader of the text must address the range of usage in an author's use of language. Traditional classification in usage reflects Aristotle, who distinguished between persuasive uses in rhetoric and imitational uses in poetics. These were themselves distinguished from referential usage in reason and logic. Linguists have refined these and refocused their emphasis.

One complete model of component senses has been summarized by Roman Jakobson and is depicted in the following scheme of the functions in language usage.[39] The model (fig. 6.2) has been slightly modified for our purposes in this book.

Figure 6.2

REFERENTIAL
(Context)

EMOTIVE	POETIC	CONATIVE
(Addresser)	(Message)	(Addressee)

PHATIC
(Contact)

METALINGUAL
(Code)

These language functions include:

a. Emotive: The expressive function, focused on the addresser, which aims at an expression of the speaker's attitude toward what he is speaking about. This has also been described as the *mood* (attitude toward subject) and the *tone* (attitude toward audience).

b. Referential: The denotative, cognitive function which is dominant in many passages.

c. Conative: A use directed toward the addressee that finds its purest grammatical expression in the vocative and imperative.

d. Phatic: Messages primarily serving to establish, to prolong, or to discontinue communication, to check if the channel works, or to attract or confirm attention.

e. Metalinguistic: The message that speaks about language to check that both speaker and audience are using the same code.

---

[39] Roman Jakobson, "Closing Statement: Linguistics and Poetics," in *Style in Language,* ed. Thomas A. Sebeok (Cambridge: MIT Press, 1978), 357.

f. Poetic: A function that is not the sole function of verbal art, but only its dominant, controlling function.

Eugene Nida suggests that meanings may be most conveniently classified in terms of two intersecting sets of factors: Cognitive vs. emotive and extralinguistic vs. intralinguistic (fig. 6.3).[40]

Figure 6.3

	Cognitive	Emotive
Extralinguistic	Referential	Emotive response to extralinguistic factors
Intralinguistic	Grammatical	Emotive response to intralinguistic factors

In the model of the author's type of meaning with implied components of traits of meaning, the language usage concerns the intralinguistic factors that the author intends in expression. It is limited to the author's intended emotive response regardless of what the response may be. In addition to the language usage, the type of meaning includes the extralinguistic factors intended by the author that the reader must share. The share in extralinguistics may be a share in imagination of a referential meaning that is based on the relation between the lexical unit and the referent. The referent may be called *denotatum,* but this denotatum alone is not the author's meaning.

Irving M. Copi has organized the basic uses of language into four broad categories.[41] These reflect the work of Ludwig Wittgenstein, who insisted rightly that there are "countless different kinds of use of what we call 'symbols,' 'words,' and 'sentences.' "[42] Wittgenstein called them language-games and listed some examples: "giving orders and obeying them, describing the appearance of an object or giving its measurement, constructing an object from a description, reporting an event, speculating about an event . . . asking, thanking, cursing, greeting, praying." It is helpful to be able to recognize some basic and comprehensive types.

Copi initially recognized three basic and general types of language uses: to inform, to express (judgment or feelings), and to direct (actions). These distinct uses influence the implications involved in an author's statement. A husband may come home from work and say, "I sure had a hard day at work." If his use was "to inform," then an appropriate response would be to seek more information. But if the use was "to express" his feelings, then his wife would do well to console him. And if perchance his use was "to direct" the actions of others, then his wife would best keep quiet. Clearly then, the same sequence of words can generate different implications of sense, depending on which language use an author chooses.

[40] Eugene Nida, *Componential Analysis of Meaning* (The Hague: Mouton, 1979), 25–26.
[41] Irving M. Copi, *Introduction to Logic* (London: Macmillan, 1968), 34–58.
[42] Ludwig Wittgenstein, *Philosophical Investigations* (New York: Macmillan, 1958), 11e–12e.

The use of "to inform" is common to exposition, description, narrative, history, and argumentation.

Information discourse is used to describe the world, and to reason about it. Whether the alleged facts are important or unimportant, general or particular, does not matter; in any case the language used to describe or report them is being used informatively.[43]

Biblical discourses having this usage include historical *narrative,* prayerful *dialogue,* doctrinal *explanation* or *exposition,* and polemic *argument.*

Other discourse types may use language to inform, but the overriding use is "to direct" action. From the authoritative position of "lawgiver," Moses *commanded* in order to direct the behavior of Israel to conform to God's will. Similarly, the prophets confronted Israel with their sin and *pleaded* with them to repent. Christ spoke with unique authority to *compel* the faith of men. And the apostle Paul at times *beseeched* men to obey due to the overwhelming compassion of God's mercy. The directional force of language governs the persuasive preaching of the prophets and the persuasive exhortation of the epistles.

The third common usage is "to express" judgments or feelings. This can have a positive sense, as to *sing* and to *praise* or to *lament.* These may be directed toward the *worship* of God or toward others to *evoke* or *arouse* similar judgment or feelings. This usage can also have a negative sense, as to *vent anger* or to *express displeasure.* The psalms are rich in the expression of judgment and feelings. So too are the prophets: Isaiah in the praise of God's glory; Jeremiah in the tears of a rejected friend; Ezekiel in the consternation of an ignored judge. The expressive use of language is common in dialogue or in persuasion; it can be both informative and directional.

But in some ways a fourth category which may be added to the three basic uses is the most interesting. Copi calls it "the *performance* utterance, the one that in appropriate circumstances performs the action that it *reports.*"[44]

John Austin classifies some subcategories of these four categories that are suggestive for biblical usage.[45] Only three of the five will be developed here, as the two others are special cases of "to inform—the *expositive,* the clarifying of reasons, arguments, and communications," and cases of "to express—the *behavitive* is the adopting of an attitude." The three we will explore are these: "the *verdictive* is an exercise of judgment, the *exercitive* is an assertion of influence or exercising of power, and the *commissive* is an assuming of obligation or declaring of an intention."[46]

The three are particularly appropriate to numerous cases where God is speaking in dialogue with men. In the verdictive, God speaks to judge the evidence or facts before the standard of moral responsibility. At issue is righteousness or guilt. God's justification of sinful believers is a verdictive statement. Many of the prophets' indictments against Israel and the nations are verdictive statements. Verdictives have an implied meaning in that they commit the speaker to certain future conduct and judgment.

In exercitives, God speaks to advocate. An exercitive is the giving of a decision for or against a certain course of action or the advocacy of it. Austin

---

[43] Copi, *Introduction to Logic,* 35.

[44] Ibid., 39.

[45] John L. Austin, *How to Do Things With Words* (Oxford: Clarendon Press, 1962), 147–63.

[46] Ibid., 162 (emphasis added).

explains, "It is a decision that something is to be so, as distinct from a judgment that it is so . . . it is an award as opposed to an assessment. . . . Arbitrators and judges make use of exercitives as well as issuing verdicts."[47] This distinction enriches our understanding of the implied force of statements about believers' rewards. God's words that believers have eternal life speak of a divine decision implying a present (verdictive) and future (exercitive) reality.

The third subcategory is perhaps the most suggestive of all. "The whole point of a *commission* is to commit the speaker to a certain course of action," writes Austin.[48] The relationship of a believer to God is enriched when the appropriate promises and covenants are read with their commissive force in regard to God the Author. Here the Word of God is recognized in its uniquely authoritative potency and force as God has committed himself to act with implications for the future. The crowds recognized the unique authoritative force in Jesus' words (Matt. 7:28–29) in contrast to others who did not speak of God as committing himself to bless them.

As interpreters we share an expectation of these various types of language usage. The problem in recognition is that a given discourse seldom is a pure or a distinct type. All well and good. Copi, however, makes a comment on biblical discourse that reflects a dangerous presupposition. According to him, when we recite the Lord's Prayer or the Twenty-third Psalm of David, "all these uses of language are not intended to communicate information, but to express emotions, feelings, or attitudes."[49] Nothing in the text suggests this negative attitude or necessitates that the use is so limited. Rather, biblical discourse, like common human discourse, serves multiple functions. Thus an appropriate conception of the use of textual design must be chosen that combines both information and expression. While it is true that both David and the Lord pray, it is also true that they both express confidence and as prophets inform the reader that God exists and that he has a relationship with them (Acts 2:30). Copi's rationalistic presupposition is part of his preunderstanding of the nature of the Bible rather than his preunderstanding or understanding of the textual language.

In the case of the biblical books as a whole, there is never a single type of language usage. Within the controlling literary concerns, there is an address of the audience and a structuring of the discourse by means of appropriate and related uses of language. In the narrative structure of the Torah, the controlling design is to teach. However, the narrative structure may also incorporate expressive statements (e.g., Gen. 2:23; 4:23–24; Ex. 15:1–18, 21; Judg. 5:1–31) or performative utterances (e.g., Gen. 3:14–19; 8:21–22; 9:1–7; 12:1–3; 15:1, 4-6). Each of these incorporated uses of language must be understood within the overarching structure of the Torah. In addition, the expressive and performative utterances do not preclude expressing information, even though the emphasis is not on information. In this fashion the unifying textual design comprehends the overall literary structure while at the same time incorporating purposeful and harmonious uses of language at appropriate points in the narrative.

HISTORICAL

Historical affirms that the textually based types of meaning refer to histori-

[47] Ibid., 154.
[48] Ibid., 156 (emphasis added).
[49] Ibid., 36.

cal realities and allude to situational features.

Hermeneutical expectations, based on the type of meaning expressed, influence one's preparation for reading an ancient text. Three aspects of these expectations will be examined, all of which involve aspects of the historical context.

1. Historical occasion context. Historical occasion involves the situation in which the utterance was spoken and the possible factors that influence the meaning. Bruce Waltke notes, "Dispensationalists have made a contribution of inestimable value to hermeneutics by their insistence on considering the situation or occasion in which a performative or commissive utterance is given."[50] The problem of apparent contradictions in Scripture would be greatly alleviated if this context were allowed to play its legitimate role. For example, Isaiah said that the Lord would not destroy Jerusalem—and he said it during Hezekiah's reign; but Jeremiah said that the Lord would destroy Jerusalem—and he said that after Manasseh's reign and during the partial repentance under Josiah. The implication is that Manasseh's influence brought a final decision in history. Similarly, when Jesus was asked about eternal life, he directed the questioner (a Jewish leader) toward his responsibility before the law of God (Luke 10:25–37); when Paul was asked about salvation, he directed the gentile questioner toward Christ and his recently accomplished work on the cross (Acts 16:31).

Two common factors are present in the historical occasion, implying limitations in the scope of statements made in history.

a. Author: The author's meaning must be examined in the historical context. Walter Kaiser writes:

> . . . let it be announced in bold relief that it is exceedingly important that the interpreter complete a thorough investigation of the biblical book's author, date, cultural and historical background. It is virtually impossible to locate the book's message in space and time without this essential material.[51]

But the question of authorship raises several thorny questions:

(1) Numerous books of the Bible are anonymous (see chap. 2).

(2) If we accept the notion of extensive editorial activity and redaction criticism, we open the door to multiple and unrelated intentions in the literature (see chap. 3). This conclusion is gaining popularity with some younger evangelical scholars. Certain critical studies seem to be marshaling evidence that cannot be overlooked. At the same time, rhetorical, literary, and canonical critical studies are finding evidence for the unity of the text at least in a final canonical form. As evangelicals, however, we must reject extreme forms of source criticism. Waltke writes:

> We ought to reject the orthodox critical emphasis on dissecting the Bible into sources not only because it is often impossible and because the work in hand constitutes a unique and unified literary achievement, but also because this emphasis rests on faulty theology. . . . The canon of Scripture that resulted from twofold divine and human activity consists not of unattested and incomplete J and P documents of a dubious E, but of the books of Genesis, Exodus, etc. These sacred books, and not the sources contained in them, constitute the Scriptures.[52]

---

[50] Waltke, "Grammatical Problems," 119.
[51] Walter Kaiser, Jr., *Toward an Exegetical Theology* (Grand Rapids: Baker, 1981), 50.
[52] Waltke, "Grammatical Problems," 91.

b. Audience: The other key historical factor in the ancient communication is the original recipient of the book.

It follows from our knowledge of the original audience that their identity is defined by the text in primarily theological terms. This does not at all deny a historical-geographical identity; that they certainly did have. But a precise knowledge of when and where they lived does not usually define the basic terms of the message. The basic terms in which they were addressed were theological in the sense of their relationship to God and only in a general sense historical (the period of history).

This general assessment may be demonstrated by the continuing uncertainty surrounding the original recipients of the Galatian epistle. While settling the issue of the North-Galatia and South-Galatia theories would specify some particular historical meanings, it would not change the essential meaning of the book. The continuing uncertainty supports our thesis that the audience as

defined contextually is known by a theological relationship experienced in a historical-geographical setting. Since the audience is addressed in primarily theological terms, our continuing uncertainty does not prevent us from understanding and applying the message of the book today.

2. Historical cultural context. G. Linwood Barney has given a helpful model for analyzing the structure of a culture (fig. 6.4).[53] He suggests that each culture is a series of layers, the deepest of which embraces an ideology, a cosmology, and a worldview. A second layer, closely related to and probably derived from the first, comprises values. Above both of these is a third layer of institutions such as marriage, law, and education. These institutions give rise to the fourth and surface layer of material artifacts and observable behavior and customs. This surface layer is the most easily described and the most readily influenced.

Figure 6.4

Material artifacts, observable behavior and customs
Institutions: laws, marriage, education
Values
Ideology, cosmology, worldview

When this analysis is applied to the culture created by God's revelation in the Old Testament, some interesting features appear. The lower two levels are determined by the express revelation of God except for some vagueness regarding Israel's cosmology. There are

clear revelatory elements in their cosmology, highlighted by the declaration that "in the beginning God created the heavens and the earth"; some statements appear to be anthropocentric observations of the earth and the heavens—"in heaven and on earth and

[53]G. Linwood Barney, a revised unpublished edition of "The Supra Culture and the Cultural: Implications for Frontier Missions" in *The Gospel and Frontier Peoples,* ed. R. Pierce Beaver (South Pasadena: William Carey Library, 1973), quoted by Bruce J. Nicholls, *Contextualization: A Theology of Gospel and Culture* (Downers Grove, Ill.: InterVarsity Press, 1979), 11.

under the earth" (Phil. 2:10)—while others reflect ancient models—"caught up to the third heaven" (2 Cor. 12:2). What role these statements have in an ancient biblical cosmology depends on determining their contextual sense. Is Paul's use of "the third heaven" sharing an idiom to refer to the presence of God, or does it intend to specify levels of heavenly orders of a physical model? Contextually, the former seems to be the case.

The two uppermost levels of the Israelite culture have been influenced more by the surrounding cultural forms. Yet many of the institutions are still the object of direct revelation in the Torah. It is interesting what scholars say about these institutions. One scholar said of the Solomonic temple, which was patterned after the tabernacle and was itself the object of revelation (1 Kings 5): "Zion with its temple was the symbol and sacrament of the presence of the living and life-creating God. By and large, Israel adopted this symbol from surrounding cultures."[54] It seems clear from the text (1 Kings 6:18; 7:13–45) that the Phoenicians had an important influence on various architectural features of the temple.

This kind of similarity between Israel's outward forms and the pagan forms raises an important question: To what extent did Israel adopt the forms of pagan religions? Waltke answers this question in part when he compares the human form (dress) of Jesus with the human forms of Israel's institutions: "While Jesus appeared like any other man, no other man spoke as he did, and while Israel's culture and literary forms resemble those of its pagan neighbors, none of the latter knew Israel's ethical monotheism."[55] But the answer also rests in part with one's commitment to the text. If we are willing to focus on the meanings that are based in the text, the cultural analogies may enrich the type of meaning expressed, yet they do not extend or change the type of meaning. Clearly this would rule out the principle of analogy of comparative religious research as being of primary or of defining importance.

3. Historical scriptural context. Scripture was another dimension of the historical culture to which the authors as men of God had access (2 Peter 1:21). They wrote in a progressively unfolded revelation. This was a determinative factor in their historical-cultural background. It seems to be a fair assumption that either a biblical author incorporated in his usage what had already been said about that subject or at least what he added was consistent with the earlier revelation.

---

[54]Othmar Keel, *The Symbolism of the Biblical World* (New York: Seabury, 1978), 112.
[55]Waltke, "Grammatical Problems," 119.

CHAPTER 7

Hermeneutical Considerations of the Task of Recognition—II

In chapter 6 we began to examine the hermeneutical criteria involved in our preunderstanding of a text, specifically the literal, grammatical, and historical premises. This discussion continues here with the premises of literary and theological knowledge.

LITERARY

Literary affirms that the textually based type of meaning is composed as a whole by the type of textual design.

1. Textual design: Defined. This hermeneutical premise seeks to focus attention on the components of textual meaning normally considered under genre. We have chosen the term "design" in order to define the components without the distractions involved in the traditional discussions surrounding the term "genre." In our use of the term, "design" is not referring to a process of forethought on the author's part, but rather to the textual product that gives evidence of designed composition.

There is considerable discussion among literary critics as to what compo-

nents of meaning define the design. Some biblical scholars seek to find matching components of structure and content in other ancient writings. Such an approach is illustrated in the respective works of V. Korosec and George Mendenhall concerning ancient treaty structure and content.[1] Korosec's original work on ancient treaties has been applied to the interpretation of the covenant structure and content of Deuteronomy. When the interpretation of Deuteronomy is compared with the ancient treaty forms, there is some degree of variation in the shared content. The question that must be raised is how much variation in content there may be while still preserving a shared design. A balanced assessment made by Cleon Rogers suggests that

> although it is evident that there was a "covenant form: in the ancient world," there is still difficulty of trying to "find" or "fit" this form into Scripture. . . . In writing of a compact history, as the Old Testament, it would hardly be necessary to reproduce a treaty text with all its formal parts. This was not done in the

[1]V. Korosec, *Hethitische Staatsverträge* (Leipzig: Rechtswissenchaftliche Studien 60 [1931]), and George E. Mendenhall, "Covenant Forms in Israelite Tradition," *Biblical Archaeologist* 17 (September 1954): 50–76.

extrabiblical historical texts. . . . Without denying or rejecting a "treaty form," it may be better to speak of "component parts of a covenant" when discussing the treaty as found in historical texts. . . . One other observation should be noted. It is obvious that Israel's covenants with God are somewhat different because the surrounding nations had no covenants with their gods.[2]

This assessment does not place the emphasis on an identity in the formal features in their entirety shared in a large number of cases, but on an identity in the shared components that define this covenant communication. These components are really generic in specifying the means, the manner, and the expression of the content of this historic covenant. In addition, Korosec acknowledges some variations in content due to the parties in the covenant relationship: God and Israel rather than two ancient nations.

Korosec's viewpoint is in harmony with a growing number of scholars who want to study the Bible simply as literature. This approach does not replace an earlier historic view exemplified by Mendenhall—in which the historic, formal features are primary—but rather supplements that approach by identifying in more general terms what role historic components of literary communication might have.

In his foundational work *The Anatomy of Criticism*, Northrop Frye identifies one general component as the kind of union or organization between grammar and logic. This concerns the literary organization in the composition of the message; it would take into account most features characteristic of literary form, such as poetic parallelism, alliteration, meter, antithetical balance, and imagery. This component addresses issues internal to the text.

Another general component concerns the terms in which an author addresses his audience, e.g., mood, tone, and purpose. This component addresses issues external to the text as expressed in the text. Frye explains that "the basis of generic criticism in any case is rhetorical, in the sense that the genre is determined by the conditions established between the poet and his public."[3]

Leland Ryken adds a third general component when he speaks of the use of language. This component is internal.

Literature uses special resources of language in a way that people through the centuries have agreed to call literary. This quality cuts across literary genres and, in fact, appears in texts that we would not consider to be primarily literary.[4]

These three components are also identified by Lars Hartman in his survey of the problem of "apocalyptic genre."[5] They may be combined and summarized as follows:

a. In *expository design* (law, wisdom, prophets, epistles) the author addresses his audience *directly,* organizes the composition to directly relate logic and grammar, and uses language in an unambiguous and direct sense.

b. In *literary design* (narratives,

---

[2] Cleon Rogers, Jr., "The Covenant With Abraham and Its Historical Setting," *Bibliotheca Sacra* 13 (1970): 249–50.

[3] Northrop Frye, *Anatomy of Criticism* (Princeton: Princeton University Press, 1957), 247.

[4] Leland Ryken, *How to Read the Bible as Literature* (Grand Rapids: Zondervan, 1984), 27. As examples Ryken cites figurative expressions in the story of Cain and Abel and metaphors in a highly theological passage in Ephesians.

[5] Lars Hartman, "Survey of the Problem of Apocalyptic Genre," in *Apocalypticism in the Mediterranean World and the Near East*, ed. David Hellholm (Tübingen: J. C. B. Mohr, 1983), 332–36.

hymns, apocalyptic visions, parables, allegories) the author addresses his audience *indirectly,* organizes the composition to rhetorically relate logic and grammar, and uses language in ambiguous and figurative senses.

While such distinct categories are helpful for definition, actual books commonly combine literary motifs in an expository framework or expository elements in a literary framework.

So the textual design is defined by three questions:

a. How does the author address the original audience? The address includes mood, tone, and aim in writing. Historical elements of time, place, and occasion are implied. Because the means and manner of the author's address relate to his reasons and purpose, the answer to this question is related to the "intent." These issues are all external to the text.

b. How does the author organize and structure his composition? The structure includes the conventional norms of a communication. These norms are of both a rhetorical kind and a direct and clarifying kind. The answer to this question is associated with the type of discourse (e.g., hymn, epistle, narrative). These issues are internal to the text.

c. How does the author use his language? The use of language in particular instances is broadly influenced by the kind of composition as a whole. While grammatical norms influence usage as a language system, so literary norms influence the particular use in the text as a whole. As with the previous question, these issues are internal.

Besides these three questions defining components of the text as a whole, there is an associated component that focuses on the reader's response. It is related primarily to the aim or purpose in writing, but it is associated with these components because it involves reading the text as a whole.

This fourth question is—

d. What is the goal in communication? This component of textual meaning is central to understanding. It involves the response that the author desires of the reader. Clues in the text either stated or implied commonly express the author's goal. This component is only an associated trait, not a defining trait of the author's type of meaning, because what the author expresses is not dependent on the reader's response. Yet the goal is basic to the reader's understanding.

The goal is also a necessary component of understanding because it is a necessarily associated trait of the type of meaning, which is biblical revelation. Since one theological theme focuses on God, every book of the Bible demands not only a cognitive response to its content but also a moral and spiritual response to the Author who speaks and about whom it speaks. Jesus said this response is necessary for understanding in a full sense (Matt. 13:18, 23).

While there is one sense in which a reader can know and understand with a simple cognitive response, in which an accurate articulation of answers to the interpretive questions is sufficient, it is adequate only for theoretical judgments about secular subjects. This is the knowledge and understanding possessed by the scholar who reads the Bible as a natural man. Because he shares in the skill and knowledge of language and communication, he can recognize biblical messages. But without a faith-obedience response there is no true understanding, nor is there the complete knowledge that follows upon response to the truth of God (1 Cor. 2:14–16). Such a theoretical kind of knowing is clearly inadequate when dealing with God's self-revelation.

It is at this point of moral and spiritual response that the Spirit-empowered person can truly understand and in time gain a fuller knowledge of the truth.

Without the Spirit's ministry of illumination, the will of man is unwilling to listen and receive what God says. So a statement of goal specifies the response which the Spirit of God works to effect in the heart and life of the believer.[6]

Several questions may help the interpreter to identify the goal:

> What responses does the author seek to gain?
>
> Are there any rhetorical devices used to gain such a response?
>
> Does the author state directly any response or imply the response in a prayer?
>
> Are the responses of the characters in the narrative included as models of response?

Additional matters related to literary design. Before we consider the defining components in detail, we need to consider further three related issues.

(1) The first issue concerns the study of the Bible with techniques developed in the study of fictional literature. Is it correct to say that

> perspectives and methods drawn from the study of fiction are inappropriate for the study of Scripture and therefore will inevitably distort the interpretation and prejudice the interpreter toward treating the gospel as fiction?[7]

This is a legitimate question and must be addressed. By way of response, I believe, first of all, that techniques of textual analysis do not determine the historicity of the documents, but they can alert the reader to recognize textual clues. Fiction may be defined as any narrative that is feigned or invented rather than being historically or factually true. So historicity is a characteristic of the written document, and the intent of historicity is discerned by clues expressed in the document. Mixing history and fiction is a characteristic of many modern novels. In these the author expands upon fact. But using this characteristic requires including textual clues, lest the author be deceptive.

Since this is the case, evangelical literary critics recognize that biblical literature is "firmly embedded in historical reality."[8] It constantly claims to be historical and has been repeatedly authenticated by modern archaeology. The historicity is not simply a fact but an integral aspect of its meaning. Roland Frye recognized that history is "always kept within a framework of interpretive significance."[9] Thus historicity is a matter of textual claim and of the author's intended meaning.

Secondly, techniques of textual analysis are used to recognize the components of meaning in the author's composition. The fact of historicity eliminates the freedom of biblical writers to invent details in a story. Biblical writers did not embellish their stories with imagined details. For example, while the highly poetic style and symmetrical arrangement of speeches in Job is an

---

[6] Both operations of the Holy Spirit in revelation and illumination function within the normal practice of human communication. Inspiration is the ministry of the Holy Spirit by which God bears along the human author to express the very verbal meaning God intends to express. Although such a process of authorship is unique and the produce is inspired by God, the product is nevertheless a written book. Illumination is the ministry of the Holy Spirit by which believers are spiritually enabled in understanding the written text. While there is disagreement on what that spiritual enablement may be (some say the Spirit operates on the will while others say he operates in the cognitive domain), it does not eliminate the interpreter from the task of reading words and construing meaning from a written text. These tasks are within the boundaries of normal communication.

[7] R. Alan Culpepper, *Anatomy of the Fourth Gospel* (Philadelphia: Fortress, 1983), 9.

[8] Ryken, *How to Read the Bible as Literature,* 19.

[9] Roland Frye, *The Bible: Selections From the King James Version for Study as Literature* (Boston: Houghton Mifflin, 1965), ix.

example of stylistic composition, the style does not violate the bounds of reasonableness in the historicity of the book. According to Ryken,

> The fact that the events themselves and even the order of the events were already determined means that the creativity of biblical writers is not seen primarily in their fictional inventiveness; rather, their conscious artistry is to be found in their selection of material according to unifying themes and with a sense of artistic proportion.[10]

These features of selection, ordering, proportionate treatment, and stylistic expression are all features of composition. The interpretive focus on God is also an aspect of composition for the prophet or apostle that corresponds to Aristotle's mode of imitation. From a human viewpoint, many compositions could only be a fictional representation of human thinking, feeling, acting, and interacting, and could be arranged around a plot or character development. From a divine viewpoint, they can be factual representations composed around a plot of God's purpose or the character development of God's dealing with men as this has been somehow revealed to the author.

(2) The second related issue concerns the components of meaning implied by a literary design. The literal tradition and this present discussion have emphasized the cognitive components of verbal meaning. But there are also emotive and volitional components. These associated components are critical to persuasion and to teaching and become defining components when the design is to persuade or to teach about a response to God. These are components of what the author does in expression. An author's appeal to the will or his use of emotion to gain a hearing for a message are often important components of meaning in the design of what the author does.

(3) A third related issue concerns a feature of the Bible's literary style that is common in different textual designs, namely, categorical statements made without qualification. The prophets delivered their messages of impending judgment at times without qualification and at other times qualified by a call to repentance. Jesus at times condemned divorce without qualification and at another time qualified it with an exception. The wisdom writers promised the righteous life, property, favor with God and man, a smooth path, physical well-being, and material prosperity (Prov. 3:1–10), yet the fully Righteous One died on a cross with none of these earthly blessings.

In each case the textual design itself may provide implied conventional qualifications. "The sage in the Book of Proverbs is looking to a future that outlasts death and his focus is on the righteous' final state of bliss. . . . Job and Koheleth by contrast directed their attention at the righteous man when he appeared to be counted out."[11]

In addition to the conventions, there are also stylistic features of design. Bruce Waltke notes the Hebrews' predilection for hyperbolic language, categorical statements, and parataxis (placing clauses or phrases one after the other without connectives). In these cases, he says, "the exegete must set the paradoxical statements side by side and attempt to infer the logic of their relationship."[12] In so doing, the interpreter acknowledges the appropriateness in some contexts for such categorical statements without implying an

---

[10]Ryken, *How to Read the Bible as Literature*, 20.
[11]Bruce K. Waltke, "Grammatical Problems," in *Hermeneutics, Inerrancy and the Bible,* ed. Earl D. Radmacher and Robert D. Preus, (Grand Rapids: Zondervan, 1984), 117.
[12]Ibid., 117.

unqualified universal. At such he also recognizes that more may be said about a given subject in which a full consideration of the subject would allow for related aspects of the teaching to be considered together and correlated. Mystery may remain in our understanding of such subjects as historic causation or human and divine responsibility. In view of this, the interpreter must be cautious about drawing implications or extending logical inferences without knowing the comprehensive teaching about the subject.

2. Textual design: Terms of address. Answering the questions that are directed at the textual design involves a careful description of what the author does in composing the text. Such descriptive statements are not in themselves the meaning of text, but they do influence one's understanding of textual usage and references to history. The more thoroughly we understand the textual conventions, the better prepared we are to consider the textual basis of the literal expectations. An adequate treatment of the variety of textual designs is beyond the scope of this book, but recent literature has contributed greatly to an understanding of the literary components of biblical texts.[13] This text will attempt to focus attention on aspects of design that ultimately influence meanings.

The terms of address seek to describe the mood and tone in which the author addresses the original audience. The clues expressing mood and tone are seldom mentioned directly in the text; thus we need to infer the terms of address. These terms fall into two broad categories: *expositional address* and *literary address.*

a. In *expository address,* the author directly identifies himself, and this implies something about the tone and the frame of the composition. In the case of the Torah, the historical occasion in the founding of the nation focuses on Moses as the source of the nation and its basic literature. The text of the Torah also introduces Moses as the author of portions of Exodus and as the primary speaker in Leviticus (1:1), Numbers (1:1), and Deuteronomy (1:1). Jesus draws upon this common knowledge in discussing the messages as identified with Moses (Luke 24:44). The counterpart to the Torah in the New Testament is the epistles, all of which establish an apostle as the author at the outset except for Hebrews, James, and Jude. In this covenantal exposition in either testament, the identity and covenant role of the author introduce a tone of authority and the initial basis of unity of what is said.

The prophets also speak directly in their sermons to the people of their day, and that too creates a tone of authority. The prophetic books present the ministry of the prophets collected in the sermons and oracles that directly address the reader. Again, their office and its authority are critical to the meaning. The prophets follow Moses in a line of authorized spokesmen who speak God's word directly (Deut. 18:15) as characterized by God's promise: "I will put my words in his mouth" (18:18).

The wisdom books of Ecclesiastes and Proverbs also address the reader directly. The authority of the author influences the tone of what is said, not because of his role or position, but because of his reputation. The author speaks as a father or mentor to an

---

[13] Brevard S. Childs, *Introduction to the Old Testament Scriptures* (Philadelphia: Fortress, 1979); Morris A. Inch and C. Hassell Bullock, *The Literature and Meaning of Scripture* (Grand Rapids: Baker, 1981); Gordon D. Fee and Douglas Stuart, *How to Read the Bible for All Its Worth* (Grand Rapids: Zondervan, 1981); John Maier and Vincent Tollers, *The Bible in Its Literary Milieu* (Grand Rapids: Eerdmans, 1979).

imagined reader who is cast as young and inexperienced.

Components of meaning are present in both prophetic and wisdom literature because a respected person speaks, although the covenant leader speaks for God while the wise man speaks from experience with God.

The mention of the author implies a frame of beginning that contributes to a sense of unity in what follows. While this unity is not explicit in the development of a message in a prophet's collections, yet the sermons and oracles do compose a selected summary of the historic message of the prophet. The unity is cast in the presence of the author. Similarly, the collected proverbs do not develop a message; but the introduction composed by an author does frame the collection of proverbs written by a number of authors.

b. In *literary address,* the author is not directly identified in the text. The meaning of the text and unity of composition rest more completely on what is written as a whole. While tradition associates the authorship with authoritative individuals, yet interpretation of the text does not include a reference to the author. What is said stands by itself as far as determining a historical context. No occasion is stated directly and therefore remains less influential for interpretation of the book's message.

The narrative materials in the Old Testament (the early prophets) and in the New (the Gospels and Acts) are self-contained stories as a whole. Luke does give more textual information about occasion, but it doesn't establish the authority of the author. Likewise, the hymns and poems of faith in the Psalms, the wisdom of Job, and Song of Songs constitute the primary section of the Writings. What they say establishes the unity of their message. Authorship became a question primarily for canonicity.[14]

3. Textual design: A mixture of textual composition and structure. In making the distinction between expositional design and literary design we are using the term "literary" in a restricted sense. In one sense it can mean any text that is written, but in the narrower sense in which we are using it, it is restricted to certain genre.

> Through the centuries, people have agreed that certain genres (such as story, poetry, and drama) are literary in nature. Other genres, such as historical chronicles, theological treatises, and genealogies, are expository (informational) in nature.[15]

Yet the Bible and books of the Bible are obviously mixed in genre. Genesis intends to give information about the beginnings of history of the earth and the Jewish people (including genealogies), yet it also intends to tell the story of Abraham's descendants becoming a family. In considering Bible books we have a continuum with both expository and literary influences. The expository influence is never lost sight of:

> In biblical literature the artistic impulse is everywhere combined with the intention to teach something about God and man. Indeed, the didactic tendency is always ready to overshadow the development of a story or poem, as when the Epic of Exodus is interrupted by long passages containing civil laws.[16]

Our responsibility at the level of recognition, however, is to determine whether a book is expositional or literary, and this decision will be based on the textual framework of the book as a

[14] Gleason L. Archer, Jr., *A Survey of Old Testament Introduction* (Chicago: Moody Press, 1964), 61.

[15] Ryken, *How to Read the Bible as Literature,* 25.

[16] Leland Ryken, *The Literature of the Bible* (Grand Rapids: Zondervan, 1974), 16.

whole. Though the book of Exodus contains extended sections of legislation (chaps. 20–23; 25–31; 35–39), yet the frame that establishes the unity of the book is narrative: the story of a family becoming God's people. So the expository impulse involves teaching what is necessary to God's people, but the narrative design frames the book and establishes the unity.

The distinction between expository and literary design involves the structural and compositional relation between logic (meaning) and grammar (form). The issue involves textual clues that indicate the relationship. The rules or procedures (conventions) of expository design purport to be clear and therefore state the relationship more directly. Conjunctions are included to express relationship, sentences are constructed to summarize key thoughts, and the sentences state directly what is intended. By contrast, the conventions of literary design aim at forcefulness and imaginative experience and therefore state the relationship indirectly or metaphorically. In Genesis, the story of Abraham's descendants becoming a family is really telling us about God gaining a people. In the narrative, the message is expressed indirectly in order to heighten the impact on the reader and his imagined experience with God.

Specifying the design of literary texts is far more necessary than the design of expository texts as an interpretive tool, yet here we will consider the design of both literary and expository books.

4. Textual design: An examination of expository composition. Northrop Frye identified expository genre as the direct union of grammar and logic that includes addressing the audience directly. Ryken limits expository to writing that seeks to tell us, as objectively and clearly as possible, facts and information about a subject. In general terms Mortimer Adler defines "an expository book as one that conveys knowledge primarily, 'knowledge' being construed broadly."[17]

The expository element of design is pervasive in Scripture and invades the whole canon, yet as we have noted, the literary element of design is mixed in abundantly. We can ignore neither aspect. All the Torah is expository in address (to teach Israel about its covenant relationship). But only Leviticus and Deuteronomy are expository in both address and composition; Genesis, Exodus, and Numbers are literary in composition. This means that three books are composed to teach indirectly while the other two teach directly in legal legislation and have a minimum narrative.

Likewise, in the New Testament epistles, the authors identify themselves directly at the outset and then greet specific historical readers. In these terms of address, the authors speak directly about the covenant blessings received in Christ; that blessing becomes the basis for directly addressing the believer's responsibilities in Christ. The tone, mood, and content are expositional, but at the same time there are literary elements that add to the force of expression. Ryken says, "The forcefulness, beauty and affective power of the New Testament Epistles are not accidental. They are the product of artistic and highly patterned prose."[18]

This expository composition guides the reader to recognize the overall structure directly expressed. In addition, propositions of an argument designed to change thinking and actions or propositions of an explanation designed to clarify and inform as a basis for

---

[17]Mortimer J. Adler and Charles Van Doren, *How to Read a Book,* rev. ed. (New York: Simon and Schuster, 1972), 60.

[18]Ryken, *How to Read the Bible as Literature,* 158.

action are expressed in the paragraphs of the text. Discourse involving description may be used in support of exposition. Naturally, the broad categories of expository genre are expressed in a form and style that is influenced by the culture and the individual expression of the human author.

The fundamental and characteristic quality of exposition is clarity. Explanation is central to the revelation of terms of covenant relation (Deuteronomy and the Epistles). One needs to explain the terms of relationship and responsibility and to explore the realm of application of the relationship in the history, in the land, and in the life of the church. Almost all teaching contains some exposition. Knowledge is the foremost requirement for the author, obtained by careful observation of experience, direct reading of the Scriptures and other sources, or as special revelation given to prophets or apostles. Explanation may also be cast in a poetic form in the wisdom psalms or in the pithy proverbial wisdom. This poetic form greatly influences the effectiveness of communication but does not diminish the effectiveness of communicating content.

Argumentation is the structural vehicle of verbal persuasion. There are invalid uses of persuasion and argumentation (1 Cor. 1–4), as in the world's wisdom, which reasoning leads to invalid and incorrect conclusions. However, there are reasons to reject sin; there are historical evidences to support the claims of Christ, and there are logical arguments to defend the truth of God's Word (Acts 17:16–34). Thus various forms of argumentation are found in the prophets or in the preaching and teaching of Jesus Christ and his apostles. One prevalent form is a supportive discourse. When Agrippa said, "Almost thou persuadest me to be a Christian" (Acts 26:28 KJV), he implied that both the logic and the emotional content of Paul's arguments were drawing him near to a state of conviction or belief.[19]

In reading expository genre, therefore, the reader seeks to understand the key terms, recognize the author's propositions, and follow the development of his explanation or argument paragraph by paragraph.

5. Textual design: An examination of literary composition. Although the principal impetus of Scripture is expositional and didactic, still large portions are literary. Again, Frye clarifies literary genre as the rhetorical organization of grammar (form) and logic (meaning). "The basis of generic criticism in any case is rhetorical, in the sense that the genre is determined by the conditions established between the poet and his public."[20] Ryken describes those conditions as "appeals to our imagination. Literature aims to recreate an experience or situation in sufficient detail and concreteness to enable the reader to relive it."[21] In clarifying the essence of literary genre, Adler makes the following comparison in emphasis.

Expository books *try to convey knowledge*—knowledge about experiences that the reader has had or could have. Imaginative ones *try to communicate an experience itself*—one that the reader can have or share *only* by reading. . . . We *experience* things through the exercise of our senses and imagination. To *know* anything we must use our powers of judgment and reasoning, which are intellectual. This does not mean that we can think without using our imagination, or that sense experience is ever wholly divorced from rational insight or

---

[19]T. R. Henn, *The Bible as Literature* (New York: Oxford University Press, 1970).

[20]Northrop Frye, *Anatomy of Criticism* (Princeton: Princeton University Press, 1957), 247.

[21]Ryken, *How to Read the Bible as Literature,* 18.

reflection. The matter is only one of emphasis.[22]

The rhetorical organization within this framework appeals to the imagination of the reader with a force that direct statement will not achieve.

In literary genre, the conditions established between the author and the reader are indirect and more subtle. "There is no such thing as direct address in literature, but direct address is natural communication and literature may imitate it as it may imitate anything else in nature."[23] So in books (Genesis) or whole texts (such as the Psalms) that are literary, "both the author and his characters are concealed from the reader."[24] Neither the author nor the characters directly address the reader. The Gospel literature comes closest to having the main character, Jesus, address the reader.

It is common in literary genre that the reader is addressed indirectly in characters' experiences in narrative accounts, and the imagery of poetry. In either case the author composes the text with the shared understanding that he addresses his reader as he identifies with the characters in the plot in the narrative or the imagery in the hymn. "There is an important sense in which the reader of biblical literature is its subject and center of reference. Biblical writers, motivated by a consciously didactic purpose, intend to tell the reader something about himself."[25]

The rhetorical structure of literary genre does not eliminate the propositional content of these sections of the biblical revelation. The message is expressed within a different structural strategy, however. "What is important about discourse structures is the fact that the structures themselves carry meaning, particularly in terms of focus and emphasis, and only rarely can one alter discourse structures without changing substantially the intent of the author."[26] Thus a discussion and clarification of the various structures of literary genre are necessary for recognizing the textual meanings.

One prominent feature of literary composition is poetry. Ryken states, "To call something poetry is to identify the special idiom in which it is written. Virtually any literary genre can be written in poetry."[27] In the Bible we find such diverse forms as poetic narrative (Job), poetic satire (Jonah, Amos), and poetic exposition and preaching (Isaiah, Jeremiah, portions of the Sermon on the Mount). It is important to consider this idiom before we consider the different forms and structures.

Barbara Hernstein Smith proposes the following as the means of identifying the idiom of poetry:

> As soon as we perceive that a verbal sequence has a sustained rhythm, that it is formally structured according to a continuously operating principle of organization, we know that we are in the presence of poetry.[28]

The pattern of rhythm is the key. Benjamin Hrushovski proposes a "free rhythm" for the Hebrew poetry which is based on "a cluster of changing

[22] Adler and Van Doren, *How to Read a Book,* 205 (italics added).

[23] Frye, *Anatomy of Criticism,* 250.

[24] Ibid., 249.

[25] Ryken, *How to Read the Bible as Literature,* 21.

[26] Eugene A. Nida and William D. Reyburn, *Meaning Across Cultures* (Maryknoll, N.Y.: Orbis, 1981), 43.

[27] Ryken, *How to Read the Bible as Literature,* 109.

[28] Barbara Hernstein Smith, *Poetic Closure: A Study of How Poems End* (Chicago: University of Chicago Press, 1968), 23–24.

principles."[29] This cluster includes the mutual reinforcement of meaning, syntax, and stress with no single element as purely dominant.

Biblical poetry recognizes the mutual reinforcement through parallelism, the dynamics of which have been nicely formulated by Viktor Shklovsky:

> The perception of disharmony in a harmonious context is important in parallelism. The purpose of parallelism, like the general purpose of imagery, is to transfer the usual perception of an object into the sphere of a new perception—that is, to make a unique semantic modification.[30]

With biblical parallelism appearing in so many lines, this kind of "semantic [meaning] modification" occurs continually. J. G. Herder observed that "the two [parallel] members strengthen, heighten, empower each other.[31]

Thus the focal feature of biblical poetic parallelism involves the matching and development from one line to the next of a new perception of an idea. This development that takes place between lines suggests to Robert Alter the basis of development in whole poems.

> I would propose that there are two fundamental kinds of structure in biblical poems, both of them following from what happens between versets within the line. On the one hand, one frequently encounters, especially in the Prophets and Job, a *structure of intensification,* a sort of crescendo development, in which certain images and ideas introduced in the first parallel versets—they often may be binary oppositions—are stepped up from line to line and brought to a certain climax. On the other hand, a good many poems are *worked out* through a *consequentiality* of images and ideas that is incipiently narrative and may include brief sequences of explicit narrative development.[32]

Kinds of Literary Compositions

Let us briefly examine the various kinds of literary compositions that we find in Scripture.

a. Narrative structure[33] tells a story that is built with three basic ingredients: setting, characters, and plot. Storytelling relates the meaning and grammar through the plot (action), which becomes the avenue through which the message is expressed.[34] It is important to repeat that the story form does not necessarily undermine historicity, for the author can tell what happened as a story rather than simply listing the events or making a record of what occurred. The author's interpretation of the events of history is reflected in the composition of the story and in his editorial comments about what happened.

The composition of historical stories limits the author to two techniques: selection and arrangement. The ar-

---

[29] Benjamin Hrushovski, "Prosody, Hebrew" in *Encyclopedia Judaica* (New York: Encyclopedia Judaica, 1971), 13:1200–12002.

[30] Viktor Shklovsky, "Art as Technique," in *Russian Formalist Criticism,* ed. L. T. Lemon and M. J. Reis (Lincoln, Neb.: University of Nebraska Press, 1965), 21.

[31] J. G. Herder, *Vom Geist der erbrischer Poesie* (Dessau, W. Germany: 1782), 23.

[32] Robert Alter, *The Art of Biblical Poetry* (New York: Basic Books, 1985), 29 (italics added).

[33] Robert Alter, *The Art of Biblical Narrative* (New York: Basic Books, 1981); Wayne Booth, *The Rhetoric of Fiction* (Chicago: University of Chicago Press, 1961); Michael Fishbane, *Text and Texture: Close Readings of Selected Biblical Texts* (New York: Schocken, 1979); J. P. Fokkelmann, *Narrative Art in Genesis* (Assen, the Netherlands: Van Gorcum, 1975); Peter D. Miscall, *The Workings of Old Testament Narrative* (Philadelphia: Fortress, 1983); Boris Uspensky, *A Poetics of Composition* (Berkeley: University of California Press, 1983).

[34] Ryken, *How to Read the Bible as Literature,* 33–86.

rangement unfolds episodes usually in chronological order, but this may be altered by flashbacks (in which the author wishes to fill in the reader with prior information) or by flashforwards (in which the reader is informed about something that is likely to happen or will happen in the future) or by juxtaposing events that may have been historically separated but are interpretively related. The selection of events in the historical sections of Scripture—which are highly selective—is an important interpretive feature, but its value as a tool is limited by our knowledge of all that actually happened. Thus in the Gospel literature and in the history of Israel's kingdom period, the knowledge of the historical period available from a number of sources increases the value of selection as an interpretive tool.

One common kind of selective emphasis is the use of dialogue in which the story lingers on one point. In addition, the author's expository comments in establishing the setting of the stories and in developing the transitions between stories or in characterization reflect the author's interpretive viewpoint further.[35]

b. Prophetic structure[36] combines the expository framework of the prophet's ministry in history along the poetic compositions of his sermons or oracles. The quality that essentially distinguishes prophetic poetry from other kinds of biblical poetry is its powerfully vocative character. In this case it is clearly God who is speaking through the prophet's poetic verse. Such communication is not only solemn, weighty, and forceful, but also densely woven with complex interval connections, mean-

ings, and implications.[37] This poetry of direct address captures the essence of biblical prophecy. Such speech is directed to the concrete situations of a historical audience, but the idiomatic form of the poetry introduces a historical scope in the language of the prophet in order to express meanings that may refer to a distant prophetic day.

The historic and the distant prophetic are combined in the intensified development within the poetic lines. While some lines seemingly refer directly to a historic invader (Isa. 1:8–9), the figurative elaboration (1:5–6) of this historical situation introduces new meanings. First, it makes the incident powerfully vivid to the imagination, but it also defines it as a flagrant instance of the folly that relates to other persistent instances in self-destructive behavior. This feature of poetic figurative generalization is important to an accurate exegesis of prophecy.

There are two principal modes of prophetic poetry: reproof and consolation. In reproof, writes Robert Alter, the effect of the language of poetry "tends to lift the utterances to a second power of signification, aligning statements that are addressed to a concrete historical situation with an archetypal horizon."[38] The Judean contemporaries of Isaiah the son of Amoz become the historic occasion of the archetypes Sodom and Gomorrah in respect to both their collective destiny and their moral character (Isa. 1:9). The figurative archetype adds to the force of reproof and implies a destiny apart from God's intervention to deliver.

In consolation, Alter recognizes a similar effect of poetic language in

[35] Uspensky, A Poetics of Composition, 6.

[36] Patrick Fairbairn, Prophecy (1850; reprint, Grand Rapids: Baker, 1980); J. Lindblom, Prophecy in Ancient Israel (Philadelphia: Fortress, 1973); J. Dwight Pentecost, Things to Come (Findlay, Ohio: Dunham, 1958); Claus Westermann, Basic Forms of Prophetic Speech (Philadelphia: Westminster, 1967).

[37] Alter, The Art of Biblical Poetry, 141.

[38] Ibid., 146.

reference to the future. Interpreters commonly dismiss apparent references to the distant future as hyperbolic embellishment of the Jewish idea of national restoration. Alter challenges this idea, using the example of Amos:

> I think that would be an unwarranted reduction in their (Amos 9:13) scope, especially if we compare these lines with visions of redemption in the prophets who came after Amos. The logic of the language of poetry brings Amos to glimpse for a moment a new order of reality.[39]

The developed intensification of the poetic prophecy leads to this interpretation of a distant, future scope of reference. While poetic idiom incorporates figurative statements of hyperbole and metaphor, the idea of poetic intensification must allow for the possibility of real climactic intensification in the ultimate resolution. This evidence, drawn from the nature of poetry, is further supported by the progress of revelation, in which there is promise of such a climax in history and in which there are other prophets who also envision a climax of like intensity.

c. Apocalyptic structure[40] strikes a balance between expository and literary genres. The framework is an explanation of the prophet's vision and of the experience the prophet has been trying to understand. But apocalyptic structure is considered literary because the text is devoted to a description of the vision seen of the future reality. The content of the vision deals with histori-

cal issues that have a future, ultimate resolution. Moreover, the structure is considered literary because of the symbolism in the vision. While symbolism has an important role in what God reveals, the view of the future does not necessarily appear in symbols. God may reveal the actual future in a fashion directly portrayed (Dan. 11; Ezek. 40–48) or at least with a mixture of the actual or symbolic (Rev. 11:1–3; 19:11–21). The white horse is a symbol of an actual divine agency, and the rider is actually Jesus Christ. The interpretive key for the apocalyptic vision is the dialogue with the divine interpreter and his explanation concerning the vision and its relation to future realities.

d. Hymnic structure[41] is a one-sided dialogue with God in which poetic imagery and statement are formed to express praise or lament.

> The frequent use of dialogue is rooted in the biblical view of man and God. In biblical literature man achieves full meaning only in relationship—relationship to God and the human community. Similarly the God of the Bible is the God who communicates–who speaks, calls, and invites human response. Dialogue is the natural and inevitable rhetorical mode for this view of man and God.[42]

Some hymns, however, are expositional in content, expressing praise for the wisdom of God's revelation. Many of the psalms are lyric poems and thus have a dramatic structure in which the

---

[39] Ibid., 156.

[40] John C. Collins, *The Apocalyptic Imagination* (New York: Crossroad, 1984); Paul D. Hanson, "Old Testament Apocalyptic Re-examined," *Interpretation* 25 (1971): 454–79; John C. Collins, ed., *Apocalypse: The Morphology of a Genre* (*Semeia* 14 [1979]); Lars Hartman, "Survey of the Problem of Apocalyptic Genre," and E. P. Sanders, "The Genre of Palestinian Jewish Apocalypses," in *Apocalypticism in the Mediterranean World and Near East,* ed. David Hellholm (Tübingen: J. C. B. Mohr, 1983).

[41] Claus Westermann, *The Praise of God in the Psalms* (Richmond: John Knox, 1965); Ryken, *The Literature of the Bible,* 121–16, 223–42, and *How to Read the Bible as Literature,* 87–120.

[42] Ryken, *How to Read the Bible as Literature,* 21.

speaker is addressing a mute but implied audience.[43]

e. Gospel structure[44] is a special case of narrative literature. The Gospels tell the story of Jesus' ministry from birth to resurrection. One distinction between the Synoptics and the Gospel of John involves the selection and arrangement of the stories to be told about Jesus. The argument that the selection and arrangement of the Synoptics can be traced to Peter's dominant ministry seems to have a great deal of plausibility.[45] By contrast, the apostle John selected events of dialogue and distinctive signs—some of which were associated with Jerusalem—and followed a distinct arrangement of major events.

The other difference between the four Gospels is the result of the expositional framework provided by each author that holds the stories together. John provides the most highly developed interpretive framework with a theological introduction (1:1-18).[46] Luke's theological exposition takes a different form; he selects prophetic, angelic, and pious speakers to interpret Jesus' advent and ministry. Luke also molds a connected account through a series of explanatory transitions that have both historical and theological meanings. There is a definite motif between prophetic anticipation and fulfillment in Christ.

Matthew provides interpretive clues in his selection of extended discourses (5–7; 13; 16–17; 24–25) and in his emphasis on the messianic and kingdom components of Jesus' ministry. Matthew, like Luke, focuses attention on fulfillment, but gives particular attention to the correspondence between Old Testament prophecy and the events in Jesus' life and ministry.

Mark's gospel seems to allow the least place for exposition as he seeks to provide a faithful record of Peter's preaching (2 Peter 1:15–19).

THEOLOGICAL

Theological affirms that the textually based type of meaning is framed by developing themes of progressive revelation.

The theological themes frame what a book of the Bible is saying because they affirm the ultimate source and reason for the recorded events of history and the ultimate basis of the teaching expressed. These framing themes are common to each book of the canon and express the components of meaning that distinguish canonical from noncanonical books. In addition, the themes state the core of a progressive revelation of what God purposes to say and accomplish in human history. As such, the content of the themes is not unique to any book. At the same time, the development of a theme is usually unique to that book.

These themes recognize the relationship of one book to another at the level of theological content. When the themes of two books are compared, the differences between the themes mark the nature and limits of *change* in the progressive revelation. Three of these themes involve changes that have marked consequences. All are introduced in Genesis 1–3:

1. The revelation of the person of God. "In the beginning God created

---

[43] Ibid., 20.
[44] Leland Ryken, "Gospels as a Literary Form," in *The New Testament in Literary Criticism,* ed. Leland Ryken (New York: Frederick Ungar, 1984); Kenneth R. R. Gros Louis, *Literary Interpretation of Biblical Narratives* (Nashville: Abingdon, 1974), 296–329.
[45] George Salmon, *The Human Element in the Gospels* (London: John Murray, 1907).
[46] Culpepper, *Anatomy of the Fourth Gospel.*

... (Gen. 1:1). While the revelation of the person of God is true from the very outset, it is incomplete. One change is to add to the reader's knowledge of God as the revelation progresses.

2. The revelation of the purposes of God. While God's actions and words are unique at a point of time in history, the purposes directing these actions and words display the *unity* of God's progressive revelation. The comprehensive purpose of God in biblical revelation is to reestablish his rule over creation through man. This comprehensive purpose is introduced in Genesis 3:15: "I will put enmity between you and the woman, and between your offspring and hers; he will crush your head, and you will strike his heel." This word of judgment addressed to the Evil One present in the words of the animal includes both promise ("I will put . . . ," "He will crush . . .") and action ("enmity").

Derek Kidner comments on God's purposes: "The first glimmer of the gospel . . . makes a debut as a sentence passed on an enemy (cf. Col. 2:15), not a direct promise to man, for redemption is about God's rule as much as about man's need."[47] Thus it does not seem inappropriate to conclude that God's comprehensive purpose in human history is to reestablish man's rule. That overcoming of the Evil One implies salvation as a component of God's accomplishment of his purpose for man.

This comprehensive purpose for human history is the source, reason, and basis of what God does and says. The initial statement in Genesis 3:15 anticipates and awaits the progressive revelation until God's rule is established through man over the Evil One and the realm of earth.

3. The revelation of God's administration of his purposes toward fulfillment. God's actions and words in history imply not only purpose, but the management of these purposes until there is fulfillment. This divine management progressed through periods of common administration frequently called dispensations. This management administers the working out of the purposes in history through chosen and responsive people in the midst of conflict with the Evil One. The various periods of administration are both effectual in God's rule and educational in preparing redeemed man to accomplish God's purpose in spite of this conflict.

There are four fundamental periods of administration:

a. Promise establishes the scope of blessing as promised in spite of the conquest of evil over men.

b. Law demonstrates the conquest of evil over men and the necessity of judgment upon the evil of men, culminating in the ultimate conquest over the Evil One by the man who had been first conquered by evil.

c. Gospel creates a body of believers who trust in the Man, Jesus Christ, and his conquest so that they may come to know deliverance from the conquest of evil in history.

d. Kingdom fulfills the full promise of blessing for those who are delivered, this fulfillment being realized under the righteous rule of the Man, the King who rules the realm of evil and creation.

The three basic themes of God's person, purpose, and administration disclose God's progressive revelation in human history as recorded in the canon of Scripture. The content of any theme is recognized through a question that is answered within a particular book. Let us look closely at these three themes.

[47] Derek Kidner, *Genesis,* Tyndale Old Testament Commentaries, ed. D. J. Wiseman (Downers Grove, Ill.: InterVarsity Press, 1972), 70.

1. The theme of the person of God: What does the book say about God?
The Bible is both a revelation *from* God about certain subjects and a revelation *of* God in relation to those subjects. While God is not the unifying subject about which the books are written, he is nonetheless a subject central to the message of each book. This is true even of books like Esther, where the name of God does not appear, or Ruth, where God is not mentioned as acting or speaking. God may legitimately be considered the center of the Old Testament in the sense that he is the origin and focus of everything done and said.[48]

Moreover, the revelation of God is progressively unfolded. Carl F. H. Henry explains this concept:

By this introduction to ELOHIM, Creator and Supporter of nature, we are brought into the arena of biblical revelation, with its progressive disclosure of EL, not amid the panoply of pagan deities but in the context of a protest against those pretenders: the one God is self-revealed as EL ELYON, the Highest; ELOAH, the Mighty One; and El SHADDAI, the Omnipotent One. Then follows his fuller self-manifestation as YAHWEH/JEHOVAH, the great proper Name of God of Israel mentioned 6,823 times in the Old Testament.[49]

This progressive revelation reaches its climax and completion in Jesus. Henry summarizes this revelation:

a. The variety of Old Testament names is replaced by the simple term "Theos/God," not—in the Christian understanding—as merely a general term, but as one informed cognitively by the cumulative context of special divine revelation.

b. The fixed center of interest in the divine name now becomes "Jesus of Nazareth," the promised Deliverer, the incarnate and exalted "Lord."

c. The promised redemptive presence of God in the midst of human need finds supreme fulfillment "in the name of Jesus"—first in the "I AM's" historical work of redemption, then in the I AM's abiding presence through the Holy Spirit continuing the work of redemption, and in the I AM's second advent to redeem creation.

d. The Old Testament concept of God as "Father" is enriched by the revelation of Jesus Christ as the "Son of God" and by the Christian experience of sonship in the Holy Spirit, the Spirit of God.[50]

2. The theme of the purposes of God: What does the book say about the reasons God speaks and acts in history?
The answers to this question are not simply what God did and said, although the answer is based on this. Rather, the focus is the narrower issue of *why* God acted and spoke. The book usually does not give direct statements of God's reasons, and when such statements are given, they may not be the comprehensive reason God acted. So in either case, reasons must be construed from what is recorded in God's words about his actions.

As an aid to recognizing textual purposes, the early revelation of God's words and works in human history (Gen. 1–3) introduces expectations of a few basic purposes. At the outset God creates the heavens and the earth, and he creates mankind to rule and inhabit the latter (1:1–2:3). The reasons for these creative works emerge in the second account (2:4-25) as God fellowships with and blesses man with good

---

[48]D. L. Baker, *Two Testaments: One Bible* (Downers Grove, Ill.: InterVarsity Press, 1976), 377–86.

[49]Carl F. H. Henry, *God Who Speaks and Shows*, vol. 2 of *God, Revelation and Authority* (Waco, Tex.: Word, 1976), 185–86.

[50]Ibid., 245–46, with personal modification.

gifts. The basic purpose of God in creation is both to rule through and *to bless* mankind, who lives in obedient fellowship with him.

In the midst of blessing, however, God *permits the Evil One* to influence the new creation and enter into conflict with God for control over mankind (3:1–7). In response to evil, God acts and speaks in *judgment* against evil as found in the serpent, the Evil One, and in mankind (3:8–24). God's word of judgment purposes to deal justly and overcome evil, thereby reestablishing divine rule over creation through man.

God's word of judgment includes choosing the woman's seed to be the *agent* in conflict with and in ultimate conquest over the Evil One (3:15). Implicit in the conquest of man over evil is the *deliverance* of mankind, as the object of God's grace, from the power of the Evil One who had so effortlessly subdued man (3:1–7). This deliverance is not without cost, but the hurt endured by man is minor compared with the death blow inflicted upon the Evil One (3:15).

Figure 7.1

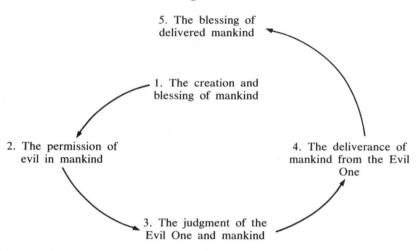

The deliverance that is implicit in the word of judgment becomes an explicit deliverance from immediate death in God's providing clothing for Adam and the naming of Eve (3:20–21). Adam and Eve, who are under the curse of death, are then *blessed* with continued life before God and offspring (4:1–2).

Thus the words and actions of God in human history are related to each other as they are subsumed under one or more of the four fundamental purposes of God in history:

To bless man over creation,

To permit evil to overcome man,

To judge evil through the agency of man, and

To deliver man from the Evil One and from evil.

These four purposes can be further related to each other in a repeating cyclical pattern (fig. 7.1).

These four components of God's comprehensive purpose to reestablish his rule through man and over mankind form the framework and pattern of early history in Genesis 1–11 (fig. 7.2).

This cycle of purpose represents no

Figure 7.2

1. Good and blessed creation (1:1–2:4)
5. Birth of promised seed (4:1–2): Cain/Abel
8. Birth of Seth (4:25–5:32) and promised line
12. Blessing to Noah (7:24–9:17)
19. Promised blessing to Abram (12:1–3)

2. Fall into sin (2:5–3:12)
6. Cain's sin (4:3–9)
9. Descendants of Cain's sin (6:1–5)
13. Shem, Ham, and Japheth (9:8–23)
16. Ham and Japheth's seed and tower (10:1–20; 11:1–4)

4. Word of promise (3:15) and mercy (3:20–24)
11. Word of promised deliverance to Noah (6:8–7:16)
15. Word of promise to Shem (9:26–27)
18. Word of promise in Abram (11:10–32)

3. Word of judgment (3:13–19)
7. Word of judgment on Cain (4:10–24)
10. Word of judgment by flood (6:6–7; 7:17–23)
14. Word of judgment on Canaan (9:24–25)
17. Word of judgment on language (11:5–9)

progress toward fulfillment of the conquest over the Evil One until the promise is introduced to Abraham (Gen. 12:1–3). But this pattern of four components anticipates the components that form the progressive outworking of God's purposes in history revealed in Genesis 12 through Revelation 21. History becomes the sphere in which the decreed conquest over the Evil One by the Woman's Seed is realized. Also, in history, worldwide blessing through Abraham's seed reaches fulfillment.

In this framework, biblical revelation does not interpret mankind's historical experience as a closed repetitive cycle, but rather as progressive cycles in the outworking of God's purposes. The promise of conquest and deliverance through the seed of the woman and of blessing in the seed of Abraham finds many partial fulfillments in the history of Israel, but ultimately will attain complete fulfillment in Christ at the climax of time. The climax is reached in two stages. After Christ's first advent there was a partial deliverance in his defeat of Satan on the cross, with the selective display of blessing through the Holy Spirit in the church. These are partial fulfillments that await the ultimate and complete deliverance and full display of blessing in history after Christ's second advent under the reestablished rule of God through Christ on earth.

These four components form the

Figure 7.3

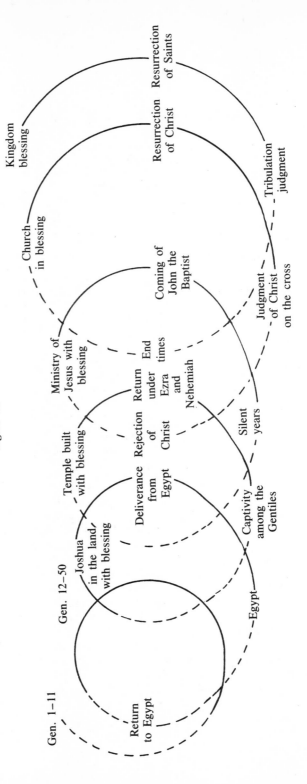

framework of the progressive fulfillment in the Bible's history, which can
be graphically represented as shown in
figure 7.3.

This model of the biblical revelation
of the purposes of God, which provides
an ultimate explanation of the events of
human history, bears a striking similarity to the perception found in Western
literature.

No introduction to biblical literature is
complete without insisting on the arche-

typal content of the Bible. An archetype
is a symbol, character type, or plot motif
that has recurred throughout literature.
One critic speaks of archetypes as "any
of the immemorial patterns of response to
the human situation in its permanent
aspects."[51]

These recurring elements involve
"immemorial patterns" of experience
in life. Aristotle called it "imitation of
life." In attempting to represent these
recurring responses to life, Ryken summarizes this "cycle" (fig. 7.4).[52]

Figure 7.4

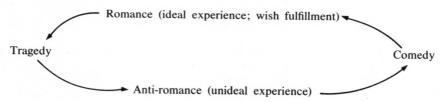

What Ryken applies to biblical literature is based on the original observation
of Northrop Frye.[53] Frye sought some
unity between the genres and modes in
Western literature including the Bible.

In looking at a picture, we may stand
close to it and analyze the details of brush
work and palette knife. This corresponds
roughly to the rhetorical analysis of the
new critics in literature. At a little distance back, the design comes into clearer
view, and we study rather the content. . . . The further back we go, the
more conscious we are of the organizing
design. At a great distance . . . we can
see nothing but the archetype. . . . In the
criticism of literature too we often have to
"stand back" from the poem to see its
archetypal organization.[54]

As Frye develops this model of overall unity in literature he sees the Bible

as the main source. In recognizing the
Bible's central role he affirms the place
of the Bible's interpretation of human
experience under God and his providential rule in Western thought. Western
literature that reflects these motifs acknowledges similarities in the ultimate
determination of human experience but
does not share in the revelation of God.

These themes form a framework
within which life is interpreted by the
biblical authors, and they are then
reflected in the textual composition.
The themes are common to either literary or expository design and thus are
pregeneric. Yet in any genre they frame
the basis for what is said and frame the
ultimate source of what is experienced
in history.

This model of progressive revelation
of God's purpose in history provides

---

[51] Ryken, *How to Read the Bible as Literature,* 22–23.
[52] Ibid.
[53] Frye, *Anatomy of Criticism.*
[54] Ibid., 140.

two additional hermeneutical advantages. It introduces an appropriate context within which to define *typology* and to describe the issues related to the *application* of the meaning of the whole canon.

a. Old Testament typology is an account of a historical event, person, or institution recorded in such a way as to allude to an earlier promise. The relationship between the account and the promise indicates that the event is a partial fulfillment of the promise (a *type* of that which was promised) which by implication anticipates an ultimate, completed fulfillment (*antitype*). For example, God promises the people of Israel that "I will be your God" (Ex. 6:7). The tabernacle in which God's glory takes up residence (Ex. 24:15–31:18; 40) is a partial and temporary fulfillment of that promise. The complete presence of God with his people is fulfilled in Christ (John 1:14), but the permanent dwelling with his people (John 14:1–3) is future and has yet to be fulfilled. That aspect of fulfillment is further developed in the Revelation.

The hermeneutical control on typology rests in the promises stated in the text that are related to God's basic purposes in history. Only promises associated with God's purposes to deliver and to bless are involved in typology. While God's permission of evil and judgment of evil are necessary to the reestablishment of his will, they are not related to the fulfillment of that reestablishment of his rule through man.

Typology is limited to promises associated with these two purposes of God. Any recorded event, person, or institution that is a type of what God promised to do according to these purposes is a valid biblical *type*. So the promise in Exodus 6:7 is related to God's purpose to bless his people and finds partial fulfillment in the tabernacle, again in Christ who tabernacled among his people, and then in the new Jerusalem with Christ and his bride in the midst of Israel (Rev. 21:2–3, 9–14). This is the final *antitype*.

b. This model is necessary for the hermeneutical discussion of the application of Old Testament messages. A message found in the Old Testament only applies to a subsequent audience because God continues to speak and act in some sense as he spoke and acted then. In one sense God spoke and acted in a unique way with a historical audience. One aspect in deciding whether God continues to speak and act in a similar sense involves the reasons for doing so. Does God continue to speak and act for the same reasons today? It is evident that God does, based on Paul's words in 2 Timothy 3:16: "All Scripture is God-breathed and is useful for teaching, rebuking, correcting and training in righteousness." It seems clear that the Scriptures could teach about what God said and did regardless, but can only rebuke, correct, or train in right actions if God continues to speak and act in a similar way. The model within which that decision is made includes the development of God's purpose to judge, to deliver, and to bless. However, *changes* in what God says and does must also reflect in the model possible changes in the way God administers his purposes in history as those purposes progress toward fulfillment.

3. The theme of the fulfillment of God's purposes: What does it say about the administration of these purposes?
In their historical outworking, all four purposes—to bless mankind, to permit evil, to judge evil, and to deliver from judgment—are present at any given time. Yet in the administration of these purposes, different priorities are given to selected purposes and different spiritual means and resources are made available at different periods in history. Central to the diversity in administration is "the Seed of the woman," who

Figure 7.5

Administration of the Purposes	Administration of Promise Genesis 12–Exodus 18	Administration of Law Exodus 19–Malachi 4; Revelation 4–19	Administration of Gospel Matthew 1–Revelation 3	Administration of Kingdom Revelation 20
Introduction of God's Purposes Genesis 1–11				
A. PERMISSIVE WILL Genesis 3:1–7	Only varies in degree due to the extent of mediated rule on earth →			
B. PRECEPTIVE WILL	PRIORITIES GIVEN IN EACH ADMINISTRATION			
1. Genesis 3:8–24 Judgment of evil		Definition of responsibility in the law; exercise judgment		
2. Genesis 3:15, 20–21 Conquest over evil through man			Proclamation of conquest realized on Cross	
3. Genesis 12:1–3 Blessing through man	Promise of blessing			Provision of blessing within righteous rule

is responsible to mediate the reestablishment of God's rule in conquest over the Evil One. Priorities reflect the need and spiritual condition of the mediator (individual or group) and the state of spiritual conflict with the Evil One.

Eric Sauer formulates the condition of the administration in different terms, but retains the central idea of distinct administrations at different times.

> It matters less what term or expression is used than to see the thing in itself. The decisive importance lies in the perception of stages themselves and in the insight into their differences and inner connections. . . . a new period begins only when *from the side of God* a change is introduced in the composition of the principles valid up to that time; that is, when from the side of God three things occur:
>
> 1. A continuance of certain ordinances valid until then;
>
> 2. An annulment of other regulations until then valid;
>
> 3. A fresh introduction of new principles not before valid.[55]

These stages of administration may be compared in more detail in figure 7.4.

a. The Promise: Each distinguishable epoch or dispensation is the outworking of a progressive phase of God's purposes introduced in Genesis 1–3, as already stated. Each stage is also characterized by additional revelation.

The first stage can be labeled "Promise." God promised Abraham and his seed that they would rule in creation apart from the influence of the Evil One. God's original promise to Abraham (Gen. 12:1–3) focused specifically on blessing rather than ruling creation. Yet implied in such a free expression of physical and spiritual blessing was the anticipation that God's rule would extend throughout an earth that was, at Abraham's time, under the dominion of the Evil One. What was implied in the promise spoken to Abraham was amplified in the promise spoken to David (2 Sam. 7). That promise, bearing the same mark of divine blessing, specified that God's rule would be expressed through the seed of David.

Whereas God's promises to Abraham fit the immediate historical needs, it anticipated the ultimate divine restoration and thus became God's means of separating mankind from the Evil One to himself. Separation from evil involves both justification (Gen. 15:6) and the righteous obedience of faithfulness (Gen. 22:1–19), but a complete separation from evil was only an unrealized ideal in the experience of Abraham and the other patriarchs. An added revelation of God was needed to accomplish that separation from and conquest over evil. Also, added revelation was needed to identify the one man (the Seed of Abraham) who was to overcome the Evil One and to accomplish God's goal in history.

b. The Law: The need for added revelation gave rise to a new phase in God's administration known as "the Law." It is clear that the stewardship of Promise had not yet been fulfilled in any final sense, so this new revelation of God was added alongside as a means of bringing Promise to its realization (Gal. 3:19–25). Thus even after the law was given, the promise was repeated for each new generation at circumcision (Gen. 17) and in the celebration of the Passover (Exod. 12–13). In addition, the promise was amplified and clarified both in the Davidic Covenant and in the New Covenant. The promise remained as the basis for justification by faith. The law was given to a redeemed nation which, under Moses, believed God's promise and was redeemed from Egypt (Exod. 15:13).

A careful reading of the law indicates that one reason for giving it was to

---

[55] Eric Sauer, *The Dawn of World Redemption* (Grand Rapids: Eerdmans, 1965), 193–194.

express God's rule among the redeemed people and thus to establish a nation set in direct conflict with evil. The law was a corporate revelation in both its scope and its form.[56] It constituted Israel as a people to be a nation under God. Its content revealed both God's righteous character and the terms by which such a God would deal with his people under Promise. The law also imposed demands on those to whom it was given, for it demanded righteous behavior in response to God and men. Obedience was established as the means to blessing; disobedience brought cursing. However, though obedience was necessary to receive the blessing, in itself it was insufficient. Only God and his promise are sufficient.

Unfortunately, Israel's experience under Law brought condemnation. The historical result of condemnation was to bring Israel, through the prophets, face to face with her sin and its consequences, which included repeated conquest by the Evil One. Such national condemnation ultimately resulted in conquest by the gentile nations.

The revelation of the law had another purpose. In demanding a righteous standard for man, a direct conflict between man and the Evil One was made evident. Out of this conflict emerged the conquest over the Evil One. The Righteous One, who was born under Law, was obedient in life to the law and remained obedient in his conflict with evil even unto death. Living and dying in faithful obedience, he was resurrected from death and exalted by God (Phil. 2:8–9). Thus the law served to distinguish and to identify the One fully separated from evil in righteousness.

In this One, the Christ, the law's demands were satisfied and the promise was fulfilled in an inceptive fashion. In his resurrection Christ conquered death and the Evil One (1 Cor. 15:12–58), and in his ascension Christ was established in a position of equal authority and glory with God.

But the results of the blessing were incomplete and not yet extended to all that God had promised. Those results still await fulfillment. In his writing, the apostle Paul anticipates the redemption of individuals from all nations who will comprise the body of Christ (Eph. 1:22–23), and he expects all creation to one day find its fulfillment in Christ (Eph. 1:10). He also anticipates national Israel's being restored to the place of blessing (Rom. 11:22–26). These expectations introduce the last two phases of the outworking of God's purposes in history.

c. The Gospel: The next phase in the outworking of God's purpose was the revelation of the gospel. With it God promised to restore a gracious rule in man, enabling him to stand firm in his conflict with the Evil One (Eph. 6:10–18). That restoration was clearly a limited but real fulfillment of God's condemnation of the Evil One stated in Genesis 3:15—limited only in the sense that Christ has not yet begun to exercise all his authority in every realm where evil displays itself. Though he has been elevated to the position of supreme authority in the heavens and earth, he has not yet claimed the title of king. He was raised from the dead (Eph. 1:20), seated in the heavenlies above all authorities in this age or in the age to come (Eph. 1:20–21), and all things are subject to him (Eph. 1:22).

He is the Christ (i.e., "the Anointed One"), but he is not yet occupying David's earthly throne. He has been declared to be Lord by God, but he is still challenged by both the Evil One and by a world of evil men (Eph. 2:13; 4:17–19; 6:10–21). He functions now as

---

[56] Walter C. Kaiser, Jr., *Toward an Old Testament Theology* (Grand Rapids: Zondervan, 1978), 56.

head only within the defined scope of the church (Eph. 1:22). No Scripture identifies him at present as the "king" of either the church or the world.

Closely connected with Christ's limited expression of authority is his activity in grace. Paul identifies at least three aspects of Christ's authoritative action in grace. First, Christ graciously brought to life those dead in trespasses and sins (Eph. 2:1, 4–5) and worthy of wrath (Eph. 2:3). Instead of abiding under the wrath of God's judgment, those persons now share an equal heavenly position with Christ (Eph. 2:6). That display of grace will make known the immeasurable wealth of Christ's grace for ages to come (Eph. 2:7). Second, Christ graciously provided for Gentiles equal access to the promise and inheritance (Eph. 3:2–6). Third, he graciously made available for his body the plunder and spoils of his conquest over the Evil One (Eph. 4:7–16).

Christ now rules in grace in the lives and activities of those who have trusted in him. He expresses his authority in the demands that he places on those believers. He exercises that authority in the person and presence of the Holy Spirit, who empowers the believers to stand against the Evil One (Eph. 6:10–20). He expects his own to walk worthy of their calling (Eph. 4:1), for his authority expressed in grace does demand obedience.

But therein lies an important change in order from Law to Gospel. Under the law the demand for obedience preceded the promise of blessing, but under the gospel the demand for obedience follows the promise of blessing. Paul first explains the exalted position in which each believer has already been placed (Eph. 1–3), then he appeals to those believers for obedience worthy of such a calling (Eph. 4–6). That is the order of the New Covenant in contrast to the Old Covenant.

Thus Christ fulfills God's purpose to reestablish God's reign in human history, although at present he does this only in a limited sense. He is in the position of supreme authority with God, yet he is still being challenged by the Evil One. He exercises his authority in a manner characterized by grace. In an evil world deserving of wrath, Christ graciously works through the message of truth and the Spirit of promise (Eph. 1:13) to redeem a possession for his praise and glory (Eph. 1:14). In that way Christ's work today enjoys a degree of fulfillment (Eph. 1:13), but there remains a future hope (Eph. 1:18).

d. The Kingdom: Paul envisions that future hope being exercised in a final phase of fulfillment known as "the Kingdom." In that final age God purposes to fully restore rule to man, enabling him to triumph over the Evil One and to accomplish the divine purposes in creation. The final age is a fulfillment of all the previous times or seasons (Eph. 1:10). In the age of Promise, blessings were expected but not yet fully experienced; rulership on David's throne was anticipated but not restored after the Babylonian captivity, and New Covenant spiritual enablement was announced but constantly challenged by evil. Those blessings will find full display in this final age.[57]

In the age of Law, conflict with the Evil One was the focus of the revelation. The ultimate victory was experienced at the Cross, but awaits a full implementation historically. That implementation will be finally achieved during the kingdom age. In the age of Gospel, redemption was realized in the forgiveness of transgression (Eph. 1:7), but believers still await full redemption (Eph. 1:14). A downpayment of the believer's inheritance has been received

---

[57] U. Cassuto, *Biblical and Oriental Studies,* vol. 1, *Bible* (Jerusalem: Magnes, 1973), 113.

(Eph. 1:14) in the gift of the Holy Spirit, but he has yet to experience the full measure of that inheritance (Eph. 1:18). These aspects of God's promise will be fully realized in the coming age.

The future age will sum up all things in Christ, who is the effective means to fulfill the purpose of God in its entirety (Gen. 3:15). Christ will also fulfill the various aspects of that overall purpose that have been stated progressively in history. In that age all the strands of history will be woven together so that the purpose of God is completely achieved, satisfying each part and filling the unified whole.

Conclusion

Having recognized the theological unity of purpose and the historical diversity of dispensational administration, we may now pose the question, How does this affect interpretation of the meaning of the text? Because what the text says does not change, the question must concern the force of that statement and its application today. Do portions of the Old Testament merely have the force of illustration or of instruction about what happened? Do they have a force of thus *said* the Lord, or thus *says* the Lord in compelling obedience?

Let us illustrate the question. The Old Testament law as a dispensation is fulfilled. What is the force of those legal portions of the Old Testament for the church? Paul says, "Christ is the end of the law" (Rom. 10:4) and also "All Scripture is God-breathed and is useful for teaching, rebuking, correcting and training in righteousness" (2 Tim. 3:16). It seems clear that the Old Testament law does not have the same force for the church that it had for Israel. It is not the law of the land for any nation today; no nation has a system of enforcing the law through God's curses and blessing. It is also not the law that was

given "until the offspring should come" (Gal. 3:19, RSV).

Christ has fulfilled the sacrifices and is revealed under law as the One having done conflict with the evil one. It is clear that the former distinctions between clean and unclean animals were set aside by God for Peter (Acts 10–11) and the church. Yet it is also clear that the law is righteous, just, and good (Rom. 7:12). The law reveals directions consistent with God's character. These are evident, not in the covenant form or in their location in the text, but rather in having a moral sense in addition to a ceremonial or civil sense. The whole law was designed to give order to the nation's life in its historical expression.

Some laws are involved with, but transcend, the historical features of the life and function of the nation. These deal with issues related to the character of God or the created nature of man in the image of God. The contents of these are repeated frequently in the New Testament, yet there is a fuller statement in the Old. In these laws the Old Testament continues to speak. The force is not just historical information, though it does communicate that. But it speaks with the force of instruction in righteous moral actions, of correction of wrong actions, of reproof of sinful attitudes and actions, and of doctrine of God's purposes and person. So while the Bible is one in authority as God's Word, the testaments are two in the force with which God speaks to the church. The theological themes thus address the theological force of the biblical message with which it is applied to the modern audience of believers (see part 4).

Every portion of Scripture is profitable, but every portion does not have equal profit. The value varies with the individual conditions and historical and national responsibilities. But the single factor that underlies the profit of Scripture is the theological themes. The theological themes are the common component in the textual meaning reflected in the theological interpretation of human experience. That textual meaning is unpacked in a component of theological focus on God's person, a component of the providential rule and mediatorial purpose of God in the human experience and a component of God's historical administration of relationship and responsibility with man.

SUMMARY

Hermeneutical considerations of the task of recognition frame the interpreter's viewpoint in two directions. From the first point of view, they cast the expectations of the textual study based on preunderstanding. One expects to find a unified and coherently expressed type of meaning in the text. That type of meaning is recognized through reading the text with a knowledge of the language, the historical setting, the textual design as a whole, and the theological categories of progressive revelation.

From the second viewpoint, the hermeneutical premises cast the categories in which the textual meaning is recognized and understood. The theological themes, textual design, and message express the meaning of the book, or at least define the type of meaning expressed. Although the full meaning is expressed only in the text of the book, these categories recognize the pattern of meaning. And the statement of the message is the first stage in the full task of interpretation.

The distinction made between the full meaning and the type of meaning is illustrated in the historic interpretation of the ministry of John the Baptist. The Bible acknowledges that John was not Elijah (John 1:21) and that John was Elijah "if they care to accept it" (Matt. 11:14). John was not Elijah in the full sense, for he was not the actual historical person, but he was Elijah in the sense that he was the same type of person and had the same type of ministry. So in the interpretation of John's gospel, John the Baptist meant Elijah for that generation even though he was not Elijah in all particulars.

That same distinction exists in the interpretation of other texts. The statement of the message, textual design, and theological themes is the meaning of the text in the sense of expressing the true type of meaning. At the same time, these statements are not the meaning of the text in the full sense. We deal with the exegesis of the full sense in part 3.

PART THREE

EXEGESIS

Introduction

Many interpreters recognize exegesis as the heart of the task of interpretation. As exegesis is the heart of the task of interpretation, so distinguishing implications that are a part of the author's intended meaning is central to the principle of exegesis. Determining these implications is important for the interpreter, as E. D. Hirsch has written:

> . . . the crucial issue—the problem of implication. Of course, this problem is not in itself more important than a good many others in hermeneutic theory, but when our central concern is validity we always have to ask whether a particular meaning is or is not implied by an utterance. The correct determination of implications is a crucial element in the task of discriminating a valid from an invalid interpretation. . . . At the center of them all is the question, Is this meaning implied or is it not?[1]

An interpreter's ability to determine the implications of the text is enhanced as he better understands the process of reading. Schleiermacher described the phenomenon this way in his distinction between understanding and not understanding: "I fail to understand anything that I do not understand as necessary." Augustine said the same thing: "I know the meaning of the signs in the text [words, phrases, i.e., forms] only if I know the sense of the sign intended by the author."

The sense intended by the author is the sense that is necessary. It is a necessary sense because it is implied by the construction of the text as it is construed as a component of the type of meaning expressed by the author in the text considered as a whole. Reading the text to interpret these necessary implications of both sense and reference is the task of exegesis.

With the task of recognition completed, the inductive study of the text is temporarily completed. Now the task of exegesis uses the tentative conclusions of inductive study to interpret the unknown or unclear constructions of the text. This aspect of interpretation, called *analysis and exegesis,* is deductive and draws necessary conclusions from the type of meaning just recognized.

Analysis-and-exegesis requires the interpreter to do a second kind of reading—a deductive reading—of the text. In an inductive reading, the interpreter reads with certain preunderstood meanings shared with the author. In a deductive reading, the interpreter reads with certain conclusions already reached about the type of meaning as a whole. Based on these conclusions, he seeks to understand the range of implications intended in the textual constructions. The range of implications thus follows necessarily from the type of meaning.

While the conclusions of interpretation follow necessarily, interpretation is by

---

[1]E. D. Hirsch, *Validity in Interpretation* (New Haven: Yale University Press, 1967), 89.

no means closed to additional readings and learning. While the cycle of interpretive readings (reading from the constructions to construe the type of the whole book and from the construed whole book to the constructions) is circular, it is not a vicious circle. It is not thus, because it does not *assume* the meaning of what it seeks to understand. The construed meaning of the type of the whole book is not assumed to be the final construct of the meaning nor is it considered to be beyond correction. Rather, it is a *working construction* from which necessary conclusions are drawn. So if the type of meaning I perceive proves to be unable to account naturally for certain constructions, that type must be modified or replaced by a perception that does account for each particular construction.

The reasoning process is not circular, but spiral. It seeks to narrow the gap between the construed type of meaning and the natural, shared exegesis of the implications of all the constructions in the text.

At this stage of study there are other conclusions that may be assumed as working premises. These include the divine authorship of the Bible understood in the framework of verbal plenary inspiration, the extent of the canon, and the appropriate application of the textual criticism to the various extant copies of the ancient manuscripts.

It should be understood that each of these assumptions must be examined on its own merits in its own discipline. But in the discipline of interpretation and exegesis these are not subject to reconsideration unless there is compelling evidence for it. And then the question to be reconsidered must be resolved in the purview of its own discipline. So we are in the process reading and interpreting the meanings of the biblical text, and none of the meanings of the text is assumed. In the inductive stage, preunderstandings of biblical meaning are brought to the task of reading, but in each case they are always subject to the readings in the text itself. My preunderstandings as well as my understandings are all subject to the test of viability in the text. This is the process of spiral reasoning.

As the reasoned interpretation of careful reading reaches a harmonious correspondence between the constructions of the text and the construction of interpretation, then the construed type of meaning is designated as intrinsic to the text. This intrinsic statement (which in chapter 5 we called "the essential summary") will then be able to unfold or exegete all the valid implications of the text.

While a theory of the process of exegesis is helpful to clarify our self-awareness of what happens, it does not ensure the successful completion of the task of distinguishing implications. This fact is aptly illustrated by I. Howard Marshall in an article, "The Problem of New Testament Exegesis," which is included in a book he edited entitled *New Testament Interpretation: Essays on Principles and Methods*.[2] Marshall defines the nature and extent of the problems in biblical exegesis and lists seven central problems, five of which concern implications of meaning in John 4:1–42. For convenience' sake we will use this same passage to show how the principle of exegesis works, and occasionally we will draw on Marshall's observations regarding the problems and their solution in exegesis.

---

[2] I. Howard Marshall, *New Testament Interpretation: Essays on Principles and Methods* (Grand Rapids: Eerdmans, 1977), 11–18.

CHAPTER 8

The Task of Exegesis

The principle of exegesis introduced in the preceding introduction can be succinctly stated as follows: *The full implications intended by the Author/author in the constructions of the text are analyzed and exegeted from the type of meaning expressed in the text as a whole, from the grammatical and historical hermeneutical premises, and from the constructions of the text.*[1]

The key term in this chapter is *implication.* The word ordinarily refers to unsaid or unexpressed meanings; "to imply" something means "to indicate indirectly or by allusion." Another recognized use, however, has the sense of "to have a necessary part . . . contain, include, or involve naturally or necessarily."[2] It is in this sense of "necessary part of the whole" that the word is used in hermeneutics. An implication is (1) a necessary component of the total meaning, (2) a submeaning necessarily related to or associated with the whole, or (3) a trait of the type.

This relationship between the part and the whole has been under scrutiny in parts 1 and 2. Part 1 introduced implications as component meanings that are intended by the Author/author. Part 2 considered how to determine these component meanings. We saw that implications are deemed intended when they are traits related to and compatible with the type of meaning expressed in the whole text. This relatedness between the implication and the type of meaning is central to the task of exegesis. And actually, it expresses itself in two kinds of relationship, which we must keep in mind as we read: (1) the relationship of the implication to a preunderstood language meaning, and (2) the relationship of the implication to the understood type of meaning communicated in the text.

THE FULL IMPLICATIONS

Implications of a construction are discussed first of all as components of

---

[1] Whenever we talk about implications we have in mind the implications of a textual construction. As we learned earlier, a construction may be any textual particular—a word, phrase, sentence, paragraph, or even a motif or plot sequence. A construction has two aspects: it is a member of a language or literary system, and it is a component of an author's composition. That is, it has a linguistic aspect and a literary aspect. Implications of these constructions must be defined in both sets of relationships.

[2] *Webster's New World Dictionary,* ed. David B. Guralnik (Cleveland: Collins, 1979).

language meanings in dictionaries and grammars and secondly as components of literary meanings perceived in literary analysis. In regard to the first, implications may have two basic relationships within the language system:

1. Defining implications are all the component meanings necessarily related to the use of the construction in its base sense. The base sense is the normal understanding of the construction when it is given without a context. These defining implications, therefore, distinguish the sense of the construction from the sense of other similar constructions in the language system.

2. Supplementary implications are all other component meanings that are potentially present in the construction but are not required to distinguish the construction from similar constructions and to define it in the language. This includes implications associated with any sense of the construction other than the base sense.

The implications of a construction known in relationships within a language system are a part of preunderstanding. To read with comprehension we must be conversant with the defining and supplementary implications of constructions of the text. However, while knowing the language is essential, it is not identical to the comprehension of the text. The language construction does not necessarily determine which implications are intended or what sense is meant in composition. This is what is involved in comprehension and in the task of exegesis. And this involves discussing the relationship between implications of constructions in the text and the type of meaning intended in communication.

A major premise underlies all the discussion of exegesis that follows, namely, that there is literary unity and logical coherence in the text of each book of the Bible. That premise was introduced, explained, and supported in parts 1 and 2. Based on that premise, all implications that are intended to be communicated are necessarily related to the type of meaning expressed in the text. Therefore the discussion does not concern whether or not there is a relationship; there always is. Nor is the discussion whether the relationship is necessary or optional; rather, it concerns how the relationship influences reading with comprehension and thus exegesis. There are two important aspects of the relationship to keep in mind:

1. Diagnostic implications are component meanings of constructions of the text that are necessary to comprehend the sense of the construction as used in the text. The diagnostic implications of composition and the defining implications of language are identical when the construction is used in a base sense. But supplementary implications can become diagnostic in a figurative sense. These defining implications are called diagnostic because they are necessary to comprehend the intended meaning. One must know them to know the textual meaning.

2. Associated implications are component meanings of constructions of the text that are necessary to fully comprehend the type of meaning of the construction as used in the text. Both diagnostic and associated implications are necessary to the type of meaning, but each has a different role. The diagnostic type defines; the associated type supports or develops the full meanings of the type of meaning. These associated implications may be implications of reference toward the world, of emotive or volitional force toward the reader, of expressive or commissive force toward the author, and so on.

To illustrate all this, let us think

about two constructions. The first construction, "Once upon a time," considered as a language unit implies only *an indefinite time in the past.* However, in the type of meaning—fairy tale—it implies something not stated: *an imagined, indefinite time in the past.* "Imagined" is a diagnostic implication of fairy tales that also helps us to understand (diagnose) what is implied by a second construction, "there was a tree," as in "Once upon a time, there was a tree." Does tree imply "trunk" or "leaves"? Knowing that we have a fairy tale, we know necessarily that the tree is imaginary. Without any other textual clues we would conclude that the tree had a "trunk" because a tree is a plant defined as a language unit by a trunk. That is part of a preunderstanding the reader brings to the text that the author would need to change if he intended a tree that is different. And in imaginary literature such as a fairy tale that is possible. However, a tree can be a living tree without "leaves"; it could be a tree in a dormant stage. Without any further textual specification the reader would have to conclude an ambiguity in statement about leaves based on what we know of the language unit, the type of meaning in the context, and the limited construction in the text.

Thus "imaginary" is a diagnostic implication, although it is not a defining implication of the language. "Trunk" is both a diagnostic and defining implication unless further text is given to change the sense. In addition, "leaves" is a possible associated implication of composition and a supplementary implication of the language without more text being given.

This model of verbal meaning is consistent with the literal tradition's conviction that all the implications are textually based. Remember that implications are textually based (1) because

they are component meanings of constructions in the text, and (2) because they are necessarily determined by the type of meaning recognized in the expression of the text as a whole.

These *implications* of the meaning must now be distinguished from the *significance* of the meaning. This distinction is necessary in order to maintain the conviction of the literal tradition. In making the distinction, we will use the term "significance" in a limited and technical way as indicated in the following definitions offered by E. D. Hirsch:

> *Meaning* is that which is represented by a text; it is what the author meant by his use of a particular sign sequence; it is what the signs represent.
>
> *Significance,* by contrast, names a relationship between that meaning and a person, or a conception, or a situation, or indeed anything imaginable.[3]

We need to clarify one point here. Significances—and there could be any number of them—must exclude the implications of reference intended by the Author/author. Meaning (including implications of reference) is textually based and is therefore capable of being determined by the text; but significance is not textually based even though it has some relationship with the text. So any significance of the meaning of the text is excluded from the task of exegesis. Yet significance is involved in using the Bible, as we will see in part 4.

The implications of reference are associated and are necessary for the communication of meaning to be completed. But they are not necessary for the textual meaning to be expressed. The associated implications of reference do not define the type of meaning, because a reader who is not aware of the actual historical reference may still imagine a general object of reference

[3]E. D. Hirsch, *Validity in Interpretation* (New Haven: Yale University Press, 1967), 8.

and still understand the sense of the text (the diagnostic implications). But they do contribute to the type of meaning by reference to what the author talks about and to whom he says it. Yet this level of understanding is not fully knowing what the author intended to say. We will say more about the exegesis of implications of reference later on.

Analysis

The practice of exegesis begins with an analysis of the type of meaning as it is expressed in the text as a whole. This analysis is actually another way of analyzing the context in terms of the text. What do we understand as a context? According to Milton S. Terry,

> The word context . . . denotes something that is woven together, and, applied to a written document, it means the connection of thought supposed to run through every passage which constitutes by itself a whole.[4]

Bernard Ramm suggests a broader definition:

> Every writer of the Bible writes in a given culture and hence a vital part of the context of any passage is the cultural background of the writer of the passage.[5]

But Hirsch offers probably the most complete definition when he says that context is "a very complex and undifferentiated set of relevant factors, starting with the words that surround the crux and expanding to the entire physical, psychological, social, and historical milieu in which the utterance occurs."[6]

If the context is "an undifferentiated set of relevant factors," it is difficult in principle to bring the influence of context to bear on the process of interpretation in any normative way. Neverthe-

less, if the influence of context is to be considered in a consistent fashion, those elements that have a possible, probable, or necessary influence must somehow be distinguished.

This is precisely what we have attempted to do by defining the "type of meaning"—that is, determining the type of meaning is an attempt to consider contextual factors in a consistent and measured fashion. The components of *goal* and *textual design* consider some of the relevant factors of context involved in the historical and cultural communication of the written document. The *theological* themes consider the relevant factors of change in the progressive revelation. The *message* seeks to consider the predication of the written context. The three diagnostic traits of theological themes, textual design, and message recognize the necessary aspects of context disclosed through the text.

Further historical and cultural factors may enrich our understanding of the text from extratextual sources, if these sources originate in a related historical or cultural setting. They have a probable influence if they enhance our understanding of meanings compatible with the type of meaning expressed in the text. We must exercise care to distinguish between a revealed, supernatural type of textual meaning and merely natural types of meaning. The two may be unrelated or incompatible (fig. 8.1).

The analysis of the type of meaning (diagnostic necessary aspects of context) involves both an analysis of the textual development as a whole and of the constructions within the text itself. Analyzing the textual development involves looking at the development of

---

[4]Milton S. Terry, *Biblical Hermeneutics* (Rev. ed. 1911; reprinted, Grand Rapids: Zondervan, 1952), 210.

[5]Bernard Ramm, *Protestant Biblical Interpretation* (Boston: W. A. Wilde, 1950), 136.

[6]Hirsch, *Validity in Interpretation,* 86.

the message and considering the relationships between the messages of multiple sections of the text.

An analysis of the development of the message initially involves determining the basic sections of the text as a whole. These sections are delineated by the expression of a complete message that distinctly advances the development of the message as a whole. The determination of these sections involves basic judgments on the development of thought that are supported by a consideration of the clues of textual design.

Figure 8.1. Possible Contexts

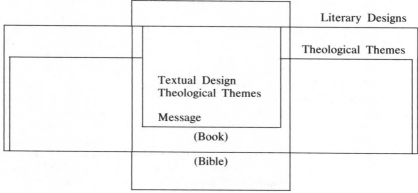

Relationship Between the
Intended Type of Meaning
Context and the Broader
Context

These clues of structural development in the text are expressed differently in an expository design than in a literary design. In an expository design there are structural markers which are directly stated as they overtly trace the reasoned development of the message. In a literary design the sections develop due to rhetorical considerations (of plot or semantic parallelism) in which the clarity of a direct statement is replaced by the force of emotional and volitional considerations of indirect or metaphorical statement. Even in this literary design, however, messages are expressed and developed in discernible sections of the text.

As he traces the development of the message, the interpreter begins to formulate an *analytical sentence outline* of the text as a whole. This outline is interpretive in the sense that the structure of the outline is analyzed in view of the development of the message of the whole text. The message of each section is analyzed as a constituent and supporting part of the overall message. That analysis will use the technique of type-logic, which we will define shortly.

The analysis of the textual design as a whole focuses on the type of relationship expressed between each constituent section. This relationship involves determining the connections and interactions between the sections. The statements of the textual design can also be

141

combined into an outline in which the statement of the design as a whole focuses on the organizing principles of genre and the outline of the sections identifies the arrangement and structure.

After the text as a whole has been resolved into an analytical sentence outline, the *constructions within the text* need to be analyzed in relation to that sentence outline. This sentence outline is an outline of the component messages. As a preparation for exegesis, the textual constructions need to be classified in terms of their relationship to these component messages. A construction is a *diagnostic component* of the message when it has been incorporated into the statement of the message and thus helps to define the message. In this case, the statement of the message reflects the collection of these diagnostic constructions. By contrast, a construction is an *associated component* of the message when it develops or supports the statement of the message in some way. It may be used to support or defend, to explain or expand, to emphasize or illustrate, and so on.

Textual constructions may have different functions and different relationships, depending on the context that is being considered. In the context of the message as a whole book, a construction may be associated with the development of that overall message. However, in the context of the component message of a section, that same construction may be a diagnostic component in the statement of that message.

Therefore the first stage in the exegesis of the text is to analyze the type of meaning into its component messages in which the relationship between these messages have been specified.

Exegesis

Biblical exegesis is the unfolding of the meaning of a passage or a book of the Bible. The Greek word *exaggeō*, from which the English word "exegesis" is derived, means literally "a leading out." The purpose of exegesis is to "lead out, set forth"—explain—an author's meaning. It is the leading out or unfolding of the full implications of the author's intended meaning.

It is common, however, for student exegetes to restrict their "leading out" to lexical or grammatical meanings found in a lexicon or grammar. This raises various questions: Which of these lexical meanings is the author's intended meaning? Which of these grammatical meanings is the author's intended meaning? Does the author intend all the options listed, only some, or only one? Every exegete must answer these questions. Every exegete desires to lead out the answers the author intended and not the answers his personal, experiential, theological, cultural, or other bias might lead him to which are not in the text. By what principle does the interpreter choose which of these linguistic and literary meanings to lead out as the author's meaning? The answer is found in the principle called *type-logic*.

Type-logic builds on the model of the interpretive spiral, reasoning from the "intended type of meaning." Type-logic attempts to "lead out" from the textual constructions all of the viable implications determined by the statement of the type of meaning of the context. Thus the initial recognition of the Author's/author's type of meaning is the starting point for exegesis.

This initial recognition suggests a word of caution. Because it offers a preliminary and heuristic construct, it will impose a perspective that will generate distinct implications of its own. The type-of-meaning construct serves to lead to new discovery based on this new perspective. So the interpreter must approach the conclusions of this preliminary construction of the type of meaning with caution, because its validity needs to be tested. It may prove to be an extrinsic construction, which means that it is incapable of meaningfully grounding all the particulars of the text. It must then be modified or rejected and a new heuristic construct considered. There will be more on this later, but first we must define the concept of type-logic.

We have taken the first step in interpretation (recognition), and we must not forget that because it is an inductive task it is subject to validation and may need revision. The next stage (exegesis) is a logical and necessary deductive task. As we have seen, exegesis is the leading out of the logical implications of the identified type of meaning. The form of the logic is a simple syllogism:

1. If the Author's/author's type of meaning is _____, and
2. If the grammatical and historical hermeneutical premises add a possible range of meaning for the textual construction,
3. Then the Author's/author's *intended implications* of textual sense or historical reference expressed in the textual construction are _____.

We will move step by step through the reasoning process. Although the term "type-logic" may connote the precision of formal logic, the precision is limited to the ordinary language usage in the text. The purpose of type-logic is not to bring precision, but rather a methodological control to the influence of the context in exegesis.

The premise of the syllogism is what was recognized as the type of meaning. It includes the separate influences of the message, the theological themes, and the textual design. Each one, in making a contribution to the type of meaning, may independently lend its perspective to exegeting the implications of the textual constructions. In addition, the general and shared premises of grammatical and historical lend a necessary perspective to the implications of sense and reference.

The textual constructions are then introduced in the conclusion. The textual construction is the basis of and the source from which all implications are drawn, since that is directly what the author wrote. That textual construction can communicate a range of possible meanings reflected in the grammatical

and historical premises. While the text is the basis of the meaning, the type of meaning as a whole is the contextual frame that provides perspective in textual usage and historical reference.

The conclusion is then completed with a statement of the actual implications intended by the author for each construction in the text. The importance of using this kind of type-logic is found in the necessary power of determination resting in the "type" of authorial usage. In this way, all the implications of the author's meaning follow necessarily from the premise of the type of meaning as expressed in the construction stated in the text.

Hirsch explains this:

From the standpoint of verbal meaning, then, all implications without distinction are governed by the type-trait model. We know that a given partial meaning is implied by an utterance, because we know that such a meaning belongs in that type of utterance. With due qualifications and in different terms, this is the point J. S. Mill made about the function of the syllogism. We come to the conclusion that Socrates is mortal, that "Socrates" implies "mortality" because Socrates is an instance of a type (man) which past experience has shown to have the trait mortality. . . . No matter how the connection between the type and the trait arose, all verbal implications are governed by some version of the formula "if the meaning is of *this* type, then it carries *this* implication."[7]

Thus textual constructions are exegeted in terms of the type of meaning of the whole context.

Author

Another key term in the principle of exegesis concerns a problem posed by I. Howard Marshall. Marshall poses the unique problem introduced by divine authorship when he writes, "The New Testament, however, poses distinctive problems because of its own individual literary characteristics and also because Christians regard it as the Word of God."[8] Having stated the general problem, he introduces a particular instance in John 4.

With the mention of the modern reader we pass, finally, to a further question regarding the interpretation of the story which may take us beyond the original intention of John. It may be illustrated by mentioning two types of exposition. One or two writers have seen in this story an example of *how Jesus dealt pastorally* with the woman in leading her to conversion. This is surely a valid interpretation of the story, but is it one intended by John himself?[9]

We ask, How can Marshall consider the interpretation to be valid if John did not intend that meaning?

Marshall answers his own question by contrasting two types of exegesis. Regarding the first type, he disputes

Bultmann,[10] who proposed to interpret the story in an existential manner. Jesus brings the woman, or any other person, to self-awareness about her being and she enters into "authentic existence." Marshall rejects these as extrinsic implications because they are implications of an extrinsic type of meaning—existential philosophy—rather than the intrinsic type of meaning—the gift of spiritual life.

Concerning the second type, Marshall reasons along with William Temple[11] that the pastoral interpretation, although left unsaid, is an implication of John's meaning. So he poses John's possible answer:

I hadn't consciously thought of the story like that, but now that you suggest it to me, I would agree that you could also understand it in that way. . . . A passage, therefore, may have a further interpretation or application which was not present to the author, but is legitimate because it can be held to fit in with his intention.[12]

In other words, a pastoral model is not defined by the text but would be compatible with some of what is said. (Then Marshall raises a related issue: Apparently, since Jesus did not intend to model the pastoral role, John may have been influenced by the needs of the first-century church to include that implication. Is it legitimate to do so? Marshall does not offer an answer to the question.)

Marshall is certainly correct in his assessment of Bultmann's type of exposition, which entertains interpretations extrinsic to John's intended meaning. John is not talking about the subject of authentic existence; he is speaking of

[7]Ibid., 90–91.
[8]I. Howard Marshall, "The Problem of New Testament Exegesis," in *New Testament Interpretation: Essays on Principles and Methods* (Grand Rapids: Eerdmans, 1977), 11.
[9]Ibid., 14 (emphasis added).
[10]Rudolf Bultmann, *The Gospel of John* (Oxford: Oxford University Press, 1971), 182–86.
[11]William Temple, *Readings in St. John's Gospel* (London: n.p., 1945), 65–68.
[12]Marshall, "The Problem of New Testament Exegesis," 14.

spiritual life in the figure of "living water." The second type is more difficult to assess. Is Marshall's openness to a "pastoral model" justified? The answer turns on a careful recognition of the author's intended type of meaning. A possible construct of John 4:1–26, 39–42 would be:

> Message: Jesus' disclosure of the woman's need draws her and the town to receive his gift of life.

Can the interpreter see a pastoral model in Jesus' ministry of the gift of life? The subject of the passage is Jesus' ministry, which consisted of disclosing the woman's need for God's life. The model of disclosure was such that it disclosed his own identity as the Christ. Her testimony was, "Come, see the man who told me everything I ever did. Could this be the Christ?" But this is a type of ministry that is distinct from the ministry of his servants. They do not have access to knowledge of a person's own witness. The minister's knowledge is not to bring people to faith in who they are as ministers. Thus this is not a model of ministry. To use the narrative as a model is an extrinsic implication. So while Jesus' ministry may have *significance* to pastoral ministry, it does not have *implications* which refer to that. God does not refer to a type of meaning to which John does not refer.

Someone who teaches this passage can, however, teach or preach about Christ's own ministry. Christ's ministry of disclosure of man's need does remain the same. The continuing means are different. Christ's drawing men to receive the gift of life does remain the same. Thus, rather than being a model of ministry, this narrative construction continues to have reference to Christ and to his offer to give the water of life. In addition, Jesus continues to address men and women who thirst for life regardless of their past. This is the meaning of the narrative. The record in

John is consistent with John's literary design (John 20:31) that in the text Jesus continues to speak and to claim men's faith.

Two important questions raised by Marshall concerning the divine and human authorship are thus clarified. First, John is not using Jesus' words to address problems uniquely raised by the church but inconsistent with Jesus' earthly ministry. Rather, John allows Jesus to continue to have the same type of ministry to needy people in the church age as Jesus did to needy people in his historical ministry. So the needs of the church undoubtedly influenced John in writing, but it did not distort the essential nature of the type of meaning in Jesus' ministry. Second, John records Jesus' disclosure of the woman's condition in order to continue to draw people in that same condition to faith in him as he discloses himself. In this manner it is God's word in John's word, God's unified sense in John's unified sense, God's continuing to address through Jesus' address of the woman of Samaria.

THE PRACTICE OF TYPE-LOGIC EXEGESIS

The practice of exegesis of any textual construction depends on its relation to the message. When we exegete constructions that are included in the statement of the type of message as diagnostic constructions, the sense of these constructions is *not* found by type-logic. Rather, their role in the text is so central to what the author is saying that the author includes in the immediate contextual development what is needed to clarify and to specify all that he intends. By contrast, other associated implications of that construction such as the historical references and emotive or willed connotations will need to be exegeted by type-logic. Moreover, constructions that are associated with the

145

type of the message are exegeted exclusively by type-logic.

This theory may well remain abstract until it is demonstrated in practice. We will take our examples either from John 4, as we have been doing, or from other evangelical literature that has been subject to occasional discussion. The examples chosen are often very troublesome, so that our treatment here may be considered inadequate; but the discussion is purposely focused to show us how the problem is resolved by this approach to exegesis. Our goal is not validation of interpretation; it is demonstration of this approach to exegesis.

1. Implications of diagnostic constructions included in the statement of the type of textual meaning

a. "Gift of God" (John 4:10): The construction "gift of God" appears directly in the statement of Jesus. Also, my construed message in John 4 includes the direct statement of "gift": *Jesus' messianic ministry of the gift of life draws the Samaritans to faith in him and draws the disciples to share his work.* In this case the term "gift" occurs in both the text and the defining statement. This occurs because the immediate context is so explicit that it defines the content of the gift. The author's textual development indicates that this is central to what he wants to say, and therefore I have recognized it as part of his message. Clearly "gift" is central to what Jesus is talking about:

4:10: the gift of God . . . he would have given

4:14: I give him [twice]

4:15: Sir, give me

In addition, the context explicitly specifies the content of the gift:

4:10: living water

4:14: water . . . will never thirst

4:14: will become in him a spring of water welling up to eternal life

So the textual construction "gift of God" that defines an aspect of the type of meaning is itself specified by the contextual development: the "gift of God" is Jesus providing life that satisfies and eternally generates itself in the one who takes a drink. The woman understands the genitive "of God" as a subjective genitive: Jesus gives the gift (4:15).

b. "Son" (John 1:18, 34, 49, etc.): Another term, with even greater ramifications, is John's use of "Son" when referring to Jesus. It is a term of such weight that it is included in the defining message of the whole gospel of John: The glory of the person, words, and work of Jesus, the Son of God, draws believers to share in his blessing of life.

But "Son" is also a term widely used by peoples of the Ancient Near East and the Greeks to refer to their gods. The question is, what informs the content of John's usage? While John shares as a preunderstanding a basic meaning of the word—namely, "a male descendant"—he is free to inform the term by his unique textual development when he has reference to Jesus and Jesus' relation to God.

John's textual development of the term is somewhat uncertain because of the textual problem in 1:18. If, however, the reading of *huios* is taken as authentic, then the first eighteen verses of chapter 1 provide a fitting introduction to the content implied in the term "Son." However, even if *huios* is not authentic in 1:18, the uses in 1:34, 49, etc., are introduced in the context of the related idea of "the Only Begotten" of the Father (1:14, 18, note).

In either case, the relationship of Jesus to the Father is introduced. John's historical and theological understanding of Jesus' divine life does not allow him to allude to the Olympian circle of gods cohabiting to give birth to gods, or the Egyptian rulers' having a positional share in God, or the Stoics' having a share in God based on the unity of mankind.[13] Nor does John's usage support merely a validation by God of an individual's claim to rule, as some have interpreted the Old Testament, or as a Jewish reading of Old Testament expectations.[14] The term "Son" as it is chosen shares a lexical range of possible cultural usage that includes "descendant" in the sense of "offspring from" and "begotten" in the sense of "bringing into being."

This One who is called Son (1:34, 49, etc.) is introduced and defined by John in 1:1–18. This Person is named "the Word" (1:1–14), "the Light" (1:4–5, 7–9), and "the Only Begotten of the Father" (1:18). In John's introduction this Person is named the Word in the sense of speaking what God says. As the Word, he is in the beginning (speaking creation into existence), he is with God (speaking with God); as he speaks, God speaks because he is God.[15] In the sense of "Speaker," he eternally shares life with the Father while being distinct in person from the Father (1:1–15). However, the Word "becomes" flesh in the sense of "takes on" human flesh (1:14). Then John summarizes, either as "the Only Begotten Son" or as "the Only Begotten God," and affirms that this One made God known (1:18).

In what sense is this One of the context begotten? He is begotten, not at a point in time when he came into being as normal humans are begotten, but he is begotten in a unique relationship of filial consciousness present because of eternal generation. This filial consciousness distinguishes him in relationship to the Father without changing his personal essence as always being God.

His flesh form does not change his essential relationship to God, but enables him to uniquely reveal God (1:18) in the humanly discernible display of glory (1:14).

So John uses the term "Son" with a basic, shared preunderstanding, but also with a special contextual development of the term.

c. "Son of God": Calvin followed an approach similar to the preceding in his interpretation of the content included in references to "God." In this case, however, a new feature appears, namely, in John's use of the term "God" (1:1–2, 6, 12–13, 18, etc.) and "Son of God" (at least 1:34). Although the term is directly included in the message of the whole book, yet John does not take the time to define his usage contextually. Similar to the case of the term "Son" previously considered, the preunderstood content is not shared with a Greek or Roman sense of god in the ancient cultures. Rather, John draws upon an understanding formulated in the progress of revelation. In this instance, where the defining term is not developed in the immediate context, interpreters must use a form of type-logic just as Calvin did. The term had been defined in prior revelation, and that revelation now defines the essential spiritual and divine content of the person of God in John's usage.

So when passages appear where human descriptions are used in reference to God (as "beget" in John 1:18), these terms must be interpreted in the context of his essential spiritual and divine being. Thus Calvin discusses the figure of "anthropopathy" in the margin of his commentary on the Psalms: "It occurs when we attribute to God human pas-

---

[13]Gerhard Kittel and Gerhard Friedrich, eds., *Theological Dictionary of the New Testament,* 9 vols. (Grand Rapids: Eerdmans, 1973), 3:334–37.

[14]Ibid., 341–53.

[15]Raymond E. Brown, *The Gospel According to John,* vol. 1 (Garden City, N.Y.: Doubleday, 1966), 519–24.

sions, attachments, and modes of life."[16] Calvin also recognizes "hypothesis," in which an immaterial object is described so vividly that it seems to stand before one's eyes as tangible and visible. So when Moses is said to speak with the Lord "face to face, as a man speaks with his friend" (Ex. 33:11), we are not to understand that God has a physical face. Instead, the description of the Lord speaking is intended for vividness and not to imply physical characteristics. This conclusion follows the application of type-logic developing an associated implication in a key term.

In summary, we can say that in this first kind of textual exegesis, the task of exegeting implications of diagnostic constructions included in the definition of the biblical message must focus on the immediate context of the construction. Two basic aspects of the task have been developed. In the first, type-logic is not necessary, since the full content of what an author intends in this diagnostic construction is expressed in the immediate context. This is illustrated in John's use of common words like "gift" and "Son." In the second, the task does use type-logic. It also involves a diagnostic construction which is fundamental to John's message, but which he does not develop in context. The author considers the term to be well-known already and thus expects the audience to share the content. In the case of terms central to special revelation, the type of meaning is drawn from special revelation rather than contemporary culture. (This instance introduces one boundary for the appropriate use of comparative methodology, which we will discuss later in this chapter.)[17]

2. Implications of associated constructions related to the statement of the type of textual meaning. Diagnostic constructions that are included in the statement of the message express implications because the author uses them in such a way as to define what he means. But many more constructions of the text expand on that skeleton of material that defines the meaning. These associated constructions relate to the type of meaning expressed, consistent with the features of unity and coherence in the composition of a whole text. They may be associated as explanation, persuasion, or illustration in expository texts; or they may be associated as various rhetorical strategies of narration or poetic composition in literary texts. In either case, the constructions are associated within the composition as a whole and are compatible with the type of meaning being expressed. In this associated role, the full range of implications is determined by type-logic, since these implications are also necessary. Calvin's interpretation in characterizing as figurative any human terms used to describe God is an example of associated constructions referring to God.

a. "Living water" (John 4:10): This textual construction is associated with the defining construction "gift of God." The "living water" is what Jesus promises to give, but there is a degree of vagueness in the language of the construction. Marshall identifies this:

The word "living," used of the water offered to her by Jesus, poses a problem. In Greek it would be used to mean "running," as opposed to "stagnant," water. This ambiguity between "running" and "living" may be significant in

---

[16]H. Jackson Forstman, *Word and Spirit* (Palo Alto, Calif.: Stanford University Press, 1962), 113–14.

[17]Tremper Longman III, "Comparative Methods in Old Testament Studies," *TSF Bulletin* (March-April 1984). In my opinion this is an example of an evangelical who has given too much weight to the comparative context.

the story. How does one get it over in English? And does the fact of this ambiguity mean that other words also in John may be used with a double sense?[18]

The first problem is, in what sense does "living" modify water? The second is, what kind of construction uses the word "water"—figurative or literal?

(1) The language of combining "living" with "water" makes it clear that the kind of construction is a figurative sense. When "living" modifies "water," it does not have the same sense as it does when it refers to "man" or "cabbage." Men and cabbages are "living or dead" in a sense distinct from water's being "living." Nevertheless, the language of combining "running" with "water" could have the sense of actual water. In this case "running" is a different figure of speech in description of "moving water." This knowledge is helpful, but the questions raised by Marshall remain: Which sense—"living water" or "running water"—did John intend? Does the ambiguity of the language usage permit John to intend a double sense of unrelated meanings?

(2) Let us handle the second problem with type-logic exegesis:

If the subject is "Jesus' messianic ministry of the gift of life,"

And if the gift is "living water" (4:10),

Then the sense of "living" is a figurative meaning associated with the "gift of life" having the sense of "life-giving" or "life-causing" water.

This sense is further clarified in the expression "whoever drinks the water I give him will never thirst. Indeed, the water I give him will become in him a spring of water welling up to eternal life" (4:14).

Jesus' point is that his gift of water gives life that presently does not exist and that gift causes this life to be continually supplied and sustained. Since the woman at the well already had physical life, this life was more than that. Type-logic can specify further implications of this water from other possible language:

If the sense of "living" is "life-giving or life-causing" water,

And if the language sense may also mean "running" water rather than "stagnant,"

Then the image "life-causing" excludes "running" as related to causing life.

The image of "life-causing water," however, is a vague image which Jesus further describes as "a spring of water welling up." The image does imply a generating capacity of the water coming from a source. But the point of the image does not imply that it gives life because it is flowing rather than stagnant, but because it is flowing from God, the life giver. So the use of type-logic reasoning from the subject "Jesus' messianic ministry of the gift of life" as expressed in context leads us to an understanding of the range of implications in the construction "living." It is the gift of life which continues and is continually sustaining because it comes from Jesus who is God.

b. "You have had five husbands" (4:18): Another rather obscure construction has been given quite incompatible interpretations and will provide a second example of interpretation of a construction associated with a type of meaning.

Since earliest times many have seen a symbolism in the number five. Origen saw it significant that the Samaritans held as canonical only the five books of Moses.[19] More recently, Hoskyns and Davey saw a polemic reference to the

---

[18] I. Howard Marshall, "Introduction," in *New Testament Interpretation* (Grand Rapids: Eerdmans, 1977), 18.

[19] "In John xiii 8," in *Die Griechischen Christlichen Schriftsteller* (Berlin: n.p., n.d.): 10:232.

five false gods of the Samaritans mentioned in 2 Kings 17:30-31[20] in anticipation of the condemnation of Samaritan piety in John 4:22. In each case there is an allegorical reference, and this implication is determined by the association with a particular type of meaning. Origen associated the number five with "the relationship with the Old Testament," and Hoskyns and Davey with "a polemic against Samaritan worship." In both cases, if that is the type of meaning with which the construction is associated, then that reference is plausible. However, Marshall argues convincingly that it is unlikely that John referred to the Philistines or that he used allegory anywhere.[21]

Exegetically it is difficult to validate either construct of type of meaning (either the relationship or a polemic) as being expressed in John 4. Instead we have suggested that the subject is "Jesus' Messianic Ministry" and it is this subject that Jesus' words must be associated with. The contextual development of the subject turns on Jesus' claim to give an inner, spiritual well of water (4:13-14). When the woman asked for this water (4:15), Jesus began to expose his knowledge of her private life (4:16-18). This construction is part of that discussion. The logic reasons:

If the subject is "Jesus' Messianic Ministry,"

And if he reveals she had five husbands,

Then this revelation is a factual statement demonstrating his messianic ministry.

Such a claim rests on the Samaritan expectations of Messiah (4:25), who would explain everything to them. Jesus had redirected the woman's expectation from a prophet imperfectly understood by the Samaritans (4:19-22) to the true revelation coming through the Jewish messiah (4:23-25). So the

woman's testimony identifies Jesus as Messiah by his capacity to reveal her private life (4:29, 39), which was consistent with their expectation of Messiah (4:25).

In these two instances, the implications of constructions associated with the type of meaning are unfolded or exegeted. In each case the range is determined by the statement of the type of meaning. Of course it is possible that our interpretive statements may not be accurate or comprehensive enough, but this issue must be settled by their capacity to unfold the implications of constructions associated with the message.

3. Implications not stated in constructions of the text but included as diagnostic of the type of textual meaning

a. Perhaps the most difficult problem in exegesis is to discern valid implications of what the text means even though they have not been stated in the constructions of the text. Such implications can be validly meant only if they follow as diagnostic of the type of meaning expressed in the text as a whole.

In John 4:1-25, the question might be raised, does Jesus' conversation with the woman mean that he is Messiah? Jesus made it very clear at the outset that knowing who he was, was important to what he said (4:10). Yet until he concluded, by way of confirmation, that he was the Christ (4:26), this diagnostic meaning of the text had not been stated. From our statement of the type of meaning—"Jesus' messianic ministry . . . draws Samaritans to faith in him"—it follows that Jesus meant to expose his identity as Messiah through his ministry. That meaning was necessary to diagnose what he meant. Jesus,

[20] E. C. Hoskyns and F. N. Davey, *The Fourth Gospel* (London: n.p., 1947), 242f.
[21] Marshall, "Introduction," 18.

then, confirmed what he meant to imply (4:26) when the woman finally made her identification (4:25).

However, that same question is appropriate in earlier sections where Jesus' ministry does not provide a statement of confirmation. Does Jesus' revelation to Nathanael mean that he is Messiah (1:44–51)? Does Jesus' changing water to wine mean that he is Messiah (2:1–11)? Does Jesus' cleansing of the temple mean that he is Messiah (2:12–25)? Does Jesus conversation with Nicodemus (3:1–15) or his conversation with the woman at the well (4:1–25) mean that he is Messiah? In each case the answer is yes, and it follows as a diagnostic meaning from the subject of the book: "The glory of the person, words, and work of Jesus the Messiah, the Son of God." The glory of these words and deeds implies that Jesus is Messiah. This implication is *intended*, even though it is not directly stated.

b. Another unstated but diagnostic implication is that "these are written that you may believe" (20:31). It again follows necessarily from the message of the book that Jesus' ministry draws individuals to faith in him. It follows from the literary design that John wrote to persuade unbelievers to become believers. It follows from the historical record of Jesus' ministry that he drew individuals to faith in him (1:49; 2:11, 23–25; 4:29, 42). It follows from the composition of the book as a whole that Jesus draws individuals to faith in him (20:31). This claim on a response of faith is necessarily an implication of each account of Jesus' ministry even though it is not stated until the end of the book. Each individual episode means "you, reader, ought to believe."

c. A final question that ought to be considered in regard to textual silence is the role of historical comparative studies and methods in exegesis. Tremper Longman explains, "At its best, comparative studies provide a deeper understanding of the OT, helping the interpreter to bridge the vast temporal and cultural chasm which separates the modern reader from the OT."[22] The question that must be faced is, how can another historical text increase our knowledge where the biblical text is silent?

The answer we will develop is this: When a text is silent concerning a diagnostic implication, or silent in the full development of any (diagnostic or associated) implication, and when the same implication is developed in another historical document, then that comparative source may fill in and deepen our understanding where the text is silent.

It is important, however, to limit the role of comparative studies in exegesis, and that role is to inform us about implications necessarily meant in the text (a diagnostic or stated associated implication) and not simply associated with the sense of the passage. As valid implications of the textual meaning, these implications necessarily follow from the type of meaning expressed in spite of the text's silence or full development in that particular. Comparative studies do enrich our knowledge of the historical realm of reference in constructions stated in the text, and therefore they enrich our knowledge of associated implications of reference.

Consider the example of how the study of Ugaritic sources in Ras Shamra has enriched our knowledge of implications in the stories of Elijah and Elisha. George Saint-Laurent has said about this contribution,

The discovered literature from Ras Shamra has become our principle source for understanding a strangely fascinating religion. . . . Now we can understand the full

---

[22] Longman, "Comparative Methods in Old Testament Studies," 5.

thrust of anti-Baalistic polemics as well as the broad meaning of Baalism itself as a deification of the forces of nature through mythology.[23]

As we will see, the book of Kings does express polemical implications in the words and themes of the text. Kings does affirm that God is greater than Baal in his control of rain, in his provision of food and oil for the widow, and in his answer with fire. These implications are clearly necessary to define the message that the reign of Ahab in the northern kingdom is challenged in the judgments of YHWH through Elijah. Our understanding of the extent and kind of challenge is enriched from a study of the Ugaritic sources.

Baal was believed to have power over thunder and lightning from texts such as the following, which presents a message of Baal: "I will create lightning that the heavens may know, thunder [that] mankind may know and the multitudes of the earth understand." The blazing, all-consuming fire which Yahweh sends from heaven, on the other hand, seems to be a lightning bolt which totally devours the altar and its contents. As Elijah has already declared: "The god who answers with fire is God indeed."[24]

So comparative studies can enrich our understanding of polemic implications already expressed in the text. In addition, the associated implications of reference when the term "Baal" or "Baal worship" is used are enriched from these Ugaritic sources.

A knottier case concerns textual silence when we are dealing with more fundamental matters. As we suggested in part 2, the meaning in Deuteronomy was recognized as expressing the terms of covenant renewal. This is evident in Moses' reference to the historical occasion in the first giving of "his covenant, the Ten Commandments, which he commanded you to follow and then wrote them on two stone tablets" (Deut. 4:13). It seems clear that Moses understood the Ten Commandments as central to defining YHWH's covenant, but what do the "two stone tablets" mean? The two tablets are related to the definition of the covenant relationship, but the meaning of "two" is never clarified in the text.

This is a second example of textual silence. Meredith Kline suggests that

a reexamination of the biblical data, however, particularly in light of extrabiblical parallels, suggests a radically new interpretation of the formal nature of the two stone tables, the importance of which will be found to lie primarily in the fresh perspective it lends to our understanding of the divine oracle engraved upon them.[25]

So Kline proposes that the role of comparative studies is to clarify wrong interpretations of implications necessary to the textual meaning but not clearly expressed in the text.

The words of the tablets are intended as a partial expression for the whole covenant. This is "confirmed by the fact that 'covenant' (berit, Deut. 4:13) and 'the words of the covenant' (Ex. 34:28) are alternate biblical terminology."[26] Therefore the two tablets of words exist to reflect something of the nature and kind of revelation of the covenant. Rather than the two tablets being Part I and Part II of a legal code, as former interpretations had construed

---

[23] George E. Saint-Laurent, "Light from Ras Shamra on Elijah's Ordeal upon Mount Carmel," in *Scripture in Context,* ed. Carl D. Evans, William W. Hallo, and John B. White (Pittsburgh: Pickwick, 1980), 134.

[24] Ibid., 130.

[25] Meredith G. Kline, *Treaty of the Great King* (Grand Rapids: Eerdmans, 1963), 13.

[26] Ibid., 16. See Deuteronomy 9:9, 11, 15; Exodus 31:18; 32:15; 34:29.

them, they are identical copies of the basic covenant terms.

So far, this conclusion follows from the type of textual expression. In addition, it "was the normal procedure in establishing suzerainty covenants to prepare duplicate copies of the treaty text."[27] One copy was deposited in the ark, which was placed in the tabernacle (Ex. 25:16, 21; 40:20; Deut. 10:2) as a witness before YHWH of his promise of blessing; the other copy was a witness before the people of their oath (Ex. 24:8; Deut. 29:1–15). The legal words were not impersonal rules of state, but the personal expression of the will of the suzerain to servants constituting a nation. The "two" tablets mean the two sides of the national, covenant relationship. So again, in a defining implication of "covenant relationship," the comparative studies enrich our understanding of the fuller implications of two tablets. These implications must be associated with the type of meaning expressed in the text.

4. Implications not stated in the text and not included in or incompatible with the type of textual meaning. The fourth alternative involves implications that are not stated in the text, but may be claimed to be associated with the type of meaning. Such claims must be rejected on one of two grounds.

The first basis is that the claimed implication is compatible with the type of meaning (i.e., not in conflict with and thus possibly related), but must be rejected as being intended by the Author/author because there is no textual basis to support the implication. It is neither stated in the text nor included in the type of meaning summary. In such a case the most the interpreter can say is that this meaning is compatible with

what the text says and may be stated somewhere else in the Bible.

The second basis is that the claimed implication is incompatible with the type of meaning (i.e., in conflict with or unrelated to) and must therefore be rejected.

In the first case the text may mean this, but in the second case the text does not mean this. Two examples will be explored.

a. One of the confusing issues in exegesis involves using historical comparative studies to enlarge our understanding of what may be associated implications. The sabbath legislation is a defining law of the Ten Commandments. As such, this word, or commandment, is understood as one term of the ten words, necessary because it is included in the statements of the text (Ex. 20:2–17; Deut. 5:6–21). Moses refers to the sabbath as the "sign of the covenant" (Ex. 31:13–17). Kline goes further when he says that "it is tempting to see in the sabbath sign presented in the midst of the ten words the equivalent of the suzerain's dynastic seal found in the midst of the obverse of the international treaty documents."[28]

The question is, does "sign of the covenant" imply the associated implication of "seal"? A seal means more than a sign. Because the text does not specify the sabbath as a seal, the only grounds for concluding this as a necessary implication is to demonstrate that a seal is a defining component of a suzerainty treaty relationship. Since this has not been shown, it is wise to follow Bruce Waltke, who says that "the sabbath sign presented . . . *may be equivalent* to the suzerain's dynastic seal."[29]

As interpreters we can accept that this historical datum is not necessary to understand the meaning of the text, but

---

[27] Ibid., 19.
[28] Ibid., 18.
[29] Bruce K. Waltke, Unpublished classroom notes on the history of Israel.

as communicators we often feel that historical background material is necessary for effective communication. It tends to enliven and create a sense of reality for what may otherwise seem abstract. But we must accept our comments on historical backgrounds for what they are. When Genesis does not express how Abraham traveled, then our discussion of ancient modes of travel must be kept as merely illustrative and possible. When Paul does not comment on conditions of life in Corinth, then a preacher who elaborates on these conditions from archaeological sources must keep in mind that he is simply setting the stage and not discussing the textual meaning.

b. Rudolf Bultmann's interpretation of the "gift of life" in John 4:16–19 to be "the Revelation as the Disclosure of Man's Being" is an example of an incompatible implication. In his desire to communicate to modern man, Bultmann introduces the existential ideas of "self-awareness" and "authentic existence" as implications associated with Jesus' message.

The question this raises is, are these implications, which are claimed to be associated with what Jesus says, compatible with Jesus' message? Since the words do not appear in the text and these ideas are not implied in the words of the text, the answer turns on whether they are included in the authentic-message of Jesus. Is authentic-existence compatible with the gift of life? They share one component in common: self-realization. But the other component makes the two implications incompatible. Authentic existence originates within oneself and is limited to personal, existential resources for realiza-

tion; the gift of God originates with God and is dependent on God's resources for realization.

Or again, is self-awareness compatible with faith? Again, they share one component in common: awareness. But the other component makes the two implications incompatible. Self-awareness is being aware of oneself; faith is being aware of Christ and depending on his adequacy.

Thus both of Bultmann's proposed implications must be excluded as incompatible with the type of message Jesus proclaims.

SUMMARY

Exegesis is surely the central task of biblical exposition, but the successful execution of exegesis rests on the foundational task of reading to recognize the type of meaning. Therefore exegesis is the task of unfolding from the textual constructions the range of implications determined by the type of authorial composition in the text. Based on the definition, the range of implications is both within the legitimate meaning of normal, cultural language usage and the intrinsic meanings determined by their necessary relationship to the type of meaning expressed in the text. Thus the meanings of the biblical text are both legitimate in general and necessary in particular.

The issue faced in the task of exegesis is the valid determination of these implications. The range of actual implications involves dealing with the hermeneutical premises to be used in type-logic. Our next task is to explore how these premises are used in exegesis.

CHAPTER 9

Hermeneutical Considerations of the Task of Exegesis—I

If the problem of implications is central to the task of exegesis, then hermeneutical premises guide the task of the interpretation of necessary implications. In the principle of recognition, the premises set the range of preunderstood expectations as one reads the text. In the principle of exegesis, the premises contribute to the understanding of the implications of textual constructions. The following hermeneutical premises have a role in type-logic in the exegesis stage reading:

1. The *literal* premise affirms what must be the framework for the task of exegesis. It affirms that the constructions in the text must be exegeted in the context of the message. Added to consideration of the message, the other hermeneutical criteria define the context with distinct emphasis from which exegesis must draw.
2. The *theological themes and textual design* define two other textually based criteria (in addition to message) that form intrinsic aspects of the context within which exegesis must take place.
3. The *grammatical and historical* premises define two broadly based

criteria that form general aspects of the context within which exegesis must take place.

These premises will now be stated and examined individually as they influence the process of exegesis using type-logic. This chapter will deal with literal, textual design, and theological themes; grammatical and historical will be the subject of chapter 10.

LITERAL

Literal affirms that the textually based type of meaning necessarily determines the reader's interpretation of any implications through type-logic.

The literal premise first arose in the historical controversy between the church at Antioch in Syria and the church at Alexandria in Egypt. This premise has in recent history been advanced in support of conservative interpretation and evangelical and dispensational theology. An important aspect of the literal premise is articulated by James Barr:

The normal use of literal is referential in scope. We are thinking about the entities or referents to which a text refers. To

155

understand the text literally is to suppose that the referents are just as stated in the text, the language of the text being understood in a direct sense.[1]

Barr has properly emphasized the referential scope of the term "literal." In his statement, however, he injects a confusing element. The referents, he says, are to be understood "just as stated in the text" and "in a direct sense." The confusing element is that "as stated in the text" may not support "a direct sense." The literal premise as we have defined it has emphasized textual basis or "just as stated in the text." That is the basic difference between literal and allegorical, according to Barr:

> "Literal" in this sense can be opposed to "allegorical." Allegorical is also referential in its scope; the difference is that the referent is other than that suggested by the direct sense of the language, being in fact known by an indirect process working from hints and hidden signals in the language.[2]

In allegory, the reference is determined by factors other than those expressed in the meaning of the text. The helpful part of Barr's analysis is the contrast between the textual basis ("as stated in the text") and the indirect basis (hints and hidden signals in the language) in the interpretation of the references. Again, however, he limits the textual basis to only a direct sense, but this does not necessarily follow. The textual clues may well support a direct sense, but they may also support a metaphorical sense as in parables or in figures of speech.

In a linguistic analysis of reading, a similar emphasis has been seen in the use of "literal." A reader interprets literal meanings "when semantic structures (textual sense) are held invariant and context or possible worlds (reference) is altered in determining that meaning."[3] This book postulates that there are two primary variables in reading: the textual or semantic sense, and the world of reference. As we read the text we attempt to match the textual sense with the worlds we know or with the possible worlds we can imagine. The meaning is the match that the reader settles on. The literal meaning is based on the textual sense being held invariant as it determines the reader's perception of the type of reference.

Problems arise in using the literal norm when the textual clues do not appear to be clear and decisive. While the literal premise is commonly associated with a direct textual sense, as Barr indicated, it cannot legislate a direct sense in the presence of conflicting evidence or in the absence of supporting evidence. At least two problem cases must be considered in using the literal premise.

1. An apparently direct sense in conflict with the known world. In a text that appears to express a direct sense, a question is raised when incongruity arises in the match with what is known about the world. Such incongruity is a valid means to identify when a construction's normal linguistic environment is juxtaposed with an unusual literary environment (such as Jesus' saying, "I am the door"). The only difference between a direct sense and an ironical sense is the incongruity with what is known in the Author's/author's world (as Elijah taunts the prophets of Baal, "Cry louder, for he is a god!"). In

---

[1] James Barr, *The Bible in the Modern World* (New York: Harper & Row, 1973), 171 (emphasis added).

[2] Ibid. (emphasis added).

[3] David R. Olson and Angela Hildyard, "Literacy and the Comprehension and Expression of Literal Meaning" (*Trends in Linguistics Studies and Monographs* 24), in *Writings in Focus,* ed. Florian Coulmas (New York: Moulton, 1981).

this case particularly, a clear knowledge of the author's world and his occasion in speaking helps to clarify the sense. In any case, a modern reader must guard against his own presuppositions about the spirit world or the reality of prophetic revelation of a future world becoming the basis of incongruity with the known world. Thus what may appear to be a direct sense can be understood as another sense when what the author clearly knows of the world is in conflict with what he apparently says.

2. *An apparently direct sense in conflict with Semitic style.* One of the common criticisms of literal interpretation is that it shows little literary sensitivity. Textual clues may be expressed in both style and genre. The clues involved in literary style are often difficult to discern. Semitic predilection to hyperbolic language and unqualified, categorical, absolute statements does raise questions about taking the expressions in a direct sense. These clues will be examined further in relation to the grammatical premise. The clues involved with genre will be considered in the next hermeneutical premise, textual design.

TEXTUAL DESIGN

Textual design affirms that the textually based type of meaning includes the conventional and stylistic meanings in the composition as a complete text that determines emotive, cognitive, and volitional implications in the force of address and the type of implications of reference to the historical realm.

Implications of the textual expressions are determined fundamentally by the message being expressed. This is so because the fundamental component of the type of meaning being expressed is stated in the message being communicated. But the same message can be communicated in different textual strategies and depending upon the textual strategy, additional implications will be intended. These implications may include the force and feeling with which the message is expressed and the direct or figurative way in which the message refers to the world and to history. These considerations are particularly important within the literal tradition, with its expectations of direct sense and reference as already discussed.

These additional implications are featured in the consideration of textual design, which will be examined from two perspectives:

1. *Textual address:* In what terms does the author address the audience?

2. *Textual composition:* In what textual strategy does the author fashion his message?

Both aspects will help to clarify the actual implications intended by the textual constructions. In these considerations, the expectations of a direct sense and direct reference will be refined by the textual design.

Textual Address

Being sensitive to the terms that the author uses to address the audience offers clues that may be important in determining the appropriate range of implications. Three general features of textual address ought to be considered.

1. Direct knowledge of the author. In certain genres of writing it is conventional for an author to identify himself (expository). Thus the author's choice of a genre and use of personal references influences the implications. The position (such as prophet or apostle) of the author lends importance and weight to the message. Where a personal relationship existed between the author and the original audience, emotive implications of concern and value are added when the author identifies himself. Pastoral letters "were written as substitutes for being present in person, and were meant to convey the apostolic presence, teaching and authority."[4] In the absence of an author's name (some psalms, epistles, etc.) the message is carried independent of a known relationship to what is said.

In addition to the force with which a message is expressed, a knowledge of the author adds to the historical information available and relevant to the occasion of writing. That issue will be further discussed under the historical premise even though it is appropriate to introduce it here.

2. Authority of the author. While the original writing of a biblical book may have been received with uncertainty about authority, that question has been resolved in the formation of the canon. And although questions of canonicity are appropriate to consider, yet in interpretation they may practically be set aside so that the text may be regarded as the very words of God. That influences implications of volitional force in exhortations and of historicity in narratives told as history.

3. Historical and theological limits of address. No biblical message is addressed directly to a contemporary audience. While each book is addressed to a historical audience, is any addressed with such particularity so as to limit the message to that historical audience alone? It is generally acknowledged that such historical factors are associated with the occasion, but commonly do not diagnose the type of meaning. So indecision about who received the Galatians letter does not prevent subsequent audiences from being addressed. By contrast, it is self-evident that Paul's message to Timothy "to get here before winter" is a message that is limited to one historical audience. This is not commonly the case in biblical epistles.

Yet the audience is addressed because of its relationship to God and in terms of its relationship to God. So Israel is addressed as a people of God existing as a nation. That national aspect of the relationship influences some of the laws stated in the text. A subsequent audience that does not share that aspect of relationship will not share that aspect of the message. This issue will be examined more fully in the hermeneutical consideration of the principle of application (part 4).

Textual Composition

The textual design also determines implications defined by the strategy of communication. These implications are influenced by some issues that are not directly stated but nonetheless are assumed as the working basis for communication. We will consider two sources of influence: cooperative maxims and generic conventions.

1. Maxims of cooperation in communication. In their study of comprehension and expression of literal meaning, David Olson and Angela Hildyard introduce a cooperative principle that works in communication. Although the maxims remain unexpressed, anyone who comprehends considers the maxim in construing the textual meaning. H. P. Grice[5] first expressed these maxims as operative in conversation. Similar maxims are present with even greater importance in written communication. These maxims may be restated in the consideration of biblical communication as follows:

---

[4]Richard N. Longenecker, "Form, Function and Authority," in D. A. Carson and John D. Woodbridge, eds., *Scripture and Truth* (Grand Rapids: Zondervan, 1983), 104.

[5]H. P. Grice, "Logic and Conversation," in P. Cole and J. L. Morgan, eds., *Syntax and Semantics,* vol. 3, *Speech Acts* (New York: Academic Press), 41–58.

a. Quantity: The composition is as informative as required. In the case of the Bible, which is highly selective, we must work with the premise that enough is said to know—although that is usually not enough to satisfy our curiosity. Historical cultural studies may help to enrich our understanding of what is implied historically in what is said.

b. Quality: What is said is believed to be true unless textual or generic clues indicate otherwise. An author has strategies to accomplish this, such as quoting an unreliable source (as demons or recognized evil men) or pressing the quality maxim (as in humor or figurative expressions).

c. Relation: What is said is relevant to the original audience in that original situation. An assumed meaningfulness and importance encourages the interpreter not to settle for some apparent but irrelevant meaning.

d. Manner: What is said is perspicuous in that it avoids unnecessary obscurity, ambiguity, prolixity, or real incoherence. Criticism of seemingly self-evident textual meaning must be replaced by deliberation and caution in reaching critical conclusions.

2. Conventions, idiom, and style in textual genre. The textual design statement constructed in the recognition stage is stated in an intrinsic form. As such, it attempts to reflect in particular the conventions of textual composition of that individual text. But those conventions are best understood at the generic level, which gives consideration to every text of that kind. Such conventions involve "an elaborate set of tacit agreements between the artist and the audience about the ordering of the art work," which "is at all times the enabling context in which the complex communication of art occurs."[6]

The critical reader who gives primary attention to problem cases must give careful consideration to these "tacit agreements" in order to exegete the range of implications intended. In addition, the modern reader must give added attention to these conventions that are no longer shared intuitively but must be shared by reconsideration. The kinds of implications involved are "derived from what is said," although they may "not be logically entailed by that expression."[7]

Prophetic Literature

Prophetic literature is prophetic revelation that reproves, pronounces judgment, and announces consolation to historical audiences in Israel. The prophet speaks through oracles or sermons that are later collected into a book of the prophet's historical ministry, written largely in the idiom of poetry and making statements of God's commitment to act in the future.

For the Greeks, oracular ambiguity was associated with Delphi and Sibyl. When Croesus consulted the Delphic oracle, he was told, "If Croesus crosses the Halys, he will destroy a great empire." With this equivocal encouragement he destroyed his own (Aristotle, *Rhet.* 3.5). In contrast to the pagan prophets stood the prophets of Yahweh, the God of Israel, who did not ordinarily indulge in this hedging of bets. However, some might characterize as ambiguous Jeremiah's prediction of destruction at the hands of an enemy from the north (Jer. 1:13; 4:6) or Joseph's interpretation of the dreams of the head butler and head baker, both of whom are told that "within three days Pharaoh will lift up your head," though in the one case this means restoration of favor and in the other, hanging (Gen.

---

[6]Robert Alter, *The Art of Biblical Narrative* (New York: Basic Books, 1981), 47.
[7]Olson and Hildyard, "Literacy," 297.

40:12, 19).[8] Joseph's lack of clarity is thus removed in the specifications in the development.

But while the biblical prophecies do not include equivocal statements, they may well involve intended ambiguity in the progress of revelation. The central question for exegesis is clearly, what in fact is affirmed by the prophet? Three aspects of prophetic composition will be examined to help in specifying implications in addition to those implied in the message.

1. Prophetic sermon structure. One overriding feature of prophetic books is that they are a collection of sermons or oracles. As a collection it represents the historic ministry of the prophet in the selective arrangement of his sermons. The message of the book, then, is not the construct of a developing argument, but rather a summary of the prophet's messages for a generation. The coherence rests, not on the logical force reached in the conclusion, but on the historical voice speaking for God on a historical occasion.

The essential component of the book is the prophetic sermon or oracle (pronouncement). The sermon itself is not constructed as a rational argument, but rather as a word of the spokesman of God that is spoken in a powerfully vocative character. The sermon is devised as a form of direct address from God to a historically real audience. Yet the word of God is represented as divine discourse with an introductory formula such as "thus says the Lord." This form of presentation differs from a presentation of God's message directly and immediately to that historical situation. This way of representing God well suits the collection of the sermons into a book for audiences to whom the prophet did not speak directly.

The structure of a sermon or oracle reflects the poetic style common to representations of God speaking. Robert Alter suggests that a "fundamental generative principle of intensification"[9] is at work in biblical poetry or oracle. The oracle involves a linear development of meaning. One image suggests a related one, or a further manifestation of the same underlying image; one idea leads to a cognate or consequent one. That linear intensification underlies the development of the pronouncement until the word of God has been delivered.

Walter Eichrodt further proposes that the prophet is a covenant spokesman who follows Moses, with whom the covenant relationship began. This role is reflected in the themes and purposes that are drawn from the covenant terms and expectations. The conditions of the Mosaic relationship having been violated, the prophet introduces themes of reproof, judgment, and consolation. As a result, the covenant context becomes the framework within which the prophet's design and message are to be construed.

a. Reproof is a word of direct accusation in which the prophet speaking for God the Judge indicts the nation for covenant violations. Alter calls it "a kind verbal buttonholing of the listener, directly calling him the names he has earned through his actions."[10] Direct accusation shades into the indirect accusation of satire. This mode is common in Amos and Jonah, where greater latitude is exercised in the use of sarcasm and irony.

b. Judgment involves the punitive consequences of moral depravity and covenant violation. Further consider-

---

[8] G. B. Caird, *The Language and Imagery of the Bible* (Philadelphia: Westminster, 1980), 104.

[9] Robert Alter, *The Art of Biblical Poetry* (New York: Basic Books, 1985), 83–84.

[10] Ibid., 142.

ation will be given to statements of warning about impending disaster and to the expectation that the warning will be realized.

c. *Consolation* involves statements of the promise of deliverance and blessing. The predominant issue emerging from these themes concerns the poetic development within the structure of intensification. How actual and real is the expectation of future blessing and deliverance? Are statements of future judgment to be understood as hyperbole or actual and real?

2. Figurative expression in a poetic style. The prophets are preeminently spokesmen of God with a *message*. So the message establishes the primary context within which the implications are unfolded. But the poetic idiom in which they speak is a consideration that must be included in the literal tradition. Thus various aspects of a prophet's use of figurative expressions must be considered within prophetic genre.

The prophet Isaiah's message is enriched with the use of metaphor as he fashions "Zion" as a woman who has lost both husband and children (Isa. 49:14–23; 54:1–8). Amos uses hyperbole to express the intensified development of his message:

"The days are coming," declares the LORD,

"when the reaper will be overtaken by the plowman
    and the planter by the one treading grapes.
New wine will drip from the mountains
    and flow from all the hills" (Amos 9:13).

The land's produce is so bountiful that the normal practices of planting and harvesting will overlap in an unnatural fashion. And each figure builds on and intensifies the thought.

We will consider figures of speech in the section dealing with the grammatical premise, but at this stage we want to focus on the development of thought in poetry in the prophetic oracle. Alter suggests that poetry

is a particular way of imagining the world—particular in the double sense that poetry as such has its own logic, its own way of making connections and engendering implications and because each system of poetry has distinctive semantic thrusts.[11]

In the prophetic system of poetry, what is the logic of the poem? A common development has the prophet beginning with a clear perception of a concrete historical threat—the armies of Assyria or Babylon—and then jumping to a horizon of ultimate threat. The problem emerges as "the prophet, for his own monitory purposes, wants to evoke these actual threats as powerfully as he can. But because this evocation is worked out through the medium of biblical verse, there is a way in which the medium begins to take over.[12]

Thus the logic of intensification culminating in the most forceful statement uses hyperbole, which departs from the actual and imagines the unreal but powerfully stated climax. So Isaiah (24:17–20) alludes to the flood as an image of judgment, and Jeremiah (4:23–27) to an original chaos (Gen. 1:2) as a powerful image of complete destruction. The question in exegesis involves the scope of actual and real judgment that is implied in the intensified image.

A typical passage is Amos's image of national restoration (9:14–15), which begins like this:

"I will bring back my exiled people Israel;
    they will rebuild the ruined cities and live in them."

---

[11]Ibid., 151.
[12]Ibid.

Alter makes a helpful point about this image:

> It is easy enough to conceive of the first two lines of the poem as merely a hyperbolic 'embellishment' of the idea of national restoration, but I think that would be an unwarranted reduction of their scope, especially if we compare these lines with visions of redemption in the prophets who came after Amos.[13]

It is important to remember that the biblical revelation begins with ultimate foundations and anticipates ultimate solutions. Written under divine inspiration, the prophet has the basis in God to refer to ultimate judgment and blessing in real and actual terms. That possibility must be kept open, and when the immediate genre does not clarify the point, then we must consider the broader context of progressive revelation, as Alter does.

3. Commissive statements of prophecy. A final consideration in the exegesis of the prophetic word concerns the sense of a prophet's commissive statements. In these, the prophet represents God as committing himself to future actions or as establishing some set of circumstances as God speaks. These statements take the form of positive promises or predictions and of negative warnings or predictions. At issue in exegesis is the question, how much does God commit himself to do? Any general expectation of hyperbole must be qualified by the fact that God is committing himself to act.

a. The sense of prediction: A basic misconception about genre concerns the distinction between predictions and promises or warnings. Willis J. Beecher has identified this misconception:

> We have been taught that the prophets uttered predictions of a coming Deliverer; that these were fulfilled in the events of the life and mission of Jesus; and that this proves, first, that the prophets were divinely inspired, and second, that the mission of Jesus was divine. All of this is true if rightly understood, but full of difficulty if we stop here. . . .
>
> The proposition that the Old Testament contains a large number of predictions concerning Messiah to come and that these are fulfilled in Jesus Christ may be scriptural in substance, but it is hardly so in form. The Bible offers very few predictions save in the form of promises or threatenings. It differs from systemized theologies in its not disconnecting prediction from promise or threatening. . . . The prevailing note in both Testaments is a multitude of specifications unfolding a single promise, the promise serving as central religious doctrine.[14]

Beecher thus makes a distinction between the type of meaning found in the more common *promise* and that found in the less common *prediction*. This distinction is supported because the meaning of the prediction is specified so explicitly in context that it allows for only one reference in the future. Though this kind of specification is not as common as promises, it is important to carefully examine one example to investigate how context specifies the one reference.

Let us choose for our example the controversial case of Isaiah 7:14.[15] A controversial passage like this involves a number of problems. In using this one as an illustration of a prediction with language that specifies, we have to make certain assumptions. The first assumption concerns the sign. All will agree that Isaiah 7:14 is related to the

---

[13]Ibid., 157.

[14]Willis J. Beecher, *The Prophets and the Promise* (Grand Rapids: Baker, 1963), 175–76, 178.

[15]Elliott E. Johnson, "Dual Authorship and the Single Intended Meaning of Scripture," *Bibliotheca Sacra* 143 (July-September 1986): 218–27. Consult this article for a complete development of the position.

sign in some fashion. The sign is given for Ahaz because of his reluctance to ask for one (7:10–13). While most interpreters take the sign to be that to which Isaiah refers—a birth in Ahaz's day—Beecher argues convincingly that the sign is the promise statement itself.[16] The second assumption is that the sense of 'almah is not determined by a study of lexical uses, though the presumption of common law and usage favors "virgin" and "virtuous" until and unless the young woman were proven otherwise.[17]

Given these assumptions, the statement made in context is seen to be very specific. Two unknowns in the historical setting provide the occasion for which the sign is given in response. The first and most evident unknown is the future destiny of the house of David (7:2). Isaiah was sent with an oracle that the house of David would survive because the impending attack of the enemy would be defeated (7:4–9). Also, Isaiah challenged Ahaz to ask God for a sign to guarantee survival (7:10–11). The second unknown arises from this oracle. Isaiah links Ahaz's future share in the house of David to his response to the oracle and the challenge (7:9).

If the sign for Ahaz is in the statement itself, then it must be two-edged: to guarantee the future of David's house, and to assure the fall of Ahaz. Those contextual constraints help to specify in a particular sense the sign of 7:14. For only a virgin conception, as strange as that might be to imagine, would remove Ahaz from the Davidic line. In addition, a virgin conception would also guarantee the Davidic line with the offspring who would be God-with-us (Immanuel) in the fullest sense. This specification of sense narrows the

statement to a prediction of a virgin conception and birth that can only refer to the conception and birth of One Davidic Son unless there were to be two incarnations.

b. The sense of promise: The promise is a broader commissive statement in the sense that it does not necessarily specify one historical reference. (In a commissive statement the Author commits himself to a certain kind of action.) The broader scope, involving fewer necessary components, in the statement of a promise does not specify the circumstances of fulfillment so completely while at the same time affirming the fact of commitment to act. Therefore a promise is potentially capable of multiple partial fulfillments before reaching a final realization of the commitment.

Beecher ends his discussion of promise doctrine with a biblical generalization about God's promise: "God gave a promise to Abraham, and through him to mankind; a promise eternally fulfilled and fulfilling in the history of Israel; and chiefly fulfilled in Jesus Christ, he being that which is principle in the history of Israel."[18] It is "eternally fulfilled" in that its fulfillment is viewed as related to the very existence of the earth and God's order of blessing for the earth in its existence. It is "fulfilling in history as Isaac, Jacob, Joseph, David, etc. receive a limited degree of blessing in Abraham." It is "chiefly fulfilled in Jesus Christ" as he is the chief recipient of the promise (Acts 2:33, 39) and the effective agent through which blessing is available to all men (Rom. 4:16–17; 3:22).

We can see that while the promise given to Abraham has one sense, it has the potential for multiple references (a chosen descendant through whom God

---

[16] Beecher, *The Prophets and the Promise,* 333–36.

[17] "The Meaning of 'ALMA (AV virgin) in Isaiah 7:14," *Princeton Theological Review* 24 (1926): 308.

[18] Ibid., 178.

blesses). Therefore any historical partial fulfillment, though genuine, is not final. Rather, God's commitment to action holds out for full and complete realization of the promise even though many roles in God's stated purpose may be shared by men in partial fulfillment of it: servant, anointed king, branch, chosen one, *Meshullam,* called one, *Jeshurun,* YHWH's son, sons of promise, *Netser, Nagidh.*

Another example of a fundamental promise that is fulfilling in history and fulfilled in Christ is Genesis 3:15. In it God promises that the seed of woman shall do conflict with the seed of the serpent and shall overcome the serpent with a head blow while only suffering a minor injury. The statement is vague at best, only guaranteeing human conflict with and conquest over the Evil One. Who, when, where, and how are all questions left unanswered. Adam and Eve thought Cain was the seed, but he was overcome by the Evil One (4:7) and in fact became the seed of the Evil One (4:8). Abel was actually the seed of the woman, but he was overcome by death in his conflict and so was replaced by Seth (4:25). That conflict continued throughout biblical history, but no descendant of woman overcame until Christ.

c. *The sense of warning:* Promise is a commitment to positive blessing. Warning is a commitment to threatening and actual judgment. The general and absolute sounding nature of the statement of warning has led G. B. Caird to conclude: "What appears to be an unconditional verdict turns out to contain an *unexpressed conditional* clause."[19] He draws this conclusion from the association in the prophets of unqualified warnings and unqualified calls to repentance. He cites Amos 3:12 and 5:14 as examples:

> As a shepherd rescues out of the jaws of a lion
> two shin bones or the tip of an ear,
> So shall the Israelites who live in Samaria be rescued
> like a corner of a couch or a chip from the leg of a bed,

but also,

> Seek good and not evil, that you may live, that the Lord of hosts may be firmly on your side.

However, is it exegetically sound to interpret an unexpressed condition when there is no textual statement to support such a condition and the type of meaning is not conditional? Earlier in Israel's relationship there were conditional warnings in the law about the coming of judgment such as,

> If you do not obey the LORD your God . . . , all these curses will come upon you and overtake you (Deut. 28:15).

Caird seeks to reconcile the apparent conflict by introducing a stylistic feature of hyperbole, but this still demands taking an unconditional statement of warning as a conditional statement.

Another approach would be to take both the warning and the offer in an unconditional sense. The judgment in the warning would fall with certainty, as a statement of God's commitment would imply. However, the offer was still available for that generation likewise to find certain refuge from God. The issues left open and unstated would be the extent of the threatened judgment and the time when it would fall. The certainty of its fall rested on the certainty of God's committing himself to act and the nature of evil at work demanding judgment.

Jonah knew that the potential for delay rested not in any implied condition, but in the character of a God of mercy. The judgment of which Jonah

---

[19]Caird, *The Language and Imagery of the Bible,* 112 (emphasis added).

warned would eventually fall on Nineveh. Yet the mercy of God forestalled that judgment on the repentant generation. While there certainly is mystery involved in the interrelation of repentance and mercy, that mystery does not demand changing the sense of God's statements of warning and offers of mercy. Both are true. Only time is needed to expose the certain execution of the Word of God.

Apocalyptic Literature

Apocalyptic literature is prophetic revelation that challenges and encourages God's oppressed people by narrating contemporary historical issues and envisioning their outcome at the end of history in terms corresponding to what the prophet saw in the vision and heard from the divine interpreter.[20] What prophetic and apocalyptic literature have in common is that both are species of prophetic revelation; where they are different is in their views of the end time. The prophet spoke to a historic audience about an impending crisis and in terms of that crises spoke of the final resolution. Apocalyptic writers spoke to a historic audience in the midst of crisis and suffering and gave that audience perspective by stepping above its own day and sharing a vision of the resolution of the conflict at the end of history.

There are several features of the composition that influence the exegesis of implications.

1. The structure of apocalyptic narrative. Apocalyptic genre involves two primary literary structures: narrative and vision. Concerning narrative, John

J. Collins states, "The form of the apocalypses involves a narrative framework that describes the manner of revelation."[21] Joyce Baldwin draws some important conclusions about this narrative framework. "In each of the books there is a clear arrangement of the material, so that it is not difficult to divide them into sections. Each begins at a given point in history."[22]

Of even greater interest is the conclusion that "the periods referred to can be identified and described, and yet the content of chapters has a universal application."[23] The events are selected and described in such a way that the problems and the characters have a representative role in that period of history and until the climax resolves the problems. Daniel and his friends represent the believing remnant testifying to God during the times of the Gentiles. The seven churches of Asia Minor were specific, historical churches, but the problems faced are normative for all who have "ears to hear." While the sequence of letters does not represent and parallel the history of the church age, the church age is characterized by these issues.

2. The structure of visions and symbols. The primary literary structure is the vision, in which God directs the attention of both the author and the reader to the end and God's resolution of historical issues and tensions. The presence of visions alone in apocalyptic literature does not distinguish it from prophetic literature, which also contains visionary revelation. But whereas the prophets had visions of insight that provided them with a theological inter-

---

[20] Elliott Johnson, "Apocalyptic Genre in Literal Interpretation," in *Essays in Honor of J. Dwight Pentecost,* ed. Stanley D. Toussaint and Charles Dyer (Chicago: Moody Press, 1986), 200.

[21] John J. Collins, *The Apocalyptic Imagination* (New York: Crossroad, 1984), 16.

[22] Joyce C. Baldwin, *Haggai, Zechariah, Malachi* (Downers Grove, Ill.: InterVarsity Press, 1972), 70.

[23] Ibid., 70–71.

pretation of the events of their day, apocalyptic visions were elaborate picture visions.[24] The imagery is distinctive. Baldwin offers an example:

Amos and Jeremiah had also seen visions of a relatively simple impressionist type, pictures which conveyed their own message. The contrast between these and the involved imagery of Ezekiel marks one distinct step in the direction of apocalyptic.[25]

This complex and sometimes grotesque imagery in visions has become the focal point in the discussion of interpretation of apocalyptic literature. Collins notes that it was Herman Gunkel who

by pointing to the mythological roots of much apocalyptic imagery . . . showed its symbolic and allusive character. Apocalyptic literature was not governed by the principles of Aristotelian logic but was closer to the poetic nature of myth.[26]

Assessing the interpretation of these visions, Collins concludes:

Biblical scholarship in general has suffered from a preoccupation with the referential aspects of language and with the factual information that can be extracted from a text. Such an attitude is especially detrimental to the study of poetic and mythological material, which is expressive language, articulating feelings and attitudes rather than describing reality in an objective way. The apocalyptic literature provides a rather clear example of language that is expressive, symbolic rather than factual.[27]

Collins's conclusion must be strongly rejected. Although the language and imagery of the vision may only sketch the outline of the reality, it is not enigmatic;[28] though the language is expressive, it does not exclude specific reference; and though the genre includes symbolism, it does not negate actual and historical reference through the symbol. This view may be defended by the line of reasoning that follows.

The concept of "prophetic revelation" necessarily includes the use of language that implies both factual information (a reference to history) and expressions of attitude and feeling. George Ladd affirms, "A final characteristic of the apocalyptic genre is the use of symbolism in declaring the will of God to people and in predicting future events."[29] Although a vision might include symbolism, this does not eliminate reference to specific events involved in the outworking of God's will, nor does it dismiss predictions of future occurrences. When the future events are designated by a symbol, the designation is not direct, but metaphorical. Yet the event designated may be historical and real. Numerous instances in the apocalyptic literature make this clear.

Daniel interpreted the vision of the image of a statue and declared to Nebuchadnezzar, "You are that head of gold" (Dan. 2:38), indicating that a symbol (head) has a real, historical reference (Nebuchadnezzar). The angelic interpreter in Daniel 7 identified the four beasts as "four kingdoms that

[24] Beecher, *The Prophets and the Promise*, 119.
[25] Baldwin, *Haggai, Zechariah, Malachi*, 71–72.
[26] Collins, *The Apocalyptic Imagination*, 13.
[27] Ibid., 14.
[28] Leon Morris, *Apocalyptic* (Grand Rapids: Eerdmans, 1972), 36–37. He quotes with approval E. Schurer, *A History of the Jewish People in the Time of Jesus Christ* (Edinburgh T. & T. Clark, 1886).
[29] *International Standard Bible Encyclopedia* (Grand Rapids: Eerdmans, 1979), 1:152.

will rise from the earth" (7:17).[30] The angel in Daniel 8 interpreted the ram as the "kings of Media and Persia" and the shaggy goat as the "king of Greece" and "four kingdoms that will emerge" (8:20-21).

In similar fashion Ezekiel was told that "these bones are the whole house of Israel" (Ezek. 37:11). The apostle John was informed of the identity of the image he first encountered (Rev. 1:12-16) when Christ said, "I am the First and the Last. I am the Living One; I was dead, and behold I am alive for ever and ever!" (1:17). Christ was not identified by name, but instead through a series of descriptions of his role and experience in history, enhancing the relation between the image and its symbols and the historical reference. Thus in the case of biblical apocalyptic, the use of images and language involve both referential and factual as well as expressive meanings.

The interpretation of symbols is central to the interpretation of the vision and central to its message. Symbols, unlike the signs of language, have no conventionally shared meanings. The meaning of the symbol must be defined exclusively from some context, and there are a number of relevant contexts upon which a symbol may draw.

The principal context is the vision itself, and the principal clue toward interpretation is the interpreting angel. This angel is sent by God to set the historical stage for the vision, and the prophet often converses with the angel as he seeks to understand the vision given to him. Thus the interpreting angel provides the primary context.

The second context is the historical setting of the prophet, which may provide the setting from which God chooses an entity to appear in the vision. For example, the steeds in Zechariah 1:7-17 reflect the means of the Persian empire for patrol and military conquest. So scrolls and beasts are drawn from the ancient world to symbolize written messages and the character of governments in the vision.

A third context is other writings in the apocalyptic literary genre that may provide a resource for recognized symbolism. The four horns of Zechariah 1:18-21 recall the horned beasts of Daniel 7 and 8. While the connection between these visions involves only the detail of the horns, yet this connection involves basic points. The horn symbolizes the demonstration of the animal's power in the kingdom of Daniel and at times represents the king or his kingdom (Dan. 7:8, 20, 24-25). Also, the sequence of four horns corresponds to the sequence of four beasts representing successive kingdoms and makes the adoption clear. The book of Revelation draws on the rich resource of apocalyptic symbolism to provide the final visions of the climax. For example, the sun, moon, and stars of the pregnant woman (Rev. 12:1-2) draw upon the symbolism of the dream in Genesis 37:9-11. Or the red dragon with seven heads, ten horns, and seven crowns (Rev. 12:3) draws upon the monster of the sea in Isaiah 27:1 and the beast of Daniel 7:7 with ten horns.

The final context would be the biblical literature as a whole from which symbols are drawn. The Edenic setting, for example, includes a number of items that reappear as symbols of a restored rule of God. The trees of life, the fruit, and the river flowing from the throne

---

[30] Collins, *The Apocalyptic Imagination*, 82. "There is no doubt that Daniel 7 is describing the persecution of the Jews under Antiochus Epiphanes. The exaltation of the one like a son of man represents the triumph of the Jews. . . . The corporate interpretation holds that the one like a son of man is merely or purely a symbol, whose meaning is exhausted by the identification of its referent."

are drawn broadly from the literature of the Bible. These are the features that characterize the apocalyptic vision.

3. The word of the divine interpreter. The word of the divine interpreter provides a brief and direct statement that orients the person who reads about a vision to an unknown future period. The interpreter directs the reader's thought so that the reader can arrange the pieces of the vision into a meaningful whole. In Daniel the detailed interpretation (2:36–45) follows a careful recording of the vision the prophet saw (2:31–35; cf. 7:2–14 vision and 7:15-27 interpretation, etc.). In Zechariah and Ezekiel the divine interpreter speaks as the vision unfolds (Ezek. 37:3–6, 9, 11–14; Zech. 1:9–11, 12–13, 14–17).

The message can be construed primarily from these direct statements. When the interpreter overlooks or ignores these direct textual clues to the meaning of the vision, he will be disoriented in his perspective. For example, concerning Revelation 12:7–11, Caird misconstrues the divine interpretation and writes:

> Later Christian tradition, by the fallacy of misplaced concreteness, treated this as a precosmic event in its own right, quite failing to recognize that John's imagery had an earthly referent, as he makes plain in the sequel: "This is the hour of victory for our God . . . the accuser of our brothers is overthrown . . . by the sacrifice of the Lamb they have conquered him."[31]

Caird is correct in rejecting precosmic event. He is also correct in viewing the word from heaven as determinative. But he does not rest with the heavenly praise. The heavenly word does not limit the reference to earth nor does it

reject the reality of the heavenly cosmic battle. The conquest in the heavenlies (12:7–9) results in "the accuser . . . has been hurled down" (12:10). The heavenly voice announces the earthly consequences of the heavenly defeat of the accuser. The full display of God's reign is now come to heaven, but earth will suffer the consequences of the dragon's presence (12:10–12).

Historical Narrative Literature

Narrative is the most dominant form of writing in the Bible. It encompasses the structuring of the Pentateuch, the early prophets, and a number of books in the Writings as well as the Gospels and Acts. "The narrative mode is uniquely important in Christianity."[32]

Historical narrative literature is a prophetic or divinely accepted interpretation of the history of God's people from a theological point of view that instructs and challenges the reader by telling the story of what happened using the techniques of narrative art. We will examine three characteristics of the literature:

1. The intent of historicity. An initial consideration must address the question whether literary composition and historical integrity are compatible? Robert Alter would answer with a categorical no. A close reading of the text, he states, does "suggest that the writer could manipulate his inherited material . . . with a kind of subtle cogency we associate with the conscious artistry of the narrative mode designated prose fiction."[33] In this construct, fictional creation or embellishment is a necessary consequence of artistic freedom and composition.

Cassuto sees a range of narrative composition with varying aims.

---

[31] Caird, *The Language and Imagery of the Bible,* 55.

[32] Amos Wilder, *Early Christian Rhetoric: The Language of the Gospel* (Cambridge: Harvard University Press, 1971), 56.

[33] Alter, *The Art of Biblical Narrative,* 32.

The Torah transcended the historian's plane, because it had a different, more exalted aim in view . . . the purpose of educating the people spiritually. . . . In the days of Solomon, . . . there was created, for the first time, historiography in the sense with which modern scholarship invests with the term, historical writing whose aim is to determine the facts as they are, and to explain how they originated and developed according to the laws of causality.[34]

Whether or not we agree with Cassuto's view as to the origin of historiography, it is clear that biblical narrative expresses a range of composition and aim. While a modern definition of historiography does not determine historicity, one concern of interpretation must be with the events of time and space the text presents. Are these necessarily embellished because there is evidence of narrative freedoms of composition?

Our confession of historicity does admit certain limitations. We are limited in our knowledge of the historical facts both from independent sources recording the events and from the textual presentation of the events, as both Alter and Cassuto argue. In addition, we are limited in our knowledge of how the facts were preserved. These limitations in knowledge have been supplemented by theories of documentary dependence and oral tradition. However, some evangelicals have challenged the accuracy of conclusions that were based on assumptions about the sources of our knowledge.

Another means of supplementing our limited knowledge begins with theological premises. Biblical narrative is written by or authenticated by a prophet or an apostle with access to knowledge that no natural model of research can duplicate. In some cases, sources are mentioned (Num. 21:14; Josh. 10:12ff.; 1 Kings 14:19). Parallel passages indicate that the same event can be treated with interpretive freedoms. This treatment exhibits selectivity and arrangement that may relate events which were historically separated in time. But this interpretation of events does not necessarily distort or misrepresent what happened or misrepresent what the events mean. Rather, a theological interpretation of what happened necessarily implies historicity when the text purports to present what happened. While there were conventions of embellishment in the Ancient Near East, there is no textual evidence that the biblical texts adopted these.

2. The structure of narrative. Narrative is story. Stories are built out of three basic ingredients: *setting, characters, and plot.* The setting simultaneously includes relevant physical, temporal, and cultural features. It relates the story to a historical context. The characters and plot work together to produce the total effect. The character is what produces the action, yet the characters are known to us through their actions. The plot of the story is the arrangement of the events around a central conflict or set of conflicts moving toward a resolution. The arrangement relates to one whole, complete action.

Adele Berlin summarizes three strategies in the development of the character in the narrative.[35] The extent of development is directly related to the role the character takes in the narrative.

a. Agent of the plot role: The author takes no interest in the person as a person. The character is presented to tell the story or to introduce the setting. In Judah's marriage (Gen. 38), a num-

---

[34] U. Cassuto, *Biblical and Oriental Studies,* vol. 1, *Bible* (Jerusalem: Magnes, 1973), 15–16.

[35] Adele Berlin, *Poetics and Interpretation of Biblical Narrative* (Winona Lake, Ind.: Eisenbrauns, 1983), 32.

ber of characters have this role—a man of Adullam named Hirah, the daughter of a Canaanite man who was named Shua, and three sons of Shua named Er, Onan, and Shelah.

b. Archetypal role: The character has a role in the plot at hand, but the role is presented in terms alluding to the divine mandate of God's theological purposes of Genesis 1-3. The basic type of role is introduced in Genesis and developed in the narrative at hand. Characters whose stories fit this pattern present a model that the reader can readily identify with and apply. So Cain and Lamech follow the tragic fall into sin of Adam. King Saul's story becomes a classic instance of such a tragic fall. Or Noah's deliverance from judgment forms the model of deliverance (1 Peter 3) that had earlier been anticipated in word (Gen. 3:15) and had been experienced in the coverings of Adam and Eve.

c. Personal role: This character is, in Berlin's words, the one "who has a broader range of traits (not all belonging to the same class of people), and about whom we know *more than* is necessary for the plot."[36] This fuller development and treatment add to the vividness of the story and the indelible imprint of the individuals on the imaginations of repeated generations. Jacob, Moses, and David are treated in the Bible as characters of this kind.

Finally, plot development involves a sequence of events based on a central conflict.

The struggle may be very elemental and physical—animal against animal, animal against environment, man against nature, man against man, man against animal. The conflict among men is a moral struggle. The conflict with God is a spiritual struggle. Each conflict resolution contributes toward reaching a climax and produces those actions and interactions that culminate in an ultimate resolution of the conflict.[37]

While conflict resolution is central to plot development, the nature of this conflict may vary from story to story. Before the nature of the conflict can be examined, the various levels of plot development must be distinguished.

The most basic level comprises small story units within a book. There is also the book level, in which numerous stories are structured together into one overall story and conflict resolution. Such narrative books may combine other literary genres within the overall story structure (such as genealogies or legislation or hymns). Along with the most basic level and the book level there is the one total book, the Bible, that tells one story. Ryken comments,

The most obvious element of literary unity in the Bible is that it tells a story. It is a series of events having a beginning, a middle and an end. Even the eternal shapeliness of the Bible is remarkable (creation-consummation). . . . The overall story of the Bible has a unifying plot conflict. It is the great spiritual and moral battle between good and evil. . . . The presence of the great spiritual conflict makes choice on the part of biblical characters necessary.[38]

At the basic story level, the plot development may vary from clear conflict resolution to a simple pair of stimulus-response roles. Within this range may be included "occasioning incident-outcome, remark-evaluation, question-answer."[39]

At the book level, the plot progression also admits to a range of develop-

[36] Ibid.

[37] Caird, *The Language and Imagery of the Bible,* 55.

[38] Leland Ryken, *How to Read the Bible as Literature* (Grand Rapids: Zondervan, 1984), 177–78.

[39] Ibid.

ments. These vary from a very loose story in thematic development to a well-crafted story combining many facets in one plot structure. Biblical narrative books admit to such a range of development, as represented in figure 9.1.

Figure 9.1

Thematic narrative   Plot narrative
1 and 2 Chronicles   Genesis
   1 and 2 Kings   Jonah
        Judges   1 Samuel
        Joshua   Exodus/Numbers
            Ezra   2 Samuel
            Nehemiah   Ruth/Esther
                      Habakkuk
            Gospels
            Acts

The role of the biblical narrator varies according to the development. In thematic development there is selection and arrangement of material along with direct editorial comment on the meaning of the events. The theme is to be construed from the editorial comments; the stories illustrate and develop the theme. In plot development, the author's role involves selecting the stories to be told, arranging the stories, and crafting each conflict as related to the unifying conflict and its resolution.

The biblical narrator, unlike the latter prophets who speak directly for themselves and God, speaks in anonymity in order to assume for the scope of his narrative a godlike comprehensiveness of knowledge that can encompass even God himself. Robert Alter writes,

> The narrators of the biblical stories are of course "omniscient," and that theological term transferred to narrative technique has special justification in their case, for the biblical narrator is presumed to know, quite literally, what God knows, as on occasion he may remind us by reporting God's assessments and intentions, or even what He says to Himself.[40]

This is a profound yet implicit testimony to the prophetic authorship of biblical narratives. The early prophets write with the authority of God, yet speak through the events and characters among whom God is at work.

At the level of the Bible as a whole, we will next consider the plot structure in terms of the theological themes of progressive revelation. These themes frame the essential conflict and reflect the relationship of each individual book to the conflict resolution for the whole Bible.

3. The art of biblical narrative. Alter discusses the unique application of techniques that are combined in the crafting of biblical stories. Having a knowledge of these techniques in exegesis will help in understanding the intended implications.

a. The technique of repetition has traditionally been used by critical scholars as evidence for multiple textual sources. Alter rejects this assumption and advances positions that rest on the *theology of causality.* One aspect of the story is to reflect *historical causality.* Narrative accounts, which are writ-

---

[40] Alter, *The Art of Biblical Narrative,* 157.

ten in the context of commands or promises of God, repeat these statements in some form to communicate fulfillment. The other aspect reflects a *linguistic causality.*

All these varied instances of artful repetition reflect in different ways an underlying assumption of biblical narrative. . . . Again and again, we become aware of *the power of words to make things happen.* God or one of His intermediaries or a purely human authority speaks: man may repeat and fulfill the words of revelation, repeat and delete, repeat and transform, but always there is the original urgent message to contend with, a message which in the potency of its concrete verbal formulation does not allow itself to be forgotten or ignored.[41]

b. The technique of dialogue appears in a narrative so as to slow down the tempo enough for us to discriminate a scene with the illusion of being present as it unfolds. This strategy is combined with narrative summary and exposition in telling the story of what happened. Alter argues that narrative dialogue is the preferred form of narrative development. It is preferred because of a *theology of language.* In the recording of a character's thoughts, the author composes a monologue. It represents an author's interpretation of how the mind relates to reality and how a character contemplates the specific possibilities of choice. Whereas attitudes of love, hate, or anger may be recorded as a narrative summary or exposition, the thoughtful consideration of choice is tied to language. It implies that willed choice is not a choice until the language is articulated.

Spoken language is the substratum of everything human and divine that transpires in the Bible, and the Hebrew tendency to transpose what is preverbal

or nonverbal into speech is finally a technique for getting at the essence of things, for obtruding their substratum.[42]

c. The art of reticence in characterization is an important consideration in exegesis. The exegete must come to grips with the economy of the account.

Biblical narrative offers us, after all, nothing in the way of minute analysis of motive or detailed rendering of mental processes; whatever indications may be vouchsafed of feeling, attitude, or intention are rather minimal; and we are given only the barest hints about the physical appearance, the tics and gestures, the dress and implements of the characters, the material milieu in which they enact their destinies.[43]

The exegete must treat the sparing use of detail to determine as many implications as intended, but no more. Again, the *theology of man* controls the outer limits of one's implications. The narrower limits are set in the form of characterization. Where the character is merely reported in their actions and appearance, very few implications are intended. The most trustworthy and wide-ranging conclusions rest in the narrator's explicit statement of what the character feels, intends, or desires.

In between these two extremes are two other general options. In the quotation of the direct speech of the character or others about him, the reader must weigh the claims in the context of the plot development. In the final case, the report of the inward speech (thought) of the character, we can be assured of his conscious intentions, but we may question his motives in view of the overall plot. Thus, in spite of the biblical reticence in detail, we can be sensitive toward the artful expression as a guide to the exegesis of implications.

---

[41]Ibid., 112.
[42]Ibid., 70.
[43]Ibid, 114.

Parabolic Literature

Parables are narrative sermons based on an interpretation of a historic issue that confronts the hearers concerning the issue. The narrative is developed through an analogy that resolves the issue in the related realms and must be related back to the historic issue.

1. The narrative structure in an analogy. Leland Ryken identifies the parables of Jesus within the literary family known as allegory.[44] The mention of allegory immediately causes concern to the biblical scholar. Adolf Jülicher in his *History of the Interpretation of the Parables of Jesus* had freed parabolic interpretation from the distortions of allegorical interpretation.[45] However, there is a distinction that must be drawn between allegorical literature and allegorical interpretation.

Allegorical literature is a form of indirect commentary about the realm of history. Unlike historical literature, it does not talk directly about actual historical events in the realm of reference. Rather, it comments on a historical situation indirectly. Allegory as a family of literature is unified by its design of indirect commentary. The different types within the family are distinguished by the form of commentary.

One kind of commentary is a story or image whose detailed characters and plot development of events comment on and relate many details to the realm of history. John Bunyan's *Pilgrim's Progress* is expressed in this form, as is the apostle Paul's allegory in Galatians 4:24–31. In both, the details represent in a studied fashion a corresponding set of concepts in the historical realm of reference. The parables of the soils (Matt. 13 et al.), shepherd and sheep, woman and coins, and father and sons (Luke 15) represent this kind.

The other kind of commentary is a story or image related to the realm of history in only one point. The kingdom parables (Matthew 13:24–50) and the short, pointed parables of discipleship (Luke 14:28–35) are of this kind.

Between these boundary cases we find all the other parables. In any case, whatever the kind of commentary, the allegorical literature expresses a single message, as Jülicher contended.

2. The sermon form. A. T. Cadoux laid down the principle that the characteristic feature of the parables was Jesus' response to life—his commentary on life.

> In its most characteristic use the parable is a weapon of controversy, not shaped like a sonnet in undisputed concentration, but improvised to meet the unpremeditated situation.[46]

With a similar emphasis, Joachim Jeremias explains their design to respond to and comment on the immediate historical situation:

> It is that the parables of Jesus are not—at any rate primarily—literary productions, nor is it their object to lay down general maxims—but each of them was uttered in an actual situation of the life of Jesus, at a particular and often unforeseen point. . . . They correct, reprove, and attack. For the greater part, though not exclusively, the parables are weapons of warfare. Every one of them calls for immediate response.[47]

3. The fictional intent. The commentary included in the parable may be

---

[44] Ryken, *The Literature of the Bible* (Grand Rapids: Zondervan, 1974), 301.

[45] Adolf Jülicher, *Die Gleichnisreden Jesu* (Tübingen, 1899), 1:203–322.

[46] A. T. Cadoux, *The Parables of Jesus: Their Art and Use* (London: James Clarke, 1930), 13.

[47] Joachim Jeremias, *The Parables of Jesus* (New York: Scribner's, 1962), 21.

fictional[48] narrative in which the details are vivid and realistic, but do not have a particular historical reference. So to interpret the parable does not involve seeking to identify the historical reference. Rather, the interpreter looks for the analogy between the historical issue or subject and the truth expressed in the parable. The gospel writer frequently identifies that historical issue. While not all the details of the parable have historical referents, they all contribute to the development of the unifying sense. Thus all details are important and must be considered, but they are not all intended to refer to the historical realm. This is allegorical literature.

4. Allegorical interpretation. Allegorical interpretation is a related but distinct matter. Here, rather than allowing the message to determine the realm of reference, the interpreter seeks to find in the details of the parable as many points of correspondence in history without any control by the message. This, of course, is an invalid approach to interpretation of meaning. However, in allegorical types of literature the author may well intend the detailed images to have many points of correspondence. So in the parable of the soils, the seed, the sower, the soil conditions, the weeds, the birds, and the fruit all have points of correspondence. But these are still determined by the message as expressed in Jesus' interpretation. The message likewise distinguishes other particulars from having any direct correspondence, as may be illustrated by who trampled the seed, by what happens to birds who eat the seed, by moisture, sun, or the differing degrees of return.

Epistolary Literature

The letters of the New Testament are ancient and cultural in form, but used in the unique functions of the early church. The early study of Adolf Deissmann focused on there being the "true letters" of the nonliterary papyri.[49] By this he meant that they were letters arising from a specific situation and intended only for the eye of the person or persons to whom they were addressed and not for the public at large. George Milligan recognized that their tone of authority and general subject matter spoke to the church as missionary or pastoral letters.[50]

1. Form of the letter. All the New Testament epistles follow a basic form shared with the ancient world. They come closest to the standard form of nonliterary "true letters."

a. An introduction, prescript, or salutation, which included the name of the addressee, greetings, and often a wish for good health.

b. The body or text of the letter, introduced by characteristic formulae.

c. A conclusion, including greetings to persons other than the addressee, a final greeting or prayer sentence, and sometimes a date.

2. Function of the letter. Richard Longenecker has recognized this as a distinctive feature of the New Testament epistle and as being shaped by two distinct functions.[51]

One function is similar to letters the Talmud speaks of as pastoral letters. In these, rabbinic authorities responded to

---

[48] For this reason, many commentators do not regard the story of the rich man and Lazarus (Luke 16:19–31) as a parable. The text does not indicate that it is a parable.

[49] Adolf Deissmann, *Light From the Ancient East,* trans. L. R. M. Strachan (London: Hodder and Stoughton, 1909).

[50] George Milligan, *The New Testament Documents, Their Origin and Early History* (London: Macmillan, 1913).

[51] Longenecker, "Form, Function and Authority," 101-111.

questions from Jews outside Israel and gave counsel. The books of 1 and 2 Corinthians, Galatians, Philippians, Colossians, Philemon, 1 and 2 Thessalonians, 1 and 2 Timothy, and Titus share the structure, idioms, contents, and tone of pastoral letters.

The other function is less influenced by circumstances and is more interested in a systematic development of the message. This function is a tractate or essay-type letter: Romans, Ephesians, Hebrews, James, 1 Peter, and 1 John.

3. Authority of the letter. Longenecker writes,

> For pastoral letters, a past relationship and present authority were highlighted while in letters of a more public or official kind, "presence" conveyed authority; and for the tractate or essay-type letters, the conversational dialogue of spoken instruction was continued.[52]

In any case, the authority resided in Christian apostles, to whom was given the right to teach and govern the church of God. Such a sense of authority and presence did not rule out the role of an amanuensis or even exclude anonymity in view of the treatment of the subject matter. But it does exclude pseudonymity. Writings that claim divine authority and purport to teach truth make pseudonymity an incompatible practice no matter what the supposed literary convention.[53]

Wisdom Literature

Wisdom literature is a mature and divinely accepted interpretation of the choices in life that are expressed in a variety of poetic forms. The shear variety of forms—including one-line aphorisms (proverbs), wisdom poems, wisdom narrative and dramatic dialogues (Job), and human love poetry (Song of Songs)—makes it difficult in a brief scope to offer any comprehensive direction in exegesis. Therefore the issues addressed will be even more selective.

1. Didactic saying. One-line proverbs intended to teach may be divided into three categories of formulation. The first two are closely related in intent but take different forms. The first is formed on the principle of *antithesis,* the second on the principle of *equivalence or elaboration* between versets. In either case, many proverbs prove to be narrative vignettes in which some minimally etched plot enacts the consequences of a moral principle.

While this happens more frequently in lines based on equivalence, it is possible for either form to exploit an underlying principle. In the case of equivalence it represents the working out of process, a course of moral consequentiality. The imagery of figurative language in such proverbs builds on familiarity. They "typically seek to convey the sort of truth that will seem perfectly 'natural' and virtually self-evident once it is well expressed."[54] In addition, the two lines of the verse may be based on intensification through a startling or vivid instance.

Bruce Waltke raises the particular problem of content involving the Lord.[55] While precepts disclose the writer's aim in the statement of a command, didactic sayings are merely a description of what is, without any comment on aim. The question is raised concerning what kind of action this description signifies. One example is Proverbs 16:1: "To man belong the plans of the heart, but from the LORD

---

[52] Ibid., 102.
[53] Ibid., 110–11.
[54] Alter, *The Art of Biblical Poetry,* 171.
[55] Bruce K. Waltke, "Grammatical Problems," in *Hermeneutics, Inerrancy and the Bible,* ed. Earl D. Radmacher and Robert D. Preus (Grand Rapids: Zondervan, 1984), 113.

comes the reply of the tongue." Does this imply that preparation should not be undertaken? Or does it imply that one should speak ultimately depending on the Lord? Waltke concludes that "the didactic saying must be interpreted by other more clear sayings."[56] The content of other proverbs that address preparation must be considered before one can properly assess the aim of individual didactic proverbs.

The third category of form is the *riddle*, in which the first verset is a syntactically incomplete or baffling statement that is explained through the second verset.[57] The baffling statement may include some perplexing, startling, or seemingly contradictory statement or image in which our attention is arrested before the tension is resolved. A shocking and illogical metaphor is first stated almost as a riddle: "A gold ring in a pig's snout" (Prov. 11:22a). That sense of shocking incongruity then carries over to the point of the riddle, making us all see with a new sharpness the contradiction of beauty in a senseless woman (11:22b).

2. Truth and wisdom narrative. The ending of the book of Job has troubled readers over the centuries. The doubling of lost property and the simple replacement of lost lives seem alien to later sensibilities. Others have seemed rather exasperated by the answers to Job's anguished questions. Questions of historicity and truthfulness plague the reader of the book.

It must be recognized that the poetic form and patterned structure leave many unanswered questions for someone attempting to deal with historicity. The message could well have been expressed in an imagined world and experience. Yet the text includes clues related to actual history, which are unnecessary if not misleading for an imagined world. The personal names imply actual people, and the geographical names of Uz (connected with Edom, cf. Lam. 4:21) and Teman (generally agreed as the place of that name in Edom) imply an actual location in eastern Edom and northern Arabia. In addition, historical experience adds to the reality of the heavenly debate and the actual divine revelation. A combination of fiction and historical reality without any clues to distinguish between the two makes it impossible for a reader to discern whether heavenly events are real or fictional, since a human reader has no immediate access to heaven to verify their reality.

The truthfulness of what is said and the answers that are given raise issues that go beyond the book's historicity. It lies outside the scope of human verification and beyond the presumed right of man to know. That may well account for the exasperation of the reader who expects an answer to the questions of justice. Yet, if the reader concedes that the answer may well be a probing of man's limits to know and to trust God and God's right to act on issues that are righteous even though outside of human experience, then truth about these limits and God's rights becomes very evident.

THEOLOGICAL THEMES

Theological themes affirms that the textually based type of meanings includes the influence of themes in the progress of revelation that contributes to the meaning of vocabulary referring to the supernatural, which informs the content of passages in the consideration of prior revelation, and which anticipates the full expression of the

[56] Ibid., 114.
[57] Ibid, 169.

content in subsequent allusions or references.

Along with the conventions included in the textual design, the theological themes are related to the conventions of biblical discourse. Ordinarily conventional implications define the "common ground" of discourse. Karttunen and Peters call them "the set of propositions that any participant is rationally justified in taking for granted."[58] In other words, conventional implications are not based on literary forms alone, but also on the content established as part of the context of the discourse.

In biblical revelation these sets of propositions include theological themes that may be assumed to be included in the revelation. Each book in the canon will include some revelation of God, the Author and participant in the actions and words of Scripture, a revelation of his purposes for acting and speaking as progressively unfolded in history and of his administration of these purposes with his people. These conventional themes decidedly influence the use of language and its intended sphere of reference. What follows is a brief examination of the use of language in the theological context of the Bible.

The Revelation of God

The biblical vocabulary for God, angels, the Evil One, and evil angels is particularly interesting since it is central to biblical revelation. One is immediately struck by the distinctiveness of the revelation of God. The Semitic peoples of the ancient world share to some extent a common vocabulary for talking about God. Frank Cross comments on the distinction:

One cannot describe El as sky-god like Anu, a storm-god like Enlil or Zeus, a chthonic god like Nergal, or a grain-god like Dagon. The one image of El that seems to tie all his myths together is that of the patriarch. He is the primordial father of gods and men, sometimes stern, often compassionate, always wise in judgment. . . . El is rarely, if ever, used in the Bible as a proper name of a non-Israelite, Canaanite deity in the full consciousness of a distinction between El and Yahweh, god of Israel.[59]

Instead El is used as a divine proper name of the God of Israel. Othmar Keel proposed to show the shared imagery in the iconography of the Ancient Near East. Yet he conceded the complete distinctiveness of the concept of God.

The ancient Near Eastern iconography of temple, king, and cultus bear a remarkable close relation to corresponding statements in the psalms. The situation is entirely different, however, in the present chapter. . . . Israel brought with it from the desert experiences . . . conceptions of God which could not be easily harmonized with the various conceptions of God prevalent in the new environment.[60]

God was exclusive and inaccessible except through the revelation of himself starting in Moses' experience. God was One, the only true God. It was in the context of these affirmations about God and his uniqueness that Israel incorporated the expressions of their world. In view of their concept of God, any shared cultural images or vocabulary of the supernatural world must first of all be defined in distinction from other cultural usages.

The distinctiveness of the biblical revelation of God is further found in the use of the term *'elohim*. While the term *'el* occurs in other Semitic languages,

---

[58] L. Karttunen and S. Peters, "Conventional Implicature in Montague Grammar," First Annual Meeting of the Berkeley Linguistic Society (15 February 1975): 3.

[59] Frank Cross, "'el," in *Theological Dictionary of the Old Testament*, 4 vols., ed. G. Johannes Botterweck and Helmer Ringgren (Grand Rapids: Eerdmans, 1978), 1:253.

[60] Othmar Keel, *The Symbolism of the Biblical World* (New York: Seabury, 1978), 178.

'elohim does not, not even in Aramaic.[61] Therefore its plural form is likely to have a biblical basis. Rather than finding this reason in the use being a plural of majesty, as there is a tendency in the Ancient Near East toward a universalism,[62] the Scripture itself provides a better reason. In the very first use in Genesis, a term is chosen that nicely conveys both the unity of the one God and yet allows for a plurality of persons. This term is used in the general sense of deity some 2,570 times in Scripture, yet it is difficult to detect any discrepancy in use between the forms *'el, 'eloah,* and *'elohim.*[63]

By contrast, in the development of the revelation of an evil one, allusion to mythological figures is common. G. B. Caird deems this of central importance: "The thesis which I shall propound . . . is that myth and eschatology are used in the Old and New Testaments as metaphor systems for the theological interpretation of historical events."[64] Caird is quick to disassociate himself from Bultmann, who would propose that mythology is the theological use of metaphor. "Since all theological language is metaphorical, his critics justifiably retorted that demythologizing would on his definition reduce theology to silence," Caird writes.[65] In distinction to this, Caird would use "myth" in a literary sense.

When I use *myth, mythical* . . . I refer to the universal instinct of any human group, large or small, to invest, almost unconsciously, certain stories or events or places or persons, real or fictional, with an uncommon significance. . . . It tells a story about the past, but only in order to say something about the present and the future. It has a literal referent in the characters and events of the vehicle story, but its tenor referent is the situation of the user and his audience.[66]

Caird would then argue that when the biblical writers refer to the power of the Evil One as Leviathan or Rehab, they are metaphorically alluding to the myths of the Ancient Near East in the creation story. Other writers also suggest this. Theodor Gaster comments on the prophets' use of mythology:

The prophets, too, employ the ancient myths in a special way. The primary function of an Old Testament prophet was to trace and expound the continuing plan and purpose of God in passing events. This involved recognizing characteristic traits of his operations, and to do so the prophets drew upon *mythological* as well as historical precedents. Thus, the defeat of Israel's enemies and oppressors could be regarded as a repetition, on the stage of events, of his mythological discomfiture of the primeval Dragon.[67]

Waltke makes a more careful distinction than Caird or Gaster in one case.

Now that we have established that Leviathan is a dragon resisting creation in the Canaanite mythology, we must raise the hermeneutical question whether the inspired poets of Israel meant that Yahweh actually had a combat with this hideous creature or whether this Canaanite story

---

[61] Gustav F. Oehler, *Theology of the Old Testament* (reprint, Minneapolis: Klock & Klock, 1978), 88.

[62] William F. Albright, *From the Stone Age to Christianity,* 2d ed. (Garden City, N.Y.: Doubleday, 1957), 213.

[63] Marvin H. Pope, *El in the Ugaritic Texts* (Leiden: Brill, 1955), 10.

[64] Caird, *The Language and Imagery of the Bible,* 219.

[65] Ibid.

[66] Ibid., 223–24.

[67] Theodor H. Gaster, *Myth, Legend, and Custom in the Old Testament* (New York: Harper & Row, 1975), 1:xxv.

served as a helpful metaphor to describe Yahweh's creative activity.[68]

He goes on to specify:

It is inconceivable that these strict monotheists intended to support their view from pagan mythology, which they undoubtedly detested and abominated, unless they were sure that their hearers would understand their allusions were used in a purely figurative sense.[69]

Ronald Allen specifies this figurative sense more clearly: "It is felt, then, that the use of the Leviathan-Tannin-Rahan motif in the Old Testament is emblematic. Yet it is emblematic of something, of a corresponding reality. Just saying that the motif is symbolic does not complete the picture.[70]

What, then, is the corresponding reality? E. J. Young explained the reality as the nations that are enemies of the Lord.

The similarity of language between Ugarit and Isaiah's text shows a very definite relationship, but how is this relationship to be explained? As in Ugarite, so also here, Leviathan is an imaginary being; but it does not follow here that in Isaiah God is represented as fighting against a mythical monster. Isaiah rather is merely employing these terms as descriptive figures of speech to refer to certain nations which are enemies of the Lord.[71]

Allen has gone even further and has accounted for more of the textual detail than Young.

The Ancient Hebrews, under the discerning hand of inspiration, occasionally adapted mythopoetic imagery for literary effect without concomitant mythopoetic ideas from their cultural milieu. One of the most graphic adaptations is that of draconic conflict, which, when used in an emblematic fashion, was a vehicle for the expression of veiled Satanology in the Old Testament. Further, there may be more than just adaptation in this motif. The universal serpentine imagery may well be explained, similarly as the universal stories of the flood, in terms of the memory of ancient people which ultimately derived from the primal encounter with the serpent in the Garden. In this case, more than just imagery is involved: The Bible is presenting the accurate account of which the parallels in the ancient world are merely corrupted derivations.

This imagery is often reflective of the exodus, but the Exodus does not exhaust the motif. The motif is seen in its full intensity when it is regarded as emblematic of Satan.[72]

These metaphorical uses of pagan terminology introduce a polemic implication.

Not Baal of the Canaanites, not Marduk of the Babylonians, not Pharaoh of Egypt, but Yahweh, God of Israel, author of Torah, triumphs. As the Creator of the cosmos, He triumphed prior to the creation, as Creator of history He triumphs in the historic present, and as Creator of the new heavens and the new earth He will triumph in the future.[73]

God's Purposes

The primary role of a biblical theology in exegesis focuses on the progress of revelation. The components of a given passage that contains descriptions of God's actions or records of God's words are defined within the type of meaning of that context. That definition

---

[68] Bruce K. Waltke, *Creation and Chaos* (Portland: Western Conservative Baptist Seminary, 1974), 13.

[69] Ibid., 14.

[70] Ronald B. Allen, "The Leviathan-Rahab-Dragon Motif in the Old Testament" (Master's thesis, Dallas Theological Seminary, 1968), 65.

[71] Edward J. Young, *The Book of Isaiah* (Grand Rapids: Eerdmans, 1969), 2:234.

[72] Allen, "The Leviathan-Rahab-Dragon Motif in the Old Testament," 89.

[73] Waltke, *Creation and Chaos,* 15.

is the task of *contextual exegesis*. Other implications of that defined meaning may be added in the progress of revelation. These implications enrich our understanding of the meaning defined, without changing the meaning as defined or replacing the meaning so expressed. This enriching of the meaning is the task of *theological exegesis*.

The relationships between passages in the progress of revelation may be recognized through the repetition of key-words, motifs in images or plots, themes, actions, or episodes. These related textual elements are understood in relation to common theological purposes. All the textual elements combine to express components of one or more of three repetitive and progressively unfolding purposes: judgment of evil, deliverance from the evil of the elect, and blessing of the delivered in righteousness. It is in the progressive revelation of the purpose that the textual elements are related. So when a term is used that expresses a component of a theme, any prior biblical revelation which also speaks to the same component of the theme may *inform* our understanding of the term. Such informing may define a term not defined in the immediate context, but it does not change the essential definition of the term contextually understood. In either case, it does enrich our understanding.

As an example, Abel's death at the hand of Cain is informed by God's pronouncement of the conflict between the seed of the woman and the seed of the serpent (Gen. 3:15). Abel is the seed of the woman. Cain is the seed of the serpent, as God had warned him that sin desired to master him (4:6–7). Abel was killed and did not fulfill God's pronouncement, and thus an expectation is created for another seed. That expectation is met in the birth of Seth (4:25–26). Similarly, the account of Noah is informed by Genesis 3:15, but Noah is delivered from God's judgment

of the evil generation through an ark. Noah does not do conflict with the evil seed and conquer, so his deliverance is not a final deliverance.

In addition to being informed by prior revelation, the meaning of the term may *anticipate* subsequent revelation. The subsequent revelation does not define the earlier textual expression, nor does it even inform the meaning. So the conquering seed of the woman (Gen. 3:15) does not mean Christ in the sense of a full and final revelation. It still means the seed of the woman who does conflict with the Evil One and conquers in spite of a wound. In that limited sense of anticipating Christ it means Christ. When the text of Genesis 3:15 is compared with subsequent revelation about Christ, there is a match in the limited sense of Genesis 3:15. This match appears again in the theological theme of deliverance from judgment of the elect seed.

One of the difficulties encountered in biblical exegesis involves exegeting passages where the anticipation is not clear. One instance in the Old Testament is Psalm 16, in which David evidently speaks of his own hope in the future. A complication arises in the apostle Peter's quoting the psalm in his Pentecost sermon (Acts 2:25ff.). He says David spoke as a prophet and he referred to Christ's resurrection. Since we believe, based on our view of Scripture, that any New Testament interpretation of an Old Testament passage is correct, if not complete, our only question is whether David means more than Christ? In passages like this psalm that anticipate a future event, we have the additional consideration of a divine as well as human author. Though it is impossible to distinguish the meanings which God meant from the ones David meant, we must consider the influence of divine intent in the expression of the textual meaning.

The theological theme involved in

Psalm 16 refers to God's anticipated blessing of the elect seed delivered from the judgment of death. That theological theme comprehends the particular message expressed in the psalm of the Old Testament text.

Walter Kaiser renders the defining message as "From such a fellowship and enjoyment of God comes . . . remarkable consequences."[74] Derek Kidner said that "the theme of having one's affections centered on God gives this psalm its unity and ardour . . . it sings of the chosen loyalty in verses 1–6, and the blessings that come to meet it in 7–11.[75] Both conceptions of the message of the passage are helpful. Any addition would simply be in clarity of wording.

My understanding of the type of message is "Rejoicing in God, who is his portion, brings his Holy One hope for resurrection." We will focus our discussion on the final portion of the message and will defend the sense "hope for resurrection." The type of meaning "hope" is expressed in these textual particulars:

"counsels me . . . instructs me" (v. 7)

"he is at my right hand, I will not be shaken" (v. 8)

"my body also will rest secure . . . you will not abandon . . . nor will you let" (vv. 9–10)

"you will fill me" (v. 11)

The type of meaning "for resurrection" is expressed in these textual particulars:

"my body . . . will rest secure" (v. 9)

"not abandon me to the grave" (v. 10)

"you will fill me with joy in your presence" (v. 11)

"made known to me the path of life . . . in your presence . . . at your right hand" (v. 11)

Thus the particulars in the text reflect a type of meaning that may be summarized: "hope for resurrection."

In Psalm 16:1–6 the personal pronouns most naturally refer to David, and the personal pronouns in verses 7–11 naturally continue to refer to David's hope in the future. Kidner comments on these implications of reference:

Admittedly some commentators see here no more than recovery from an illness (cf. Isa. 38:9–22); but the contrast in Psalm 49 and 73 between the end of the wicked and that of the righteous supports a bolder view. And at its full value, as both Peter and Paul insisted (Acts 2:29ff; 13:34–37), this language is too strong even for David's hope for his own resurrection.[76]

Walter Kaiser interprets the implications with a somewhat different sense. He writes, "David expects to arrive safely with his immaterial and material being in the presence of God."[77] In each case the implications of reference are determined by the interpreter's perception of the type of message in reference to David.

The exegesis of biblical prophecy and typology, however, introduces another future dimension of reference. The message that referred to David may also refer to Christ. It must be affirmed strongly that the enlarged context of progressive revelation does not change the defining sense of the original passage. Its textual defining sense remains determined and unchanged. Additional implications of reference often become evident to a human reader in the unfolding of revelation. Thus Kidner adds, "This language is too strong even for

[74] Walter Kaiser, "The Promise to David in Psalm 16 and Its Application in Acts 2:25–33 and 13:32–37," *Journal of the Evangelical Theological Society* 23 (September 1980): 223.
[75] Derek Kidner, *Psalms 1–72* (London: InterVarsity Press, 1973, 83.
[76] Ibid., 86.
[77] Kaiser, "The Promise to David in Psalm 16," 226–27.

David's hope of his own resurrection. Only he whom God raised up saw no corruption."[78] Does this reference to Christ change Kidner's understanding of there being one message? Kaiser states plainly that it should not.

> Therefore he rested secure in the confident hope that even death itself would not prevent him from enjoying the face-to-face fellowship with his Lord even beyond death, since that ultimate *hasid* would triumph over death. For David, this was *one word*.[79]

It is not clear how this was one word or one message. In reference to David, the sense is resurrection ("expects to arrive safely with his immaterial and material being") and eternal life ("enjoying the face-to-face fellowship"). In reference to Christ, the sense is simply resurrection ("ultimate triumph over death").

Kidner seems to suggest a change in sense. "Peter quoted this closing paragraph of the psalm, from the LXX, as a prophecy of the Messiah, for whom alone such words would be perfectly and literally true."[80] Does Kidner mean that in reference to Christ, the literal sense is true while in reference to David, perhaps a figurative or changed sense is true? Kaiser affirms that it is only one sense. But his exposition of this one sense is not clear. In reference to David, Kaiser writes of both resurrection and eternal life; in reference to Christ, he writes only of resurrection. In his Pentecost sermon Peter argued that David had not yet arisen but surely enjoyed eternal life. Thus, in the case of Psalm 16 it must be clarified how one sense is retained in reference to both David and Christ.

As has already been suggested, the defining sense of the passage is: "Rejoicing in God, who is his portion, brings his Holy One hope for resurrection." That sense does not change in the progress of revelation. In reference to David, God's holy one, it refers to resurrection; in reference to Christ, his Holy One, it refers to resurrection. While the sense of the psalm is one, some implications in reference to David and in reference to Christ are distinct.

When David affirmed that "I have set the LORD *always* before me" (16:8), it was true to a limited degree. In 1 Samuel 21:10–15 and 27:1–12, David took refuge with the Philistines, namely, with Achish of Gath. In 2 Samuel 11, David took Bathsheba. To the limited extent or degree that any sinful man can have allegiance to God, David could and did. But Messiah did without limit. Kidner recognizes this distinction,[81] but limited reference does not equal figurative reference with a change in semantic domain. Similarly, when "your Holy One" (Ps. 16:10) identifies both the author David and Christ, it refers to David in a limited degree. Whether the term is active ("one in whom God manifests his grace and favor") or passive ("one to whom God is loyal, gracious, or merciful"), it is unlimited in reference to Christ and limited in reference to David. This distinction in fullness of implications of reference is crucial to the development of the psalm.

It was these very limitations in accomplishing God's purposes through David (Ps. 16:5–6; Acts 13:36) that necessitated God's instructions and counsel (Ps. 16:7). This instruction and counsel enabled David to know and to speak as a prophet (Acts 2:30). As a prophet he anticipated his own death in spite of God's portion and lot (Ps. 16:8–10; Acts 2:30; cf. 2 Sam. 7). But God would make known to him, the holy

---

[78] Kidner, *Psalms 1–72,* 86.
[79] Kaiser, "The Promise to David in Psalm 16," 229 (emphasis added).
[80] Kidner, *Psalms 1–72,* 86.
[81] Ibid.

one, the way to life and blessing at his right hand (Ps. 16:11). In addition, David's hope included the knowledge of the fully Holy One or Favored One. This knowledge came by prophetic instruction (Ps. 16:7). David's personal hope was limited in comparison to this One who would fully inherit God's favor. In a limited reference, David would not be abandoned to the grave; to a limited extent, he would not see decay. David would not remain in the grave eternally; he would not see decay eternally. Moreover, as a prophet he also saw the One who would experience the full extent of resurrection. In the one statement there were two references. The full sense of the language refers to Christ, and in some limited but corresponding sense it also refers to David. It is accurate to say David's hope is a hope in Christ the Heir.

While David the prophet knew the truth clearly enough to write, it is doubtful that he knew the full implications in reference to Christ or even to himself. While he knew the fact conveyed in his words, the type of meaning "hope for resurrection" undoubtedly involved implications he was unaware of. In this way David was unaware of all that he was saying. This issue of limitations in the human author's awareness is crucial to biblical exegesis when we consider the progress of revelation.

Two kinds of authorial ignorance are possible.

1. Ignorance with regard to the subject matter. As David spoke of death—both his own and the Holy One—there was much about that subject beyond which he spoke. He did not necessarily know the historical means, the historical occasion, the full reason, or the time of death. Similarly, there were many details about the subject of resurrection

which even believers with a completed canon know, but which David undoubtedly did not know. The interpreter must not confuse his own greater knowledge of a subject with the interpretation of an author's meaning. This greater knowledge is not relevant to the exegesis of the passage. While there is a valid application of the "Canonical Process Approach to the Psalms" developed by Bruce Waltke,[82] the confusion between subject matter and the author's type of meaning must be kept clearly in mind. Waltke says that

> The Antiochian principle of allowing but one historical meaning that may carry with it typical significance, is an inadequate hermeneutical principle for the interpretation of the psalms. . . . By the canonical process approach I mean the recognition that the text's intention becomes deeper and clearer as the parameters of the canon were expanded.[83]

If Waltke abandons the one historical sense, he is in danger of failing to define the type of textual sense as historically expressed. Then when additional aspects of the subject matter are mentioned in the progress of revelation, it is possible that implications that are not anticipated may be read back into the Old Testament textual meaning. The scope of the Author's/author's intention must not be separated from the affirmations in the text. The fact that God knows every subject in all its possible relationships is not doubted by an evangelical. This knowledge clearly transcends any human author's knowledge of any subject. We must distinguish the progressive revelation of the subject matter and the further revelation of the meaning stated in the passage.

---

[82] Bruce K. Waltke, "A Canonical Process Approach to the Psalms," in *Tradition and Testament,* ed. John S. Feinberg and Paul D. Feinberg (Chicago: Moody Press, 1981), 3–18.
[83] Ibid., 7.

2. Ignorance with regard to the author's meaning itself. E. D. Hirsch addresses the obvious question:

How can an author mean something he did not mean? The answer to that question is simple. It is not possible to mean what one does not mean, though it is very possible to mean what one is not conscious of meaning. That is the entire issue in the argument based on authorial ignorance. That a man may not be conscious of all that he means is no more remarkable than that he may not be conscious of all that he does. There is a difference between meaning and consciousness of meaning, and since meaning is an affair of consciousness, one can say more precisely that there is a difference between consciousness and self-consciousness. Indeed, when an author's meaning is complicated, he cannot possibly at a given moment be paying attention to all its complexities.[84]

In regard to Scripture, the possibility of the human author's ignorance is very important. As already postulated, the human and divine authors share in the composition of the message of the text. This understanding of the message sponsored the writing of the text by the human author. God, however, in authoring the revelation not only originated the defining message and all the textual particulars through the human author, but at the same time was aware of all the implications and all possible references. It is possible that the human author did not share this knowledge, as Peter seems to assert in 1 Peter 1:10–12. Nor does this limitation allow for erroneous knowledge.

But the possibility of this kind of human ignorance is not recognized by Walter Kaiser. In regard to 1 Peter 1:10–12, he asserts:

Does this text teach that the writers of Scripture "wrote better than they knew"? Indeed it does not. On the contrary, it decisively affirms that the prophets spoke knowingly on five rather precise topics: (1) the Messiah, (2) His sufferings, (3) His glory, (4) the sequence of events . . . and (5) that the salvation announced in those pre-Christian days was not limited to the prophet's audiences, but it also included the readers of Peter's day.[85]

Kaiser then adds that the prophets "searched intently" without any success about the *time* when these things would take place. He concludes that

this passage does not teach that these men were curious and often ignorant of the exact meaning of what they wrote and predicted. Theirs was not a search for *meaning* of what they wrote; it was an inquiry into the *temporal* aspects of the *subject,* which went beyond what they wrote.[86]

If we grant Kaiser that the unknown meaning was simply a matter of time, then the issue is this: Does this type of meaning, "spoke of the grace that was to come to you," imply time? To answer the question it is necessary to examine specific passages, for Peter's statement only implies indefinite future time. It is true that numerous *promises* also do not specify or imply specific time. Even promises of imminent action do not imply a known time. Jesus affirmed that only the Father knew the time of the second advent (Acts 1:5–7). However, the *prediction* of Daniel 9:24–27 does specify the time of the "Coming Prince" in numerical terms. Thus Daniel, at least in this instance, wrote beyond what he knew.

The prophets themselves expected to

[84]E. D. Hirsch, Jr., *Validity in Interpretation* (New Haven: Yale University Press, 1967), 22.

[85]Walter C. Kaiser, "The Single Intent of Scripture," in *Evangelical Roots,* ed. Kenneth Kantzer (Nashville: Thomas Nelson, 1978), 125.

[86]Ibid., 126.

find a notation of time in the prophecies. This is an example of an implication of reference in what they said which they did not know. So it seems quite clear that the human writers knew accurately the defining sense of what they wrote. Had they lived at the time of Jesus Christ, they could identify Jesus as the Coming Prince based on the true sense of what they wrote. This is, in fact, what the gospel writers did in reference to numerous Old Testament prophecies. But they were limited in the fullness of their knowledge to the type of meaning that they spoke. God, who spoke in the prophets, did not share such a limit in knowledge.

What we are saying, therefore, is that the *author's intention* expresses a *single, defining textual meaning of the whole*. The single meaning is capable of implying a richer sense and a fullness of reference. This is not *sensius plenior* (i.e., many unrelated or contradictory senses) but *sense singular* as related senses expressed or implied in the affirmations of text. Yet it also recognizes the possible characteristic of *references plenior* (many related references). This is the case with Psalm 16 as explained by A. Vaccari: "The words of verse 10 apply to both David and Christ in their proper sense yet in a fuller sense to Christ who rose from the dead, while David's body knew corruption but will not be subject to *eternal* corruption."[87]

S. Lewis Johnson affirms this conclusion: "We should not be surprised that the authorial will of God goes beyond the human authorial will."[88] And J. I. Packer agrees, albeit with a qualification:

God's meaning and message through each passage, when set in its total biblical context, exceeds what the human writer had in mind. . . . the *sensius plenior* which texts acquire in their wider biblical context remains an extrapolation on the grammatico-historical plane.[89]

While both Johnson and Packer recognize the need to keep the historical-grammatical premise under control, they also concede that divine implications of meaning may transcend the historical setting. The solution we propose is to consider the progressive revelation of the purposes of God as the additional context in which the full implications are exegeted.

The Administration of God's Purposes

Another aspect of the common ground of Scripture is that any passage of Scripture implies something about God's administration of his purposes at that time in history. When that same portion is read and understood in a later period of administration of his purposes, the question is raised, How is that portion to be read? Frequently readers of the legal literature are encouraged to read the law spiritually rather than as a legal code. A proper reading of the law at one time in history was as a legal code, but is this a proper exegesis for Gentiles living under gentile government and worshiping God in the church?

When the children of Israel read the law as a legal code, they read it as a unit. It was a composite legislation, providing direction for Israel as a nation and for Israelites individually. Moreover, ceremonial legislation offered forgiveness from the Lawgiver based on a

[87]Leopold Sabourin, S.J., *The Psalms* (New York: Alba House, 1970), 270.
[88]S. Lewis Johnson, Jr., *The Old Testament in the New* (Grand Rapids: Zondervan, 1980), 50.
[89]J. I. Packer, "Biblical Authority, Hermeneutics and Inerrancy," in *Jersualem and Athens,* ed. E. R. Geehan (Philadelphia: Presbyterian and Reformed, 1971), 147–48.

system of animal sacrifices. While the law was given through Moses, grace and truth came through Jesus Christ (John 1:17). After the coming of grace, the law no longer remained a legal code for the believer. Forgiveness thenceforth came through Christ. The believer today is responsible to the law of his land and to the truth revealed in Christ. However, the laws of the biblical text can be read and understood as they were intended and then applied in righteousness and justice. So although the code as a whole has been done away with as a code for a nation, the truth and righteousness continue to speak.

This sense of truth and righteousness is not different from its original sense. "Though the Lawgiver presented His commands absolutely and concretely, He intended them to be interpreted according to the Spirit of a personal relationship with God" (Deut. 6:5), Waltke writes.[90] So while the law forbade the Hebrews to marry Canaanites,

we find in the narrative of the book of Joshua that God approved the marriage with the Canaanite prostitute Rahab; and though the law excluded a Moabite from the congregation of Israel for ten generations, God smiled with favor on the faithful Moabitess, Ruth. Even as a national code, the law was administered by God on the basis of his relationship with individuals. This did not violate the righteousness and justice of the law, but admitted Gentiles who became believers who were otherwise cut off.

Today these legal distinctions of race and sex and economic status are done away with in Christ (Gal. 3:28). So the Old Testament is read in view of God's administration of blessing in the church. In Israel, God's blessing was mediated in the national structure under the law; in the church, God's blessing is administered in Christ through righteousness.

The discussion of exegetical premises will continue in the next chapter and deal with grammatical and historical.

[90]Waltke, "Grammatical Problems," in *Hermeneutics, Inerrancy and the Bible,* ed. Earl D. Radmacher and Robert D. Preus (Grand Rapids: Zondervan, 1984), 112.

CHAPTER 10

Hermeneutical Considerations of the Task of Exegesis—II

This chapter continues the discussion of the hermeneutical processes involved in the task of exegesis. Three premises have been dealt with: literal system, textual design, and theological themes. The two that remain are the grammatical and the historical.

GRAMMATICAL

Grammatical affirms that the textually based type of meaning has implications of sense that are consistent with the natural norms of language usage.

In considering the grammatical norm, various examples of usage will be examined to explore the implications of sense intended in each construction of the text. James Barr limits the literal interpretation to the sense directly stated, but we have argued that literal interpretation must be sensitive to the sense as it is stated in the text. Therefore we will devote our attention to the textual clues that lead us to conclude a wider range of textual senses. In any case, type-logic is to be used in determining the implications of the sense intended.

Then we will examine the different problems faced in each of the various senses. Two general obstacles to writ-

ten communication through language are present: (1) *vagueness* is an inescapable quality of language and a particular problem in written communication that does not have a specific historical context; and (2) *ambiguity* is a characteristic of speech in which a construction may bear more than one meaning and we are left in some doubt as to which meaning is intended.

While ambiguity involves the polysemy of language (multiple sense of the dictionary definitions of words and of the grammatical classification of constructions), there can also be a deliberate exploitation of multiple yet related meanings. The obstacles of vagueness and ambiguity are complicated in biblical hermeneutics by Semitic idioms that are common to Hebrew and even biblical Greek but foreign to the intuitive thought of a modern Western reader. An idiom is a normal usage to the native speakers of the language. Among the possible forms of expression, one is regarded as "normal usage," and this is the idiomatic way of saying it.

Many idioms are merely matters of style (use of verbs and tenses, use of adjectives, particles, etc.), but some are more closely related to thought. G. B. Caird focuses attention on two—hyperbole and absoluteness, and parataxis—which have a far-reaching influence on the interpretation of implications.

As stated earlier, type-logic governs the analysis and exegesis of the grammatical sense. The textual clues are involved in the textual constructions to be exegeted. The various senses to be considered result from type-logic.

Casual Sense

In a linguistic analysis of reading, the casual sense is the most common type of interpretation among inexperienced readers. In this, the textual sense is made to match the historical object. When asked what a word means, the reader will point to an object. That object is what the word means.

This approach to interpretation runs contrary to the premises of exegesis and type-logic. Yet at times the author uses a term in a technical sense. No matter what context or what occasion, it is always used to refer to a given and shared referent. It is a "technical term" in the author's vocabulary. So Paul uses "man of lawlessness" (2 Thess. 2:3) and Joel uses "the northern" (Joel 2:20) as technical terms with fixed referents. This is reflected in the author's message and enables the reader to increase his understanding by further examination of the referent.

But this is not a normal phenomenon. Authors commonly use terms differently in a variety of contexts. Care must be taken not to associate such fixed meaning with literal use or even with an author's usage. This approach often reflects a lack of linguistic awareness to the textual clues.

Direct Sense

In the context of the author's message, a direct sense of a textual construction follows directly as an expression and development of the message. Also, the sense directly matches and adequately expresses the historical referent, the author's emotive expression or volitional command. In spite of the general clarity in many instances of the direct sense, the vagueness of language and the ambiguity of expression may still raise problems.

1. The vagueness of generalization. General terms are less precise than particular ones: "tree" is less precise than "maple," "craftsman" than "potter," "weapon" than "spear," "sin" than "covetousness." Yet general terms are indispensable to organizing and relating our experiences. It is not true that the Hebrew language is deficient of general terms, but biblical style commonly avoids overgeneralization. Narrative style features the particulars of stories and accounts. Proverbial literature includes moral instruction, but it also has teaching by instance and illustration (Prov. 6:16–19). Poetry exploits the imagery of the particular (Ps. 22:6–8, 12–18; Isa. 11:6–8). The legal codes have at their core a body of case law (Ex. 22:1–23:19) involving the use of synecdoche.

By contrast, a desire for greater preciseness may be an attempt to avoid what is already known in general. This was the case of the lawyer who came to Jesus and wanted him to define "neighbor" with greater precision. In the parable of the good Samaritan, Jesus showed his listeners that the lawyer knew enough to identify a neighbor, but was simply unwilling to follow what he knew (Luke 10:25–37).

2. The vagueness of abstractions. Caird identifies the vagueness of abstractions as a problem of indeterminate meaning. "Some abstract terms are of such a high degree of generality that on close scrutiny they are found to have no clearly defined referent."[1] This seems to be the problem Paul referred to in speaking of "quarreling about words" (2 Tim. 2:14). Such constructions in other contexts and on other occasions had conveyed clear meanings, but now they were used polemically or carelessly as slogans and had lost any clear referent. Besides these, there are many important abstract terms in the New Testament such as "love," "truth," "knowledge," or "righteousness" for which the content is unclear. John's and Paul's epistles are particularly problematic in the use of abstract terms. Thus careful lexical studies of the semantic field and contextual studies of type-logic will help to clarify the sense.

3. The ambiguity of polysemy of language. The value of type-logic again appears clearly when the lexical and syntactical properties of language are unable to resolve ambiguities of usage. The faulty expectation of numerous students is that learning the biblical languages will eliminate this ambiguity. Though biblical languages may recast the range of ambiguities in their original form, they do not eliminate them. One example is the verb "to be," which in English, Greek, and Latin may be used either in statements of existence or, in Hebrew, as a copula. In each of these languages, statements with the copula remain ambiguous unless we know the contextual message:

If the subject is "the law's condition," then "Is the law sin?" (Rom. 7:7) has the sense of identity; or

If the subject is "Jesus' person," then "no one *is* good except God alone" (Mark 10:18) has the sense of attribute; or

If the subject is "the work of the flesh," then "the mind of sinful man is death" (Rom. 8:6) has the sense of cause or sequence; or

If the subject is "the expression of a human tongue," then "the tongue also is a fire" (James 3:6) has the sense of resemblance or equivalence.

In each case, the ambiguity is the result of the polysemy of linguistic forms used in inexplicit fashion. The exegetical use of type-logic can clarify the ambiguity and specify the intended sense.

4. The ambiguity of functional use. Further ambiguities arise out of the use to which words and constructions are put by an author. Again, type-logic provides the basis in the context for resolving the ambiguity even though the language itself does not appear clear. While no functional ambiguity exists in biblical books as a whole, examples do exist within narratives or arguments in the epistles. Caird lists five, but some are clearly resolved in context.[2]

a. Oracular ambiguity: The face value of Joseph's words to the butler and the baker appear to be directly stated: "within three days shall Pharaoh lift up thy head" (Gen. 40:13, 19, KJV). Yet there is ambiguity in the term "lift up"—which means "restore" for the butler and "removal" for the baker. Caird is clearly in error to suggest that Joseph allowed the ambiguity to remain, for Joseph specifies the sense in context that removes any ambiguity: "restore you to your position" (v. 13) and "hang you on a tree" (v. 19). So while such ambiguity may well be present in other literature, Caird has not proven a case in Scripture.

b. Ironic ambiguity: The words of Caiaphas are an example of dramatic irony: "You do not realize that it is better for you that one man die for the people than that the whole nation per-

[1] G. B. Caird, *The Language and Imagery of the Bible* (Philadelphia: Westminster, 1984), 92.
[2] Ibid., 103–8.

ish" (John 11:50). Such dramatic irony assumes a double audience. Caiaphas assumed the one Jewish audience in which the subject was understood to be "a Roman invasion of Jerusalem." John, by contrast, saw Caiaphas in the position of the high priest and realized that God intended to speak to another audience to whom John's gospel spoke. This audience understood the subject to be "the wrath of God upon sin."

John's gospel keeps two audiences in mind throughout: the historical audience who rejected Jesus, and John's audience for whom he wrote to accept Jesus as the Christ (John 20:31). So "dramatic irony is one of the most prominent stylistic features of the Fourth Gospel."[3] John regularly considers Jesus' words and works both as natural and as supernatural phenomena.

John also develops Jesus' explanation of the meaning of the feeding of the five thousand. As a natural phenomenon, it is understood as "the feeding and satisfying of man's hunger" (see 6:22–27). Jesus presses the audience and the readers of the Gospel to understand this as "a heavenly provision"—which involves both "the bread" and "the Giver of the bread." Men are invited to believe in the One whom heaven gives (6:29) to be the source of heaven's gifts for men (6:35–40).

Such ironic ambiguity may appear to support two meanings in the text. In fact, it does not; rather, it supports two understandings by two different audiences. One audience understands the message only in natural terms, which is inadequate. Both Jesus and John develop the supernatural and spiritual aspects of the meaning that must be considered to understand the message correctly. So there is an ambiguity, but this is not a barrier to the communication of an interpretation of Jesus' actual message. Instead, the use of dramatic irony adds to the force with which the message is communicated.

c. Parabolic ambiguity: The parables of Jesus are a similar type of communication. On the surface the words seem to be intended to be read in a direct sense. Yet one audience sees them as absurd, and a believing audience hears them in terms of Jesus' intended subject. The believing audience rejects the absurdity of the direct sense and searches for additional clues in Jesus' meaning (Mark 4:9–12).

In similar terms, Nathan's parable (2 Sam. 12:1–10) has an apparent ambiguity until the subject is accurately recognized. If the subject is "a wealthy landowner's behavior," as David at first understood, then the landowner deserved judgment. But in what Nathan added, the subject became "David's own taking of Bathsheba from Uriah." That clearly is the subject; no ambiguity remains once the analogy is recognized.

d. Exploratory ambiguity: Some authors use grammatical ambiguity to force readers to explore more fully the range of related components of sense. In 2 Corinthians 5:14 (KJV), the genitive "the love of Christ" is left unspecified in that it may mean either objectively "my love for Christ" or subjectively "Christ's love for me."

> Paul's argument is that love for Christ entails love for our fellows, so that the one cannot exist without the other; and that when we love our fellows, it is not merely we who love, but Christ who loves through us; so that all human love which is genuine is the indwelling of Christ.[4]

e. Associative ambiguity: In this form, the same words seemingly stated directly are associated in different senses to heighten the rhetorical force of the statement. Nathan's prophecy

---

[3] Ibid., 104.
[4] Ibid., 106.

concerning David's house (dynasty) and God's house (temple) in 2 Samuel 7:5–11 or Paul's explanation of the church as God's house (household, building, temple, dwelling) in Ephesians 2:19–22 are examples. In both instances, the contextual type of meaning clarifies the sense and leads to the rhetorical force.

f. Hyperbolic ambiguity: Numerous statements of Jesus illustrate absolute and unqualified statements that appear to be direct statement, but may involve hyperbole. Hyperbole is a common figure of speech that involves overstatement for emphasis. Examples of Jesus' words:

". . . does not hate his father and mother . . ." (Luke 14:26)

"No one can serve two masters. Either he will hate the one and love the other . . ." (Matt. 6:24)

"The man who loves his life will lose it, while the man who hates his life . . ." (John 12:25)

The ambiguity is resolved by establishing the subject about which Jesus is talking: "competitive desires" (Luke 14:26) or "commitment" (Matt. 6:24) or "surrender" (John 12:25). In the context of such a subject, the implications of force in overstatement become clear.

Different conclusions arise among interpreters because they disagree on the extent of the use of hyperbole in prophecy. Are statements of "cosmic collapse" to be taken in a hyperbolic sense or in a direct sense? Again, the ambiguity must be resolved in type-logic with the message of that context limiting the imagery.

g. Parataxis ambiguity: Parataxis is the placing of propositions or clauses one after another without indicating by connecting words the relationship between them. The opposite construction is hypotaxis, in which there is a main clause and subordinate clauses whose relationship is clearly indicated with a

connecting particle. In parataxis that relationship must be interpreted from clues in the type of meaning expressed in the context of both lines or broader. Type-logic is used here also.

This discussion has focused on the use of language that appears to be stated in a direct sense. Yet even in these cases we have seen that there may be vagueness and ambiguity in the apparent textual expression. The biblical illustrations have briefly demonstrated how these problems may be recognized and how the sense may be interpreted.

Indirect Sense

An indirect sense is recognized when the direct sense creates some tension with the conventions of textual design or theological themes. Then the interpreter must ask what additional implications are meant through the shared conventions. In such cases the relationship between what is said and what is meant is not directly stated. As an example, a teacher comments, "Someone is talking," and the child recognizes that the teacher is not merely describing a situation but is also requesting silence. The child recognizes this from the conversational maxim of "quantity." The teacher did not need to describe the situation in order to teach while she would desire to control the classroom. So the child asks how this statement helps to control the classroom. He recognizes that indirectly she is requesting silence.

In the same way, readers of biblical narrative recognize that more is being said than merely a report of what happened. Such a report would be either *redundant* (quantity), based on what they already know from oral tradition or other written sources (the books of Kings and Chronicles), or *irrelevant* as a word from a prophet of God. That realization does not necessarily lead to the conclusion that what the writer includes in the narrative is not historical or does not correspond to what actually happened.

Some would advance this conclusion about historicity as they seek to develop further the indirect expression of meaning in the narrative portions. Robert Alter writes,

> What a close reading of the text does suggest is that the writer could manipulate his inherited materials with sufficient freedom and sufficient firmness of authorial purpose to define motives, relations, and unfolding themes, even in a primeval history, with the kind of subtle cogency we associate with the conscious artistry of the narrative mode designated prose fiction.[5]

Alter recognizes from a close reading that the narrative is more than a report of the external and natural events that were observed. Instead, the author works with what happened to interpret the meaning of these events. Yet Alter does not acknowledge that the prophet with access to the revelation of God could well go beyond his sources in the interpretation of their meaning without necessarily misrepresenting what happened. As a spokesman for God the prophet would have access to know the motives of men (Amos 4:13) and the mind of God (1 Cor. 2:10–12). However, based on a model of natural human authorship, this sort of control over a knowledge of events and men is seen only in prose fiction.

Alter goes on to posit what that interpretive perspective would be: "The ancient Hebrew writers, as I have already intimated, seek through the process of narrative realization to reveal the enactment of God's purposes in the historical events."[6] This common ground (convention) shared by the author and the reader of expecting theological interpretation in biblical revelation enables the reader to interpret those implications beyond a mere report of narration. Through the theological themes and the conventions of narrative composition, the reader is able to recognize the subject and complement of a narrative and to exegete the full range of implications from the events narrated, the persons characterized, and the dialogue recorded.

The difficulty in the exegesis of narrative arises from the ambiguity in the modes of indirect expression and in the vagueness of an economy of expression. Economy of expression in a narrative account is both an occasion of vagueness for unanswered questions and an opportunity to recognize a selective silence of a purposeful kind. Erich Auerbach has focused on the sparingly sketched foreground of biblical narrative that somehow implies a large background dense with the possibilities of interpretation that are left only to imagination.[7] By contrast, Alter focuses attention on the specific means through which that "somehow" is achieved. As Roman Jakobson has correctly recognized, the poetic function (of which narrative is an instance) has two basic modes of arrangement in composition: selection and combination.[8]

Alter suggests that the purposeful selectivity of means is dictated by the biblical view of man. "Every person is created by an all-seeing God but abandoned to his own unfathomable freedom, made in God's likeness as a matter of cosmogonic principle but almost never as a matter of accomplished

---

[5] Robert Alter, *The Art of Biblical Narrative* (New York: Basic Books, 1981), 32.
[6] Ibid., 33.
[7] Caird, *The Language and Imagery of the Bible*, 93-94.
[8] Roman Jakobson, "Closing Statement: Linguistics and Poetics," in *Style in Language,* ed. Thomas A. Sebeok (Cambridge: MIT Press, 1960), 358.

ethical fact."[9] Alter's overstatement and theological problem should not blind us to his point. While the narrative is composed with economy, it is designed to reflect the mystery between God's will and providential guidance, and human freedom and man's fallen condition.

Another factor in the selection and economy of the biblical narrative is the "tension between the divine plan and the disorderly character of actual historical events . . . between the divine promise and its ostensible failure to be fulfilled."[10] It is in this respect that implications of biblical typology appear in a narrative. A record of an event, person, or institution contains typological implications when it occurs in history as the outworking of divine promise previously given. A typological account appears as a historical, partial fulfillment of that which was promised—which itself anticipates in the telling of the partially fulfilled the complete fulfillment in the antitype.

In addition, there is the ambiguity of indirection. Alter comments:

> There is a horizon of perfect knowledge in biblical narrative (i.e., God's knowledge) but it is a horizon we are permitted to glimpse only in the most momentary and fragmentary ways. The narrator intimates a meaningful pattern in the events through a variety of technical procedures, most of them modes of indirection. In the purposeful reticence of this kind of narration, the characters retain their aura of enigma. . . . At the same time, however, the omniscient narrator conveys a sense that personages and events produce a certain stable significance.[11]

Besides the Old Testament narratives, the Gospels, and Acts, indirect sense is expressed in the poetic hymns of the book of Psalms, the poetic discourses of the prophets, and the indirect expression of wisdom in Job and the Song of Songs. In each discourse, structures similar to techniques of selection and arrangement in the conventions of textual design and theological themes express their message and the implications of sense indirectly.

Metaphorical Sense

A metaphorical sense is recognized when the direct and normal reference of a term or literary unit is transferred to a second referent in order that the second may be illumined by the reader's knowledge of the first. The first serves as a lens, through which the second can be seen and which frequently evokes powerful emotions along with it.

Thus, in a metaphoric statement such as "John is a chicken," a reader knows that John is not literally a chicken (a person is not normally a bird), but "rather has some of the secondary properties associated with chickens, such as cowardice."[12] With such a limited text as this illustration provides, the metaphor is recognized simply in the discord created between the normal sense and reference of chicken and the textually stated reference of John. But a very basic question arises from the broader consideration of what identifies a metaphorical construction.

A. What kind of construction do we have?

There are six kinds of clues to indicate figurative construction that apply to metaphorical sense. The more com-

---

[9] Alter, *The Art of Biblical Narrative,* 115.

[10] Ibid., 33.

[11] Ibid., 158.

[12] David R. Olson and Angela Hildyard, "Literacy and the Comprehension and Expression of Literal Meaning" (*Trends in Linguistics Studies and Monographs* 24), in *Writings in Focus,* ed. Florian Coulmas (New York: Moulton, 1981), 299.

mon uses of figurative language are embedded within the literary whole and associated with the type of textual meaning. They function in a supporting role and are recognized by clues within the immediate context. Caird developed some specific contextual clues "in which an author may expressly indicate that he does not intend his words to be taken literally."[13] Among them are explicit contextual statements, impossible literality, low correspondence with direct sense and the reference, the degree of imaginative exploitation, the ramifications of the author's own imagery, and juxtaposition of images. It will be helpful to our consideration of the task of exegesis to examine some of these in detail.

1. An explicit contextual statement. Several different explicit clues are the clearest clues to follow. Terms of comparison (*hosper . . . houto,* etc.) are often used to introduce analogies. Paul does so in epistolary literature, providing a supportive illustration (Rom. 6:19; 1 Cor. 15:28; Gal. 3:15). A simile provides an explicit textual clue. A genitive construction where there is a semantic conflict between the basic (literal) senses of the two nouns identifies a metaphor:

"the *sword* of the *Spirit*" (Eph. 6:17)

"the good *fight* of the *faith*" (1 Tim. 6:12)

"*bread without yeast,* the *bread* of *sincerity* and *truth*" (1 Cor. 5:8).

Being associated implications, the implications intended are determined by type-logic. As an example, in Romans 6:19 the analogy is drawn between a natural presentation of one's members to service and a spiritual presentation of one's members to service. The point and extent of the analogy are not clear. Is it simply the fact of presentation, or is it the manner or time or conse-

quences of presentation that is implied? Type-logic would reason as follows:

If the message of Romans 6:15–23 is:

The motivation for obedience under grace arises from the fact of slavery and the consequences of enslavement to righteousness, and the analogy of presentation in slavery is used,

Then the fact of presentation alone is intended.

2. A semantic conflict in the direct, basic sense. This type is a bit more difficult to recognize, but it is initially recognized intuitively and at "first blush" when the direct senses seem to clash. Jesus frequently used conflicting literal senses to startle his hearers to listen and to reflect on the meaning. In Matthew 7:3–5, a *plank* and an *eye* are incompatible senses. But *plank* contrasts with a *speck,* which often gets lodged in one's eye. Likewise, in Matthew 23:24, *swallow* and *camel* are conflicting senses. The sense of hyperbole or overstatement startles one to face the seriousness of the rich man's problem.

Two gospels record Jesus' words of common theme in a figurative construction and a literal construction. In Luke 14:26, Jesus says, "If anyone comes to me and does not hate his father and mother. . . ." The sense of *hate* and *father and mother* create a semantic conflict. In Matthew 10:37, Jesus says, "Anyone who loves his father and mother more than me is not worthy of me. . . ." In Luke's gospel, Jesus speaks to startle apathetic disciples; in Matthew's, Jesus speaks to clarify for willing disciples. In Luke there is a figurative sense; in Matthew it is a literal sense.

In parallel, Amos refers to the *personal God* as a *lion* and a *Sovereign Lord* (3:8). Hosea likens *Ephraim* to a *dove* and *the Lord* to a *bird-catcher*

---

[13]Caird, *The Language and Imagery of the Bible,* 186–97.

(7:11–12). These senses create semantic conflict as the prophets seek to vividly portray the relationship between God and Israel.

3. A high development of figurative sense. Caird comments, "There is no surer index of the linguistic awareness of an author than the degree to which he exploits imaginatively the ramifications of his own imagery."[14] When Ezekiel seeks to "confront Jerusalem with her detestable practices" (16:2), he expresses it in the extended metaphor of a foundling saved at birth, nurtured, and then married by a passing stranger. The figurative sense engenders implications of compassion for the stranger and repulsion for the ungrateful loose woman (16:3–34).

In both his personal experience and his description of God and the elect people, Hosea develops two fundamental metaphors. One metaphor is based on his family experience. The prophet's marriage experience and his marriage contract are analogous to God's love experience with Israel and their covenant (Mosaic) contract (Hos. 1–3; 4:1–6; 6:4–10; 11:12–12:2). The metaphor is associated with the defining type of theological relationship. The second metaphor concerns father and son associated with the promise in the election of their relationships (1:10; 11:1). These two metaphors are associated with the two aspects of relationship to God: responsibility and privilege.

4. The juxtaposition of a number of images. One vivid image alone may clearly convey any semantic conflict. In Psalm 89, when the psalmist meditates upon the Davidic covenant relationship, he uses a number of images to reflect the facets of relationship: Father, Rock, and Savior (v. 26). Each metaphor refers to an aspect of the relationship:

life-shared spiritual authority, substantial foundation, and delivering person. Then, in developing the royal theology the psalmist adds the metaphor of appointment: he is Son and firstborn by appointment and shared life. Solomon shared God's life to a degree (2 Sam. 12:24) and received his appointment (1 Chron. 28:5–6). The early church recognized the full share Christ had in God's life (Mark 9:7, eternal generation) and his appointment to the throne (Rom. 1:3–4; Heb. 5:5).

The other question that arises in the task of exegesis is this:

B. What implications are intended in this metaphorical construction?

After the metaphor has been identified, the comparison needs to be clarified and specified. It is in specifying that the implications are exegeted. But before we turn to specifying, we should consider the nature of comparison. Caird lists four classes to which all points of comparison belong:[15]

1. What are the common points of comparison?

a. Perceptual comparison: Caird states, "These may appeal to any of the five senses." Many of these comparisons are directly stated in a simile. "The cloud above the tabernacle looked like fire" (Num. 9:15).

b. Synaesthesia comparison: This, Caird suggests, "is the use in connection with one of the senses of terms which are proper to another, as when we speak of sharp words (Isa. 49:2; Acts 15:39; Heb. 4:12)."

c. Affective comparison: These, according to Caird, "are those in which the feel or value of the affect or impression of one thing is compared with that of another. The hearts of Joshua's

---

[14] Ibid., 189.
[15] Ibid., 145–60.

troops turned to water (Josh. 7:5), i.e., their courage ebbed away."

d. *Pragmatic comparison:* In this, Caird explains, "we compare the activity or result of one thing with that of another." For example, he writes, "the throats of the wicked gape like an open grave and with the same implication for their victims" (Ps. 5:9). This is the nature of comparison in Isaiah 42:2–3, which describes the manner in which the Servant brings forth justice. The objects of judgment are portrayed by the inanimate *bruised reed* and *smoldering wick*. The actual objects of judgment act like a fragile bruised reed and a faltering, sputtering flame about to go out. Yet, in judgment the Servant would not crush the reed or extinguish the flame. Thus Matthew applies this to the manner in which Jesus judges his generation (Matt. 12:15–21). In establishing justice, Jesus does not physically challenge the Pharisees' right to reject, nor does he force them prematurely to decide as he cautions his followers not to proclaim his identity.

2. What are the specific points of comparison? Specifying the points of comparison is the task of exegesis. As type-logic controls the analysis and exegesis of each sense, so it controls the specification of the points of comparison. Psalm 23 builds on the basic metaphor "the Lord is my shepherd." The identity of the metaphor is clear; the word "shepherd" belongs to the semantic realm of animal husbandry (normal reference), but it is juxtaposed to the thought pertaining to a transcendent, spiritual Being. The point or points of comparison could be affective comparison (the comfort and strength of the Lord's presence) and/or pragmatic comparison (the leadership and direction of his presence). The actual points of comparison would be deter-

mined by the message of the psalm. If the subject of the psalm is "David's relationship to the Lord," then both the affective and pragmatic points of comparison are intended. If, however, the subject were narrower—"David's future steps"—then the pragmatic comparison would be intended.

Several examples will be developed to illustrate the identification and exegesis of metaphor. The first example is chosen to illustrate the control that the message must have for determining the extent of the implications involved in the figure of speech. Rather than using a metaphor, hyperbole is chosen because it is particularly sensitive to the extent of implications.

Let us consider Isaiah 13:9–11, as quoted by Caird, and his comments on the passage:

> The Day of the Lord is coming indeed,
> that cruel day of wrath and fury,
> to make the earth a desolation
> and exterminate its wicked people.
> The stars of heaven in their constellations
> shall give no light,
> the sun shall be darkened at its rising,
> and the moon refuse to shine.
> I will bring disaster upon the world
> and their due punishment upon the wicked.

Caird comments:

> When we read on, it becomes apparent that what the prophet intended to describe, under the symbols of world judgment, was the end of Babylon's world, the coming destruction of Babylonian empire by the invading armies of Cyrus the Mede.[16]

It is clear that Isaiah has in mind the historical judgment of Babylon (13:1) by the Medes (13:17). But it is also clear textually that the scope of judgment transcends the historical referent. There are references not only to the end of the world, but also the end of wick-

---

[16]Ibid., 113–14.

edness: "I will put an end to the arrogance of the haughty and will humble the pride of the ruthless" (13:11). It is interesting that Caird omitted that portion of verse 11 from his quotation. The scope of judgment is described both in natural and spiritual terms as the Day of the Lord. In the initial consideration the natural may be seen as hyperbole in the historical reference, but the spiritual makes no sense when it is regarded as hyberbole. Rather, the spiritual scope of judgment must be literal and refer to some ultimate judgment. This introduces the concept of "double reference."

Caird argues contextually from the historic judgment of Babylon (13:1) by the Medes (13:17). The argument goes:

If this refers to the historic judgment of Babylon

And the historic judgment is limited in scope,

Then these statements of unlimited scope must be figurative and hyperbolic. He takes the figurative constructions as associated and not as defining. The message is defined only by historical statements concerning Babylon on the Medes.

However, a broader consideration of historical and spiritual statements in defining the message casts the issue of limits in a different light:

If the literary design is to persuade Ahaz (king of Israel) to trust YHWH by arguing for his control of national and spiritual forces,

And the text states that "to make the earth a desolation" and "exterminate its wicked,"

Then the integrity of YHWH rests in his control of wickedness.

While the references are influenced by wickedness expressed in Babylon, they are not limited to wickedness expressed

at one period of Babylonian history. Therefore, although the initial reference is to the historical display of control, the ultimate scope in overcoming wickedness leads the reader in the progress of history to complete realization and to expect a future and final display of the wickedness of Babylon being judged in the Day of the Lord. So the text has a single sense, but it has the potential of multiple reference. Yet in each historic reference, the sense remains unchanged with respect to the defining and necessary implications of sense and reference. Associated implications will be fuller in the final fulfillment than in the historic hyperbolic reference.

Such prophetic contexts in which metaphors are difficult to identify and interpret are all too common. We will look at two examples. One will serve to help identify the presence or absence of a metaphor; the other will illustrate the exegesis of a metaphor.

A continuing question in eschatology involves the interpretation of the reference to a thousand years in Revelation 20:2-3. Some claim that it is a metaphor, while others say it should be taken in a direct sense. Bruce Waltke raises the issue:

I think that it is fair to say that premillennialists, who believe in a future Jewish kingdom on this earth, tend to minimize figures of speech in the prophetic language. Moreover, they tend to ignore the symbolism in apocalyptic literature. . . . the premillennialist's conviction that the Jewish kingdom will last precisely 1,000 years is based on one passage in the Apocalypse (Rev. 20:1–9) notorious for its symbolic use of numbers, and in spite of the fact that elsewhere 1,000 is used for an indefinite extended period of time (cf. Ex. 20:6; Deut. 1:11; etc.).[17]

Waltke contends that those who see an actual rule of Christ on earth tend to

---

[17]Bruce K. Waltke, "An Evangelical Christian View" (Unpublished paper presented at the Evangelical Jewish National Conference, December 1980), 13.

incorrectly see various figures of speech as referring directly to actual experiences in that future reign. In this way they fail to feel the force of the immediate context, which changes the interpretive decision. The unfortunate aspect of this is that no hermeneutical criterion is absolute. The decision about the presence or absence of a metaphor must weigh a number of criteria.

The criterion of a normal reference would support a direct sense. It is not at all unusual to refer to a historic experience of a period of reign with a number of years. While the enemy and the conquest are spiritual, referring to Satan, this does not exclude a historical expression in a number of years of this conquest. Although the literary genre alerts the interpreter to look for symbolic senses, the immediate context does not support that expectation. John describes the thousand years as both the length of the imprisonment (v. 2) and the time of peace on earth (v. 3). In addition, when an indefinite time does occur, it is so described: "set free for a short time" (v. 3). Thus the description can be taken as natural and straightforward. As such, apocalyptic genre does not eliminate literal numbers in spite of a use of numbers in a symbolic sense. So the very time of the judgment is repeatedly described in actual years ($3\frac{1}{2}$) or days (1,260) in correspondence to Daniel.

Thus weighing the criteria of natural reference and literary genre does not lead one to identify a metaphorical sense in the thousand years.

The second example will illustrate how to interpret an accepted metaphor. It is necessary to note the controlling role that the message plays in exegesis of a metaphor. The message identifies the type of meaning of the authorial expression of the context. Within this contextual type of meaning, the particular figure in question can be investigated to see if there is a metaphorical reference consistent with the message. So it is interesting how Waltke approaches Isaiah 42:3: "a bruised reed he will not break, and a smoldering wick he will not snuff out." There is no question about the identification of metaphor in "reed" or "wick." Waltke then notes:

> the poet asserts three times that the LORD will bring justice to the nations (vv. 1, 3–4). Into this clear context he throws the line "a bruised reed he will not break, and a smoldering wick he will not snuff out" (v. 3). Thus he places inanimate objects (reed and wick) into the context of salvation history of the nations.[18]

Waltke thus correctly recognizes the metaphors. But when he introduces "salvation history" as the type of meaning, does he accurately express the contextual theme of "bring justice"? This seems to be a broadening of the idea of justice to salvation. "Salvation history" is more clearly supported as a theological construct than as a contextual construct.

The comparison in Isaiah 42:2–3 is a pragmatic comparison. These verses express a type of meaning that describes the manner in which the Servant brings forth justice. The objects of judgment are portrayed by the inanimate "bruised reed" and "smoldering wick." The actual objects of judgment act like a fragile, bruised reed and a faltering, sputtering flame about to go out. Yet, in judgment the Servant would not crush the reed or extinguish the flame in considering the rights of these individuals. Matthew applies this to the manner in which Jesus judged his generation (Matt. 12:15–21). In establishing justice, Jesus does not obliterate the Pharisees' right to reject, nor does he force them prematurely to decide as he

---

[18]Ibid., 12.

cautions his followers not to proclaim his identity.

Therefore, when Waltke applies "the context of salvation history of the nations," he concludes that "the broken spent objects represent nations that will be 'repaired' and 'rekindled' through the Servant's spiritual ministry."[19] However, when the contextual type of meaning is used—"the Servant of the LORD will bring justice to the nations (vv. 1, 3–4)"—then the activity is not "repairing or rekindling," but rather "respecting the right to a fair trial" in spite of their weakness before the true Judge.

This faithfulness to the demands of justice also fits with verse 2, in which a raised voice or quarrel is an illustration of attempts to get one's own way in spite of justice. Thus, only when the proper message controls the use of the metaphor does one understand the specific implications and points of correspondence.

Another example from Waltke provides a clearer distinction between his interpretation and a premillennial interpretation. The passage is Isaiah 11:1–9, in which "the wolf will be the guest of [Heb., *gur*] the lamb" (v. 6).[20] Waltke rejects a "pedestrian way" or a "character of rule" as a type of meaning. That would lead to Charles Ryrie's interpretation of "Messiah's reign in the yet future millennial kingdom, which will be characterized by harmony in the whole creation (Rom. 8:18–22)."[21]

Instead Waltke adopts "salvation history among men" as the type of meaning. This leads "to a picturesque portrayal of the harmony that will exist among men when the tyrant turns to the meek for salvation."[22]

A complicating problem arises, since the situation described in 11:6ᵃ is developed further in 11:6ᵇ–9. Waltke warns against allegorizing this development.

> No attempt should be made to relate these species of animals with specific types of people; that would subject the text to allegorizing. The amplification serves to evoke the full extent of harmony that will exist during Messiah's righteous rule.[23]

However, the metaphor of pragmatic comparison of wild creatures tamed in salvation is complicated by introducing the little child. Though wild animals may act like unregenerate mankind, within what type of salvation history may the little child leading the formerly wild animals be associated? This development of the metaphor is incompatible with the type of "salvation history." It may, however, be associated with "the rulership of Messiah" type in which the defenseless and weak will walk in harmony under Messiah's rule.

As a final support, Waltke states:

> The poet concludes by safeguarding his text against literalism: "The earth will be full of the knowledge of the LORD as the waters cover the sea" (v. 9). Since animals cannot know God, it becomes absolutely clear that mankind is in view.[24]

Is not Waltke himself guilty of literalism? The prophet affirms, "The ox *knows* . . ." (1:3). Is it not possible that donkeys and oxen know the source of their life even as wild animals know the vicious, destructive, deadly ways of their wild nature? Would it not again be possible to exegete knowledge associ-

---

[19] Ibid.
[20] Ibid.
[21] Charles C. Ryrie, *The Ryrie Study Bible* (Chicago: Moody Press, 1986), 933.
[22] Waltke, "An Evangelical Christian View," 12.
[23] Ibid.
[24] Ibid.

ated with the type of "Messiah's righteous reign"? Animals will know the source of life and harmony in Messiah's reign. Men will know in a personal relation, but not to the exclusion of animals. Thus the overall type of "Messiah's righteous reign" introduced in 11:3–5 adequately relates all the particulars. There is no need to incorporate "salvation history."

3. What distinguishes correct from incorrect implications? For the final example of metaphor we will consider an extended metaphor called parable, and in so doing we will study how to distinguish correct from incorrect implications. The parable is a unique kind of narrative because the message clues are expressed not just indirectly, but metaphorically. For our exegetical example we will use John 15:1–17. There Jesus speaks directly about one realm (vine, branches, husbandman), but actually he intends to refer to another realm (Christ, disciples, God).

This example serves also to highlight the role of the message in the exegesis of a parable. The message determines the range of implications, and valid exegesis of implications may involve changing a statement of the message until we find the one that corresponds with the textual data. The process goes like this:

For the author, the type of meaning of the whole is a given—that is, he knows what he wrote or spoke about. But for the interpreter, any formulation of the type of meaning of the whole is a tentative construct subject to validation. As one reads the words of the text, a construct of the type of meaning of the book begins to take shape in the interpreter's thinking. The construct is useful to the extent that it relates the sequence of meanings. If a word or a construction is reached that does not fit, immediately the reader should be alerted to reconsider the type of meaning he has been considering.

E. D. Hirsch explains what this involves, and in doing so he distinguishes between extrinsic genre and intrinsic genre. By *extrinsic* Hirsch means a preliminary judgment that under further examination of the context proves to be false according to the writer's meaning; *intrinsic* connotes an understanding of genre that proves to be correct.*

> Now, an interpreter can use any type idea heuristically to get at the meanings of an utterance. Sometimes, in the course of interpretation, he will find that his original type idea must be discarded or drastically revised (extrinsic type), but usually he does not find this necessary. Almost always, he begins with a type idea which is vaguer and broader than the intrinsic idea of the utterance, and, in the course of interpretation, merely narrows this idea and makes it more explicit. A preliminary genre idea that is vague and broad is not, however, necessarily extrinsic, but rather, a heuristic tool that has not yet been sharpened to the fine edge necessary for determining all the meanings of the utterance. . . . An extrinsic is a wrong guess, an intrinsic genre a correct one.[25]

Although this process is difficult to reconstruct in the abstract, it can quite readily be understood through an illustration. Taking again the parable of Jesus in John 15:1–17, we will test two statements of the type of meaning side by side through the practice of type-logic. In so doing, we will discover how a type of meaning can introduce faulty, incorrect implications. (See figure 10.1.)

As the interpreter reads with either type of meaning in mind, he will read in the text the expressions of fruitlessness or the Father throwing the fruitless branches away. The implications un-

---

*Remember that we have been using the term *type* essentially as a synonym for *genre*.

[25] E. D. Hirsch, Jr., *Validity in Interpretation* (New Haven: Yale University Press, 1967), 88.

Figure 10.1

Textual Design (Example I)

To remind the disciples of their relationship by illustrating with an old analogy

Message

The essence of the disciples' relationship with Christ depends on his abiding in Christ, the Vine.

Application of Type-logic

A. 1. If the subject is the essence of the relationship and bearing fruit is necessarily based on abiding (15:2, 4) . . .

   2. Then fruitlessness proves a break in the essential relationship.

B. 1. If the subject is the essence of relationship and the nonabider is thrown away . . .

   2. Then the essence of the relationship is broken for the nonabider.

Textual Design (Example II)

To introduce the disciples to their new relationship by refashioning an old analogy

Message

The functioning of the disciples' relationship with Christ depends on his abiding in Christ, the Vine.

Application of Type-logic

A. 1. If the subject is the functioning of relationship and bearing fruit is necessarily based on abiding (15:4) . . .

   2. Then fruitlessness proves a break in the function of the relationship.

B. 1. If the subject is the functioning of relationship and the nonabider is thrown away . . .

   2. Then the functioning of the relationship is broken for the nonabider.

folded by the type I statement cause conflict with the doctrine of eternal security if the branch is a genuine believer originally. The implications unfolded by the type II statement cause conflict with either the doctrine of perfectionism or the doctrine of perseverance. The type I disciple, a nonabiding branch, has lost his relationship. The type II disciple, a nonabiding branch, has become a nonfunctioning relationship. These two implications, generated by meanings of type I and type II, are incompatible, since both cannot be true of a disciple at the same time. Thus, if these statements (type I and type II) exhaust the possible interpretations, then one statement must be wrong (extrinsic), the other right (intrinsic).

In this case, the intrinsic statement is not disclosed by its ability to clarify all the implications of the text. Both statements are capable of clarifying the figure; the particulars of the figure may

be brought to support either statement. "Abiding," "bearing fruit," "cleansed by his word," and "being in the Vine" fit nicely with either the subject of a "function in relationship" or "the essential relationship." "Withering," "fire," and "burning" are strong figures whose meaning rests on the statement of the type of meaning in the whole parable. The validation statements are distinguishable in the broader theological context of the doctrines of eternal security or perfectionism or perseverance. (The weighing of the evidence for this example will be pursued in more detail in part 5 on validation.)

Accurate exegesis is logically dependent on an accurate recognition of the type of meaning. It necessarily follows that an indefinite or erroneous recognition of the author's meaning leads to indefinite or erroneous exegesis. Thus the interpreter's recognition of the type of meaning must remain a tentative and preliminary construction until its accuracy is validated.

HISTORICAL

Historical affirms that the textually based meanings have implications of reference, allusion, expression, or volition that correspond to the textual sense as the Author/author intends.

In the task of exegesis, associated implications of reference need to be unfolded as well as the diagnostic implications. Type-logic is again the tool by which the corresponding realm of reference can be determined. The use of type-logic leads us to conclude that the implications associated with the realm of reference are based on the message and the textual design. The textual design specifies the terms in which the audience is addressed (reference) and the literary conventions implying reference and the use of language. These uses (direct, indirect, metaphorical) of language indicate the way the author intends to speak about the world. The textual design is the broadest framework within which the type of reference is determined. Therefore this section will be organized around the different textual designs and examine the normal range of implications. This is the final stage in our consideration of the task of exegesis.

The Exegesis of Implications of Reference

In the complete exegesis of the textual meanings, implications of historical reference are just as necessary as implications of textual sense.

This point becomes clear in the narrative of the apostle Philip and the Ethiopian eunuch related in Acts 8. The Ethiopian was reading Isaiah 53. He understood the sense of the passage. It spoke of one led like a sheep to the slaughter who was silent; the person's life was taken as he was deprived of justice. This much the Ethiopian understood. His question was, "Who is the prophet talking about, himself or someone else?" (v. 34). In other words, is the author referring to himself in the third person, or is he referring to someone not identified historically in a textual form?

"Then Philip began with that very passage of Scripture and told him the good news about Jesus" (v. 35). *If* Isaiah 53 spoke of God's substitutionary sacrifice for sin, then God referred to *Jesus.* This was an implication of reference. It was an associated implication of the type of prophetic meaning expressed by Isaiah. As it was essential for the Ethiopian to understand that implication to understand fully what the prophet said, so understanding implications of reference are necessary in any case of textual interpretation. The meaning of the implication of reference is not found in the object to which the writer refers, but in the type of reference that relates the textual construction to the historical referent. Isaiah means "Jesus in the sense of a silent, willing sacrifice, slaughtered not for his own guilt but for the sins of the world he bore." The prophet does not include in his meaning "Jesus who was born in Bethlehem of Mary, or who was anointed to be the Davidic king."

Before the practice of exegeting implications can be considered in general, let me issue some important reminders. The first is that the realm of reference does not define or determine the type of meaning being expressed; the text is the basis of the type of meaning being expressed. Thus the task of recognition must begin with the text. On this ground, G. B. Caird's direction seems premature: "In interpreting the words of others the first task is the identification of the referent."[26] Instead, the first task is recognizing the sense in the text as a whole, considering only an imagined reference.

The second reminder is that references to a realm of reality are not limited to an informational or cognitive use of language. While an informational use of language almost exclusively deals with a realm of reference (denotations), it should not be implied that other uses of language do not.[27] For example, an expressive use of language such as "Ouch!" implies some problem. If there was no associated physical or emotional problem, the meaning of the expression would surely be difficult to determine.

With these things in mind, we are ready to examine different aspects of reference.

1. A statement referring to particular, historical facts as the exclusive reference. This is the common form of reference in the discourse structure of historical narrative. It could involve a reference to natural events ("In the fifteenth year of the reign of Tiberius Caesar") or to supernatural events ("the word of God came to John the son of Zechariah in the desert," Luke 3:1–2). It can describe events by referring directly to the observable events: "With a loud cry, Jesus breathed his last" (Mark 15:37). Or the same event can be described from an interpreted theological framework: "Christ died for our sins" (1 Cor. 15:3). The interpretation neither diminishes nor necessarily distorts the reference to the historical event.

The discourse structure of predictions of future events in prophetic literature has this same particular reference.

These predictive statements are so specific in reference to particular persons or things that they are not transferable. The detailed nature of the textual qualifications in the reference predicts one historical fulfillment. A clear example of this is found in Micah 5:2. The qualifications of reference:

a. "Bethlehem Ephrathah": In 1 Samuel 17:12, David's father Jesse is described as an Ephrathite from Bethlehem in Judah. Ephrathah appears to have been the district in which Bethlehem was located; the places are identified in Genesis 35:19; 48:7; and Ruth 4:11. Ronald Allen adds to this, "The very names 'house of bread, fruitfulness' conjure up visions far different from the present spectacle. Surely the omens of prosperity that clustered round such names were not destined to die out in the squalid nadir of Assyrian occupation."[28]

b. "Though you are small among the clans of Judah": The size of this little clan is a specific detail in historical reference that also becomes a symbol for God's future purposes.

Who could have dreamed that so unimportant a place would breed a David? Of all the clans of the tribe of Judah, the Ephrathite clan around Bethlehem would hardly supply a respectable army unit at times of tribal levy (Heb. "*alepe,* units of fighting men supplied by *mishpahot* or *phraties,* tribal subgroups"). How strange that God summoned the man of His choice from so insignificant a source![29]

c. "Will come for me": The language anticipating this future ruler clearly reflects God's first words to Samuel when God chose David: "I have provided *for Myself* a king" (1 Sam. 16:1, AMPLIFIED).

---

[26]Caird, *The Language and Imagery of the Bible,* 10.

[27]Ibid., 20.

[28]Ronald B. Allen, *The Books of Joel, Obadiah, Jonah, and Micah,* New International Commentary of the Old Testament (Grand Rapids: Eerdmans, 1979), 342.

[29]Ibid., 342.

d. *"Whose goings out are of old"* (mine): The word for the future is backed by the heritage of the past. The appearing of this ruler is to be validated by hereditary right; the same root is deliberately taken up and used again ("out of you will come . . . whose goings out").

e. *"From days of eternity"* (mine): While the parallelism may be synonymous, as Allen and the New International Version ("from ancient times") affirm, it is also possible for the term to be taken as an additional qualification. Keil and older commentators have taken this as an enigmatic reference to Christ's deity in birth. Such synthetic parallelism would certainly limit the statement to prediction and enhance the paradox of this leader. These are statements about a particular person, with a particular origin, and a particular relationship that are clearly not transferable.

2. A general statement that refers to any member of a class. This kind of reference is at the other end of the spectrum in particularity. Whereas the first statement talks about particular people and events and refers to only one realm of reference, this statement talks to a class, or group, of experiences or practices. These involve general statements that can properly be applied to any member of a class.

In the discourse structure of the *proverbs,* the statements address themselves to categories of experience of learners as "simple" or "wise" or "fool" or "scoffer." They then express normative truths appropriate to the experience of the learner. Similar proverbial statements appear in the Gospels. "It is easier for a camel to go through the eye of a needle than for a *rich man* to enter the kingdom of God" (Luke 18:25).

The *promises* in the Beatitudes of Jesus are addressed to a class of people described by experience: "Blessed are *the poor in spirit,* for theirs is the kingdom of heaven" (Matt. 5:3).

Warnings and promises in covenant statements are addressed to citizens within national or spiritual covenant relationship. There are warnings of this nature in Deuteronomy 4:25–26: "After you . . . have lived in the land a long time—if you then become corrupt and make any kind of idol, . . . you will quickly perish from the land." The warning is to the class of corrupt idolmakers in their practice. Or consider Deuteronomy 27:16: "Cursed is the man who dishonors his father or his mother." The curse falls on the class of ones whose practice is a dishonor to God. Or in the category of blessing, Deuteronomy 28:1: "If you fully obey the LORD your God and carefully follow all his commands I give you today, the LORD your God will set you high above all the nations of the earth." The blessings are promised for the class of obedient ones in their practice. These promises and warnings are prophetic statements, although the statements of prophetic literature may often be more specific.

By contrast with the preceding, the next three categories of reference form intermediate positions between the extremes of the first particular and the second general reference.

3. A statement with a particular reference in mind, but the particular historical reference is in some way representative of other instances. To illustrate this aspect of a particular reference, consider Isaiah 29:13:

"These people come near to me with their
   mouth
   and honor me with their lips,
   but their hearts are far from me.
Their worship of me
   is made up only of rules taught by
   men."

Caird comments on this passage as follows:

> When Jesus says, "How well did Isaiah prophesy about you hypocrites" (Mark 7:6), He is not suggesting that Isaiah was gazing into the future across eight centuries, but rather that in speaking of his own generation Isaiah might equally have been speaking about the contemporaries of Jesus: "Isaiah might well have been prophesying about you."[30]

In the terms of address in condemnation, Isaiah spoke against Ariel concerning hypocritical worship. These terms applied again in Jesus' day as the situation reappeared in history. After Israel was restored to the land, Isaiah spoke again and continued to speak. Again Isaiah's audience was addressed in terms that represented the spiritual condition of Jesus' day. In addition, Jesus quoted Isaiah 6:9–10 as fulfilled in God's national hardening ministry (Matt. 13:14–15; Mark 4:12; Luke 8:10).

4. A statement with a descriptive reference to a theological role, without a reference to the personal identity in the text. Caird compares this type of reference in the human perspective to a situation-vacant advertisement: "It describes in some detail a person whose identity is not yet known to the writer."[31] While the writer does not know the historical, personal identity of the individual, he does know his identifying role traits. In this sense the human author, if he were to see this figure appear in history, could recognize or identify him. Thus, according to Caird's illustration, the servant of the Lord (Isa. 53) has been determinately identified though not personally known to Isaiah.

Numerous other instances of this type of prophetic discourse occur. The first reference to "seed of the woman" (Gen. 3:15) provided enough to begin a search for the One of God's reference. Adam and Eve at first thought it was Cain (Gen. 4:1: "a man"). However, Cain was overcome by the Evil One in conflict (Gen. 4:7). Thus God warned Cain, "If you do what is right, will you not be accepted? But if you do not do what is right, sin is crouching at your door; it desires to have you, but you must master it." The conflict anticipated in the judgment (3:15) appeared, but Cain was defeated as he slew Abel (4:8).

Similarly, "the seed of Abraham" (see Gen. 12:7), "a prophet like me" (Deut. 18:15), and "the son of David" (2 Sam. 7:12) all specify the individual without giving full historical, personal identification. The historical authors and readers know enough to await the outworking of events and to test the individual of their generation who might fulfill the promise. History demonstrates that in each case God ultimately referred to Jesus the Christ. Each historical candidate demonstrates by his actions in history that he is not the One to fit the role of divine reference. This was precisely the case of Psalm 16. David was to fulfill a role in history that his own sin limited. David will fulfill his role through One who will preeminently fulfill that role. In Christ and in resurrection, David would be raised to fulfill God's purpose.

5. A statement with a knowledge of the defining sense and immediate reference, but without a knowledge of the full sense and ultimate reference. "The Old Testament is full of such words, and a part of its inexhaustible usefulness to us lies in its 'majestic mendi-*

---

[30]Caird, *The Language and Imagery of the Bible,* 57.
[31]Ibid., 57.

cancy.'"[32] The description of the mighty words of God and their consequences are a part of the prophetic discourse and its progressive unfolding.

Redemption is a good example as the word is first used in the book of Exodus. YHWH promises, "I will redeem you with an outstretched arm and with mighty acts of judgment" (Ex. 6:6). While God clearly refers to the enslavement of Egypt from which Israel would be set free with mighty acts of judgment, the context implies that there would be more. In the biblical cases of promised words of God, God fully grasped what men only experienced in limited degree. So God adds certain consequences in the ultimate realization: "I will be your God. Then you will know that I am the LORD your God" (6:7). The scope of these consequences anticipates a redemption from personal judgment of sin (Gal. 3:13) and ultimate national redemption of Israel (Isa. 52:3-4) from judgment. So when Israel sang of redemption (Ex. 15:13), she only grasped it to a limited but true degree. The peoples' understanding was certainly true—because God also said so—but it was not completed or fully understood.

Another example of this use of particular reference involves the discourse structure in prophecies referring to "the Day of the Lord" in prophetical literature. The prophets had a near referent in mind. Joel, who probably was historically the first prophet to use the term, clearly anticipated the day to be near (1:15: "Alas for that day! For the day of the LORD is near"; or 2:1: "for the day of the LORD is coming"). Yet the general scope in the description of the judgment and the scope of unprecedented spiritual blessing to be accomplished are such that Paul can say that the day of the Lord had not yet come (2 Thess. 2:2–3). Though there was a historical

judgment within one hundred years of Joel (722 B.C.), it did not exhaust the scope of what God purposed to accomplish in judgment and blessing. Nor did national judgment through Babylon in 586 B.C. So Paul could anticipate the day as still future in A.D. 55. The historic instances are fulfillments in limited degree and thus representative in kind, but the prophecy still anticipates a full degree of fulfillment.

The tabernacle introduced many aspects of worship and priestly ministry that ultimately refer to either Christ or his ministry. Other aspects refer to heavenly order, in which Christ is presently functioning. In each case of implications of reference, the influence of theological themes and textual design in biblical revelation generate necessary meanings of reference. The simple argument goes like this:

If the theological theme is to reveal God who speaks,

And the textual statement involves this scope;

Then the realm of reference must consider God's authorship of the statement.

What must be hyperbole in normal human authorship may not necessarily be with God as the Author as we consider the progress of God's revelation.

If the biblical textual design has these conventional norms,

And this textual statement appears;

Then the discourse sense and terms of reference of the statement must be _____. In each case the theological themes of the canon and the textual design of the canon and textual design of the genre determine the potential realm of historical reference.

---

[32] Ibid., 58.

The Reference of the Narrative Structure

When historical details are associated with narrative structure, they specify the nature and realm of the author's reference. Thus the exegesis of the meaning of narrative literature includes determining the implications of the historical realm of reference. This task involves first of all recognizing the indirect narrative sense and only then exegeting the implications of reference. Recognizing the historical sense involves answering the questions, *What* happened? *Who* was involved? and *When* and *where* did it happen? The narrative sense involves the interpretive questions, *What* does this mean? and often *Why* did it happen? In the absence of any of these historical clues in the setting of the narrative, it is very likely that the narrative would have a fictional framework.

In parables and allegorical structures, the answers to these historical questions are unimportant to understanding the meaning. The characters remain nameless, and the time and place do not matter. Nevertheless, what happens represents realistic issues from the historical realm because parabolic events refer to an actual historical realm but with a distinct intent. For example, in the parable of the soils, Jesus talks about a sower, seed, and different soil conditions, but refers to a proclaimer (at first Christ), the Word, and different responses to the Word that is heard. While each textual particular contributes to the sense of the parable's message, the message controls which particulars metaphorically refer to the realm of reference. So in the interpretation of parables, the clues of the textual sense precede any exegesis of the implications of historical reference.

A necessary implication of the theological themes of what purports to be historical narrative is historicity. Fiction in any form, in which fact and fiction are intermingled in an undistinguishable fashion, is inconsistent with divine authorship of a historical-appearing account. The interpretation of historical events or periods of history by a biblical author does not require that he write a fictitious expansion of history. Whereas such fictitious embellishment may be common to certain human interpretations of historical issues, it is by no means necessary. And when one considers the contribution of the divine Author, correspondence between the clues of the text's meaning and the intended realm of reference is necessary unless the biblical narrative gives textual clues that it includes fiction.

We must exercise caution in order to recognize within the realm of historicity the primary issue of accurate recording. Such accuracy in recording does not imply the moral integrity of every action performed, nor does it imply the truthfulness of what every character says in a recorded conversation.

There are a number of instances in which the intention of God differs from that of his agent or messenger. However, in each case God used these agents in spite of themselves:

Joseph's brothers: "You intended to harm me, but God intended it for good" (Gen. 50:20)

The Assyrians as a punitive rod (Isa. 10:5-11)

Cyrus as God's anointed servant (Isa. 45:1-4)

In the story of Job, what Satan intends as temptation God uses as test. The same may be said of the temptations of Jesus. In view of God's use of them despite their evil character, we must conclude that Caird's assessment is invalid: "It is reasonable, then, to question whether the messengers of God have always correctly understood his intentions."[33] Rather, the speakers in the narrative of Scripture must be interpreted in terms of who they are, from what position they speak, and what they say. Some statements must be viewed as having a negative contribution and other statements as contributing positively to the message of the book. Such considerations are particularly important in the interpretation of Job or Ecclesiastes.

The Sense and Reference of Typological Narrative Structure

A unique expression of biblical narrative involves prophecy through history in which Jesus Christ is uniquely albeit indirectly identified with certain characters and even events and things. Christ is identified with these characters not as the *object* of God's purposes who receives God's blessings or curses, but as the *agent* of God's redemptive rule and purposes of history. As in all historical narrative, the record refers to historical characters, events, and things, but the record—also in an indirect prophetic sense—refers to Christ.

This prophetic sense of reference in historical narrative is commonly recognized in the broad context of the progressive revelation of the canon. God's purposes and direction in redemptive rule are introduced early in God's promises to act through man (*agent*) to overcome the Evil One and to bless (Gen. 1–12).

As these purposes begin to unfold and take shape in the events of history, God introduces various agencies of his will to accomplish his purposes. Each person, institution, or event serves to genuinely though only partially fulfill his purposes and promises. In the sense that each agency fulfills his promise at least in part, that instance is at once a historical fulfillment and a historical

anticipation of the ultimate Agent. As Christ comes and reads the text, he finds himself addressed indirectly in a genuine and complete sense as the ultimate and single effective Agent of all God's purposes. The typological sense is the historic partial fulfillment that implies and anticipates a historic ultimate fulfillment of God's promise. The typological reference is Christ—the antitype.

While the meaning thus resides in the intended type of meaning of the Old Testament, the interpreter may not recognize the full implications of meaning of the Old Testament until he reads the New Testament. But the meaning does not arise from the New Testament. It is genuine meaning of the Old Testament recognized in the context of the completed revelation of God's purposes. In the history of biblical hermeneutics, four defining characters have been identified in Old Testament typology:

1. Providence. Old Testament narrative accounts are written in a form indicating the outworking of God's purposes and promises in history. Aspects of God's purpose find expression in the record of the historical instance of fulfillment. It is God's providential outworking of his purposes that casts the historical event, character, or institution in a form related to a future event.

2. Historicity. This narrative account refers to actual persons, events, and institutions. The fact that they also have a fashioned role in the outworking of God's purposes and in the narration of the historical instance in no way diminishes their historicity.

3. Resemblance. The historical event is a real and distinct historical event or personage. Yet in certain respects that are an outworking of God's purposes and a partial fulfillment of God's prom-

---

[33] Ibid., 60.

ises, it resembles the antitype of complete and final fulfillment. Thus the Passover lamb resembles the substitutionary sacrifice of Christ and the individual application of the benefit of the shed blood. God purposes to redeem Israel from Egypt through judgment on evil based on his promises to Abraham. God worked out his purpose through the provision of the lamb. God's ultimate redemption will be accomplished through the provision of Christ. The resemblance is twofold: the satisfactory substitute and the application of the blood by faith.

4. Dissimilarity. Old Testament typological instances are distinct in their individuality from Christ. But they are dissimilar in the extent and effectual fulfillment of God's promise. The blood of the lamb spilled provides no efficacious satisfaction in dealing with the judgment of sin. While the lamb's substitution took God's judgment of the Israelite in the form of an animal death, Christ's substitution took God's judgment effectively in the offering of his own life. This dissimilarity in extent and effectiveness of fulfillment of God's purposes in no way diminishes the resemblance in limited but assigned fulfillment.

The focus of the agency is primarily on Christ. He is seen as the agent doing conflict with the seed of the serpent in Abel or in David (Pss. 22; 45; 89); as the agent bringing the promised people into blessing in Joseph or in Moses; as the agent mediating blessing to God's people in Noah or Moses; and as the agency for approaching God in the tabernacle and the sacrifices. While the focus on typology is primarily on Christ, it also includes historical in-

stances of the seed of the serpent in David's enemies (imprecatory psalms), in Cain, and in Antiochus Epiphanes (Dan. 8; 11), etc.

SUMMARY

The constructions in the text are the focus of attention in the task of exegesis. The issue concerns unfolding implications that the Author/author intended. The hermeneutical premises provide these controls:

1. *Literal* affirms that implications are based in the text. This translates into finding this basis in the constructions construed in the context of the message. While the message interprets the immediate textual context, the next two hermeneutical premises also provide broader textual bases.

2. *Literary* affirms that the textually based meanings are determined by the textual forms—both the conventions of design and the composition of design.

3. *Theological* affirms that the textually based meaning is determined by the textual content—the conventional expectations of the revelation of God in relationship with man in history.

4. *Grammatical* affirms that the textually based meaning conforms to the author's use of language in unfolding the range of implications of sense.

5. *Historical* affirms that the textually based meanings include implications that refer or allude to a historical realm. In addition, an Author/author also expresses himself in history or wills to direct historical audiences.

PART FOUR

APPLICATION

Introduction

Any exposition and interpretation of the Scriptures is incomplete until it includes application. This scope of interpretation is demanded by the normative design and authority of the Bible. David reflects on the application of God's revelation in Psalm 19. The application is discussed in terms of the effect that the revelation has on the life of mankind. This effect is first portrayed in the image of heat in natural revelation: "nothing is hidden from its [the sun's] heat" (v. 6). Natural revelation simply speaks of the limitless power and unchanging control of God in space and time in which the sun displays its glory and its heat searches man out. The effect of this search, by implication, burns until mankind recognizes its own insignificance before the greatness of God.

By contrast, David abruptly introduces God's written revelation, which has an evident and opposite effect of raising people to a relationship with God. It restores the soul (v. 7a), makes wise the simple (v. 7b), rejoices the heart and enlightens the eyes (v. 8). These effects for a person who is insignificant before God are absolutely essential to him or her and are the vital climax of spoken revelation from God. And these effects come into existence only through application of God's Word. For David, God's law was written to be applied. No interpretation of God's revelation would be complete until a person is challenged by these effects.

In a parallel passage in Psalm 119, the psalmist meditates on the excellencies of God's law. Among other figures, the law is a *lamp* to enlighten one's steps and clarify the direction of one's path (v. 105). Jesus speaks similarly of the relevance of his Word to life. His Word mediates eternal life to the one who believes in God, who sent Christ (John 5:24). Abiding in Jesus' Word brings a knowledge of the truth. This truth shall set men free (John 8:31–32). Having demonstrated his love for his disciples, Jesus promises blessing to those who act on his words (John 3:16–17).

In 2 Timothy 3:15–17, the apostle Paul gives an extensive statement concerning the value of all Scriptures applied to life. Scripture as a whole and in each part continues to be profitable. Its profit lies both in making us wise to salvation and in instructing us as to what God wants us to do. This is the common object of interpretation. In addition, its profit extends to reproof of the believer in error. Finally, it prescribes correction in how to get right and training in how to stay right.

The author to the Hebrews speaks of the active, penetrating power of a written, ancient Word. It discerns and judges the motives and plans of a person's heart (Heb. 4:12–13). It thereby relates God's eyes to the designs and activities of man's inner thoughts and designs. James, in a similar vein, sees Scripture as a *mirror* that accurately reflects the reality of a person's life for reflection.

Nothing in these texts indicates that they are the result of different tasks unrelated to interpretation of meaning. The meaning of the Word intends to be related to and to effect changes in believers' lives.

While the study of the biblical message is closely related to the interpretation of the text's meaning, this study involves distinct aspects. These aspects may be clarified in the use of the term *apply*.

1. *Does this apply to me?* This question focuses on the *relationship* of a message to an audience. When the author originally spoke, he intended to say something (message) to an original audience. As a subsequent audience, we raise the question whether the message relates to us in the same way that it related to the original listeners. The factors involved in this relationship are theological, historical, and cultural. These factors will be considered both in the task of application and in the hermeneutics of application.
2. *How do I apply this?* This question focuses on *my response* to the message. Have I put into practice the instruction, the correction, or the training in righteousness? This involves the crucial role that obedience plays in application.

These two distinct senses reflect two aspects of the application of the Author's/author's intended meaning. The initial aspect concerns determining the nature of the relationship. The logical completion of application involves obedience to the Word of God. In regard to the latter, James speaks with great clarity: "What good is it, my brothers, if a man claims to have faith, but has no deeds?" (2:14) or "As the body without the spirit is dead, so faith without deeds is dead" (2:26). There can be no application without works. A careful analysis and discussion of the action demanded without the action is an abortion of God's Word implanted.

The task of application as a portion of Bible study must focus attention initially on the relationship of the Author's/author's intended meaning to the contemporary reader. This properly entails the effect that Scripture should have in the life of the reader, but this effect is only realized when it is translated by obedience into experience. So application is the task of relating the Bible's authoritative message to people today so that God may use it to change lives. On this basis let us consider the principles involved in the task of application.

CHAPTER 11

The Task of Application

Application is the task of relating what God has said to modern man. This task involves working with theological, historical, and cultural factors. These aspects of the task will be incorporated into three principles and one corollary.

Principle No. 1: We apply the textual message of the passage or principles implicit in the message.

Since application is the completion of the interpretive task, it must relate the meaning of the passage. It is that meaning which the interpreter states most completely in the message. The message then sets the limits in content for the applicational principles. The principles may develop components of the message, but must avoid including meanings that are not said or implied in the message. These principles must develop or generalize something of what was said in the message and are therefore limited to what is said.

An interesting example of misapplication occurs when the disciples attempt to apply some words of warning from Jesus (Mark 8:14–21). Jesus tells his disciples, "Watch out for the yeast [leaven] of the Pharisees and that of Herod." The disciples make no attempt to interpret the message, but immedi-ately state a principle of application based on one word, "yeast." Their principle is, Jesus is rebuking us "because we have no bread."

The principle does relate, since the disciples brought only one loaf into the boat (8:14) and it is relevant to their need. But it is unrelated to Jesus' message. That message is, the Phari-sees and Herod's skepticism toward Jesus (8:11–13) ought to be rejected in view of what he did (8:1–10). "Yeast" is a metaphor referring to the skepti-cism of the leaders that may well spread to influence everyone. The leaders failed to see the miracle in the feeding of the four thousand. The irony in the disciples' application is that they share the same skepticism, failing to relate Jesus' power to feed four thousand to their forgetfulness.

At issue here, in the task of applica-tion, is the disciples' failure to apply the message of Jesus. Instead they apply a principle based on one word wrongly interpreted. That kind of problem is all too common in application. The prob-lem is to attempt to apply a principle before or without interpreting the mes-sage in the passage. So the first princi-ple is that we apply the message which has first been interpreted.

Some people question the need for considering the message in the application, and others question whether the textual message is applicable for any but the original audience. At issue is the general scope of the textual message that was addressed to a historical audience about a historical situation. Is such a textual message general enough to include an address to a contemporary audience and to consider a subject relevant to a modern situation? At first glance it does not appear that many textual messages would be general enough to be relevant. All the biblical books address ancient historical audiences and speak about historical subjects.

The question, then, is whether there is any basis for broadening the scope and relevance of the textual message. A corollary question raises the issue of the authority of any broadened message we may construct. As a basis for finding answers, we propose the following clarifications. The issues introduced here will be developed in chapter 13.

a. Whatever changes in scope and relevance are proposed, *the original message does not change.* The textual message remains in its identity as the message of the passage. In the history of hermeneutical thought, attempts to change and broaden the message usually took the form of spiritualizing or allegorizing the textual meanings. In *spiritualizing,* most historical and natural components of the textual message are dismissed and only the spiritual core of relationship with God is kept. Then a spiritual principle is formed based on this core. In *allegorizing,* components of the message are related in a relevant fashion to modern concerns, but this relatedness disregards the textual content of the message. We reject both of these traditional approaches by maintaining the integrity of the textual message as the basis of application.

b. The initial basis for broadening

what may appear to be the limits of the textual message involves *the conventions of textual design.* The author submits to conventions in his composition that broaden his intended scope of reference from what may appear in an initial textual reading.

c. The scope of a textual message is expressed in *the textual context* of the passage. However, most textual messages relate to normative themes of progressive revelation. These normative themes form the broader canonical context within which the textual message is expressed. This context helps us to discern what is normative in the textual message and provides the contextual perspective within which to relate an Old Testament message to a New Testament believer. This important canonical consideration is the basis of the second principle.

Principle No. 2: We apply a canonical message based on the textual message, which is understood in its normative aspects according to the theological themes of God's purposes then and which may be completed by additional canonical revelation.

We have said that the initial question we must address concerning application deals with whether the biblical messages relate to the modern world. The essence of our answer rests in the second principle. A textual message may be applied in and to the extent that it expresses aspects of God's normative acts toward the accomplishment of his purposes for restoring his rule through mankind in history. These aspects of the textual message become the base of a canonical message. These basic aspects of a textual message in the Old Testament form the basis of the authoritative message that continues to speak to New Testament age believers. But the New Testament age believer is not limited to the basic aspects of an Old Testament message; the canonical message may be enlarged or completed by subsequent, related revelation. The complete explanation of the formation of the canonical message awaits a further consideration of several issues.

It is important to remember that the textual message does not change. The meaning of the original text does not change even though it is related to the broader, progressive revelation of the whole canon. The original meaning of the text is expressed in the passage. It is expressed in terms of historical and theological meanings. In some passages, the historical components of the message are necessary to its application and thus limit the scope of relevance of the textual message. These messages are limited to an original audience, as when God said to Moses, "Take off your sandals, for the place where you are standing is holy ground" (Ex. 3:5), or when Christ told the disciples to untie the donkey and her colt and bring them to him (Matt. 21:2–3), or when Paul told Timothy, "Do your best to get here before winter" (2 Tim. 4:21).

These historical limitations are not included when we consider biblical books as a whole. As these books were selected to be included in the canon, their message and most messages within the books were recognized as continuing to relate to subsequent situations. This is because the theological components of the messages are the basis necessary for application, and these components are capable of being related to normative theological themes.

While it may yet appear that the Bible contains a multitude of unrelated messages, yet in the progress of revelation, God's actions are primarily connected to four related purposes as he works toward reestablishing his rule through mankind over the world and evil. In the progress of revealing these works and words of God, the messages are either clustered around or encompass several of these purposes as they

are unfolded and developed toward fulfillment. These four themes were introduced in chapter 6.

a. The permission of evil purpose: messages of tragedy.

b. The judgment of evil purpose: messages of judgment.

c. The deliverance of the elect from judgment purpose: messages of salvation.

d. The blessing of the delivered purpose: messages of blessing.

These messages expressed in individual texts can be understood in the context of God's purposes and the normative aspects that contribute in some way to one or more of these purposes. It is these aspects of the textual message that are relevant to the church age.

Based on these normative aspects, the textual message now continues to speak. But frequently more is said about the subject in the progress of revelation until the purpose is fully accomplished in history. The additional revelation may be added to complete an early textual message. This new canonical form of the message may be related with authority. Within these basic message types, each message unfolds the progress of revelation in a different fashion.

The message of tragedy remains essentially unchanged in history. Subsequent instances of messages of tragedy may add fuller details and emphasize different aspects of tragedy, but they do not change the essence of tragedy. There is no fulfillment. What is tragic at the beginning of history remains tragic whenever repeated. Nothing is more tragic than Adam's fall.

A judgment message is reported in each age as God acts to limit the nations' and the peoples' expressions of evil. This historical message of judgment features the nations balancing each other and mediating judgment until the Day of the Lord, when God will finally judge evil. On that day the Lord himself assumes judgment as he establishes justice in national judgment of Israel on earth (Ex. 32:34). Subsequent prophetic messages announce the arrival of the Day of the Lord anticipated in the near future and in history delineated in the full scope of judgment of all wickedness.

The message of deliverance has two aspects: the promise of a deliverer (agent of deliverance), and the description of the work and reception of deliverance (object of deliverance). The message of the deliverer is progressively unfolded from an initial generic expression to repeated expressions in fuller detail that clarify and specify the reference ("seed of the woman," "seed of Abraham," "son of David," etc.). The message of the work of deliverance is also progressively revealed from a typological experience to the actual spiritually completed experience (redemption, propitiation, etc.). The message of the reception of deliverance relates to historical accounts of individuals (or nations) who are delivered (justification, regneration, redemption) by faith. These accounts are followed by accounts of the walk of those as being delivered from the power of evil (sanctification) by means progressively revealed (promise, law, etc.).

The blessing message is commonly associated with God's mediated rule on earth in some degree. The fullest display of such blessing appears when the kingdom of God's rule through man is most completely established, as when the Evil One is bound. Yet the promise of blessing reveals the generic pattern of ultimate blessing, which is then followed by messages describing the historic instances of partial fulfillment. In each case, a sufficient display of God's mediated rule is associated with the partial display of blessing. The turning point in history came when "the seed of the woman" (Jesus Christ) conquered Satan on the cross. Upon his resurrection, "the Son of Man" (Jesus Christ) was seated to participate in the Father's rule mediated on earth in the power of the Holy Spirit. The message of ultimate blessing is anticipated with Christ's return as King, as in his reign the fullness of blessing is realized.

A textual message is then understood according in its normative aspects according to the theological purposes of God. The result of such understanding is a canonical message whose initial content is defined by the textual message and whose historical content and scope are determined by God's continuing purposes to act and speak in history. This understanding may be illustrated from the textual message of Genesis 15:6: "God's response to Abraham's faith accounted it to him for a righteous standing." The content deals with God's response to faith, while the scope deals with Abraham and his righteous standing. The scope is broadened as we conclude that God's historic action is related to one of his normative purposes.

If God purposes to deliver all believers from the conquest and judgment of evil

And God's response to Abraham's faith accounted it to be a righteous standing for Abraham before him,

Then God's response to everyone's faith accounts it to be a righteous standing for that person before him as the Judge of evil.

The conclusion of this broadened scope of historic content rests on the assumption that all God's words and actions in history are purposeful and molded to fulfill his ends for creation history. As historic and particular actions of God and mankind can be related to God's purposes, their normative scope can be understood. This is the focus of the second principle.

This conclusion stated with normative scope is a canonical message of application. A given message may imply more than one principle, but however many principles are involved, it is these principles that are applied to the modern believer. Yet a person who seeks to apply the principle must make one additional consideration. He must compare and contrast the administration of the purpose of God *then* with the administration of the purpose of God *now*. This is the issue addressed in the third principle.

Before we deal with the third principle, however, let us consider another example and the conclusion we can draw from it.

A more difficult case than Genesis 15:6 is the message in Leviticus 15:31: "Separation from uncleanness must be maintained by Israelites lest they die for defiling God's dwelling among them." This message speaks of man's response to God. Yet it involves a defilement that concerns historical features of God's dwelling in the tabernacle among Israel. Various causes of defilement are listed: venereal discharge (Lev. 15:1–13, 15), emission of semen (15:16–18), menstrual flow (15:19–30). Some of these are natural and some are unnatural, involving disease, but all bring defilement in the presence of God and worship. The purpose of God is to either judge or bless Israel through his dwelling among them. He blesses those who keep themselves clean and judges those who disregard cleanliness and become unclean. God's purpose—to judge his own in disobedience and to bless his own in obedience—remains unchanged in history. The administration of that judgment and blessing today is no longer associated with his earthly dwelling in the tabernacle and these old covenant stipulations.

Later in history, when God was present in Jesus, the uncleanness of prostitutes and the woman with the issue of blood never separated them from Jesus' grace, indicating that the uncleanness was more symbolic than intrinsic. The symbolic uncleanness seems to be an absence of respect for the created human capacity to produce life and a presence of concern for the infections involved with its abuse. The message of Leviticus may be stated: "Disregarding God's gift of reproduction of life defiled one in God's presence in the tabernacle." However, the determination of an appropriate response today awaits the consideration of the next principle. So while the purposes of God for his own remain unchanged, the administration is so changed that the understanding of the principles with their added meanings must also consider the related manner of application.

The approach prescribed in the second principle acknowledges two important features of biblical revelation.

First, God continues to speak in the whole Bible. This truth is based on messages expressed in particular texts, but understood as principles seen in the context of the theology of revelation in the whole canon of Scripture. The four component purposes of progressive revelation may appear to cause an unnatural reduction; the diversity and historical richness of all that God said and did in the whole of the Bible may seem to be threatened. Yet the approach neither reduces nor limits the content of the message or principle of a particular passage, but only seeks to determine what elements in the message should be understood to be normative according to God's comprehensive and generic purposes. The historically specific message is examined in theological context. That theological context identifies some aspects of the message that relate to God's normative purposes. Other aspects of the message may not relate due to changes in God's historical administration through man.

Second, God spoke to a historical audience in a way that was relevant and authoritative, because it was he who was speaking. Yet that same message speaks to numerous other historical audiences in a relevant fashion in a related, always authoritative manner. This related manner is addressed in the third principle.

Principle No. 3: We apply the canonical message so understood by relating God's administration of his purposes then to his administration of his purposes now.

The textual message is not only completed by additional revelation, but is also to be modified by the changes in God's administration. The administration of God's purposes involves stages of history in the progressive fulfillment of his word and purposes. At each stage of fulfillment there is a period of history in which different purposes of God are changed in their relative priority and in which a new covenant relationship establishes different responsibilities and privileges. These periods of history may be as few as two—the Old Testament and the New Testament—but are naturally identified as four dispensations (as developed in chap. 7). This dispensational model provides helpful hermeneutical criteria for the preaching and application of the whole canon. The two cases already introduced will provide an illustration of the use of this third principle.

In the example of Genesis 15:6, the administration then involved:

God promises a land to Abraham and his seed, and Abraham believed that God would raise a seed from his own dead body and Sarah's to receive the land God promised.

The administration now:

God promises new life in Christ to all who would believe in him, and we believe that God raised Christ to life from the grave, through whom we receive the new life God promised.

In the case of Abraham (Gen. 15:6), the relevance of the message is understood in God's evident purpose to deliver and bless believers. However, the relation between God's deliverance and blessing then and now involves both God's priorities at a time in history and progressive fulfillment. God's priority *then* was the establishment of the elect line within a land (nation) from whom the Seed would arise. *Now* the Seed has come through whom life is offered to the elect people from all nations. The priority now rests on gathering a people with new life. These differences in administration influence the content of what is preached and applied from an Old Testament passage. We preach Genesis 15, which provides the initial content of the message. In our preaching we express what is promised, to whom it is promised, and the content of what is believed about God from the texts of the New Testament. This is canonical exposition and application.

The second example (Lev. 15:31) provides further instruction. God's purposes for judgment and blessing of his own continue. However, understanding the message in view of the theological purpose does not say the same thing to the church as it did to Israel, because God administers his purposes in such different ways.

The administration *then* is related to Israel's national covenant existence in which God dwelt enthroned in their midst in the tabernacle (Ex. 40). That administration began to change when the temples (1 Kings 8; Luke 1:8–9) were destroyed (586 B.C. and A.D. 70).

The administration *now* is related to the believers (both Jews and Gentiles) existing under the gentile government and gathering in local churches, with God dwelling in heaven as well as indwelling individual believers. In addition, with Christ's death on the cross, the administration of the law has been fulfilled (Rom. 10:4). This administration was given through Moses, but the grace and truth administration came in Jesus Christ (John 1:16–17). Grace and truth in the message of the gospel replace the earthly tabernacle. Believers now draw near to God and worship in the grace of Christ's finished work and in the truth of Christ's revelation of God and his work on the cross (John 4:23–24; 14:6). The change in the physical structure of worship (tabernacle on earth) means the former physical condition of uncleanness of the worshiper no longer defiles one who worships in spirit and truth.

So the message of Leviticus 15:31 does not apply to the New Testament believer. Yet the Old Testament is profitable to him. While the message of Leviticus 15:31 does not correct or train in the righteous approach toward God, it does instruct (2 Tim. 3:16). God is defiled by those who abuse sexual practice or disregard normal sexual functions; he is honored by those who respect the normal, human sexual functions and positive sexual behavior. So a woman who is having her period is not separated from collected believers' worship as she was in Israel. However, it would still be wise to encourage separation from the infection of a person with a contagious sexual disease, though he is not separated from God.

In this construct, the understanding of the message according to the theological purpose does not read spiritual causes for defilement into a passage that talks about physical causes for defilement. That would involve changing the meaning by adding unrelated meanings (i.e., spiritualizing the meaning). Normal sexual union by married partners does not imply evil or sin. The worshiper under the old administration who was unclean through proper sexual union did not defile God because he sinned, but because he disregarded the restriction God established. This restriction no longer exists under grace and truth. However, one who fails to separate from evil does defile God, but this is taught in the New Testament (1 Peter 1:14–16) and in the Old (Lev. 11:44–45; 19:2; 20:7).

Corollary: In the historical transitions between administrations, God may act sovereignly and uniquely to conclude the old administration and introduce the new one.

The task of application involves using the three principles. These principles are used to relate the actions of God at one time in history to appropriate actions of God at the time of the reading. They are also used to relate appropriate responses by believers to God at different times in history. These principles are based on the understanding that God administers his purposes consistently at different periods of time. In Scripture we have concluded that there are at least four periods of distinct administration of God's purposes as he reestablishes his mediated rule in history over creation through mankind (see also figure 7.5 on page 128).

Promise	Genesis 12 to Exodus 18
Law	Exodus 19 to Malachi 4, with conclusion in Revelation 4–19 to national Israel (Dan. 9)
Gospel	Matthew 1 to Revelation 3
Kingdom	Revelation 4–22 and other references in specific portions

Overlapping these periods of normative administration are periods of transition in which God chooses not to work according to the norms alone but may introduce unique actions. These transitional periods can be drawn thus:

a. Transition between Promise and Law: Selected portions of Exodus–Joshua. The unique works of God involve his work through Moses and Joshua in bringing the promise to occupy the land to completion and in introducing and validating the revelation of the law.

b. Transition between Law and Gospel: Selected portions of Kings, Ezra, Nehemiah, and the Gospels and Acts. The unique works of God begin with the prophet Elijah and continue with Elisha, but focus on Christ and his apostles. God worked in Elijah and Elisha to introduce judgment under law and in Christ to fulfill the law as well as working in Christ and through the apostles to introduce the gospel ministry (grace and truth). Certain of God's actions are unique in this period, because they are exclusively involved with the fulfillment of personal judgment under the law (death on the cross) or with the introduction of the gospel message (validating miracles, signs, and wonders).

c. Transition between Gospel and Kingdom: Selected portions of Revelation. The final transition, like the others, involves some unique acts of God. The events entail the fulfillment of the gospel age as well as the fulfillment of the law at a level of national judgment. These include actions of God in the rapture of the church and in the judgment of nations (both Israel and gentile nations). In addition, the work of God in the second coming of Christ introduces the kingdom. These actions of God are not commonly confused in application, but they do clearly illustrate the point being developed.

In concluding our discussion of the principles of application, let us examine briefly two passages that illustrate the use of the corollary. The first is a beatitude from the Sermon on the Mount (Matt. 5:5). The message is plain: "Those with a meek spirit will share with Christ as an heir of the earth in his kingdom." The theological purpose in what Jesus said is to introduce and offer new blessing available in Messiah. The question in application concerns the administration of the blessing in history, but the passage does not deal directly with that issue.

The original audience of disciples expected the "inheritance of the earth" to involve an earthly share in Messiah's kingdom, which they expected to appear on earth with the presence of Messiah. In the progress of revelation, Jesus' messianic claim was rejected by national Israel, but he was received by heaven and enthroned at the Father's right hand (Acts 2:33–34; 3:21; 7:55; 9:4–5). While the expectation of such a future inheritance remains for the meek in Israel, is there any application of this promise for the meek disciple in the church today?

The administration of this promise *today* rests on the extent to which Jesus has entered into his inheritance of the earth. There is a continuing debate over the existence and condition of Jesus' kingdom today, but most would agree that his kingdom does not extend to political control over the earth or any portion of the earth. Thus the promise *does not have* an administration today. However, there is a *hope*. As joint heirs with Christ (Rom. 8:17), believers hope to share in Christ's future inheritance of the earth. The administration of that sharing depends on Christ's sharing with the meek in Israel and the meek in the church. The meek in Israel have the right by promise made effectual in Christ, and the meek in the church have the right only by virtue of relationship and association (body) with Christ.

A second example concerns the response of man to God in the gospel age.

When Jesus is asked about inheriting eternal life, he responds in an unexpected fashion (Luke 10:25–28). The message may be summarized: "The one who meets the law's demands will live by what he does." We might have expected Jesus to invite the lawyer to believe in him. Jesus' theological purpose and administration was to conclude the administration of the law in which terms of responsibility with judgment under law invite one indirectly to seek mercy.

Today such an answer would be inappropriate, for the age of law has already been concluded. The fact that men must face the judgment of God on their sin remains true (Rom. 1:18–3:20) but the message of eternal life is focused on Christ and his satisfaction of God's judgment (Rom. 3:21–30). So today the message of eternal life directly refers to Christ. The message as understood theologically would thus involve an implication of mercy that is left unstated. That implication alone is normative, since no one is willing to follow the law in all respects just as the young ruler was not. Thus an exposition of Luke 10:25–28 would focus on the young ruler's need for mercy. The content of such mercy is further clarified in the progress of revelation, in which belief in the Lord Jesus Christ would be one's only basis to be saved from God's judgment of sin. Therefore the message of Luke 10 expresses an important content even though its application is clarified and specified in the progress of revelation.

CHAPTER 12

Hermeneutical Considerations of the Task of Application

The hermeneutics of application examines the relationship between the biblical message and the modern audience. The task of exposition for the church-age audience is not limited to one text alone, as Peter's and Paul's messages in Acts make clear. The need to consider a canonical context is particularly important when preaching or teaching from passages in the Old Testament, the Gospels, and Acts. This is true because these messages relate to a modern audience with the help of the progress in revelation.

However, this relationship must be given careful consideration. The hermeneutical criteria guide us to discern the relationship properly and to monitor possible limitations in the relationship. Without this guidance and control, inadvertent problems often crop up. As we work on the task of application, the hermeneutical premises both guide in the task and monitor the exegesis of the relationship to a modern audience.

Literal system is based on the goal of the Author's/author's intended meaning and affirms that there must be limits in the relationship between the text and the application. This relationship is limited by the message expressed in the text even for the original audience and

by the theological context of the whole canon for the modern audience. Since God authored the text as well as the whole canonical context, he may well continue to speak beyond the original audience as recognized in the perspective of the whole canon. This meaning to be applied is distinct from other judged significances.

Theological themes considers those themes related to determining what God continues to say and do. A comparison of the theme in the Old Testament passage with the content of the theme in the New Testament determines what progress has been made in the revelation of that theme. In addition, when the message is understood in the context of that theme, the reader can determine any changes in the message that are necessary for a New Testament application.

Textual design specifies the terms in which the readers are addressed. In an oversimplified sense, the Bible addresses one audience, the believing people of God. However, in a more specific and accurate sense the Bible addresses audiences in theological and/or historical terms that may specify or limit the message.

Historical specifies the role that historical and cultural factors have in the relationship of the message to the modern audience.

Monitoring the task involves a consideration of fundamental questions related to the task of application.

Is this an application of textual meaning or not?

How does the biblical author apply other portions of the Bible?

Does this passage apply to this audience? On what basis does it apply?

Does this message change when it is applied to a contemporary audience?

These questions and the issues involved will be considered in the hermeneutical premises.

LITERAL

Literal system affirms that textually based principles of application are limited by the generality and scope of the message understood in the context of the canon and are distinct from other significances of the meanings of the text.

Since throughout the Bible its authors repeatedly attest to the necessity of applying the Scripture to life, the task of exposition and the scope of interpretation must include application. Traditional literal hermeneutics did not give much attention to application. Its perspective is captured in the maxim, "One interpretation and many applications," implying that these two are unrelated tasks. Interpretation was viewed as a task that was controlled and objective while application was less controlled by the text and subjective as judged by relevance.

In one sense, the polarity between literal and allegorical in the history of interpretation has demonstrated the contrast between interpretation and application. Allegorical interpretation attempted to relate or apply the Old Testament to situations that were not directly anticipated in the text. Although its approach and strategy had elements in common with Greek interpretation, it found prominent expression in both Judaism and Christianity. However, in each case it did not have the rigor or control that literal interpretation had, and thus it led to objectionable excesses in interpretation. James Robinson writes on this score:

Thus the history of hermeneutical theory has in each case been determined by a very practical dimension: the necessity of man *to act in the present,* and yet *to act correctly* in terms of traditional norms. For hermeneutics itself is rooted in man's historicness, namely the call placed upon him to encounter the history of the past in such a way as not to deny his own existential future and present responsibility.[1]

Daniel Patte adds a comment consistent with this understanding—but note how his use of the terms *exegesis* and *hermeneutic* is different from mine:

The process of interpreting a text—a single phenomenon—can be viewed as including two approaches: *exegesis* and *hermeneutic*. Exegesis aims at *understanding the text* itself, while hermeneutic attempts to elucidate what the *text means for the modern* interpreter and the people of his culture.[2]

This perspective was first stated by Krister Stendahl in his now-famous article "Biblical Theology" in the *Interpreter's Dictionary of the Bible*. A basic hermeneutical debate today is found in the contrast between the two questions,

---

[1] James M. Robinson, "Hermeneutics Since Barth," in *The New Hermeneutic,* ed. James M. Robinson and John B. Cobb, Jr. (New York: Harper & Row, 1964), 8.

[2] Daniel Patte, *What Is Structural Exegesis?* (Philadelphia: Fortress, 1976), 3 (emphasis added).

"What *did* Scripture mean when it was written?" (the aim of traditional hermeneutics) and "What *does* Scripture mean to us today?" (the aim of "the new hermeneutic"). In Stendahl's construct, exegesis has become a historical discipline. Gordon Fee comments,

A new way of "hearing" Scripture was forced upon us. How is a statement spoken to a given historical context, in response to a specific historical problem, the Word of God for us, whose context is so different? How, or when, does something that it culturally conditioned become transcultural?[3]

A. C. Thiselton is justifiably critical of the emphasis given in the new approach.

Whilst the new hermeneutic rightly faces the problem of how the interpreter may understand the text of the New Testament more *deeply* and more *creatively*, Fuchs and Ebeling are less concerned about how he may understand it *correctly*.[4]

Though it is true that in traditional hermeneutics greater attention should have been given to the relevance and application of the meaning, such an emphasis should not exclude the question of accuracy of interpretation as in allegorical application. The foundation for authoritative application must be an *accurate and valid understanding* of the author's intended meaning. Both facets must be considered as aspects of the task of interpretation. One facet is the *foundation,* the other the *natural and necessary expression;* neither should be confused or excluded lest the task be distorted.[5]

In challenging the traditional scope of interpretation, the new hermeneutic has run the risk of forfeiting the Bible's authority as expressed in the message of the passage. It not only diminishes the task of valid interpretation, but also distorts that task. E. D. Hirsch challenged this distortion and responded to the new hermeneutic of Hans-Georg Gadamar by distinguishing between the *meaning* and the *significance.* The distinction was introduced to clarify the limits of the task of interpretation. But Hirsch's distinction has proven confusing when related to the Bible. Many evangelical interpreters who have adopted Hirsch's distinction have equated interpretation with meaning and application with significance.[6] But this in fact misses the point of Hirsch's distinction. His distinction is not between what is *meant* to be related and what is *not meant* to be related.

The important feature of meaning as distinct from significance is that meaning is the determinate representation of a text for an interpreter. An interpreted text is always taken to represent something, but

---

[3] Gordon D. Fee, "Hermeneutics and Common Sense: An Exploratory Essay on the Hermeneutics of the Epistles," in *Inerrancy and Common Sense,* ed. Roger R. Nicole and J. Ramsey Michaels (Grand Rapids: Baker, 1980), 163.

[4] A. C. Thiselton, "New Hermeneutic," in *N.T. Interpretation,* ed. I. Howard Marshall (Grand Rapids: Eerdmans, 1977), 323. Ernst Fuchs and Gerhard Ebeling are two scholars of the new hermeneutic.

[5] J. Robertson McQuilkin, "Limits of Cultural Interpretation," *Journal of the Evangelical Theological Society* 23, no. 2 (June 1980): 121. McQuilkin has also emphasized the important relation and distinction: "To preserve the independent authority of the Bible I feel it is necessary to clearly distinguish the two activities of interpretation and application. And interpretation must be the ground for application, not the other way around."

[6] Walter C. Kaiser, "The Single Intent of Scripture," in *Evangelical Roots,* ed. Kenneth S. Kantzer (Nashville: Thomas Nelson, 1978), 136; Perry B. Yoder, *Toward Understanding the Bible* (Newton, Kans.: Faith and Life Press, 1978), 26ff.

that something can always be related to something else. Significance is meaning-as-related-to-something-else.[7]

Hirsch's point is to establish the relationship between the textually determinate stability of meaning and the textually freed flexibility of significance.[8] In the special case of biblical meaning, we have sought to establish that God's Word was meant to be applied. This application was not meant only for an original, historical interpretation but was understood by David or Paul—much later than Moses—as meant to be applied for them. So in the case of the Bible, the meaning expressed in the text is a determinate *type* of meaning that is commonly stable and not dependent on what generation makes valid application.

The difficulty we encounter in using Hirsch's distinction is that the terms *meaning* and *significance* are themselves confusing. "Meaning" was chosen because of its association with textual expressions; "significance" was chosen because of its association with the relevance to the reader. However, they create confusion because "meaning" can imply meaningfulness to the reader and "significance" does not exclusively imply meaningfulness to the reader. Hirsch desired to distinguish meaningfulness from different points of view and on different grounds or bases. Let us pursue this distinction further.

Meaning views meaningfulness from the author's point of view in the textual composition. The issues and subjects are defined by the author. The problems are chosen and clarified by the author. Having determined this, the interpreter then takes the pattern of the author's type of meaning and relates or applies it to the shared type of issues and problems of the world of the interpreter.

Significance, by contrast, regards meaningfulness exclusively from the interpreter's point of view. The interpreter defines the issues. He articulates the problems. From his viewpoint of issues or problems he seeks to find relationships with the textual meanings. The meanings of the text are meaningful as they are relevant to his problems. The meanings that fit into the interpreter's solutions are examined; other meanings are disregarded. In this way the interpreter selects and chooses and thereby imposes his perspective on the textual meanings.

Besides the distinction in viewpoint, there is a related distinction regarding the bases of meaning and significance, as Hirsch explains in discussing the interpreter's relationship to the author:

> When we construe another's meaning, *we are not free agents.* So long as the meaning of his utterance is our object, we are completely *subservient to his will,* because the meaning of his utterance is the meaning he wills to convey. Once we have construed his meaning, however, we are quite *independent of his will.* We do not have to accept any longer the values and assumptions he entertained. We can *relate his meaning* to anything we want and *value it as we please.*[9]

That is, the basis of meaning is the author, no matter what interpreter applies that meaning. The basis of significance is the interpreter, since different interpreters judge significance in relation to issues in their experience. The authority of the meaning is the authority of the author and his message. The authority of the significance is the

---

[7] E. D. Hirsch, Jr., *The Aims of Interpretation* (Chicago: University of Chicago Press, 1976), 79–80.

[8] Ibid., 80.

[9] E. D. Hirsch, Jr., *Validity in Interpretation* (New Haven: Yale University Press, 1967), 142 (emphasis added).

authority of the interpreter and his argumentation for significance.

In the meaning of Scripture, the Author/author wants his message to relate and be meaningful in the lives of the hearers/readers. Thus the task of application is part of continuing interpretation. But this task is distinct from the task of judging significance. The applied meaning has its basis in God and has the authority of "thus says the Lord." It involves the realization of the goal and the theological and textual design in the intended effect of communication.

Both meaning and significance can be truthful. But since each rests on a different basis, the ground of the truthfulness is different. In application of meaning, the meaning is true because God has spoken truthfully. In assigning significance, the significance is true because the interpreter has reasoned in a valid fashion. Thus an accurate interpretation of textual meanings becomes the initial test of authoritative application of meaning. Valid reasoning from various possible sources of truth becomes the test of authoritative judgment of significance. The Bible does not validate the truthfulness of significances as it does meanings; it may only validate aspects of a discussion of significances. The Bible only considers aspects of the discussion of significances while it establishes the truthfulness of the message related to any subject about which it speaks.

Further, the application of meaning does not rest on the Bible's addressing modern man directly in the immediate issues of his modern circumstances. Rather, as the Bible addresses a type of meaning it implies issues that are in the modern world. For example, in the type of meaning of murder, this biblical meaning applies to abortion as the tak-

ing of human life since the fetus is a human life. In the type of meaning of creation, the biblical meaning applies to some scientific questions of the origin of the world. In the type of meaning of sinful man, the biblical meaning applies to issues in modern political theory concerning the value of checks and balances or the limits of personal power. In each case, where the type of issue or question or subject is addressed by the Author, the application of that meaning enjoys the authority of the Lord in speaking to that matter in contemporary life.

The judgment of significance concerns issues or subjects that the Bible does not address. The Bible does not speak to the type of political system in the gentile world. The Bible does not speak to a type of historical geology or a scientific system of creation. The Bible does teach about subjects included within a consideration of historical geology or origin of the earth, which issues may have significance in a system constructed in modern science on separate grounds.

In summary, *significance* is judged from the interpreter's point of view on the basis of his needs or subjects framed in his day. *Meaning,* by contrast, is applied from the Author's point of view on the basis of his speaking and defining the subjects that correspond to the interpreter's needs.

The distinction between meaning and significance is admittedly a theoretical construct. As a theoretical construct of the interpreter's acts of attention, it does not commonly reflect actual experiences. Hirsch acknowledges that

usually we cannot even understand a text *without perceiving such relationships,* for we cannot artificially isolate the act of construing verbal meaning from all those other acts, perceptions, associations, and judgments which accompany that act. . . . Nevertheless, we certainly can isolate or at least emphasize a particular goal for our activity.[10]

Although this distinction may be foreign to our experience, it is a necessary distinction in tasks in which we want to understand what the Author/author intended to mean. In this instance the interpreter is relating the meanings the Author intended to refer to in the reader's realm, a task called *the application of meaning*. The other task of the interpreter is relating subjects and issues from his world to the author's textual meaning; this is called *judging of significance*. This distinction forms the basis for identifying the two distinct principles: the principle of application of meaning and the principle of judgment of significance.

Moreover, while this distinction is theoretical, failure to make the distinction has led to confusion. Allegorical interpretation and many instances of midrash are in fact instances of significance. In addition, modern practices of the new hermeneutic and various examples of liberation theology are different instances of significance. A failure to make this distinction may lead to one of these confusions.

These two principles will now be examined in relation to the literal premise. The principle of application concerns the basis and range of principles implied in a message to be applied— what can be genuinely applied with the authority of "thus says the Lord." The principle of significance is important because many of a Christian's decisions

are involved in the significance of the Bible's meanings.

A. The Basis of Principles of Application

1. The approach to application in terms of principles. It is common to begin to think about application in terms of *principles,* an approach that has been widely adopted by evangelicals. Roy Zuck summarizes this approach:

Principles, often stated in single sentences, serve as bridges between interpretation and application. Latent in the text, they summarize the essence of a Bible passage in terms that are applicable to a broad spectrum of readers and situations.[11]

J. Robertson McQuilkin also supports this strategy: "The contemporary emphases on deriving principles from Scripture and emphasizing the function of Scripture are certainly legitimate."[12] Both writers follow the work of Bernard Ramm:

The proper alternative to spiritualizing the Old Testament is to *principlize* the Old Testament. To *principlize* is to discover in any narrative the basic spiritual, moral, or theological principles. These principles are latent in the text and it is the process of deduction which brings them to the surface. It is not an imposition on the text.[13]

So there appears to be a general consensus among evangelicals that principles drawn from the Bible become the basis of application. However, the validity of the approach in the literal tradition depends on the *textual basis*

[10]Ibid., 140 (emphasis added).

[11]Roy B. Zuck, "Application in Biblical Hermeneutics and Exposition," in *Walvoord: A Tribute,* ed. Donald K. Campbell (Chicago: Moody Press, 1982), 26.

[12]J. Robertson McQuilkin, "Normativeness in Scripture," in *Hermeneutics, Inerrancy and the Bible* (Grand Rapids: Zondervan, 1984), 221.

[13]Bernard L. Ramm, *Protestant Biblical Interpretation,* rev. ed. (1956; reprint, Grand Rapids: Baker, 1970), 199–200.

for the principle. Among evangelicals there exists a wide variety of approaches to establish the principle that reflects the traditional division of the task of interpretation and the task of application. We will critique these approaches by means of examining the textual basis for the principle. When the proposed principle does not have an adequate textual basis, the statements are merely judgments of significance and not applications of meaning.

2. Criticism of the form of the Bible as the basis for principles. A principle, by definition, refers to any generalization that provides *a basis for reasoning* or *a guide for conduct* or procedure. In Ramm's approach, the form of the Bible includes principles latent in the text that need to be brought to the surface. Such a conception is necessary because the Old Testament is an ancient text that expresses historical meaning. The interpretation of this historical meaning *is limited to* the historical. In the face of this limitation, the principle of application, though necessarily related to interpretation, is disjoined, since the principle expresses normative rather than historical or particular experience and general time reference applicable to any day and not just that day, in addition to being unlimited in reference to other audiences.

The question that arises in response to this is simply, "How does the interpreter generate and establish such general principles from particular, historical instances?"

a. The latent principle form of the Bible is a vague notion. Ramm sets out to answer our question by stating and defending a principle[14] which affirms that "the Bible is more a book of principle than a catalogue of specific directions." He explains that the Bible contains an excellent blend of general and specific principles for Christian living. "The *emphasis* in Scripture is on moral and spiritual principles, not on specific and itemized lists of rules for moral or spiritual conduct."[15]

Ramm's principle is both hopeful and disconcerting. It is hopeful in that it assures us that at least a major part of the Bible is of general value. But it is disconcerting in its vagueness in that it does not identify or tell the interpreter how to identify from the text what is of abiding value and what is of limited value for the modern reader.

This vagueness of identification is complicated by Ramm's hazy distinction between principles and specific rules. For example, Paul commands "husbands, love your wives" (Eph. 5:25). In Ramm's view, it would appear that this is a specific rule in that it limits a man's husband-kind-of-love to one woman; but at the same time it is a general principle as a guide for the behavior of every husband in Christ who has lived since Paul for all his responses to his wife. Thus Ramm's view of the general form of the Bible is seriously limited in its usefulness because it makes vague distinctions that are difficult if not impossible to use. Unfortunately, Ramm does not give any specific examples.

b. The latent principle form of the Bible is a misunderstood notion. Ramm's principle is also seriously marred by his attempts to support its truth. He advances two reasons in support of his emphasis on principle rather than specific rule.

(1) "If it were entirely specific in its practical teachings, then it would be provincial and relative."[16]

---

[14] Ibid., 186–90.
[15] Ibid., 186.
[16] Ibid.

Ramm is saying that the Bible must contain generalized principles because if it did not, it would be so historically tied as to be irrelevant to the reader. This argument assumes that the Bible is universal and therefore contains principles rather than specifics. Ramm neither defines nor defends his premise concerning the universal relevance of the Scripture, although this assumption is one that an evangelical would readily grant. My criticism is with his assumption that universality requires the presence of principles latent in the specifics of the text. Although Ramm does not clarify the specifics, he does see an illustration of one in the fact that Paul did not have a "classification of sin solely in terms of specifics and therefore in terms of the culture of his day."[17]

In Galatians 5, Paul lists a catalog of sins: "sexual immorality, impurity and debauchery; idolatry and witchcraft; hatred, discord, jealousy, fits of rage, selfish ambition, dissensions, factions, and envy; drunkenness, orgies, and the like" (5:19–21). The list is certainly specific in the sense that the terms are not so general as to be interchangeable. The classifications refer to distinct kinds of sin that may refer to many specific acts of that kind.

While it is true that Paul could have referred to an individual and private experience of sin which had a particular cultural form, even if he did this he would have to use words with shared meanings with the audience to be able to communicate even in his own culture. What makes Paul's reference to sin general rather than specific is that he expressed himself in terms with shared meanings. Thus, often the generality or

shareability of the Bible's message is the result, not of a unique emphasis on principle, but of its being a written revelation in terms *shared* by other people. In addition, its universality is explained by its subject matter. The subject of sin in its defining essence is not cultural but theological. It may have unique cultural expressions (as the Old Testament makes abundantly clear and Paul's list includes), but in its essence and nature it involves rebellion against God. And that problem is universally present among men of every culture.

In summary, Ramm has emphasized the generality and particularity in the form of the Bible. While it is true that the Bible speaks of timeless truths, this is not because of a unique form with latent principles, but because language uses shared types of meaning and because the Bible talks about a unique subject matter—theological revelation.

The second reason Ramm advances to support the emphasis on principle in Scripture goes as follows:

(2) "If it were a legal code of rules, then the Bible would foster an artificial spirituality, and indirectly sponsor hypocrisy."[18]

Again, Ramm is guilty of confusing form with content and in the confusion commits a grievous error. Since most would agree that the Old Testament law is a legal code,[19] Ramm's reasoning means that it is partly responsible for artificial spirituality and hypocrisy. This is clearly unacceptable (Rom. 7:12). Rather, the specific form of a command does not predispose one to seek acceptance in outward performance, i.e., legalism. It simply specifies the response that must arise in faithful obedience on a particular issue. The contrast between

---

[17] Ibid.

[18] Ibid., 187.

[19] For a helpful discussion of the role of law in the Old Testament see George E. Mendenhall, "Ancient Orient and Biblical Law," *Biblical Archaeologist* 17, no. 2 (1954): 26–46; *idem,* "Covenant Forms in Ancient Israelite Tradition," *BA* 17, no. 3 (1954): 50–76.

letter and spirit does not refer to the specific or general form of expression, but instead to the nature of the revelation. The letter demands that law be placed on the heart; the spirit refers to the law's having been placed or written on the heart.

c. *The latent principle form of the Bible is a misused notion.* This faulty view of the form of biblical revelation leads to confusion in attempting to generate general principles. Ramm suggests that *deduction* brings the general principle to the surface from particular instances. But this is confusing, because deduction always reasons from a general premise to a particular conclusion that logically and necessarily follows.

This confusion can be illustrated as follows:

> Numbers 15:32–36 instructs Israelites that if they gathered wood on the Sabbath they would be stoned. The meaning may be stated, "If an Israelite does not follow God's commands explicitly, God will punish him." Since this is part of the Mosaic law and the Mosaic law has been abolished, that command is not directly relevant to Christians. But the underlying principle is relevant. Deduced from the passage and confirmed by other Scriptures is the principle that "God punished disobedience."[20]

But how can we conclude from this passage any more than that Israel ought to punish anyone gathering wood on the Sabbath? Does this text support a principle any broader than "Israel ought" to punish "anyone"?

Perhaps there may be some form of disobedience which, because of mitigating circumstances, God would not punish. Walter Kaiser[21] points out a case

concerning Aaron and his sons that they alone were to eat of the sacred bread of presence (Lev. 24:8–9). Yet the Lord not only approved of Abimelech's offering that untouchable food to hungry David and his famished men (1 Sam. 21:1–6), but he used it to reinforce his own practice of performing emergency deeds of mercy on the Sabbath (Matt. 12:1–5; Mark 2:23–25; Luke 6:1–4). So while the law appeared to allow no exceptions, it actually had a *ceteris paribus* ("other things being equal") understood.[22] And thus the general principle that "God punishes disobedience" does not follow necessarily from Leviticus 24:8–9; mitigating circumstances may have prevented the uniform enforcement of this particular law.

For Ramm and those who follow him, the basis of the principle found in the form of the text sponsors abuse. The abuse is found in principles that say more than the text says and supports. As in the case of Numbers 15:32–36, the text does not control the range of application (i.e., Israel ought to punish anyone gathering wood on the Sabbath); instead, the interpreter's statement dictates the scope (i.e., God punishes disobedience). Clearly the message of the text involves punishment limited to the nation Israel and Sabbath violation. The principle involves punishment necessarily coming from God and that directed against any and all disobedience.

Based on the text, should we believe that punishment will fall from God on any and every instance of disobedience (i.e., an envious thought, a dishonest word, an angry response, etc.)? Or, should Israel not punish individuals found desecrating the Sabbath? And,

---

[20] Zuck, "Application in Biblical Hermeneutics and Exposition," 28.

[21] Walter C. Kaiser, Jr. "Legitimate Hermeneutics," Summit papers of the International Council on Biblical Inerrancy (Oakland, Calif.: ICBI, 1978), 6.25.

[22] J. Oliver Buswell, *A Systematic Theology of the Christian Religion* (Grand Rapids: Zondervan, 1962), 1:368–73.

was their punishment not the punishment of God? What is the difference? The principle of application (God punishes disobedience) says more than the text and therefore generates applications that are not based on this text. They are therefore not grounded in the form of the text. Some other basis has been included to generate the principle, and this we will consider in the next section.

3. Criticism of theology as the basis for principles. While Numbers 15:32–36 or Leviticus 24:8–9 do not generate a broader concept of "disobedience" by themselves, our theology does provide a basis for such a generalization.

What in fact generates the principle is a combination of numerous instances that judge particular instances of disobedience from which an *inductive* conclusion is drawn. An induction based on different instances of disobedience can lead to the conclusion that God punished disobedience. But induction cannot generate a necessarily universal conclusion or principle unless it is based on an exhaustive or representative number of cases. Wisdom literature acknowledged the truth that God punished disobedience, but Job struggled with his friends' attempts to treat that truth as a universal cause for suffering applying to his case. The answer for Job came in a revelation of God's purposes and character, although Job never found out what the actual cause of his sufferings was.

The premises informed by the truth of God's character and the normality of his purposes form the basis for truly universal principles of application. That same issue is expressed in Jesus' handling of Leviticus 24:8–9. Although God normally punishes disobedience, he did not in David's case because of the unique administration of the divine purposes as David and Christ were rejected by the leadership.

This recognition of the influence of theology has been advanced in varying forms by a number of scholars in an attempt to provide the normative textual framework within which a particular can be used as an instance of that principle. Richard Longenecker explains:

> New Testament ethics should be defined as prescriptive principles stemming from the essence of the gospel and usually embodied in the example and teachings of Jesus. . . . Its principles, I argue, are to be taken as normative. The way those principles were put into practice in the first century should be understood as signposts.[23]

The particular instance of practice did not provide the norm in itself, but the theology of the gospel did. Kaiser also recognizes the norm of theology.

> Therefore, there is an absolute loyalty in Scripture to the principles founded in the nature of God or the ordinances of creation: yet, there is more flexibility in applying those other commands such as sanitary laws, dietary laws . . . [and] ceremonial regulations.[24]

Kaiser acknowledges distinctions in the theological basis for a principle. When that basis is God's person and purposes as known in creation, the principle is normative. When the basis is the way God directed men at various times and cultures, then the principles are not normative without other considerations.

Gordon Fee seeks a solution to the application of biblical particulars by similar means.

> One should note whether the matter in hand is inherently moral or nonmoral,

---

[23] Richard N. Longenecker, "The Hermeneutics of New Testament Social Ethics" (Unpublished paper, n.d., 13, 15).

[24] Kaiser, "Legitimate Hermeneutics," 6.25.

233

theological or nontheological. Although some may differ with my judgment here, it would appear that eating food offered to idols, head covering for women when they pray or prophecy, women teaching in the church, and Paul's preference for celibacy, are examples of issues not inherently moral; they may become so only by their use or abuse in given contexts.[25]

Fee also sees the basis for application in the inherent moral or theological character of the application. If the action commanded in the text is not moral or theological, the action may be changed as the occasion or culture changes.

The position advanced here is convincing; theological content is at least related to a consideration of the textual basis of application. The problem introduced in using theological context as a basis of application, however, is that the theology may add information to or subtract information from the textual basis that is contained in the passage. So Fee judges women's head coverings to be a nonmoral and thus nonnormative issue in spite of Paul's statements regarding it as having a theological basis (1 Cor. 11:3, 7, 10). Of course, if our theology is correct, our application will be *biblical,* but it may not be an application of *the truth of that passage.* So it is apparent that theology will necessarily have a role in application, yet it is not the ultimate basis of the principles to be applied.

4. Criticism of culture as the basis for principles. Another approach to the problem of generating universal principles of application inductively was developed by Charles Kraft among others. He has sought to ground the principles not in theology, but in culture. Like Ramm, Kraft distinguishes between the

specific and abstract form of material in a cultural matrix.

> With respect to the head covering versus the "do not steal" commands, likewise, we have statements at two different levels of abstraction. "Do not steal" is a general command that occurs in every culture. Analysis of the meaning of this common form culture yields slight culturally conditioned alternative understandings within a fairly narrow range.[26]

Kraft does *not* follow some who then reason: the range of abstraction or universality is based on the presence in other cultures of the essentially same form of ethical value; where a culture does not share that value, then in that culture the biblical command is no longer relevant. In response we can say that while this inductive approach is a way of generating generality, it seriously impairs biblical authority. McQuilkin comments:

> The problem of distinguishing between that which is universal—of enduring authority—and that which is not is the question of authority. If culture determines—that is, if only those items that are found universally in all cultures are accepted as God's universal will—then culture is the authority, not Scripture.[27]

This approach is clearly unacceptable to one holding an evangelical view of biblical authority. This is not to say that culture is not a factor in application, but that it does not determine the universality of application.

Kraft, by contrast, would use cultural norms to inform both meaning and application. One such cultural principle would be: "Christians should live according to the rules of the culture (as long as they do not conflict with Christian principles)."[28] Based on this norm,

[25]Gordon D. Fee in *Inerrancy and Common Sense,* 74.
[26]Charles H. Kraft, "Interpreting in Cultural Context," *Journal of the Evangelical Theological Society* 21 no. 4 (December 1978): 363.
[27]McQuilkin, "Limits of Cultural Interpretation," 118.
[28]Kraft, "Interpreting in Cultural Context," 365.

he concludes two opposite cultural practices: "Woman should learn in silence in Greek culture (1 Tim. 2:11)" and "Woman may speak up in mixed groups in the U.S.A."[29] The disturbing thing about this is that the senses of the two applications are in direct conflict in spite of Paul's stating that his basis for the command is biblical and theological (1 Tim. 2:13–15).

In cases where culture is used as the basis of principle of application, the principles are again more correctly judgments of biblical significance rather than applications of biblical meaning. In the two instances of the use of culture, biblical commands (1 Cor. 11:1–2 or 1 Tim. 2:11) are judged to have relative significance in view of modern culture and therefore the biblical meaning is changed.

5. Proposal of message of the text understood in the context of the progress of revelation as the basis of principles of application. An alternative to these approaches to principlization does exist. Rather than seeking to deduce a principle "latent in the text," "inherent in the meaning," or "underlying the text," one can seek principles implied in the message expressed in the text. The generality of message of a passage understood in the context of the canon determines the possible range and kind of principles which that passage implies.

Since the subject matter of most biblical messages is either the words and actions of God or man's response to God, these messages relate to God's generic purposes in history. This relationship may prove to be normative or historically limited by the administration of these purposes. In either case, the unique expression of content is based on the textual development of the

passage. Thus the basis of the application rests in the type of meaning the author intends as expressed in the text. Some components of the message may be generalized, based on the relationship to the theological purpose of the canon, but theology does not thereby become the basis of the message.

These factors in the application of the biblical message are precisely at issue in Paul's interpretation and application of Deuteronomy 25:4. Paul identifies the issue in 1 Corinthians 9:9–10: when Moses writes about "oxen," does God also intend to write for "us"? The word "ox" or "oxen" certainly does not lend itself to such an interpretation or generalization. On what basis, then, did Paul generalize? He did not somehow deduce a principle that is latent in the text. Rather, Paul recognized a type of message that is expressed in the textual design of the law, in the textual particulars of the context of Deuteronomy 25:4, and related it within a broader theological context.

In identifying that textual design we must first recognize that this is a command in the literary genre called "apodictic laws." Fee and Stuart comment,

> The law is paradigmatic—it sets *a standard by an example,* rather than by mentioning every possible circumstance. . . . The statements in the law were intended as a reliable *guide* with general applicability—not a technical description of *all* possible conditions one could imagine.[30]

When Moses referred to oxen, did he intend to exclude donkeys? It seems clear that he did not, because the sense of the command does not distinguish one kind of animal from another. The point was not to draw distinctions between animals but to use one animal as an example of our attitude toward

---

[29] Ibid.

[30] Gordon D. Fee and Douglas Stuart, *How to Read the Bible for All Its Worth* (Grand Rapids: Zondervan, 1982), 140.

"creatures who serve someone else's interests."[31]

In addition to the literary genre of the verse, the context refers to certain kinds of issues. The immediate context has to do with a number of social laws such as exemption from military service (24:5), the taking of millstones in pledge (v. 6), kidnapping a person (v. 7), leprosy (vv. 8–9), loans (vv. 10–13), protection for hired servants (vv. 14–15), personal responsibility (v. 16), protection of the weak and defenseless (vv. 17–18), the law of gleaning (vv. 19–22), and the limits of corporal punishment (25:1–3). "Creatures who serve" (25:4) are having their interests guarded, as is common to the needy in these commands (24:5–25:3). S. Lewis Johnson suggests, "It is plain that the commands are directed toward the inculcation of care and consideration toward the poor, the weak and the defenseless."[32]

Thus the author's message in Deuteronomy 25:4 would be: "Creatures who serve should have their needs met in their service." The message of the text refers to "creatures," which could imply oxen, donkeys, or human beings. Paul can understand the principle that "a minister has the right to have his needs met in the ministry" (cf. 1 Cor. 9:4–6) with the authority of "thus said the Lord" (1 Cor. 9:8). This is true because the principle is implicit in the message of the law (1 Cor. 9:10). The subject "creatures who serve" is understood as a "minister," and the complement "in their service" is understood "in their ministry" in the progress of revelation. In the progress of revelation, God's blessing was experienced in the productivity of the land then, while now it is experienced in the spiritual blessings gained by Christ. In addition, "his own" includes the nation served by animals *then* and the church served by ministers *now*. The administration has changed from the law to the new covenant, but the law involved is not unique to an old covenant administration that has been put away. Rather, the law expresses a fair dealing with the needy servant, which is consistent with righteous dealings in the new covenant.

This conclusion rejects the position that "the text is given a further spiritual or moral sense."[33] Instead, the "righteous sense" is expressed in the old covenant and merely applied as consistent with the righteousness of the new covenant. In addition, this fairness is evident in the military, for the farmer, and for the shepherd (1 Cor. 9:7, 10); each has the right to live on what he receives from his work. The application is not deduced from a principle underlying the text or a sense added to the text; it is a principle that Paul addressed to a particular case and that was implied in the message expressed in the law of Moses.

This instance of Pauline exegesis and application is a good example of what should be normative practice in interpretation. At times the message itself in its entirety will be applied. These implications are often expressed directly in particulars in the text. At other times the implications may not be stated in the text and must be expressed in the interpreter's own words. The important issue is that the content of the principle must be controlled by the message expressed in the text. This is the textual basis and control of application.

The statement of the implication to be applied can be written in the form of a principle. The principle is stated with the degree of generality allowed by the type of message, which includes the theology of God's purposes and admin-

---

[31] "Ox" is taken figuratively for one member of a class.

[32] S. Lewis Johnson, *The Old Testament in the New* (Grand Rapids: Zondervan, 1980), 44.

[33] Ibid., 48.

istration. It is also stated with the degree of particularity needed in the situation of the interpreter. Thus "oxen" in the type of message means "creatures who serve someone else's interests," while in the principle of application it in particular implies "ministers of the gospel." This application of the truth of the Mosaic law does not place one under the Mosaic system but serves as an example of the profit of all Scripture.

Not all literary and linguistic texts express a type of meaning with the same generality. Some biblical material is tied to historical, cultural, and theological particularities. Consider the following: Paul commanded Timothy to come before winter (2 Tim. 4:21) or commanded the church at Thessalonica to pray for him (1 Thess. 5:25); Jesus commanded his disciples not to bring a purse, bag, or sandals (Luke 10:4) and then commanded them to bring a purse, bag, and a sword (Luke 22:36). These messages with very particular references do not imply a principle of application for anyone beyond the original audience. They may be used to illustrate a truth taught in some other passage, but this is not the application of the message of the passage under consideration. Timothy's coming before winter does not mean others should serve or that others should serve within time limits. Nor does the Thessalonians' prayer for Paul imply that churches ought to pray for their leaders. Nor does Jesus' command mean that all disciples ought to carry or not carry purse, bag, or sword.

Paul's general statement of the profit of God-inspired Scripture is established in the message expressed in the text. The explication of the full dimensions of the application of the whole Scripture demands more careful examination of any other applications.

The conclusion established in the literal tradition is that the message of the Author/author should determine the limits in the content of the principles to be applied. This message is in contrast to any principle merely related to the text other than by interpreting the Author's/author's intended type of meaning. These principles related to the text are uniformly judgments of significance.

The form of the Bible as emphasizing principle rather than specifics provides no foundation for expecting to find a principle implicit or inherent in a particular text. Rather, the foundation is discovered in the intention of the Author to continue to speak as found expressed in the textual message of the author's passage when the message is understood in its canonical and theological context. Principles of application are implied in the message and are formulated after considering appropriate theological, historical, and cultural factors. We will consider each of these factors in connection with the hermeneutical premises.

B. The Basis of Significances of the Meanings

The principle of significance in a literal tradition must be distinguished from the application of meaning. This principle may be stated: *Other significances of the author's message are judged to be relevant in view of the contemporary subjects, issues, and problems.*

Let us examine this principle piece by piece.

1. Other significances of the author's message . . . In our discussion we have distinguished *judgment of significance* from *application of meaning*. The two constructions are not antonyms, so the distinction is not one of contrast. Instead, their distinction is an attempt to identify or classify the kind of authority in the relevance or meaningfulness an interpreter sees in the message.

a. Application of meaning refers to the activity of relating the Author's/author's message. As long as we are applying another's meaning, we are not free agents. As long as the meaning of the author's utterance is our object, we are completely subservient to his will in whatever he expresses. Thus application is central to a believer's obedience of God's will. Application is central to preaching and proclamation of "thus says the Lord" and "thus commands the Lord." Application refers to the task of relating the Author's authoritative message to the believer. It remains the climactic aspect of the task of interpretation. This accuracy is concerned with faithful recognition of the full scope of the message intended—no more and no less. The outer limit of "no more" is the point at which the principle of judgment of significance comes under consideration.

b. Judgment of significance is not an activity of textual interpretation, but an aspect of personal evaluation in which textual messages are weighed and integrated into a personal worldview. All biblical messages are relevant in some respect. The relevance seen by modern audiences is seldom limited to what the author intended; in many cases it goes beyond what the author ever intended.

A few illustrations may help to clarify the distinction in the authority of relevance. Two young men, Jim and Bill, both overweight, are rooming together as each pursues an advanced degree in chemistry. Jim receives a letter from his fiancée and shares part with Bill. He reads, "Thanks for the flowers on the anniversary of our engagement. . . ." This meaning applies to Jim and his fiancée. But it is related by Jim's roommate to his own situation. In two weeks Bill's girlfriend will celebrate her birthday. Bill thinks to himself, "It would sure be nice to send my girlfriend flowers." Bill's thought of sending flowers is not part of the intended meaning of Jim's fiancée's letter; it is not in the author's intended meaning. It is *significance*.

This anecdote introduces a trite distinction and perhaps even an irrelevant one when the Author is God and "the letter" is the Bible. Is there any child of God who is not addressed by the Bible? The application of the messages found in the whole Bible rests on the fact that the messages are at least addressed to the people of God. This is the foundation of the principle of application. We will see that certain historical and cultural factors may influence the application, but the analogy that the church, in reading the Old Testament, reads "someone else's mail" is not valid. Still, the example of Jim and Bill illustrates significance not simply because the message is intended to speak to a certain audience, but because the relevance was not in the sense intended in what the letter said.

Another example will shed further light on the question of significance. Jim's letter from his fiancée continues, "I've just read about the results of a new chemically controlled diet that claims to deal with the metabolism problem you have. It would be good if Bill and you tried the diet." This message written to Jim is intended to apply to Jim, but Bill is also included. Moreover, although the message is addressed to include Bill, it may not relate to Bill's problem of being overweight. The message addresses the chemical control of metabolism, which is Jim's particular problem, but Bill's problem may be overeating, lack of exercise, or some glandular disorder. The limited scope of the message of the letter means that it may not apply to Bill's problem, but Bill would have to decide whether it has any application or significance to him.

The kind of judgments Bill faces in regard to Jim's letter are the kind of issues commonly faced in biblical exposition.

Let's consider a biblical example to complete the analogy.

An interpreter who is interested in the ethical questions of truth-telling finds a textual message in Exodus 20:16: "You shall not give false testimony against your neighbor." The ethical questions are wide-ranging. The question that the interpreter faces in Exodus 20:16 concerns the breadth of the subject addressed in the text and the relationships in which it applies. Brevard Childs offers this answer:

> The commandment is directed primarily toward guarding the basic right of the covenant member against the threat of false accusation. The original commandment is, therefore, not a general prohibition of lying, but forbids lying which directly affects one's fellows.[34]

U. Cassuto, by contrast, supports extending the subject to include "testimony contrary to the truth" and emphasizes that the relationship extends beyond Israelite citizens to include "strangers," and it thus implies "all men."[35]

From Cassuto's interpretations it seems clear that the type of subject includes "lying about another person's reputation." Within this subject the truth applies to the modern believer. There is no limit on the relationship; truth must be spoken about any person to any other person. Similarly, truth is measured in one's testimony to reality about the person in spite of the relationship to that person.

Obviously there are many other issues with respect to truth-telling that must be answered, but the truth of Exodus 20:16 would only have significance (not application) for developing a comprehensive answer. So in cases like this the distinction between application of meaning and judgment of significance concerns the scope of the type of subject addressed in the text.

Another concern of significance is the relationship constructed between certain components of the text's message and other fields of knowledge. Various components of the message can be studied in their significance to a field.

One important field of New Testament study is the life and ministry of Jesus, including such related studies as the chronology of his life, the origin of Matthew's gospel, a gospel author's life and profession (like Luke), or problems faced in the early church indicated in the Gospels. None of these subjects is addressed as a subject in the biblical text, but the text contains content related to the concerns of each study. The Gospels are certainly a primary source for the study of the subject of the life and ministry of Christ, but if that subject were to be studied in its entirety as John indicates (John 20:30), other sources would need to be consulted or assumptions would need to be made to account for information crucial to the study of life and ministry that is not found in the Gospels. The study of these subjects, then, is study in significance.

By contrast, an interpretation of one gospel writer's account of Jesus' ministry would be simply a matter of textual interpretation. The subject of Jesus' historical ministry is not addressed comprehensively as a biblical subject and thus is a study with judgments of significance. Or in the case of Luke the historian, the scanty evidence that Luke provides about himself must necessarily be supplemented with other historical sources either written about Luke or written about general subjects related to Luke, e.g., ancient physicians and historians.

---

[34] Brevard S. Childs, *The Book of Exodus* (Philadelphia: Westminster, 1974), 424.

[35] U. Cassuto, *A Commentary on the Book of Exodus* (Jerusalem: Magnes Press, 1967), 247–248.

Clues to the composition of Matthew are found in the text, but such a study must surely be related to other synoptic gospel documents and to other historical sources dealing with authorship of Matthew before any conclusions can be drawn. And in related study, the study of the occasion of Matthew's gospel must include textual data, but also include related historical witnesses associated with early extant manuscripts and historical problems in the church.

As studies in textual significances, these studies all constitute valid study of a field of knowledge. But the conclusions of the studies of significance are not interpretations of the meaning of the text, nor do they have the same authority in ministry as "thus says the Lord."

2. . . . Are judged to be relevant . . .
In regard to significance, the interpreter judges meanings in the text as being relevant to subjects and issues in his world, that relevance not being intended in the type of meaning expressed. Significance is judged in relation to the Author's/author's message, but selects and enlarges upon points of chosen interest. The significance of an issue may be enlarged upon in its relation to another writer's thought, the thought of another era, a wider subject matter, or an alien system of values.

Significance has received prominent attention in the history of interpretation, but unfortunately it has not always been distinguished from the text's meaning. The resulting confusion has produced unneeded frustration and conflict. An early example can be found in the work of Aristobulus, who was one of the precursors of Philo (late first century B.C.). Austin Farrar says of Aristobulus, "He is the first to enunciate two theses which were destined to find wide acceptance and to lead to

many false conclusions in the sphere of exegesis."[36] The most important of these two principles is that "all the tenets of Greek philosophers, and especially of Aristotle, are to be found in Moses and the Prophets by those who use the right method of inquiry."[37]

This so-called right method was *allegorical interpretation,* which is clearly a judgment of significance of Moses and the Prophets. The interpreter begins with the tenets of the Greek philosophers, which he proceeds *to relate* to Moses through the allegorical method. The truth and authority of this relationship between Moses and Aristotle depends on the validity of the interpreter's argumentation. When significance is distinguished from meaning and is identified as being Aristobulus's or Philo's relating to Aristotle and Moses, it is a legitimate avenue of study. But when significance or allegorical interpretation is claimed to be a method to understand Moses, it is "eisegesis" and illegitimate. And that is precisely the character of allegorical interpretation.

3. . . . In view of the contemporary issues and problems. Whereas there is a defining context for application—namely, the theological character of biblical revelation and the textual data—a different context controls the judgment of significance. Whereas application uses the biblical categories to relate their meaning to the same categories in modern life, judging significance uses the categories of contemporary issues or philosophy to relate back to biblical meanings. These categories may be broader than biblical terms, or they may introduce alien issues into the discussion. A few instances may help to clarify the nature of the principle and the direction that our thought will take. Although the examples are dated, it

[36] Austin Farrar, *History of Interpretation* (Grand Rapids: Baker, 1961), 129.
[37] Ibid.

seems that clarification of thought often comes only through looking at particular cases.

An example of significance in the current scene is flood geology. As a biblical discussion, the question of a universal flood is a question of understanding Moses in Genesis. Interpretively, the scope of the flood is an implication of the text of Genesis. However, for those who agree on a universal flood, its role in a system of historical geology is a judgment of significance. How does the biblical teaching of a universal flood *relate* to an interpretive system of historical geology? Flood geology is one answer that is consistent with biblical revelation. But there may be other geological schemes consistent with biblical revelation in which the universal flood is not seen to have such a determinative role. These judgments find their authority in geological argumentation, not in the authority of Moses or of God. Judgments of significance can be true, but their truth is recognized and tested on a different basis from meaning.

Another example may be found in theological studies. Biblical theology seeks to identify subjects raised by the individual scriptural authors or within the Scripture as a whole. It then collects all that an author says about that subject or all that all biblical authors say about that subject. These studies are interpretive of the text's meaning. It is only when these data are arranged into a system that questions of the character of the study arise. If the system is an attempt to reflect a biblical system, evidence is needed that this system is based on biblical data. This too is an interpretive study. However, if the system introduces issues raised in the world of the interpreter and if the system is organized and arranged around these issues, such a systematic theology would be a study of significance. In the latter category are the theologies of Karl Barth, Rudolf Bultmann, and Paul Tillich.

Liberation Theology

A particularly important example of significance in theology has arisen in the wake of contextualization: liberation theology. The following summary and assessment reflect the very helpful analysis of Harvie M. Conn.[38] It is hoped that the four issues in the assessment will demonstrate the nature of significance in liberation theology.

a. Origination and orientation of the theological interpretation. Conn says, "Liberation theologians insist that theology must start, not with theories and not with views from above, but with 'the view from below.' All theology is necessarily partisan. It starts 'where the pain is.' "[39] So it is clear that the contemporary issues of socioeconomic oppression in Latin America and racism among the blacks set the agenda and define the issues. This is even at the expense of acknowledging the possibility of a biblical theology that is transcultural.[40] Conn goes on, "The commitment does not focus on the poor as objects of the gospel's concern. The poor become the subjects of the gospel, the artisans of a new humanity— shapers, not shaped."[41]

Hugo Assman acknowledges that in

---

[38] Harvie M. Conn, "Theologies of Liberation: An Overview" and "Theologies of Liberation: Toward a Common View," in *Tensions in Contemporary Theology*, ed. Stanley N. Gundry and Alan F. Johnson (Chicago: Moody Press, 1976), 327–436.

[39] Ibid., 395–96.

[40] Bruce J. Nicholls, *Contextualization: A Theology of Gospel and Culture* (Downers Grove, Ill.: InterVarsity Press, 1979), 37–52.

[41] Conn, "Theologies of Liberation: An Overview" and "Theologies of Liberation: Toward a Common View," 396.

liberation theology there is "the epistemological privilege of the poor."[42] Supposedly, their view of life is not skewed by special interests. But of course it is just as skewed, though with different values than the wealthy. Therefore liberation begins with what exists and refuses to accept the status quo of that.

b. *Basic definition of concepts and issues.* "The strategy of liberation theology is to recover the meaning of God language within the context of history. Any separation between the revelation of God and the history of mankind must be overcome."[43] Thus the concrete situation of history in the here and now provides the primary *context* of interpretation of meaning. Basic biblical words—"kingdom of God," "salvation," "redemption"—are not defined in the biblical text and applied to history; instead they are defined in history and then related in varying degrees to the Bible. Conn writes:

"The mission of the church is to be defined in terms of history and historical struggles for liberation," they argue. Any theological model that locates the meaning and purpose of history above and beyond the concreteness of the historical now is idealistic, a relic of abstractional rhetoric. Even the eschatological dimensions within which theology seeks to function must be rooted in the present.[44]

c. *Philosophical direction in thinking.* Conn writes:

In the past, theological tools forged in the North Atlantic community have usually drawn on philosophy for their structure. Questions posed to them have come from philosophy. How can we believe in God in an age of science? How can we believe in the unchangeable God in a world of flux? But liberation theologians are driven to create tools from other disciplines in the face of different questions: How can we believe in God in a society that crushes the poor, that redefines the black into something less than a person? How can we believe in God as personal when everything in the world conspires against one's own personality? The demands of a concrete situation cause the liberation theologians to feel compelled to social analysis and the disciplines of sociology, politics, economics, and modern history.[45]

Social sciences and political philosophies like Marxism appear in varying roles among liberation theologians. At the minimum they are an instrument of social analysis. As such they frame the questions, set the priorities, provide the test of efficacy of their obedience—they assume a role of determining meaning. In a more dominant role they can set the plan for political action. Here they propose the kind of answers to the questions that have been framed. The greatest influence would be to fashion one's very worldview with its values and goals in life. In this sense, one would be completely secular and remain Christian only in name. This problem is not unique to liberation theology, but also exists in other theological systems in which philosophy has defined the agenda.

d. *Liberation's basic commitment.* "Praxis" is a term borrowed from Marx and oriented by the Latins especially to a Marxist analysis of society. It describes the circular traffic always going on between action and reflection—engagement in the world in transforming action.

In "the first act," praxis, we commit ourselves to the renovation of society on behalf and alongside the poor and the

[42] Hugo Assman, *Practical Theology of Liberation* (London: Searde, 1975).
[43] Carl Braaten, *The Flaming Center* (Philadelphia: Fortress, 1977), 145.
[44] Conn, "Theologies of Liberation: An Overview" and "Theologies of Liberation: Toward a Common View," 397.
[45] Ibid., 398.

black . . . In "the second act," theology, we reflect on what transpires because of the first act and seek to bring our praxis into juxtaposition with the revelation of God in Christ. Theology then "is not a theory we impose on our life and world, to which we expect our life and our world to conform; it is our way of thinking, as Christians, about what is going on in that life and world."[46]

Conn's analysis of liberation theology sees it as judging significances between the divine message and the problems of contemporary man. The authority and the truth in the approach are not derived from Scripture, although Scripture is involved. Liberation theology's truth rests on its accurate analysis of the problem and in the sources used in and the content of the proposed solution.

While we may readily recognize truths in its analysis of society, the theology fails to be true as a balanced biblical analysis. Only the application of the truth sourced in biblical theology to the needs of contemporary man bears divine authority and truth as a solution. The truth is not the imposition of a theory, but the application of a revelation. Its validity rests in its origin and solution from God. While constructs of biblical theologies may reflect the imbalance and shortcomings of the interpreter and thus need correction that comes from the whole body, a biblical theology remains the only valid Christian source for a solution.

Contemporary Issues

Recognizing the distinction between meaning and significance helps to clarify the nature of the discussion and the kind of agreement to be expected among Christians. Many discussions of current issues would benefit from distinguishing whether they deal with

meaning or significance. A number of issues serve to illustrate this distinction.

a. Ethics: Ethics as a subject concerns conduct that may be either personal or social and that can be judged right or wrong. The Bible has much to say about the moral judgment of human actions. But inherent limitations make it impossible for any book, even Scripture, to speak on all possible moral situations. No statements of Scripture propose to give an all-inclusive system of moral judgments. Therefore the question in a work on hermeneutics is: Is a Christian ethical system a matter of biblical interpretation, or a study in the significance of biblical teachings?

(1) One interpretive approach seeks to develop a system of ethical judgments as an expression of the holy character of God (1 Peter 1:14–15). In this approach any action is judged as to whether or not it is an implication of holiness. But few if any people have adequate knowledge of the type of meaning "holiness" to allow them to see the ethical implications of holiness in every choice of action of the twentieth century. Perhaps it is a lack of knowledge of Scripture that prevents us from reasoning interpretively from the character of God to right moral actions. In some instances, attributes of God's holiness are involved in his moral decisions (John 1:14). Since God's holiness remains a rather vague concept, and no comprehensive development of the concept of holiness in terms of ethical action exists in the Bible, therefore different and conflicting systems of ethics all claim to have their basis in the Bible. In this sense, ethics is not an *interpretation* of the *meaning* of God's character as a basis for an ethical system.

(2) A second interpretive approach is theonomy. Theonomy affirms that "the Christian is obligated to keep the whole

---

[46]Ibid., 400–401.

law of God as a pattern of sanctification. . . . [it] has a central and eradicable place in any genuinely Christian ethic.[47]

It would seem likely that the Mosaic law may express such an ethical system. Moses expressed the core of the law in ten commandments (Ex. 20:1–17; Deut. 5:1–22). His exposition of the law focuses on a love response toward God (Deut. 6:4–9). Jesus identified love directed to God as the first commandment and love directed toward others as the second commandment. Compared with these there are none greater (Mark 12:28–31), for in a sense they express the generic whole of the Ten Commandments: love for God (commands 1 to 4) and love for other people (commands 5 to 10). The content of such love is sketched generally in the Ten Commandments, which emphasize respect for God's rights and other people's rights. That content is particularized in other laws. Is that a biblical ethical system for modern man?

As indicated earlier, theonomy does not give proper attention to progressive revelation and the fact that believers in Christ are no longer under a system of law obligation (Gal. 3:10–15). Yet the truth and righteousness of God's law is revelation suited to a believer's sanctification. He is obliged to obey law mediated in Christ (1 Cor. 9:21). Norman Geisler introduces a logical objection to such a system built on universal laws. He poses a question that introduces a conflict in ethical norms: "Is it ever right to lie to save a life?"[48] In other words, within a system of biblical norms of righteous behavior no resolution is provided whether truth-telling is ever more important than life-saving. So in order for a system to exist, some consideration must be given to the significance of the collection of biblical ethical righteous laws somehow related as a system.

(3) Another approach is to abandon any attempt to develop a system as a whole. Some ethical questions require reasonings from other fields of knowledge related to the biblical teachings. These answers would be considerations of the significance of biblical teaching in broader areas of question. Still other ethical questions are considered directly in Scripture, and these may be handled as *interpretations* of scriptural *teaching*. Also, some broad teachings of Scripture may cover ethical choices by implication, as in abortion. Though modern practice was never considered in ancient times, abortion still is an implication of murder.

So an important issue in these moral judgments concerns the proper formulation of the questions and issues. Depending on how the question is formed and which issues are emphasized, different relationships to the Scriptures emerge. On the modern subject of "the test-tube baby," the questions raised and issues addressed have a wide range:

(a[1]) The technique of laboratory fertilization
- If life begins at conception, what happens if someone wants to cancel the experiment and dumps it into the sink? Or what happens if the experiment starts well but then aborts. Who is responsible?
- It would tend to mechanize the marriage act.
- There are risks associated with transfer from laboratory to implantation in the mother's womb. These would include relying on hormones to prepare the womb and help maintain the pregnancies. The hormones could well produce congenital abnormalities.

[47] Greg L. Bahnsen, *Theonomy in Christian Ethics* (Nutley, N.J.: Craig Press, 1979), 34.
[48] Norman L. Geisler, *Ethics: Alternatives and Issues* (Grand Rapids: Zondervan, 1971), 13.

- Christian ethics cannot be determined by medical technology. Fallopian tubes, like the Sabbath, are here for the benefit of moral human beings created in God's image. The basic issue is validity of conception control, whether in aiding or in preventing such conception.

(b¹) The use of the technology. Of even greater moral implication are the questions associated with man's control over his technology.

- The ethical significance of the use of any medically sound method within a covenant of marital fidelity depends chiefly on the motivation of the users, because human beings do not actually create life either inside or outside test tubes.
- The possible use of surrogate mothers for women not desiring to become pregnant. This changes the whole concept of mothering a child. Other similar problems arise as selective pools of genes or genetic manipulation are used to produce a "super race." In addition, the potential for single parenthood introduces a new concept of family.

Thus many ethical questions involve complex analysis of the problem that defines the judgment for the interpreter. Depending on his analysis of the issues, an interpreter may judge how the truth relates to the questions.

Other, similar issues arise from the explosion of technological capability.

b. Politics: Numerous political questions call for responses from Christians. When they turn to Scripture, do they find themselves making *application* or *a judgment of significance?* In *Sojourners* magazine, one writer highlights the following questions:

How do biblical teachings about lifestyle *relate* to energy resource choices and underlying assumptions of economic expansion? How does U.S. energy policy affect the stewardship of world resources

and the hope of biblical justice for all humanity?[49]

The accuracy of the editors' judgments of significance rests both on their understanding of biblical teaching on lifestyle and hope and the construct of the condition in a secular nation. The application and significance of these judgments become the basis for political action. Where there are issues of significance, Christians can reasonably disagree. This suggests that Christians can have different political convictions without affecting their Christian unity.

THEOLOGICAL

Theological affirms that the textual message and the principles of application must be understood in the canonical context of the theological purpose then and now, and applied according to God's theological administration now in comparison with then.

1. Understanding the message in the context of theological purpose then and now. Historically, the role given to theology in attempts to apply Scripture has fluctuated, sometimes being visible and sometimes appearing to be a hidden agenda. In the discussion that follows we will contrast the role of theology over against allegorization and spiritualization in interpretation; we will also refute the charge of importing a foreign theological content.

Theological terms in application are necessary because even after the type of message has been interpreted, it is not always evident what meaning this message may have for a subsequent reader. Particularly troublesome are passages from Old Testament narratives. Fortunately the apostle Paul used instances from Exodus 13–17 and Numbers 10–15 to warn the Corinthian believers of the potential for discipline

---

[49] *Sojourners* (June 1978).

in spite of their spiritual privilege. This Pauline use is particularly relevant because in it Paul refers to the design of this Old Testament narrative: it was written "for our instruction" (1 Cor. 10:11, NASB). This instruction is more than information given as a report about historical events; these events are interpreted in the perspective of God's purpose to judge evil and of his way of doing so with his people in spite of their relationship to spiritual blessings.

This theological purpose specifies the norm according to which God acts in history. The contextual type of message in Exodus and Numbers might be stated: "God's blessed people, Israel, are judged in death in the wilderness when they set their hearts on evil things." The Old Testament context does not imply in the immediate text that God would do this again. So Paul developed dimensions of shared meaning understood in the context of the theological purpose in God's dealings. It is not strange that he recognized the parallels in spiritual blessing of the Israelites then and of Christians now.

On 1 Corinthians 10:1–4, Leon Morris comments: "Notice the fivefold repetition in these verses of the word *all*. Stress is thus laid on the fact that without exception the Israelites received the tokens of God's good hand upon them."[50] It is strange, however, the way Paul described Israel's spiritual blessing; he does not find its origin in the textual expressions of the Old Testament narratives. C. K. Barrett comments on the strange constructions:

If this interpretation of the Old Testament story had already been given (Red Sea as a kind of baptism), Paul's argument is easier to understand for in fact the Israelites are represented by the Old Testament as having crossed the sea on dry land, so that the comparison with baptism is not one that would readily come to *mind*. . . . *Into Moses,* however, has no Jewish parallel; it was presumably made up by Paul on the basis of the Christian formula, *into Christ.*[51]

It is evident that Paul understands the Old Testament narrative in a *perspective* of a common view of spiritual blessings. The Old Testament historical blessing was real, but it was interpreted by Paul to be applied in the perspective of God's common purpose in history. The shared perspective *focuses attention* on theological similarities, but neither ignores nor denies the historical distinctives (Moses, Manna, rock). It is in this perspective of common theological purpose that Paul understands that this message *applies* to the Corinthians. The application and the warning of judgment rests on the repeated, normative activity of God toward his covenant people in history.

Paul's reasoning rests on the shared theological purposes present in both testaments of the canon. The basic theme is to reveal God (see part 2). It is not revelation as historiography, however. Where it refers to history it does so factually within the ancient conventions of historical reference. It is not revelation as scientific theory, although when it refers to issues in common with science, it is true. It is not revelation as a philosophy of life, though as its message unfolds there is a philosophy of life implied. It is a revelation in the initial sense that the common *focus* of Scripture is on God. This means that God speaks as the Author of Scripture but also performs as the central Actor in history.

As God the Author continues to

---

[50] Leon Morris, *First Epistle of Paul to the Corinthians* (Grand Rapids: Eerdmans, 1958), 140.

[51] C. K. Barrett, *First Corinthians,* Harper's New Testament Commentaries (New York: Harper & Row, 1968), 221.

speak the message of the Old Testament, so God the Actor is the *focus* of the *content* of Scripture. In a comprehensive study of the relationship between the Old and New Testaments, D. L. Baker examined the terminology used in discussing the unifying factor in the context of the Old Testament.[52] In brief, he divided the terminology into two groups of terms: (1) centre, *Mitte,* central point, focal point, heart, central element, essential and normative elements, vantage point, and (2) unity, unifying principle or theme, central theme or concept, primary structuring concept, essential root idea, essence, fundamental principle, or message.[53]

At the heart of Baker's distinction is the difference between *vantage point* or *focus* and *subject.* The focus may not be directly mentioned in the text but nonetheless controls and unifies both content and structure. Content is selected and interpreted from that focus and as such provides an unstated unifying factor. So the author interprets history, seeing God as the principal determining Actor in the events. By contrast, *subject* is what is mentioned in the text and what the text develops in expressing its message. The message of the passage states the subject that is expressed in the text. Numerous subjects are central to the biblical revelation: salvation, redemption, the monarchy of David, the ministry of Elijah, Israel's covenant relationship, Abraham's separation to God.

The unity of the Old Testament is not a unity in subject, but a unity in focus. Similarly, the unity between the Old Testament and the New Testament is a unity in focus. While numerous subjects are discussed, they are unified around a focus on God and his actions in history. Wilhelm Vischer suggests that this theological statement of unity may be stated even more accurately as a Christological unity in biblical revelation: Christ the Word and the ultimate agent of God's dealings and revelation.[54]

Yet the theological purpose does not inform in the sense of altering or distorting the textual sense. Rather, the message is understood in its historical content, but also as an expression of a canonical revelation. Thus the interpreter does not ignore the physical and national aspects of Old Testament meaning and generalize a principle of only spiritual factors as in spiritualization. Nor does it change a physical or national reference to a spiritual realm as in allegorization. The reasoning is as follows:

If the text reveals God's purpose *then* compared with the same purpose *now,*

And if this is message *then,*

Then these are shared implications (principles) of that message understood with normative content according to the purposes of God.

As an example, Paul reasoned in 1 Corinthians 10:1–13 in this fashion:

If, in separating a people to himself, God judged his peoples' sin *then*

and continues to judge his peoples' sin *now*

THEOLOGICAL PURPOSE

---

[52] D. L. Baker, *Two Testaments, One Bible* (Downers Grove, Ill.: InterVarsity Press, 1976).

[53] Ibid., 379-80.

[54] Wilhelm Vischer, *The Witness of the Old Testament to Christ* (London: N.p., 1949).

And God's blessed people, Israel, are judged in   MESSAGE
death in the wilderness when they set their hearts
on evil things,

Then these principles of application follow *now:*

believers must not set their hearts on evil things (v. 6),
believers must not be idolaters (v. 7),
believers must not commit sexual immorality (v. 8),
believers must not test God (v. 9),
believers who think they stand secure must be alert lest they fall
[be judged] (v. 12).

Therefore, theology in which God works repeatedly according to comparable and progressively fulfilling purposes, determines the application of the whole Bible. This is not a spiritualized interpretation in which physical and natural factors in Israel's relationship to God are generalized to spiritual factors. Rather, the interpretation is based on normative purposes of God in history that involve what God did and said then to what God does and says now in relation to the same purpose.

The message is the textual basis for the content of the principles, and the theology provides the context for enlarging the range of reference that applies with the authority of "thus says the Lord."

However, the illustration of Paul's use of Exodus and Numbers also includes additional features. These features consider the uniqueness of the two situations and weigh what influence they have in application. They are both theological, due to the progress in revelation and history-culture. We will examine these in the historical premise.

2. Application according to God's theological administration now in comparison with then. The application of the biblical messages may vary in history because God administers his purposes differently in time. Any evangelical theological position would recognize a difference in administration before Christ died and after he died, arose, and

ascended to heaven. Messages expressed in the Old Testament were applicable in an *immediate* theological sense to the original audience in that everything in the text addressed to them was administered by God in their lives. The message had direct theological pertinence to them even though God may have intended to bring fulfillment of his purpose many years later.

Even later Jewish audiences that were still in the land would be addressed in an immediate theological sense in spite of changes in time and even culture. When Israelites were taken captive in gentile lands, the first fundamental theological changes occurred. No longer could the text be applied directly; Jewish hermeneutics arose to address this condition. Then, after Jesus Christ came, the messages no longer applied in an immediate sense. The fulfillment of God's purpose in Christ was so fundamental that any Old Testament message would thereafter be applied and administered by being *mediated in Christ.*

Following a similar argument, we find that the messages of the Epistles are addressed and administered in a theologically immediate sense to church-age believers because God continues to administer his purposes the same way today in spite of the changes in culture and historical circumstance. Some evangelicals would also argue that the message as expressed historically in the

Gospels must be mediated and administered in view of the finished work of Christ, and that the message of Acts must be mediated and administered in view of the normative work of Christ expressed in the Epistles. The reason for this role of theology is that the period of the Gospels and Acts involves, historically speaking, a transitional period in God's administration of his purposes.

To summarize this point, the application of the biblical message or principle may change in history. This is because God administers his purposes differently due to their progressive fulfillment. A central issue in biblical hermeneutics involves the application of an Old Testament message, and that is the main concern of this section.

While that message applied *immediately* when addressed to Israel, it is now applied as *mediated in Christ* when addressed to the church. However, different theological traditions view the message mediated in Christ in distinctive ways and thus apply incompatible principles. We will briefly describe these theological traditions, examine their roles in hermeneutics, and evaluate them to find a suitable model for authoritative application. Each tradition holds a position on the relationship between Israel and the church. Since the message was first addressed to Israel and then to the church, its application will be influenced by that relationship.

Israel and the Church

1. Israel and the church considered essentially identical. In this view, the church and Israel are *spiritually* identical as the people of God. The *theological* differences arise as the message is mediated in Christ in different constructs of God's administration of his purposes in the church age. So Israel is a type of the church that fulfills God's purposes in distinct ways.

a. Theocracy: The goal of the Old Testament message is fully realized in the rule of God in a Christian-governed society. It views the church as the antitype of Israel in the fullest sense. God administers his purposes in Christ through the political and righteous rule of the church. The clearest expression of this interpretation in history appeared in Calvinism in Geneva. Kenneth Latourette commented:

> It was Calvin, then in his late twenties, the youthful author of the *Institutes*, who was induced by Farel to help him with the Reformation in Geneva. The two worked closely together and sought to make of the little city a model community, organized in such a fashion that church and state worked together in harmony. After a little less than two years, in April 1538, they were banished for refusing compliance with what they regarded as improper interference of the civil authorities in the church's sphere.[55]

The political climate changed in September 1541, and for nearly twenty-five years Calvin was the dominant figure in the city.

> Under Calvin's leadership, close cooperation between church and state was carried through. . . . He had the discipline of community morals and the sumptuary legislation enforced which in theory had long been advocated by the Roman Catholic Church.[56]

In this theocratic position, the church is addressed *spiritually* as identical with Israel and *theologically* as the antitype of Israel in both a moral and a political sense.

---

[55] Kenneth Scott Latourette, *A History of Christianity* (New York: Harper Brothers, 1953), 757.
[56] Ibid., 758.

The political cast of the Roman Catholic Church today is an attempt to express a similar theological position. The flaw in this construction lies in the lack of textual evidence that the church is a fulfillment of the national and political promises addressed to Israel during the times of the gentile government (Dan. 2:37–45; Mark 12:17).

b. Theonomy: The goal of the Old Testament message is the rule of God in a society ruled by divine laws. Like theocracy, theonomy views the church as the antitype of Israel; but by contrast it recognizes the valid separation between church and state when the state is secular. Thus the political parallels between Israel and the church are limited. God administers his purpose in Christ by restoring his rule over his people in his law and, through them and their political support, gradually over secular society.

The biblical support for theonomy, according to Greg Bahnsen,[57] rests in the abiding validity of the "Older" Testament legislation for Christian ethics in exhaustive detail. This conclusion rests largely on Bahnsen's exegesis of Matthew 5:17–19, in which Christ "confirmed" the law for the age between his advents.[58]

This technical sense of *plērōsai* as "confirm" (v. 17) is chosen because it is the exact opposite of *kataluō* as "void, abolish, abrogate, annul" (also v. 17). While Bahnsen's exegesis is linguistically possible, it ignores two important contextual questions:

(1) What indication is there that Jesus was speaking of any broader fulfillment or confirmation than for himself? ("I have not come to abolish [the Law or the Prophets].") And what is the nature of his relation to the Law and Prophets? If he only spoke for himself, then in what sense would he approve it for fulfillment in this age?

(2) Why did the law need to be confirmed, ratified, or established? Had it not been confirmed at Sinai (Ex. 24)? If God had confirmed it then, what further confirmation was needed?

Moreover, theonomy's attempt to apply the law consistently in full detail in a secular society faces some major problems. First, Bahnsen treats the ceremonial aspect of the law as valid today in a different sense from the moral and civil law; this difference is fundamental, but has no textual basis in the Old Testament. The difference does emerge in the progress of revelation, since Christ's first advent "fulfilled" in himself the sacrificial role for sin that the ceremonial sacrifices anticipated (Heb. 10:11-14). Thus Bahnsen concludes that "we *must* identify and distinguish ceremonial observance *from* moral requirement."[59] Most evangelicals would acknowledge the validity of this change today.

Second, in civil legislation Bahnsen fails to distinguish any difference between God's appointment of theocratic mediators in the Old Testament (Deut. 17–19; 2 Samuel 7, etc.) and his appointment of gentile rulers in the time of the Gentiles (Dan. 2:37–45; Rom. 13:1–7). While they share a common responsibility for righteousness, they do not share a similar covenant relationship with God. In what way can secular civil magistrates be responsible for or expected to achieve the righteous demands of the law? Even Israel, the redeemed people, could not achieve that righteousness. Furthermore, the ethical demands theonomy places upon the church have an unclear relation to the state. Thus the position is unclear in specifying how the church and the state

---

[57] Bahnsen, *Theonomy in Christian Ethics.*
[58] Ibid., 39–86.
[59] Ibid., 213.

are addressed by the Law and the Prophets. Also, in what sense is the church, a nonpolitical entity in a secular state, a fuller realization of the civil rule of God's law than Israel, a political entity?

In summary, the Christian is addressed *spiritually* as identical with Israel and *theologically* as the antitype in the rule of law.

c. Spiritual repetition: The goal of the Old Testament message is realized in the rule of its spiritual and moral truth in the lives of believers. In this construct the church is the antitype of Israel but only in the sense of fulfilling a spiritual heritage. This is true theologically because God's administration of his purpose is fulfilled in the spiritual rule of Christ in heaven over believers. The message of the Old Testament is applied by changing the meaning in the sense that the meaning is either limited to spiritual implications or the natural and physical references are allegorized to apply to spiritual realms.

The result is that the meaning of the message is changed. In the promises, the blessing of a land, of physical and national bounty, is set aside, and spiritual blessings mediated in Christ replace them. In promises of a future for Israel, these promises are seen to be voided by the nation's rejection of Christ or are seen to be fulfilled in eternity in a new heaven and new earth.

Such a conclusion, however, ignores Paul's anticipation of a future for Israel in history. In Romans 11 he speaks of a temporary grafting of the Gentiles into the olive tree of Israel's heritage, which will be followed by a future time when all Israel will be saved. In the Law, the civil (political state) and ceremonial (cultus) aspects of the law are seen as no longer valid for Christians, while the moral aspects are valid. However, unless there is a recognition of a fundamental change between the old covenant and the new, the Old Testament

text provides no evidence for such a distinction between moral and civil aspects of the law.

A hermeneutical system of interpretation that applies only moral and spiritual meanings allows the theology to inform the Old Testament message. Theology determines not merely how the message is used today, but what changes in the message are appropriate for today. In this construct some of the authority of the Old Testament meaning is lost.

2. Israel and the church considered spiritually related, but theologically distinct. This construct regards the two peoples as spiritually related as the people of God, but theologically distinct as serving different ends in God's administration of his purposes. In this view, the church is not the antitype of Israel but a people of God formed of Jew and Gentile, while Israel was set aside (Rom. 11; Eph. 2–3). The goal of the message of the Old Testament is to be finally fulfilled in Israel so that the message is defined in the Old Testament text. Yet the message of the Old Testament is useful for the church (1 Cor. 10:6, 11) as God works consistent with the Old Testament purposes in the administration of his purposes in the church age.

This construct of the administration of God's purposes in distinct ways at different periods in history is part of a dispensational theology. It recognizes that some of God's purposes do not change, while others change in the priority given to them because of the progressive fulfillment of his purposes in history. As we saw in part 2, the four basic periods given priority were Promise, Law, Gospel, and Kingdom. This construct will be used to examine how the Old Testament message may be applied by the church.

Dispensational theology has an important and distinctive role in the hermeneutics of application. All evangelical theology affirms that God and his basic purposes in history are unchanging, but different constructs are used to explain their progressive fulfillment. Dispensational theology specifies one model, and that model influences the application of Old Testament messages.

This role of theology may be clarified by again examining Paul's case in 1 Corinthians 10:1–13. The fact of judgment is established in the message and the continuation of judgment in a biblical theology. The Old Testament text makes clear that God administered judgment on his people by taking their lives in the wilderness so that they could never enter the inheritance of the land promised. In the New Testament, Paul *adds* new revelation as a new covenant apostle concerning God's administration of judgment *now:* "I myself will not be disqualified for the prize" (1 Cor. 9:27) and "you don't fall" (1 Cor. 10:12).

In other words, God's new administration involves *new* information. The church-age interpreter does not share Paul's position of receiving new revelation, but accepts the additional revelation from a construct of New Testament theology. So the interpreter finds the message in the Old Testament, understands the continuing implications in the perspective of a theological purpose, and uses that message with the necessary *added* revelation about God's administration of his purpose in the church age.

In the creational roles of the family (Gen. 1–2) and the creaturely conflict with evil (Gen. 3), God's purposes in human, earthly history are introduced, but are not advanced toward fulfillment. In Old Testament promises and law, God's words and actions begin to make progress toward fulfillment; distinct administrations are introduced.

God's promise to Abraham (Gen. 12:1–3, 7, etc.) promise is addressed immediately to Abraham and the patriarchs in spite of the generations that were to follow before it would be fulfilled. The same promise was addressed immediately to Israel in Moses' generation with the *added* revelation of the law. The promises would apply immediately as God used the law as a means by which to bring Israel into the promised blessing. Likewise, the promise was addressed immediately to Jesus, an Israelite, who is now "exalted to the right hand of God, he has received from the Father the *promised* Holy Spirit" (Acts 2:33–34; Heb. 1:8–9, 13).

Now the promised blessing is *mediated in Christ:* "he . . . has poured out what you now see and hear" (Acts 2:33), as "God . . . has blessed us in the heavenly realms with every spiritual blessing in Christ" (Eph. 1:3ff.). When teaching the Old Testament promise, we would understand that it was being applied in Israel's history and preeminently applied to Christ, who now applies it to us out of his supply. In addition, it will ultimately be applied to Israel as a whole, mediated in Christ as the goal of the Old Testament promise is fully attained.

The law was added alongside and addressed immediately to Israel by Moses. The priestly ceremony was applied in the tabernacle, the civil legislation in the national life, and the moral and spiritual legislation in both personal and public life. Because they were Israelites, the law addressed Jesus and his family immediately, and they applied its legislation (Luke 2:21–24, 41–50; 5:14; 10:26–27, etc.). So when Jesus said that he came not to annul but to fulfill the law (Matt. 5:17–19), he meant "fulfill" in the sense of reaching the goal and realizing the end through obedience (Matt. 5:21–48). That goal and end had been identified by God as the obedient ones of Israel becoming his "treasured possession . . . a kingdom of priests and a holy nation" (Ex. 19:5–6).

Although Jesus personally realized these purposes through his obedience, no national group realized this corporate goal. Rather, Jesus' obedience to the law brought death administered by the national leaders who were responsible to exercise the law's curse. However, in his obedience Jesus also received the promise from the Father in his resurrection to life and his ascension to honor.

Thus Jesus is the end of the law (Rom. 10:4) in the sense that in him the goal of the law is realized. This realization takes place as the Law and the laws of the Old Testament are now mediated in Christ. The ceremonial sacrifices for sin prescribed in the law are no longer needed, since the nation had offered the Sacrifice to bear the law's curse (John 11:49–53; Heb. 9:9–14). The curse of law no longer threatens man, because Christ accepted that curse himself (Gal. 3:13–14). The righteous, just, and good demands of the law are also mediated in Christ (Rom. 7:12) in several ways.

While civil aspects of the law are difficult to identify in particular, it seems irrefutable that this legislation existed as the structure for the nation of God. Israel existed as a political entity among the nations. It had uniquely a theocratic political system in which God was enthroned as King in glory (Ex. 40; 1 Kings 8–9). In bringing judgment to Israel, God temporarily removed his glory from Israel and the right to national independence for Israel. In turn, God deposited the right to world rule with the Gentiles (Dan. 2:37–45). The Jewish people returned to the land as a worshiping community (Ezra); they had no king or independent national authority (Nehemiah).

When Christ came, he claimed the rights of a political kingdom, but never exercised political authority. Today he shares a coregency with the Father as Melchizedek, but exercises no civil authority (Acts 2:34–35; 3:20–21). In-

stead, civil responsibility "gives to Caesar what is Caesar's and to God what is God's" (Matt. 22:21). Thus those civil aspects of the law are not mediated in Christ unless they have moral implications of responsibility to God or other men. Civil responsibility is defined in Christ by the country of which the believer is a citizen. So the Christian advocates righteous laws in his land, but without the expectation that God's rule will thereby be restored. In an ultimate fulfillment, Christ will mediate the civil aspects of law when he returns to earth to rule over the nations through Israel.

The moral aspects of the law apply as mediated in Christ. Yet they apply not simply as the *older* covenant, but as the *first and old* in distinction to the *superior and new* (Heb. 8:6–10:18). They are not an immediate moral code, because the legal demands have been nailed to the cross (Col. 2:11–17). The legal demands have been satisfied, but in the law God continues to speak truth, righteousness, and justice. It addresses the believer mediated as new covenant responsibility as God promises to place the law upon their hearts (Ezek. 36:27; Jer. 31:33). In this responsibility the believer can be taught, corrected, and instructed in righteousness and justice by the message of the Old Testament laws.

In the example of Numbers 15:32–36, one found gathering wood on the Sabbath must die. The application must be controlled by the type of meaning. The message might be: "One dishonoring God with work on the Sabbath rather than worshiping him must be put to death." Additional revelation from theology in the new covenant would specify means of worship and judgment in the church in God's administration of his purpose to judge those who dishonor him by failing to worship. The fact of judgment is determined in Numbers 15; the means of violation and judgment are determined in New Testament theology. Both would be involved in the application of the Old Testament message today.

Dispensational theology anticipates that the goal of the law (Ex. 19:5–6) in its ceremony, civil, and moral aspects will be realized in the future, mediated in Christ through Israel (Isa. 54). Then what was fulfilled on a personal basis will be fulfilled on a national basis consistent with Old Testament expectation.

LITERARY

Literary affirms that the textual message addresses the reader in terms established in the textual design, addresses subsequent readers in the same type of terms but appropriate to God's later administration of his purposes, and calls for a response consistent with the goal.

The essential terms addressed in each book of the Bible are theological, since it is ultimately God who addresses an audience in the biblical text. However, a distinction must be made for some narrative literature (e.g., Gospels) in which messages are included in the text that address historical audiences included in the book who are distinct from the readers of the book. The application of these historical messages must be treated in a distinct way from the message of the book or other messages in portions of the book.

1. Terms of address. There are three essential components to the terms of address.

a. The theological relationship in which God addresses the reader in the message. There are three distinct theological relationships. While no book as a whole addresses unbelievers, there are messages in the books in which God addresses them. These can continue to be addressed to unbelievers, for numer-

ous verses in John's gospel are used to proclaim Christ's promises to them. All other messages and all books either address the reader in an old covenant relationship (Old Testament) or in a new covenant relationship (New Testament). Today messages addressed to old covenant audiences must be applied and administered in new covenant relationships. So the three relationships are unbeliever, believer in old covenant relationship, and believer in new covenant relationship.

b. The theological role in which the message addresses the reader. There is a wide range of roles in which messages address believers. In the New Testament, the Gospels address the reader in his role as a disciple of Jesus with many responsibilities in life; the Epistles express the role of members of the body. In the Old Testament, the Torah and the prophets address the reader in his role as a citizen of Israel with its various responsibilities (king, prophet, priest, citizen, etc.), the Psalms as worshipers, and the wisdom books as managers of life. When these messages are applied today, apt changes must be considered in the roles of believers in God's administration of his will.

c. The historical and cultural factors in which the message addresses the reader. The historical and cultural factors will be considered under the hermeneutical premise of historical.

2. Used with a view toward response consistent with the goal. The goal investigated in part 2 of this book was defined as necessary to the understanding of the reader, but not necessary to the meaning of the text. This means that the text specifies a range of responses determined by the type of meaning without specifying the particularity of each individual response. The question that arises from this is, What is the basis for authority in the individual and particular response?

The answer is that the authority rests in the Scriptures and in the ministry of the Holy Spirit. The first issue needing clarification concerns the degree of particularity resting in the Scripture. The degree of particularity can be illustrated in considering the principles of application from the message of Ephesians 5:25 in the context of 5:23–33. The message may be stated: "Husbands must love their own wives as Christ loved the church." Some principles of application may be stated thus:

(1) A husband's love ought to be self-sacrificial.

(2) A husband must share his salary unselfishly.

(3) I must stop purchasing books before we pay our bills.

These principles become successively more particular and individual. Principle no. 1 is implied clearly in the message. Christ's love is defined in context as self-sacrificial love ("gave himself up for her," v. 25). No. 2 is often implied in the message because "self-sacrificial" implies "sharing one's salary unselfishly." However, it introduces a trait not necessary though commonly associated with the husband: being the wage earner or even primary wage earner. No. 3 is consistent with the type of meaning in the message, but involves a number of new defining components. "I" by definition may be implied by "husband"; that is part of the meaning of the message. But "purchasing books" is a particular that is part of a given reader's "individual experience." Although it is associated with "sharing his salary," it would only be suggested by the individual practice. So it is consistent with the type of meaning, but rising only to the level of principle because of the individual reader's experience.

These conclusions seem to follow for this line of thinking:

a. The authority of the response rests with the Scripture when it is a diagnostic component or a clearly associated component of the textual message. This response is accompanied by the Holy Spirit's conviction of the truth. This is the level at which the preacher can express and claim "thus says the Lord."

b. The authority of the response rests with the Scripture when the component is associated with the type of meaning, but brought to consciousness by the Holy Spirit in reference to the individual's experience. The preacher can suggest this principle, but the Holy Spirit personalizes the conviction.

While the authority of the Word and the Spirit is associated with both principles, the individual role of the Holy Spirit is much more evident in the second. Humans must be very cautious in claiming divine authority to direct individual experiences and should be able to demonstrate how these experiences are consistent with the goal and message of the text.

3. The conventions of textual design. The scope of a textual message is influenced significantly by the shared conventions of the textual design. Biblical genre has a normative intent shared to some extent by great literature, in which the occasional and situational intention of private communication is absent.

The intent includes normative implications because of the conventions shared in the design and content of the textual expressions. As already examined in parts 2 and 3, these conventions are assumed aspects of composition that must be shared by the author and the audience in order for communication to be completed. It might be appropriate to review the discussion of textual design before proceeding further (see especially chap. 7).

At this point we are interested merely

in illustrating how conventions impinge on the scope of the message. At issue in the study of the text is the scope of the subject of the passage. For example, in the *case law* of Deuteronomy 25:4, "oxen" is the stated subject, but not the subject of the law. The conventions of case law intend the case to represent a category of violated individuals.

Jesus' *practical instruction* in Matthew 5:22 concerns specific subjects such as *raca,* or "you fool," which are intended as illustrations. This intent is discovered, in the convention of practical instruction, to move between the general truth and the particular illustration and application. The general message concerns "any derogatory term."

In regard to a historical book like Genesis, the Hebrews interpreted it as *torah,* implying normative history of some kind. So the accounts of the patriarchs are recognized as composed according to normative roles: Abraham the father of faith, Jacob the prototype of the nation's character (recognized in his name "Israel"), and Joseph the chosen deliverer of his family.

Other textual designs, such as *wisdom,* also have conventions conveying normality. In wisdom, the wise man talks about what generally holds true. This literary genre helps to set the scope of the subject of the text.

HISTORICAL

Historical affirms that the textual message does not change with changes in history or culture unless the message is based on historical or cultural factors.

While the Bible addresses its reader primarily in terms of a relationship to God, its original audience was addressed in a particular historical and cultural context. This context needs to be considered in the use and application of the ancient message. All members of the original audience had a common historical and cultural context, which we shall refer to as a context shared by the original audience in a *related* fashion. Because all subsequent audiences have a different historical or cultural context, they are addressed in a *distinct* fashion.

This observation raises two questions that need to be addressed in the task of application:

- To what extent does a change in history and culture change the content of the message?
- To what extent does a change in history and culture change the use and application of the message?

Two theses answer these questions:

1. Even though the Bible, in form, is essentially a historical book expressed within a variety of ancient cultural milieus, modern man may still understand the message. This fact was introduced in part 2 and formed the basis of a number of the aspects of the initial task of preunderstanding. Even though people in the original historical culture understood many of the communication cues immediately, modern man is not innately separated from their meanings. We must do sufficient research to bridge the gap of understanding. We must work in order to share the cues that the original audience understood with little effort, and some cultural cues may even be beyond the limits of our knowledge of the setting.

But these obstacles are not sufficient to make the task of recognizing the meaning of the text impossible (2 Peter 2:21). In the case of biblical research, growth in knowledge has helped significantly to increase the modern reader's preunderstanding of the ancient culture.

2. The historical and cultural form of the Bible does not necessarily distort the truth of the type of message, or limit or change the application of its pre-

scribed or implied practices. The question of whether culture distorts the truth of the message of Scripture can be considered in the broader framework of issues introduced in contextualization. So we will briefly discuss contextualization in an attempt to understand better some of the issues at work in biblical studies.

Stephen A. Grunlan and Marvin K. Mayers have expressed what "contextualization" means in plain terms:

> When a person has been raised in one culture as a Christian and enters another culture to bring the gospel, the person brings more than just the gospel. The person is bringing his or her cultural understanding of the gospel and cultural manifestation of it. In other words the gospel has been contextualized in the culture of the Christian. . . . As we introduce the gospel in another culture, we must attempt to lay aside our own cultural understanding and manifestation of the gospel and allow understanding and manifestations of the gospel to develop in the light of the host culture, that is, to become contextualized.[60]

It is not difficult to see how the idea of contextualization raises a host of questions. One set of questions may be directed to the truth of the biblical message. How can the original, ancient writer, conditioned by cultural and perhaps erroneous views of reality, express God's Word truthfully? Does the cultural baggage of the original author not limit the truth of what is said?[61] Then again, another set of questions concerns the relevance of the biblical practice. How can the modern reader, with a host of modern cultural concerns

find relevance in an ancient message cast in ancient values and concerns? Bruce Nicholls, writing from the perspective of world missions, comments,

> The concerns of the advocates of contextualization are valid. As well as addressing the gospel to the traditional cultural values, we must take into account contemporary social, economic, and political issues of class struggle, riches and poverty, bribery and corruption, power politics, privileges and oppression—all the factors that constitute society and the relationship between one community and another. . . . Contextualization is part of a wider theological debate. The shift from the issues of indigenization [which tended to use a more traditional approach to culture] to those of contextualization is part of a much wider theological concern for understanding the function of the church in the world.[62]

The questions must be addressed in the *use* made of the Bible by modern man.

> A central issue in today's theological debate is how we use the Bible. . . . How we use the Bible will depend on our understanding of the nature of the authority of the Bible and on our understanding of the hermeneutical task in our approach to contextualization.[63]

Nicholls acknowledges that evangelicals at the Lausanne Conference on World Evangelization (1974) accepted the authority and power of the Bible. He then specifies the issue more directly: "The pressing issue now is one of hermeneutics and questions raised by the cultural conditioning of our theolog-

---

[60] Stephen A. Grunlan and Marvin K. Mayers, *Cultural Anthropology: A Christian Perspective,* 2d ed. (Grand Rapids: Zondervan, 1988), 26. See also Grunlan and Mayers's quotations from the *Willowbank Report* of the Lausanne Committee for World Evangelization (1978) in *Cultural Anthropology,* 27–28.

[61] Ibid., 27.

[62] Nicholls, *Contextualization: A Theology of Gospel and Culture,* 21–22.

[63] Ibid., 37.

ical understanding."[64] He admits the possibility of transcending one's own preunderstandings drawn from one's historical and cultural situation (as discussed under thesis 1 above). In his summary Nicholls affirms the possibility of knowing truth as expressed in ancient cultural forms and finding relevance as it is a Word from God.

> In conceptual terms there is an inseparable relationship between the content and the form of the Word of God. Both are overshadowed by the Holy Spirit so that the inscripturated Word is the authoritative Word that God intended. This biblical content-form carries its own objectivity. It is not dependent on the relativity of the interpreter's own culture or the culture into which he contextualizes it.[65]

We agree that the form of the Bible does not necessarily distort the truth of the message or the relevance of the issues addressed in spite of their arising in an ancient culture. Furthermore, Nicholls's conclusion is supported by a theological argument and an ancient language argument.

Theologically, as God's appearance in human flesh did not distort or diminish the manifestation of his deity, so the human form of Scripture does not necessarily distort or diminish the communication of truth as a revelation from God. The divine is veiled but truly revealed. The Word of God is occasioned in an ancient but real relationship. This revelation is thus true and relevant in these respects.

Linguistically, as a vehicle to express truth, ancient language forms are not inferior to modern language forms. To be sure, they are different, and ancient conceptions of reality were different from modern conceptions. However, in the Bible it is the divine source of the message that determines its truth (2 Peter 1:20–21). While modern language has a richer technical vocabulary enabling greater precision in communication about the natural world, all languages are able to serve in an acceptable fashion to express God's self-revelation within the natural world of Genesis 1–2.

In addition, the historical and cultural form of the Bible does not necessarily limit or change the practices prescribed and thus change the biblical message used in the modern world. While the text may be historically conditioned, the historical occasion for the message does not preclude comparable historical situations in the church where the message can be applied. And while the text may be culturally conditioned, the cultural form does not limit its truth and authority as God's Word to subsequent cultures. This aspect of thesis 2 will be supported by four propositions:

a. The *meaning* of a practice should be understood within the historical and cultural forms of the practice. In other words, culturally and historically conditioned practices generally have no supracultural meaning. Norman Ericson expressed a form of this proposition when he defined the criteria for contextualization.

> Cultural events and objects often have no intrinsic worth, but rather have the value and significance attributed to them by the common mind of the society. It is not so much the object or the action, in many cases, as it is the meaning of the object or the action.[66]

Thus the baptism of John in the river Jordan meant something in the Jewish culture familiar with washings and ritual practices. In the case of a biblically prescribed or commanded practice, the

---

[64] Ibid., 38.

[65] Ibid., 45.

[66] Norman R. Ericson, "Implications for Contextualization From the New Testament," in *Theology and Mission,* ed. David J. Hesselgrave (Grand Rapids: Baker, 1978), 80.

prescription is normally not given without a theological explanation of the cultural form. Whether the cultural practice is the tabernacle institution or believer baptism, the meaning of the practice is textually defined in the context. Or, to put it differently, it is commonly revealed sufficiently for repetition of the practice to occur with meaning. So when the Lord ate "the Last Supper," the meaning for later shared participation was carefully revealed. The meaning was not simply borrowed from or dependent on a cultural practice, even though a common cultural form was used. Indeed,

> The Hebrew culture of the Bible . . . is not just a culture alongside any other culture, but it became a unique culture that carried the marks of the divine-human interaction. In the providence of God this culture was able to faithfully carry the uniqueness of the divine message of creation, sin, redemption, and supremely the incarnation and resurrection of the divine Son.[67]

The uniqueness of this culture as well as the culture of the church body is the result of revealed meaning that has molded its forms and customs. Further understanding of such biblical practices may be enhanced by added knowledge of historical and cultural cues, but usually they have a theological base.

b. If a theological basis is given for a practice and the practice *teaches* theological truth, then a change in culture provides no basis for a change in practice. Thus, while the ancient cultural practice involves ancient cultural symbols, these symbols should not be replaced by equivalent symbols in the new culture. This is true because the meaning of the symbolic practice is defined by the teaching in the text, and the practice is knowingly chosen to teach theological truth. In the case of the Lord's Supper, the two elements

(unleavened bread and Jewish wine) carry meaning as symbols of Christ's death. Although the symbols were chosen from Hebrew culture and the passover meal, they were chosen to relate to the old theology and also to teach new theology. To seek to change them to cultural equivalents runs the risk of distorting their theological teaching.

Translation of language signs is different from translation of cultural practice. Both language forms and cultural practices are cultural signs or symbols, but language signs are part of a larger language system. Modern culture also has a language system that is different in degree but not in kinds of meanings. These two systems of signs make translation possible that works toward expression of equivalent meanings. No such systems exist to control and direct the translation into equivalent practices.

It should be evident, however, that a change in culture demands teaching the theological basis for and meaning of the practice. A repetition of the practice without this teaching would be meaningless form. For example, it is possible that there are missionaries for whom the original elements of the Lord's Supper are not available. Does this prohibit their practice of the Lord's Supper? Common sense suggests that the teaching must supersede the form; but it also suggests caution against using such an exceptional instance as the basis for one's normative practice. The normative practice should be drawn from the biblical text.

If we accept in principle the practice of substituting cultural equivalents, the danger of abandoning prescribed form of response involves the related problem of losing or distorting the type of meaning. Perhaps the form was chosen for theological reasons which the interpreter does not yet perceive or which

---

[67]Nicholls, *Contextualization: A Theology of Gospel and Culture*, 46.

are related to other biblical usage. If the chosen form is abandoned, the unknown implication involved in the form will be forever lost. This is the very real danger, especially when the form has become culturally unpopular. For example, in the case of headcovering (1 Cor. 11), the basis for the form must be clearly demonstrated to be nontheological before the form itself can be dismissed without possible loss of theological truth taught in the apostolic practice.

One additional feature merits attention. In epistolary literature the theological basis for a practice is usually easy to recognize. However, a simple narrative record of apostolic practice, such as celebrating the Lord's Supper from house to house (Acts 2:46) or on the first day of the week (Acts 20:7), may not clearly share the theological basis that is being taught by the practice. This is particularly true when the record of the practice is not associated with direct teaching. At the very least, apostolic practice would seem to be a wise course to follow. At the greatest, the theological purpose and administration associated with the whole narrative may provide theological implications to give support for following or not following an apostolic practice based on God's changing administration of his purposes. Yet the interpreter must also be open to the possibility that God was working uniquely in his purposes in the apostolic practice. Therefore we must exercise great care to arrive at an accurate recognition of the type of meaning in the narrative account and to use that message in application.

Some scholars have challenged this proposition. Paul Jewett[68] argues that the human author might be so culturally conditioned in his authorship that he has prescribed erroneous cultural practices. In spite of the theological basis for the practice, conflicting cultural values have crept into the biblical text in some cases. In the case of woman, Jewett says that Scripture teaches both their equality with and their inferiority to men. Other evangelical interpreters have flirted with the proposition that cultural conditioning has led to the adoption of culturally popular ideas that may be in error. For example, Alan Johnson comments on 2 Peter 3:5–6:

> Most commentators point out that Peter was alluding to the accounts of creation and the flood episodes in the Book of Genesis (1:2, 6–7; 7:6–24). He seems to have reiterated the ancient cosmological perception of the world being "formed out of water." It is true that some commentators explain this statement as a reference to the earth being separated from the water (Gen. 1:9). However, what if Peter was in fact referring to a view of cosmology which he shared with the ancient world but which no one today would hold as correct? How do interpreters handle this difficulty?[69]

Johnson's proposal that Peter refers to a faulty cosmology has two evident weaknesses. First, there is little if any historical evidence for that cosmology's being present in the first century. We know of Ancient Near Eastern cosmologies, but there is no evidence that they were current in the first century. Second, the wording and type of meaning correspond so closely to Genesis and that reference is so widely accepted that there is little reason to even entertain an alternative suggestion. As such, it provides no support for a thesis of cultural conditioning introducing error or faulty values into the biblical teaching or text.

[68] Paul K. Jewett, *Man as Male and Female* (Grand Rapids: Eerdmans, 1975).
[69] Alan Johnson, "History and Culture in New Testament Interpretation," in *Interpreting the Word of God,* ed. Morris A. Inch and Samuel J. Schultz (Chicago: Moody Press, 1976), 140.

c. If a theological basis is given for a practice and this practice *illustrates* a theological truth, then a change in culture is an occasion for a new illustration. The distinction between the second and third propositions is the distinction between *teaching* and *illustrating*. In a practice that teaches theological truth, the particular components of the practice are present in text as teaching the truth. To change the components of such a practice would imply a change in its teaching.

The practice related to the tabernacle is a good example of a practice that teaches. Every piece of furniture and every action of the priest is present to teach truth. In the case of a practice that illustrates, the teaching of the message is started separately from the teaching of the practice. Thus it is possible that numerous types of practice would be appropriate as illustrations of the teaching.

An example of a practice that illustrates is meat offered to idols (1 Cor. 8–10). Paul presented the teaching first: "knowledge causes pride, but love builds up" (8:1–3). That teaching was to guide the many possible decisions, and one decision that illustrated the teaching was the practice of eating meat offered to idols. The practice of avoiding eating the meat should be recognized as an instance of love even though one knew it meant nothing; it should not be viewed as a prescribed practice to teach love superseding knowledge.

There are many types of questionable practices that illustrate the application of knowledge and love. A more difficult instance to recognize is footwashing (John 13:1–17). The teaching involved Christ's cleansing ministry of forgiveness, which was necessary to have a part with him. Jesus illustrated that ministry in washing his disciples' feet. When he then commanded them to wash each other's feet, he explained, "I have set you an *example* that you should do as I have done for you" (vv. 14–15). He meant that they too should humbly serve one another by forgiving one another. Such service may take numerous types of activity as different historical needs for forgiveness arise. The washing of feet and the bath appropriately taught in symbol what type of redemptive service Jesus would provide (13:10–11), but only illustrate in symbol one type of service for his disciples.

d. If a historical or cultural basis is prescribed for a practice, then a *change* in historical or cultural context is a sufficient reason for limiting or changing the practice. In this case, the historical basis involves addressing the reader in historical terms in the historical context. Several variations of the application of this proposition have been proposed, and we will look at some representative examples.

(1) The historical or cultural issue addressed is so particular that the practice prescribed is not normative. The reader is addressed in very particular historical or cultural terms associated with a particular practice.

Several interpreters have developed an argument of this form concerning the role of woman in the modern church. Douglas Moo's affirmation that "in every age and place: Women are not to teach nor to have authority over men because such authority would violate the structure of created sexual relationship and would involve the woman in something for which she is not suited" called forth a response based primarily on this argument.[70] Philip Payne's response can be summarized as follows:

---

[70]Philip B. Payne, "Libertarian Women in Ephesus: A Response to Douglas J. Moo's Article, '1 Timothy 2:11–15: Meaning and Significance,' " *Trinity Journal* 2 (1981): 169–97;

Our brief overview of 1 Timothy 2 shows how thoroughly Paul's comments are aimed at the specific situation that Timothy faced in the Ephesian church. Although theological principles may be derived from Paul's handling of their situation, we need to be careful lest we mistake God's direction through Paul to the church at Ephesus in their practical historical situations as though he would give identical directions to every church in every age and culture.[71]

Moo responds that while the *occasion* is surely historically unique, the *situation,* with its set of selected circumstances to which an author intends his words to apply, can be repeated. Sufficient historical evidence is not available to limit the circumstances to which Paul wrote to one historical occasion.

> We conclude that his [Payne's] reconstruction of the Ephesians' side of the "conversation" lacks sufficient evidence in the texts and fails to provide an adequate explanation of the nature of Paul's "reply." Yet sound hermeneutical procedure would require that there be very good evidence for any local situation which is held up as a factor limiting the application of a biblical command. Otherwise, one could limit the applicability of virtually *any* biblical text simply by suggesting possible local circumstances behind it.[72]

Charles Ryrie feels that such evidence does exist in Jesus' teaching on divorce (Matthew 5:32; 19:3–9) to limit his reference to a "local Syrian problem."[73] In particular, *porneia* denotes marital relations within the forbidden degrees of Leviticus 18. Ryrie acknowl-

edges that *porneia* may mean (a[1]) adultery, (b[1]) unfaithfulness during the period of betrothal (see Matt. 1:19), or (c[1]) marriage between near relatives (Lev. 18).[74] Yet he follows the historical word study of W. K. Lowther Clarke.[75] Ryrie concludes that the reference is technical and limited to marriage between near relatives:

> *Porneia* here means *marriage within the prohibited Levitical* degrees. . . . But for a decade or two, especially in places like Antioch, where Jews and Gentiles met and where the agitation which led to the decree arose, *marriage within the prohibited degrees* was a live issue, and *porneia* was the word by which it was known.[76]

Again, the caution of Moo stands. Does "very good evidence for the local situation" exist so that the application may be limited?

(2) The historical or cultural issue addressed is normative, but the terms of relationship in which the audience is addressed necessarily limit the scope of the practice prescribed. The clearest instance of this kind of limitation toward application is found in Paul's second epistle to Timothy. Although this is the most personal of all the New Testament epistles, readers recognize that Timothy is being addressed as a minister in the Pauline tradition. Thus numerous specific commands are broadly applied to others who share ministry in that same Pauline tradition: "the things you have heard me say in the presence of many witnesses entrust to reliable men who will also be qualified to teach others" (2:2).

and Douglas J. Moo, "The Interpretation of 1 Timothy 2:11–15: A Rejoinder," *Trinity Journal* 2 (1981): 198–222.

[71]Payne, "Libertarian Women in Ephesus," 189.

[72]Moo, "The Interpretation of 1 Timothy 2:11–15." 218.

[73]Charles Caldwell Ryrie, *The Role of Women in the Church* (Chicago: Moody Press, 1970).

[74]*Ryrie Study Bible* (Chicago: Moody Press, 1978), 1346.

[75]W. K. Lowther Clarke, *New Testament Problems* (New York: Macmillan, 1929), 59–60.

[76]Clarke as quoted by Ryrie, *The Role of Women in the Church,* 47.

The modern reader has not shared the historical experience of hearing Paul speak in person, but he may share the same type of relationship in hearing Paul speak in the epistolary composition in the canon. We apply "endure hardship" (2:3) similarly in spite of our absence from the spiritual and religious conflicts of Ephesus. Even without being able to identify the specific quarrels to which Paul refers, the modern minister can apply the words, "Warn them before God against quarreling about words; it is of no value, and only ruins those who listen" (2:14).

But when Timothy is addressed *because* of his historical relationship to Paul, the commands implying this relationship are necessarily limited. So we apply "do the work of an evangelist" (4:5), which does not depend on a personal relationship to Paul, but we cannot apply "do your best to come to me quickly" (4:9), which does depend on this relationship. The issue of expressing loving concern for brothers in need is certainly normative, but this passage of the text does not command that normative behavior for anyone else. Paul and Timothy's case becomes an illustration of truth taught and action commanded in other passages. Those other passages become the authoritative basis for application. In this passage, since the historical, personal relation is included in defining the relationship in which Paul writes, the command is necessarily limited.

Another more problematic instance of this kind is the Pauline references to "greeting with a holy kiss" (1 Thess. 5:26; Rom. 16:16). Rather than immediately seeking a cultural equivalent for a practice more acceptable to the practice of modern American church, the interpreter must first examine the historical scope of the command. In both epistles, the command occurs at a location in the book where the author is addressing concluding words and greetings of a

very personal nature. The commands are based in part on Paul's personal relationship to the church that he addresses. The other commands in the surrounding context are necessarily impossible to obey. For example, modern brothers can no longer pray for Paul's personal ministry and life, as his audience was urged to do in 1 Thessalonians 5:25. Paul no longer makes an effort to have the letter read publicly to all the brothers (5:27). Similarly in Romans, he can no longer greet individual believers who lived in the ancient city of Rome (16:3–15). Thus it seems that the command is addressed exclusively to the ancient audience, who were to greet the other brothers for Paul, who wrote the letter. Nor can the type of meaning be generalized based on the text to command heartily greeting the brothers; it remains an illustration of such hearty greeting that befits the believing family. But the command to greet with a holy kiss is limited to those who historically greet one another for Paul.

Perhaps certain commands in the narrative portions of Acts also warrant this kind of interpretation. Of particular interest is the command of Peter, addressed to the Jewish generation who rejected and crucified Christ, to "repent and be baptized . . . for the forgiveness of your sins" and "save yourselves from *this* corrupt generation" (Acts 2:38, 40, emphasis mine). There is the impression that that historical generation awaited imminent catastrophic judgment. Then the same terminology appears to another son of that generation, Saul: "be baptized and wash your sins away" (22:16). In these cases the reason for baptism and washing away of guilt is related to the historical issue of a Jewish generation that rejected God's own Son. This conclusion arises in part from a comparison of the teaching in these contexts with other teachings about the reasons for baptism.

SUMMARY

The Bible is a Christian's book in which the Scripture as a whole is inspired and profitable. At the same time the biblical books were written to ancient audiences living at various times in biblical history and in ancient times of human history. The fundamental hermeneutical issue involves monitoring the relationship of a biblical message to a modern audience. Three conclusions summarize the monitoring of this task:

1. The biblical message of the Old Testament theologically understood is used consistent with the way God's purposes are administered in the church. These purposes are administered or "mediated in Christ." Such "mediation in Christ" is understood differently in various theological traditions, and these differences are reflected in possibly conflicting applications of the Old Testament message. This textbook supports a dispensational construct of the theological sense of "mediated in Christ."
2. The biblical message of the New Testament theologically understood is used consistent with the theological administration mediated in Christ for the practice in spite of historical or cultural changes. While the historical and cultural context is fundamental to a preunderstanding for the recognition of meaning, in biblically prescribed practices with a theological basis this basis introduces normality to the practice.

Two exceptions are proposed. If a theological basis is given for the practice, yet the practice itself is not related to the diagnosis of the teaching but is merely associated as an illustration of the teaching, then a change in culture gives occasion for a new illustration. Or, if a practice is prescribed or recorded without any theological basis present, then the historical or cultural form of the practice is not necessary for response to that practice.

3. The validity of a particular response rests on the shared authority of the text and the Holy Spirit. The text's authority extends to any valid implication of response implied in the message of the text as addressed in the text. The Holy Spirit's authority includes any response consistent with the message and the goal of the text and relevant to the real spiritual needs of the situation.

PART FIVE

VALIDATION

Introduction

Evangelicals agree that what the Bible says, it says with authority and in truth, yet they have experienced frustration in coming to agreement on what that truth may be. They have faced further frustration in seeking to convince their world of what that truth is.

As a result of that frustration, many evangelicals have abandoned any attempt to verify what the Bible says as truth, let alone render judgment on validating one interpretation of the Bible or another. In place of rigorous discussion on this matter, they seek to respond to issues on which they can hope to agree, such as abortion or affirmations of inerrancy.

As useful as that strategy may be, it avoids the central issues that evangelicals have long held dear: the truth and authority of the Bible's message. It is wise to seek a strategy before the world that defends the truthfulness and authority of critical messages like the gospel or abortion. It is also imperative that evangelicals continue to discuss the relative merits of various interpretations and seek to validate one interpretation as the truth in problem passages.

Some strategy of validation is needed that can enable evangelicals to talk together about the relative merits of incompatible interpretations and to begin to gain a broader agreement on issues that remain under discussion. Even if agreement is not reached, greater clarity can come in identifying the reasons for continuing disagreements. This clarification would certainly make important contributions toward realizing a practicing unity within the body of Christ; and it would support the important goal of placing believers under the authority of Scripture in its message.

Most scholars would agree that the verification of one interpretation among a number of incompatible interpretations is a task of hermeneutics. The premises of hermeneutics are the product of the science of hermeneutics, but because they are general they are incapable of determining particular meanings with objectivity. Thus personal judgments are introduced to choose particular meanings and thereby introduce a subjectivity. These subjective decisions, according to some, plunge the task of interpretation hopelessly into personally based judgments. And so the question arises, How can I as an interpreter be objective in the use of general premises to determine particular meanings?

"Literal interpretation" is frequently advanced as the means for bringing such objectivity to this task. The interpreter chooses the literal sense, and therefore his interpretation is not based on subjective criteria. For example, consider this statement from F. F. Bruce:

> The Gospel of John in particular lent itself to allegorical exegesis. This is not surprising because even today many readers of the narratives in this Gospel are left with a feeling that John is saying more than meets the eye. . . . If commentators are not content to confine themselves to literal and surface meaning, their symbolic interpretations are likely to reflect their own mode of thinking rather than the evangelist's intention.[1]

Bruce's use of "literal" (in a sense different than that used in this text) is an attempt to provide objectivity by introducing this general rule of interpretation. But it is clear from Bruce's "confine themselves to the literal and surface meanings" that such a general rule can be forced on specific instances and would not allow for the textual clues that the author provides for meanings other than "literal and surface" ones. E. D. Hirsch has concluded that "a truly general rule will fail, . . . to guide us in a specific case, and a practical rule—that is, a specific and concrete one—cannot be truly general: it may or may not lead to the valid conclusion."[2]

So the literal rule of interpretation (with normal usage) is actually a provisional guide or a maxim, a rule of thumb. "In the absence of compelling indications to the contrary we follow them because they hold true more often than not. In other words, the practical canons of interpretations are preliminary probability judgments based on past experience."[3] To put it plainly, the literal, or normal, clear sense is to be chosen because past experience has shown that more often than not it is a correct choice. This approach has its basis in common sense.

The important point to realize about such a "literal" rule or maxim is that it guides a *probability judgment*. This is a judgment of the merit of an interpretation based on the weight of evidence in its favor. "Literal" brings the evidence of previous language uses to the new and unknown usage in the text the interpreter is studying. This has value because the construction's previous usage is quite likely to have a bearing on the meaning the author intended in the text we are interpreting.

The "literal" rule, however, should not be understood to be a rule with legislative authority to designate objective meanings in the text. As a guide to a probability judgment, "literal" identifies the meaning that is *probably* to be chosen *unless* there is compelling contextual evidence to the contrary.

Such maxims are the most common features in hermeneutics and remain profitable to the extent that they are used with thoughtful consideration. Maxims such as "the perspicuity of Scripture" and the application of "the analogy of faith" are generally true. Yet the ultimate ground for our knowledge of a text's meaning should not rest on general maxims, but on the consideration of evidence related to that particular passage. What is needed is a logic of validation of an interpretation of the particular passage.

The "literal norm" or "maxim" does introduce an important fact in such a logic of validation. By its very nature, the act of understanding involves generating hypotheses of the author's intended sense. There are no methods that can guarantee the accuracy of the hypothesis. There are no "always works" rules for

---

[1] F. F. Bruce, "The History of New Testament Study," in *New Testament Interpretation*, ed. I. Howard Marshall (Grand Rapids: Eerdmans, 1977), 23.

[2] E. D. Hirsch, Jr., *Validity in Interpretation* (New Haven: Yale University Press, 1967), 202.

[3] Ibid., 203.

generating correct insights. The maxims or methodological activities of interpreta-tion are only relevant when we begin to test and criticize our hypotheses. *While there is no method or maxim for generating correct interpretative hypotheses of the author's intended type of meaning, there can be a critical process of validation.* Thus Hirsch casts the focus of the discipline of hermeneutics, not on the methods of construction, but on a logic of validation.[4]

The "literal norm" was an attempt to bring the weight of a probability judgment to bear to validate the meanings understood. Therefore the logic of validation is a logic of probability. The only limitation of the "literal norm" is that it attempts to relate a valid probability judgment in general to particular instances that may or may not apply. By contrast, Hirsch proposes a strategy for informed probability judgments about particular cases.[5]

The logic of validation relates a series of principles in the discipline of hermeneutics as follows:

1. The principle of recognition involves an interpretive hypothesis regarding the type or class of meaning expressed in the text.
2. The principle of exegesis provides not only an unfolding of meanings expressed in the text that are implicit in the type of meaning recognized, but also a test of correspondence and consistency for the recognized meaning as expressed in the text. The test examines whether the type of meaning as a whole comprehends coherently all of the particular meanings in the text. This test has limited value in validation because all interpreta-tions of the whole tend to have a self-confirmability. All the particulars either "fit" or "can be made to fit" the type of meaning as recognized. Thus additional tests of validation are needed.
3. The principle of validation is the critical testing of the probable accuracy of the proposed interpretation of the textual meaning. It deals with the critical defense of the probable interpretation. Having its base in shared common sense, the reasoning does not compel agreement by the force of philosophi-cal certainty, but rather by the weight of the evidence in search of a legal kind of certainty. This principle will be defined and its practice examined in the chapter that follows.

What was originally introduced as a problem of subjectivity in the process of interpretation is now seen more clearly to be a problem of probable accuracy. A constructive approach to resolve this uncertainty involves the logic of validation.

---

[4] Ibid., 207.
[5] Ibid., 203.

CHAPTER 13

The Principle of Validation

The foundational goal in Bible study is to know the meanings of Scripture. Reaching that goal is thrown into question when different interpretations of the meaning of a passage are in conflict with one another. Hermeneutics is the discipline that deals with the principles of interpretation and that focuses attention on resolving these problems. One approach to handling the problem of conflicting interpretations begins by sitting in judgment on one's capacity to know or by assuming a skepticism toward the scope of what can be known from an ancient document in a modern perspective. This approach finds expression in the critical use of interpretive principles and reflects the judgmental perspective implicit in a Kantian and rationalistic worldview.

This textbook chooses a different strategy and perspective, namely, the author's initial right to speak and be understood. That right is reflected in the choice of our goal of interpretation: to know the author's intended meaning. It also formed the basis of the first principle of interpretation, discussed earlier: to recognize the author's type of meaning as a whole.

This right to know, even with an ancient document, and the correspond-ing right of an author to speak and be understood rest securely in a biblical worldview. As a foundation for valida-tion, we must affirm the essential ele-ments that define this worldview. Four key terms for us are *probability, cer-tainty, uncertainty,* and *critical.*

A BIBLICAL WORLDVIEW FOR HERMENEUTICS

1. Man created in God's image and sharing language with God as a lan-guage speaker is capable of knowing God and the world. Man, as created, is designed to know God and his world. This capacity to know rests in the shared image between God and man; it is expressed in language as man com-municates with God and his fellowmen and talks about God and his world. An objective and real knowledge rests on the correspondence of language mean-ings with the world and God about which man speaks. And the corre-spondence between language and real-ity finds its origin in Creation as God spoke the world into existence. God's words spoken set the pattern in which the world took form and appeared in substance. So in the biblical worldview, language is the basis of the created world and the vehicle of communication within creation.

At the Fall, man's sharing in God's image was distorted, but not lost. Similarly, his capacity to know was distorted, but not lost—distorted in both the enslavement of his will and the darkening of his mind. His will was enslaved to the lie that he could be like God (Gen. 3:5).[1] His mind was darkened by the knowledge of evil added to a knowledge of good (Gen. 3:22). As a consequence of this sin, man died (Gen. 2:17; 5:3–5). Thus, in one sense he knew about God, but in another, he did not know God and was separated from him until God reestablished this relationship (Gen. 3:21). Fallen man's knowledge of God was intuitive and mediated in creation (Rom. 1:19: "since what may be known about God is plain to them"). But it was distorted by the lie of Satan and ineffective for a relationship with God.

The moral consequences of man's fall into sin further complicated man's knowledge of God. Man was created to know in dependence upon God and as the agent of God's will. But after the Fall, man knew good and evil. As the Evil One crept to Cain's door, the knowledge of hatred and murder arose and ruled Cain. Ever since, natural man has been powerless to control the knowledge of evil as he has attempted to establish himself as autonomous from and equal with God.

While man's capacity to think logically was unaffected by the Fall, his willingness to think logically was distorted (1 Cor. 2:14). He now no longer thinks and reasons in relation to God, but thinks and reasons in relation to himself as the center and focus of life (Rom. 1:18–23).

Since all knowledge is not known in relation to God but in relation to man, knowledge is distorted. Knowledge dealing with ultimate causation or basic origins must find answers in man or his imagination. Likewise, the essential nature of created reality is no longer known in the context of and in the revelation of God. So attempting to see reality only in relation to itself or in relation to man will necessarily be incomplete and thus distorted.

Man's knowledge is further complicated by his capacity to comprehend. Since man is finite in his essence and knowledge, all his comprehension of an unknown is bound by *probability* judgments.[2] Aristotle saw man's reason proceeding from preexisting knowledge—what Aquinas called "rational and discursive." Discursive reasoning influences man's comprehension as he gradually comes to know. In the case of Adam in the garden, he gradually came to know as he named creature by creature; each new name was chosen in relation to what he already knew as he named woman in relation to his knowledge of himself. If, by contrast, man could comprehend the unknown in its own true and total identity, such probability judgments would be unnecessary. But in reality man's probable knowledge of the unknown may need to be corrected, modified, or even totally abandoned in favor of a new interpretation of the unknown.

So in hermeneutical theory, fallen

---

[1] So, although they knew God (Rom. 1:19–21), they refused to treat Him as God in glory and thanksgiving.

[2] Probability, as we will see later, does not measure the truthfulness of a statement, but rather our degree of assurance in claiming truth for it. This distinction is important in discussing problems in logical terms. "A statement that is only probably true has the same truth that is possessed by a statement that we regard as certainly true. . . . Degrees of probability are not measures of the truth of a statement, but only measures of the assurance with which we can determine its truth" (Mortimer J. Adler, *Aristotle for Everybody: Difficult Thought Made Easy* [New York: Macmillan, 1978], 157).

man's knowledge may be distorted or inaccurate in the process of comprehension. The distortion of fallen man's knowledge is corrected when men find a base for their thinking in the special revelation of Scripture. The Bible's revelation provides such a context to ground man's knowledge and reject the epistemology of Kant. Moreover, in the communication of the Bible to man, we must consider the discursive nature of man's reading and learning. The probability judgment in interpretation does not concern whether a reader *can* know, but whether he *does* know what the Author/author has said.

This probability refers to the judgment of the validity of an interpretation of an object (such as a biblical text) to be known. Its validity is based on the weight of evidence in favor of an interpretive option. As more evidence is known in favor of an option, the greater becomes the probability that the interpretive judgment is accurate. *Certainty* in knowledge refers to the kind of criteria met and the weight of evidence in favor of an interpretation. (These criteria will be examined later.)

Critical refers to the stance taken by the interpreter in reference to his knowledge of the object to be known. This stance is a chosen position of his right, capacity, and achievement in coming to know another's communicated meaning. Because this book is attempting to work within the framework of a biblical worldview, it will not take the stance to sit in judgment on either man's right and capacity to know or on the adequacy and accuracy of the biblical revelation to be known. So along with rejecting Kant's epistemology we will reject certain practices of what is called "critical inquiry." For example, textual emendation of readings that are difficult to interpret are forthrightly

rejected. By contrast, textual criticism (lower criticism), the merits of optional textual readings supported in extant manuscripts must be weighed and the text form determined to the best degree of our present knowledge.

Moreover, principles of source criticism will not be used to "correct" the interpretation of one Gospel in view of a proposed original expression of another Gospel record or in the proposed document such as Q. Historical reconstructions of the ancient world that are based in part on Scripture and in part on other ancient sources must not be used to override the apparent sense of a textual interpretation.

However, legitimate criticism of interpretations of the text may be helpful and in fact necessary. An interpretation may claim to know a literary or historical meaning from the text. Further scrutiny, using some critical methods, may demonstrate that the meaning claimed is not valid at all. So interpretations that claim that the Bible sees the earth as the spatial center of the universe will on closer literary scrutiny clearly disclose that a spatial meaning is not intended at all. This approach is consistent with the position reached by Donald Guthrie on critical inquiry:

> There is a decided difference between a scholar who accepts the divine origin of Scripture and inquiries into its historical and literary origins and a scholar who begins his critical inquiries with the assumption that there is nothing unique about the text and who claims the right to examine it as he would any other book. The former is not simply submitting the text to the bar of his own reason to establish its validity, but assumes that the text will authenticate itself when subject to reverent examination. His stance of faith and critical inquiry in no way invalidate each other.[3]

---

[3] Donald Guthrie, "The Historical and Literary Criticism of the New Testament," in *Biblical Criticism: Historical, Literary and Textual* (Grand Rapids: Zondervan: 1978) 87.

2. Spiritually enabled man is capable of knowing God and his Word.

a. The first aspect of spiritual enablement is *divine self-revelation*. Being in a spiritually dead position, man has no access to God or an adequate knowledge of him apart from his revelation of himself. The special revelation found in the Bible and in Christ is absolutely essential for fallen man's knowledge of God.

b. The second aspect of spiritual enablement is *the individual's ability to know*. This spiritual enablement is referred to in Scripture under various terms and concerns various issues in thought. The Spirit convicts the world of sin, righteousness, and judgment (John 16:5–11). There is a question whether the Spirit ministers immediately in the thinking of the world or mediately through the evangelist and his message; but it remains the Spirit's ministry. The issue concerns the world's response or willingness to respond to truth. It is in that sense that the world is not capable of knowing. The Bible states that natural man wills to suppress the truth which may be plainly known about God (Rom. 1:18–20). It is not that man cannot reason logically or that he cannot conceive of God (Rom. 1:21: "although they knew God"), but that he *will not* respond to him as God. In a similar line of thought, Paul argued on Mars Hill that in their poets (Acts 17:28) the Greeks knew more about God than they were willing to acknowledge in their images (Acts 17:29).

This capacity to know God is directly specified in the promises of the new covenant: "No longer will a man teach his neighbor, or a man his brother, saying, Know the LORD, because they will all know me, from the least of them to the greatest" (Jer. 31:34). Jeremiah affirms that all men living under the terms of the new covenant will know God. In distinction to the terms of the old covenant, in which all natural sons were responsible before God, now only Spirit-taught individuals will have a relationship and the corresponding responsibility before God. Thus Jesus affirmed, "No one can come to me unless the Father who sent me draws him. . . . It is written in the Prophets: 'They will all be taught by God.' Everyone who listens to the Father and learns from him comes to me" (John 6:44–45). The focus is on the proclamation of the truth associated with the Spirit's drawing. Without the Spirit's enablement to know God, there is no knowledge involved in a relationship with God.

Spirit enablement also involves "illumination," construed to refer to subsequent responses to the truth. This is also a matter of the will—a willingness to believe and to act (1 Cor. 2:12–16). The spiritual man is one who responds to the truth in thought, faith, and obedience, and such response enables him to make subsequent "judgments about all things" (1 Cor. 2:15). It seems clear that those judgments include accurate understanding of the Word of God (Matt. 13:18, 23). This Spirit-enabled response to truth already received prepares us for fuller and richer understanding of additional truth.

3. A biblical view of knowledge is based on the determinate nature of that which is to be known. Biblical revelation bears witness to a fact that has been underlying this whole study. In order for objective knowledge to exist, the object to be known must be capable of human comprehension in its determinate identity. The Bible bears witness that this is true of God. God is One— not many, not everything, not nothing, but One personal being. He is known by a revealed identity, knowable truly though not completely; knowable to the extent of his self-revelation. This is a portion of what is referred to in the phrase "what God has freely given us"

(1 Cor. 2:12). That phrase bears remarkable similarity to Moses' words *"The secret things* belong to the LORD our God, but *the things revealed* belong to us"* (Deut. 29:29, emphasis mine).

In this way God's revelation *in words* is capable of determination and knowable. Both the world that God spoke into existence and his verbal, special revelation bear limits on the capability of knowing corresponding to language. The written revelation is the primary aspect of "what God has freely given." The knowable nature of the Bible is implicit in its very condition as written communication.

Authors write to be understood; they write about subjects that may be known. Therefore, any exception to this normative condition of the written revelation is noteworthy. Daniel closes his record of God's revelation with God's word concerning both him and the future generation: "Those who are wise will shine like the brightness of the heavens. . . . But you, Daniel, close up and seal the words of the scroll until the time of the end" (12:3–4). The implied contrast is between those who read the prophecy and become wise, and Daniel, who must close the prophecy until the end time. Then the wise will read it and know God's revelation because they will match the cryptic revelation with the end-time events.

Thus the very condition of a written revelation implies that those who read it may know what it means. This knowability of Scripture is based on the determinate limits of its content in spite of its supernatural subject matter. Physical and natural subject matter are not the only objects of knowledge that are determinate and thus knowable. Ideas and concepts of the supernatural realm of reality are also determinate and can be known through special revelation.

In the context of this biblical worldview, the principle of validation may be defined as follows: *A valid interpretation of the textual meaning is one that is critically defended.* We will explore various aspects of this definition in terms of hermeneutics.

THE LOGIC OF VALIDATION

Valid, in distinction to *verified,* is the term we will use to describe the kinds of tests to be applied to interpretations. "Verification" is a broader term than "validation" and represents the more ambitious task of testing and demonstrating that an interpretation is true. Hirsch explains the distinction in a section he calls "the survival of the fittest":

> To verify is to show that a conclusion is true; to validate is to show that a conclusion is probably true on the basis of what is known. From the nature of the case, the goal of interpretation as a discipline must be the modest one of achieving validations so defined. But it also follows from the nature of the case that conclusions, based on greater knowledge, are more probable than the previous conclusions it has rejected.[4]

In other words, the difference between validation and verification is the difference between a probable certainty and an unquestioned certainty that a particular interpretation represents the author's meaning. Probability involves not the degree of truthfulness in the text, but the degree of assurance we have about an interpretative statement concerning the text.

The veracity of Scripture is not at issue here. Our discussion begins at the point of accepting the Bible's witness to its own nature as true. This leaves us with the narrower task of validation rather than the broader task of verifica-

---

[4]E. D. Hirsch, Jr., *Validity in Interpretation* (New Haven: Yale University Press, 1967), 171.

tion; we are seeking merely to show that an interpretation is probably accurate on the basis of correspondence to what is known in the text and in the historical and cultural context.

Principles of Probability

The general analysis of the logic of validation of verbal interpretation was first stated by Hirsch.[5] He identifies three issues involved in principles of probability.

1. The basic fact about a probability judgment is its uncertainty. The judgment of meaning is directed toward a verbal statement which is partly unknown and which may never be known with full certainty. It is important that we clearly understand what is meant by *certainty* and *uncertainty.* There are at least three kinds of criteria to which the term "certainty" may be applied.

a. Philosophical or formal certainty: "Philosophical certainty has to do with formal arguments that are so logically tight and compelling that to deny the conclusion would be to yield to manifest irrationality and absurdity."[6] This kind of certainty obtains or follows within the framework of the formal relationship of propositions. For instance, "2 + 2 = 4" and "If he is a father, then he is a parent" are logical truths; their logical certainty is not controversial, given shared definitions and uses of words and signs. Absolute certainty is limited to the formal relationships between propositions.

However, even in such a common proposition as "all men are mortal," the certain truth of that proposition does not necessarily follow. While the relational property of the famous syllogism concerning Socrates[7] is absolutely certain, the truth of this major premise concerning "all men" is not, since we have not experienced "all men" to test their common mortality.

b. Practical certainty: In spite of the theoretical possibility that one man may be born who would not be subject to death, yet a practical certainty concerning that proposition is shared by all men. In common usage, we speak of being "sure" or "certain," which describes a sense of confidence or assurance. This certainty arises out of continuing contact with evidence supporting a given proposition; it can manifest relative degrees of intensity, for it is more or less influenced by a mixture of doubt.

c. Moral certainty: The third variety of certainty characterizes the burden of courts of law when jurists speak of "reasonable doubt." In literary interpretation this concept involves a more formal critical testing of the evidence supporting various incompatible interpretations. In contrast to philosophical certainty, which admits no *rational doubt,* moral certainty allows no *reasonable doubt* that may be established by the *weight of evidence.* In law courts considering criminal cases, evidence may be sufficiently weighty to impose moral culpability. In literary interpretation, evidence may be sufficiently weighty to impose a critical moral certainty in favor of an interpretive ver-

---

[5] Ibid., 173–98.

[6] R. C. Sproul, "The Internal Testimony of the Holy Spirit," in *Inerrancy,* ed. Norman L. Geisler (Grand Rapids: Zondervan, 1979).

[7] The classic syllogism goes as follows:

> *Major premise:* All men are mortal.
> *Minor Premise:* Socrates is a man.
> *Conclusion:* Therefore Socrates is mortal.

See Adler, *Aristotle for Everybody,* chap. 17, for discussion of syllogisms.

dict. B. B. Warfield reached this conclusion concerning the authority of Scripture and the weight of the testimony favoring that interpreted meaning from Scripture.

> The exact relations of the "proofs" to the divinity of Scripture, which Calvin teaches, was sufficiently clear to be caught by his successors. It is admirably stated in the Westminster Confession of Faith. And we may add that the same conception is stated also very precisely by Quenstedt: These motives, as well internal as external, by which we are led to the knowledge of the authority of Scripture, make the *theopnuesty* of Sacred Scripture *probable,* and produce *a certitude which is not merely conjectural but moral.* . . . they do not make the divinity of Scripture infallible and altogether indubitable. . . . That is to say, they are not of the nature of *demonstration,* but nevertheless give *moral certitude.*[8]

We can attain moral certitude in many interpretive verdicts. The weight of the evidence is sufficient so as to remove "reasonable doubt" in favor of a given interpretation. While Hirsch calls the initial probability judgment an informed guess, once that interpretation has been critically tested and validated, it carries a moral certainty. And such removal of reasonable doubt is based on a common sense weighing of the evidence.

2. *"All members of the same class will tend to act in the same way."* [9] This fundamental axiom and assumption, as stated by Hirsch, underlies all probability judgments. It has already been used as fundamental to the development of the principles of recognition and exegesis of the type of meaning. Because it is a fundamental axiom, we need to reflect on its use in the theory of literary interpretation and defend its essential validity.

This assumption is far from arbitrary and can be easily defended. The idea of a class in itself entails an idea of uniformity at some level, for we subsume different individuals under the same class only because we observe that those individuals are the same in some respects—the respects in which the same become the defining characteristics of the class.[10]

In other words, the model of a type with defining traits exists in a biblical worldview as a necessary implication of the language base of creation and of communication between persons. Language is a system of shared meanings based on the classes, categories, or types of meaning tending to act in the same way; otherwise they cease to share meaning.

For one application of this fundamental axiom, we have proposed that literature can be classified from a number of different shared meanings or traits. A class of literature may be defined by only one shared meaning component; an individual piece of literature may be determined in its own identity by three defining components.

These components—the theological themes, textual design, and message—determine the meaning intrinsic to that individual writing. No two pieces of literature would share these same three components in equal particularity and specificity unless they were exact copies. A synoptic statement corresponds to the same type of meaning, but without sharing in the particularity of the same words.

Classes of literature can be formed in sharing one or more components that

---

[8] B. B. Warfield, *Calvin and Augustine* (reprint, Philadelphia: Presbyterian and Reformed, 1956), 74.
[9] Hirsch, *Validity in Interpretation,* 176.
[10] Ibid.

admit certain shared unity along with elements of diversity. The biblical canon is a class of writings that share common theological themes. This means, among other things, that they have divine evidences in common: a divinely authenticated author, a content with a focus on God, a literary text capable of analysis into affirmations which are consistent within the whole canon and which correspond to the historical realm as well as sponsor the testimony of the Holy Spirit as read by a believer. Classes can also be formed by subject, as in a library collection, or by textual design, as in studies of literary genre. Or classes can be formed by using two defining traits as in biblical narrative, the Gospels, or doctrinal epistles.

It is worth noting in passing that the application of the axiom to literature has been challenged by Benno Landsberger in the field of Old Testament comparative studies.[11] Another criticism of Old Testament comparative studies has come from theology. Greg Bahnsen and Gerhard Maier argue against using historical analogy in interpreting Scripture.[12] Bahnsen also objects to the use of extrabiblical materials to elucidate the Bible, viewing this as a threat to the doctrines of the sufficiency and the perspicuity of Scripture.[13]

Nevertheless, comparative studies in both the Old and New Testaments have applied the basic axiom for a long time, but not always the same way. Older evangelical comparative studies sought to find parallels in *subject matter* and build their case on similarities. For example, the early discoveries by Assyriologists of the Babylonian creation (Enuma Elish) and flood stories (Table XI of the Gilgamesh Epic) were used to support the legitimate meanings of the biblical accounts; differences in meaning were contrasted to highlight the distinct biblical content. Contemporary evangelical comparative studies, by contrast, lay greater stress on the similarities and differences in the *textual design* and call this method the "contextual" approach. This method seeks to use "the entire Near Eastern literary milieu to the extent that it can be argued to have any conceivable impact on the Biblical formulation."[14]

The direction of such comparative studies may well press the axiom to the point that implications drawn from the divine authorship of a text are being challenged. In an evangelical discussion on the interpretation of Ecclesiastes, an interpreter has drawn the following deduction from three shared elements of literary design.[15] The text opens with a self-introduction that is formally similar to that of Qohelet's speech in the text of Ecclesiastes:

What is of special interest here is that in both cases the first-person speaker was long dead by the time these compositions

---

[11] Benno Landsberger, "The Conceptual Autonomy of the Babylonian World," in *Sources and Monographs on the Ancient Near East* (Malibu, Calif.: Undena, 1976).

[12] See Greg Bahnsen, *Theonomy in Christian Ethics* (Nutley, N.J.: Craig, 1979), 573; and Gerhard Maier, *The End of the Historical-Critical Method* (St. Louis: Concordia, 1977), 51.

[13] Cited in Tremper Longman III, "Comparative Methods in Old Testament Studies," *TSF Bulletin* (March-April 1984): 6. Longman here refers to Bahnsen's critique of views expressed by Meredith Kline.

[14] Ibid.

[15] Ibid., 7–8. The main part of Ecclesiastes (everything except the prologue [1:1–11] and the epilogue [12:8–14]) contains the words of a figure given the name "Qohelet," a transliteration of the Hebrew. Longman writes, "What is of great interest is that there are a number of texts written in Akkadian which are autobiographies and also structured in this tripartite manner. The texts are didactic autobiographies."

came into existence. In other words, both Ecclesiastes and the Cuthaean Legend are fictional autobiographies. Naram-Sin lived in the twenty-second century B.C. and "Qohelet" *clearly represents* Solomon who lived in the tenth century B.C. . . . Ecclesiastes [was composed] centuries after Solomon.[16]

The question that must be raised is this: Does Ecclesiastes share enough with the Akkadian model to classify it an "autobiography" and in particular a "fictional autobiography"? The advice Hirsch gives for applying the axiom is worth considering for our response:

> The more we know about the object [the verbal text], the narrower and more reliable we can make the class. Then, on the basis of what we know about other individuals belonging to the same class, we make a guess that the unknown traits of any such object will be the same as the corresponding traits for most individuals in the class—more often than not.[17]

When the class shares a common textual design, certain conclusions legitimately follow only concerning the diagnostic traits of the textual design: an author's address of the audience, discourse structures, and language usage. Other commonly associated traits that do not diagnose the design do not necessarily follow. In the case of biblical application, shared textual design cannot contradict necessary components of the theological themes.

This means that regarding our example from Ecclesiastes, it is questionable whether the discourse structure or the scope of subjects treated could be considered "biographical" even though there are first-person references. It could more easily be considered "didactic testimony." In addition, to posit fictional autobiography when the text "clearly represents Qohelet to be King of Jerusalem," at least raises questions

about the integrity of such statements. And a lack of integrity contradicts necessary components of the character of God and what he says. So in the application of the axiom, the correspondence between classes in terms of diagnostic traits must be determined first. It also follows that the more that is known about the class of meaning, the more reliable are the judgments to be made about the unknown elements of the class.

In a valid application of shared textual design, Deuteronomy can be compared to the suzerainty-vassal international treaty. The comparison is established in terms of the resemblance in diagnostic components of Moses speaking for the benevolent YHWH to his delivered vassal. A bilateral covenant is expounded in which obligation is placed on the vassal for benefits already received and in anticipation of blessing to be received. Also, the language used shares a similar covenant vocabulary and the structure follows a treaty form.

3. The narrowing of the probability judgment increases our certainty about the meaning of the unknown traits of the object. Two questions lead us to this principle:

> What, probably, are the unknown traits of the textual meaning?
>
> How probable is it that our judgment of their meaning is accurate?

The likelihood of our judgment being accurate

> will increase the more we know about our object and the more narrowly, by consequence, we can define the class to which it belongs. If we narrow the class so that our object becomes almost identical with other known objects (the more of them the better), then we can be less and

---

[16]Ibid. (emphasis added).
[17]Hirsch, *Validity in Interpretation*, 176.

less doubtful about the remaining unknown traits of our objects.[18]

This conclusion is self-evident in stating that *the judgment of an unknown meaning has higher probability of being accurate if the interpreter knows more about the type of meaning.* There are three kinds of knowledge of the type of meaning, each of which will increase the probability of an interpretive judgment in a distinct fashion.

a. The better the interpreter knows the particular book, the more likely the unknown will be known. Associated with a better knowledge is the narrowness of this knowledge to conform to the actual particulars of the book. Thus a knowledge of the theological themes in terms of a revelation of God's person, his purposes in history, and the administration of the purposes defines the theology of God's person and works in this revelation.

Knowing the textual design involves the author's address of the historical audience, the discourse structure, and the use of language. The message is known in the subject and the complement. Knowledge of these diagnostic traits that correspond to the expression of the text as a whole summarizes the type of meaning intrinsic to that book. A knowledge of the book in these terms increases the probability in the accuracy of the interpretation of other unknown particulars and difficulties.

b. The better the interpreter knows the class of books (design) or the class of subject matter (doctrine), the more likely the unknown will become known. The knowledge of the class of books is formed basically in terms of textual design and theological themes. The greater our knowledge of historical narrative, both biblical and extrabiblical, the more likely we are able to judge the unknown particulars in Genesis or

Acts. (The cautions that have been raised in regard to extrabiblical literature are still appropriate, however.) The knowledge of the class of subjects commonly deals with doctrines expressed in different books rather than the subjects of books. The Gospels or Kings and Chronicles are obvious examples of the same subject.

The probability of the interpreter's judgment of an unknown component of a subject increases with the number of instances he knows.

c. The better the interpreter understands the unknown component, the more likely his solution of the unknown will be accurate. There are two steps to gaining understanding of an unknown component: identifying and defining what is unknown, and diagnosing what relation the unknown trait has to the type of meaning.

(1) In the first step, we reach a level of maturity in understanding in being able to identify what is known and what is unknown. Clearly one place to begin is in asking the basic interpretive questions of the type of meaning. These questions direct an interpreter's attention to textual content.

In answering these questions the interpreter may discover that his limits in knowledge are of a preunderstanding kind. He can recognize what the answer in the text involves, but he does not share any knowledge of that kind of subject matter. This is where formal education comes in.

Or the reader may discover that the limits in his knowledge are of an understanding kind. He does not recognize how the author answers the questions in what he has written. Repeated reading seeks to address this need.

And, of course, the lack of knowledge could involve both preunderstanding and understanding. Continued read-

[18]Ibid., 178–79.

ing and reading widely on the subject are the best remedies for these needs.

(2) In terms of the second step, we must ask, How frequently is the unknown a trait of this type of meaning? Is it a diagnostic trait and thus necessary to know in order to understand the type of meaning, or is it an associated trait and thus enriching in our knowledge of the type of meaning. In most cases in biblical literature, a knowledge of the exact date of authorship is not diagnostic to a knowledge of the type of meaning. In many cases a knowledge of the personal identity of the human author is not necessarily diagnostic.

For example, the dispute on authorship for the book of Hebrews influenced the decision concerning canonicity, but the identity of the author is unnecessary for knowing the type of meaning. It is sufficient to recognize the implied author of the textual composition. By contrast, if we do not know the subject or the complement, our knowledge of the type of meaning in that book is deficient to the point of not knowing. It is necessary to know the subject in order to understand the meaning of that book. We may know many things about the book, but we do not know the book without knowing the subject and complement.

Interpretive Evidence

Having surveyed Hirsch's three principles of probability, we turn to one remaining issue regarding the probability judgment of validation. This involves the relative weight of our knowledge in supporting an accurate interpretation. That is, we need to translate knowledge to best knowledge.

The support for our judgments comes from the interpretive evidence. The first question concerns the nature and amount of support needed for a critical or moral certainty. It is generally accepted that the amount and nature of support is sufficient to make practical certainty our initial goal. This interpretive evidence is that evidence which was found to be internally consistent in the exegesis of the implications of the text from a construct of the type of meaning as a whole.

The subsequent question concerns the moral certainty of a judgment or conclusion. With our finite knowledge it is not possible to achieve unquestioned certainty except when an interpretation can be proven false. Disproving or discrediting any view requires only finite knowledge. This process of eliminating a probability judgment is clearly more suited to testing a scientific hypothesis than an interpretation of a biblical text. The two criteria for a good scientific hypothesis are that it fits the observable data and it predicts unobserved future events as the outworking of certain determined and related factors. It is easy to discredit such a hypothesis: either new data render it unfit, or the predicted events do not appear. By contrast, an interpretive hypothesis of a verbal text does not predict conclusions about a new set of data in which the interpretation can be repeated.

However, verbal interpretation can be discredited when an interpretive hypothesis violates an accepted shared norm of language meaning between the author and the original readers. In this vein, the Jehovah's Witnesses' interpretation of John 1:1—"the Word was *a god*"—can be discredited. The statement is a clear violation of the syntactical norm of an anathrous noun in a predicate nominative position. In Greek syntax, the absence of an article does not imply indefiniteness. Thus this interpretation can be discounted.

Similarly, interpretations that violate shared literary norms or historical factors in the original communication can be discredited. So if Deuteronomy is a covenant statement in the form of suzerainty treaty, we would not expect it to include an unrelated Palestinian covenant in Deuteronomy 30:1–10. A second covenant would be incompatible with an overall treaty design and meaning. Another example: A spiritualized interpretation, which ignores historical references or hymnic conceptions of Solomon and the Shulamite in the Song of Songs, violates the norms of the original composition.

In each example the interpretation can be discredited because the shared norms of the original composition have been violated. However, most competent interpretations cannot be discredited or disproved on these grounds; we are quite likely to encounter competing and often incompatible interpretations that are all viable. And frequently, evidence appears to be divided between the competing interpretations, i.e., each interpretive construct seems to have some independent evidence in its favor. Therefore some means is needed to weigh the relevant evidence.

> Thus, the crucial problem in judging between disparate interpretation is usually the comparative weighing of relevant evidence. We must be able to conclude that the evidence favoring one hypothesis outweighs the conflicting evidence favoring its rival. . . . We need principles for determining the admissibility (i.e., relevance) of evidence and the relative weight of evidence.[19]

A general principle emerges from these considerations: *The most accurate interpretation always explains most evidence, but that evidence must also be the most relevant evidence.*

Let's explore this principle.

1. Determining admissible evidence. Any verbal text is a complex of numerous meanings and meaning components. The question involves how many of the textual meanings provide relevant support to an interpretive hypothesis. Hirsch writes,

> Since an interpretive hypothesis is always a probability judgment, it follows that the evidence which is relevant to that judgment must have some function in affecting the probabilities involved. . . . It follows from this structure of all probability judgments that evidence will be relevant which helps define the subsuming class and which increases the number of instances within the subsuming class.[20]

a. Evidence defining the type of meaning. When interpreting a book or a portion of a book, the particular meanings are relevant evidence if they define the type of meaning. Four issues are at stake: subject and complement of the message, theological themes, and textual design. Any textual meanings expressing any of these four aspects of the definition of the type of meaning are relevant evidence in favor of that interpretation. A particular instance may help to clarify the concept. In James 1:2–11 a number of different subjects are mentioned:

1:2	various trials
1:3	tested faith
1:4	endurance (of testing)
1:5	lacks wisdom
1:6	ask in faith

1:7	ask with doubting
1:8	doubting man
1:9	poor man
1:10–11	rich man

[19] Ibid., 182–83.
[20] Ibid., 183–84.

Suppose that an interpreter chooses "tested faith" as the subject of the message in this passage. Verse 3 provides direct evidence for that subject. Some other verses may say something about "tested faith," and they can be taken as evidence supporting the choice: "various trials" provide the test of faith; "endurance" is the result of tested faith; "lack of wisdom" is often associated with a test to faith; "poverty" is also clearly associated with a test to faith. But are "riches" associated with a test of faith? In what way is "riches" related to either the subject or a complement?

b. Evidence increasing our knowledge of the type of meaning. Our hypothesis of an interpretation that considers "riches" as an instance of a type of "tested faith" would be enhanced if we knew more of what is entailed in tested faith. Does James consider "wealth" a test of faith elsewhere (cf. 2:2–3; 2:14, 16; 4:13–17; and 5:1–5)? Is not "wealth" a "blessing from God"? How can a blessing be a test of faith? Does our knowledge of other defining aspects of the book increase the likelihood that James writes to Jews of the first century who placed an inordinate value on wealth, or increase the probability that wealth can be a test of faith? In this way, our increased knowledge about the type of meaning and about the related types of meaning will unearth relevant evidence either to support or to discredit an interpretive hypothesis.

All textual evidence is relevant evidence for either the diagnostic traits of recognition and definition of the type of meaning or the associated traits related to or occasionally implied in the type of meaning. Of greater interest is the question of the relevance of extrabiblical data as evidence. Clearly, extrabiblical data cannot be evidence to directly contribute to define the traits of the type of textual meaning. However, it may provide evidence to increase our knowledge of the type of meaning.

Several interesting examples have recently been posited to increase our knowledge of an author's textual design and language usage. Robert Gundry argues that a knowledge of the way Jewish Midrash explains the Old Testament texts increases our knowledge of the "haggadic and midrashic techniques" used by Matthew in relating historical events.[21] But again one is left wondering whether we are really dealing with the same type of discourse structure. Even in a most general consideration, is commentary on a known text and commentary on unknown historical events or sources the same kind of commentary? Commentary that seeks to explain or illustrate what is already known assumes the reader's knowledge. But commentary on what is not known must necessarily inform the reader about what is not known before it can explain or illustrate. So Jewish Midrash and Matthean commentary do not share a necessary point. The original readers did not necessarily know about the events of Jesus' life about which Matthew comments.

Similarly, the literary parallels between Ecclesiastes and "the Akkadian didactic autobiographies" share enough to enable a commentator to conclude that modern attempts to turn Qohelet the skeptic into Qohelet the preacher of joy fail miserably because the "eat, drink and be merry" statements (2:24–26; 3:12–14; 3:22; 5:18–20; 8:15; 9:7ff.; 11:7ff.) are passages of resignation, not optimism.[22] Can such an unqualified assertion be sustained as a type of statement of resignation when Qohelet

---

[21] Robert H. Gundry, *Matthew: A Commentary on His Literary and Theological Art* (Grand Rapids: Eerdmans, 1982).

[22] Longman, "Comparative Methods in Old Testament Studies," 8.

adds "this is a gift of God" or some parallel thought (2:24; 3:13; 5:18; 9:9)? Must the type of meaning stated in Ecclesiastes not include a qualification to any possible trait of resignation? And would that qualification not be appropriate to a preacher who appreciates food as a gift from God? The type of meaning must never be defined by the extrabiblical type that creates a conflict with the data and evidence of the text. The type of meaning of "resignation of fate," is distinct from, if not incompatible with, the type of meaning of "resignation of a God-given lot."

2. Weighing the admissible evidence. What do we do when we face two or more incompatible interpretations that unfold conflicting or unrelated implications? The crucial issue, according to Hirsch, is the "problem of directly conflicting evidence. Normally the interpreter is faced with the dilemma that some independent evidence favors one hypothesis, while other independent evidence favors its rival. This is the normal state of affairs in interpretation."[23]

The problem of conflicting evidence takes two forms. The normal situation is when, say, ten textual facts support message A and fifteen other pieces of evidence support message B. The weight of evidence in this case by sheer number favors message B. But do numbers alone equal weightiness? Some textual facts are clearly more weighty than others.

The second form of the problem is more difficult to resolve. Here the same item of textual data is claimed as support for message A and for message B. Which one does it support with more weight? The principle Hirsch suggests is that "the evidence of the narrower

class is always the more weighty—no matter what the frequencies are within that class or any broader one that comprises it."[24] This principle may in turn be reduced to two working principles, or guidelines:

a. The principle of support: The weight of the evidence is heavier in support of a narrower statement of the type of meaning. The issue involves the same piece of data that has greater weight in support of the narrowest construct of the type of meaning.

Both Rudolf Bultmann and C. K. Barrett claim *meinate en emoi*, "abide in me," as evidence in support of their interpretation of John 15:1–8. Bultmann, on the one hand, conceives of the subject as "consistency of faith," citing "the first part of the discourse, verses 1–8, in an exhortation to constancy of faith."[25] Barrett, on the other hand, writes, "The union [of believers] with Christ is the theme of the present and of the next section. Only in Christ can Christians live."[26] Barrett's conceived subject, "union in Christ," is almost coincidental with the evidence. Constancy of faith, however, is a broader concept defined in part by "abiding in him." While faith is certainly associated with "abiding" or "remaining," it does not necessarily imply "staying with." Thus the evidence "abide in me" weighs more heavily in support of "union" as the narrower class than "faith." Since the evidence is central to the section, there is a strong probability in favor of "union" or "living union" as the subject, based only on this piece of evidence.

The principle of support deals with pieces of evidence, in contrast to the second principle.

b. The principle of source: The

---

[23] Hirsch, *Validity in Interpretation,* 181.
[24] Ibid., 185–86.
[25] Rudolf Bultmann, *The Gospel of John* (Philadelphia: Westminster, 1971).
[26] C. K. Barrett, *The Gospel According to John* (London: SPCK, 1955), 203.

weight of the evidence is heavier when drawn from the narrower type of meanings. The narrowness of the type of meaning is judged in relation to the author's text. Under this principle, the author's use of a term in the text has greater weight than the use of the term in the New Testament generally or in the Septuagint. Thus evidence from the immediate authorial context of the book is weightier than usage in other books by the same author, other biblical usage of the same subject, or extrabiblical usage regarding the subject or design. In each successive source context removed from the author's text, the weight of the evidence decreases.

In assessing the weight of evidence, both principles—support and source—must be applied. The principles may be in conflict in determining the weight of any piece of evidence, but the resulting weight is what must be considered.

The Resulting Certainty

In biblical interpretation, understanding the message communicated involves varying degrees of certainty that the message recognized is accurate. These *degrees of certainty* need to be identified and the basis of each specified. The distinct *kinds of certainty* have already been defined earlier in this chapter. In literary interpretation, there is not the philosophical certainty that one obtains between propositions. Rather, literary interpretation is akin to legal interpretation in that it reaches only a moral certainty. The degree of moral certainty rests on the nature and the careful adjudication or weighing of the evidence.

The question we must ask is, Has sufficient evidence been critically examined to *remove reasonable doubt* about the accuracy of the interpretation? Or is there merely *a preponderance of evidence* favoring one interpretation after critical adjudication? Two factors are at issue in establishing moral certainty: the nature of the critical adjudication, and the quantity and weight of the evidence. We can distinguish three degrees of certainty.

1. A practical certainty in biblical knowledge rests in the consistency of thought in recognizing and exegeting the Scripture's message. As a believer *I can know that I know* through Spirit-directed consistency of thought in interpretation.

a. Any discussion of biblical interpretive certainty rests first of all on the Holy Spirit's illumination. Without the Spirit's ministry overshadowing the process, there could be no certain knowledge of Scripture. In the context of the Spirit, *practical certainty* rests on the consistency of thought. Consistency seeks to make explicit each step in one's thinking such that all relevant data are considered in proportion to their relative weight and role in the author's thought.

This method of interpreting consistently recognizes a full use of contextual details, always in harmony with the Scripture's teaching as a whole. The issue in practical certainty centers in the nature of critical testing; the test is one of internal consistency. The method does not attempt to weigh any evidence from outside the text or compare alternative interpretations. Practical certainty concerns only a true knowledge, not a full knowledge. The message can be known truly even though it may not be known fully without years of research and a more complete knowledge of the historical and cultural setting. In addition, the message may be known truly even though all alternative interpretations have not been considered. The practical certainty focuses only on the interpreter's work and not on the history of interpretation.

b. This conception of certainty is

described as "practical" to refer to its sphere of application. Like other forms of human knowledge, it operates as a basis for normal life and action. I live in a world that I take at face value. (I do not prove a chair exists before I sit on it.) The knowledge gained allows me to live and grow even though I may not be able to demonstrate what I know in practice to be true. While there are occasions when such knowledge is inadequate or even misleading, this does not invalidate such dealing with life from having a practical application. Though such practical certainty is insufficient in itself, it is not thereby disqualified as knowledge with valid application. However, its limits must be considered and included in my knowledge.

c. Spiritual illumination does not ensure that a man will recognize God's truth. History demonstrates that men of God, regenerated and led by his Spirit, have not all adopted the same or even compatible understandings of all of God's Word. Presumably the Spirit guided or was guiding them all to the true meaning of a text. But for some reason at least some of them adopted ideas derived from their own explanation or from their own thought world instead. Because the Spirit of Truth (John 16:13) does not author error, we conclude that the interpreters erred in invalidly adopting their own ideas. The possible reasons why they erred are numerous: insufficient time spent reading, rational errors, insufficient preunderstanding, willful rejection of what is clear, to name a few.[27] Yet spiritual illumination is the foundation of the knowledge of Scripture. Thus it is the indispensable ingredient of any degree of certainty.

d. A conviction of practical certainty does not presuppose omniscience. A person who claims to truly know one thing does not thereby claim to know everything. It is not necessary to know all things completely before we can know one thing truly. Nor does true knowledge presuppose autonomous knowledge; but that is the perspective of the philosopher who seeks to ground all knowledge within himself, independent of other foundations.

e. A conviction of practical certainty based on the Word of God does not preclude teachability. We can be taught by living teachers or by the commentary tradition. But the basis of such teaching must rest on the Word and the ministry of the Spirit. This teaching may help us come to know, or it may challenge the accuracy or completeness of our knowledge. For this reason, Apollos, who was "a learned man, with a thorough knowledge of the Scriptures," spoke with great fervor and boldness in the synagogue at Ephesus. He was obviously a man speaking with conviction, yet open to being taught "more adequately" (Acts 18:24-26).

2. A moral certainty in biblical knowledge rests in the validation of thought in the history of interpretation. As a teacher or scholar, I can demonstrate that I know through a critical test of interpretations found in history.

a. "Any interpretation of Scripture must have adequate justification."[28] Bernard Ramm introduces this critical test of interpretation in Protestant Biblical Interpretation. To this statement he adds, "The grounds of the interpretation must be made explicit." In locating "adequate justification," the role of other interpretations from the past must be considered. An interpretation is not

[27] Robert LaBreche, "A Guideline for Recognizing Valid Interpretation of Scripture" (Unpublished research project, Dallas Theological Seminary, n.d.), 4-5.

[28] Bernard Ramm, Protestant Biblical Interpretation (Boston: W. A. Wilde, 1950, rev. ed. 1956), 101.

true simply because a majority subscribe to it or because it is the historic position. But the ground of these interpretations must be compared with the ground for current or alternate interpretations. This process of judging the most adequate grounds for an interpretation is called "validation."

b. *This conception of certainty is described as "moral" to refer to the elimination of reasonable doubt in a person's interpretation.* The term *moral* does not imply that we seek to defend our construct at any cost, but that we seek the construct that is most adequately defended. Adequate defense demonstrates the validity of our practical certainty in knowledge by the weight of evidence in favor of one interpretation. It must be acknowledged that some interpretations, given the present state of knowledge, will yield no more than a preponderance of evidence. In this case our interpretation is only morally probable.

In practice the distinction between moral certainty and moral probability rests in the principles of probability and the weight of evidence. It may be helpful to sketch the aspects of these factors associated with each category.

(1) An interpretation would be *morally certain* when—

(a¹) A clear defense of the defining traits of meaning for the whole book demonstrates that they are to be preferred. The weight of internal evidence demonstrates clear preference and not simply compatibility as in practical certainty.

(b¹) A broad demonstration of harmony and compatibility within classes of literature with shared design. These classes would be drawn primarily from biblical sources, but secondarily from extrabiblical sources. Moreover, there should be harmony and complementary teaching in shared classes of subjects or doctrines.

(c¹) The known problem areas that remain do not concern the defining components of the text's meaning. There may well be unanswered questions of a historical or cultural nature or even in demonstration of historicity. But since these problems do not deal with primary evidence concerning the meaning of the book, they do not need to undermine a moral certainty in the knowledge of the book's meaning.

(2) An interpretation would be *morally probable* when—

(a¹) More than one construct of defining components for a book can be demonstrated to be viable and to have plausibility. Commonly the evidence is divided, with one construct being supported by a portion of the textual data and another construct being supported by different textual data. The probable preference is the most plausible.

(b¹) Either because of a lack of available instances of the same type of design or because of a lack of research, there is only a limited demonstration of the same class of design and an equivalent treatment of subject matter. These limitations in demonstration further hinder gaining a clear certainty.

(c¹) The problem areas do include some fundamental components defining the text's meaning. The interpreter must await further research to demonstrate a broad harmony in classes of design or in the usage of terms. Instances of *hapax legomena* in the Old Testament are particularly dependent on additional research in the field of meaning in the usage of terms.

c. *An adequately defended construct does not establish truth.* Rather, truth is established both in the fact of biblical revelation and in the demonstration of correspondence with reality. An accurate construct of the message expressed is true. An accurate interpretation is one that corresponds to the meanings which the author intends to express in the text. Such an accurate interpretation of textual meaning is true because its source is God's revelation. This truth is demonstrated in the correspondence between (1) the message and theology so understood, and (2) the reality about which the text speaks.

3. Doctrinal certainty resides in the perspicuity of Scripture. This concept means that the Scripture repeatedly teaches a truth which believers can know and to which they can affirm their agreement in knowledge.

a. Doctrinal statements commonly combine three distinct kinds of subject matter or doctrinal issues.

(1) The central teachings of the gospel that define Christianity. If these truths were to be changed, the very nature of Christianity would be changed. These truths are first principles of a defining sort that cannot change without changing the identity of the faith, i.e., the Gospel.

(2) The foundational truths on which the faith rests. While these truths do not define the faith, they form its reasonable and necessary basis—for example, the nature of Christ's person or the nature of Scripture, etc.

(3) Truths that are in question in a given period in church history. Examples for the latter twentieth century are the charismatic gifts, church leadership, and woman's roles.

b. Doctrinal certainty assumes both practical and moral certainty. The issue is not really the nature of the critical adjudication. The test of consistency of teaching on a doctrine within the canon as well as the critical weighing of the evidence both favor the doctrinal interpretation. The repeated teaching of the truth tends to reinforce the truth understood so that it is seen more clearly and then taken to be almost self-evident.

We are not concerned here whether some truths are taught clearly and some with obscurity. The issue involves the repeated teaching of the same truth. The weight of evidence favoring that truth as understood simply multiplies, bringing a consensus on interpretation.

c. Doctrinal certainty also involves systemic harmony and unity. Some truths that are not taught as frequently as the truths of the gospel may nevertheless have other canonical forms of support. Though they lack the support of *repeated* teaching, they have the support of *related* teachings. There is a conviction that "the whole counsel of God" is revealed and profitable for the church. These related teachings harmonize in a consistent and supportive system of truth taught as a unified whole counsel of God. While such a system must be always recognized as a human interpretive construction, we must still acknowledge its value as a confirming evidence in doctrinal certainty.

The perspicuity of Scripture is certainly evident in the teaching of the defining truths of the gospel. The truth is expressed directly and repeatedly. The foundational truths may appear more often in an implied form. While they are taught directly, they more often appear in supporting the development of other issues, but in this supportive role they appear repeatedly.

The truths that have historically been called into question may not be taught either directly or repeatedly. With these, doctrinal affirmation concerning these issues must retain a recognized nature of support. So a doctrinal statement includes defining truths,[29] founda-

---

[29] Bruce Waltke questions the scope of truths to be held as first principles and as a part of dogmatic theology. He contends that a dogmatic doctrinal statement should include only the core of historically agreed-upon truths. However, a discussion of a doctrinal statement

tional truths, and historically distinctive truths.[30]

SUMMARY

This chapter had been devoted to the definition and description of the principle of validation. While there is no method or principle for generating correct interpretations, there can be a critical process of validation. For evangelicals, this process must be determined and its tasks defined within a biblical worldview.

The development of the principle determined that a valid interpretation of the textual meaning is one critically defended. Such a critical defense rests on the logic of validation, which is described in three ideas:

1. The logic of validation is based on principles of probability, which are simply issues of common sense. Hirsch characterizes the interpretive or probability judgment by a fact, an axiom, and a conclusion.

   a. The basic fact concerning any probability judgment is its uncertainty.

   b. The axiom affirms that all members of the same class will tend to act in the same way.

   c. The conclusion affirms that in narrowing the degree of uncertainty, the interpretive judgment of the unknown meaning has a higher probability of being accurate if the interpreter knows more about the type of meaning.

2. The logic of validation reaches conclusions dependent on the weight of the interpretive evidence available. Hirsch outlines three corollaries about the final conclusion and the weight of the evidence.

   a. The most accurate interpretation always explains the most evidence that is relevant.

   b. The weight of the evidence is heavier in support of the narrowest statement of the type of meaning.

   c. The weight of the evidence is heavier when the evidence is drawn from the contexts closest to the author's text.

3. The logic of validation brings an interpreter to a specific kind of certainty from his initial uncertainty. Three kinds of certainty have been proposed: practical, moral, and doctrinal.

---

provides an agreed-upon foundation of first truths upon which the group is gathered and those truths it needs to accomplish its tasks.

[30] Mark A. Noll, "Who Sets the Stage for Understanding Scripture?" *Christianity Today* (23 May 1980): 16. There is a tendency today to regard doctrinal statements as sharing in an antiquated, static, and mechanistic dogmatism. Noll suggests this:

Baconism [Noll's term for the worldview of Newton, Bacon, and the Scottish realists] was mechanistic: its model was the carefully constructed watch; the newer science was organic: its model was the growing plant. Baconism was static and antithetical: scientific conclusions were fixed and could be stated dogmatically, once and for all; the new science was developmental and synthetic: scientific conclusions were expected to change over time and often included considerable ambiguity or mystery. Baconianism was realistic—our minds took reality from the external world; the newer science was often idealistic—our minds shaped perception of the world.

It must be remembered that truth about God is absolute in the sense of being true without exception. It does not change. Thus, when the Bible speaks of God and this is the source of doctrines, these doctrinal truths can be stated in a final form. However, caution must be exercised, since doctrinal statements are the interpretive constructions of man and so capable of including error, of being inadequately conceived or stated. They are also capable of growth as the church's knowledge of the Scripture grows. So while truth is certain and absolute, men's knowledge of truth is not in every case equally absolute or final.

CHAPTER 14

Procedures in the Principle of Validation

The principle of validation assumes, in the literal system of interpretation, the possibility of self-critical and rational thought. It is not rationalistic, because it does not rest solely on rational presuppositions. But it is rational in the sense that it holds that one interpretation alone corresponds to the author's intended meaning and that a judgment among incompatible options can be reasonably reached at least in principle, if not always in practice.

This approach toward the choice of an accurate interpretation rejects two extremes. On the one hand, an *optimistic* approach tends to minimize the choice of an accurate interpretation, because it views divergences in interpretation as not representing genuine conflicts in thought, but merely differences in emphasis or perspective. Clearly, these kinds of differences do exist within interpretation, but there are also more basic differences that involve incompatible interpretations.

On the other hand, a *cynical* approach tends to magnify differences in interpretation to the level of irreconcilable conflict. The cynic reasons that an interpreter's sense of conviction cannot be changed because it rests on his personal aptitude, and his choice of a reading must be ascribed to personal preference. Hirsch writes that 'the cynic naturally prefers his own competent reading to that of another, yet he openmindedly recognizes the right of another to be just as blithely closed-minded as himself.'[1]

On the surface these two positions appear to share a common spirit of acceptance and openness. In fact, both have surrendered the possibility of accurate interpretation as a rational possibility and responsibility.

The literal tradition does not recognize such a surrender. However, this is not a claim that the application of the solution to particular cases is either easy or fully clear in all instances. So we have a double purpose in this chapter in developing the literal approach: we both describe the procedure and demonstrate its application with a particular problem passage. It is hoped that this will specify and clarify the nature of the application of the solution in principle. The passage we will use is a

---

[1] E. D. Hirsch, Jr., *Validity in Interpretation* (New Haven: Yale University Press, 1967), 168.

recognized unit in the gospel of John, namely, John 15:1–17. It was chosen because it has generated incompatible interpretations. The branches broken from the vine have been viewed (1) as mere professors, (2) as genuine believers who lost their lives, and (3) as genuine but unfruitful believers. These are three mutually incompatible interpretations of a *crux interpretum,* or problem textual construct:

There are two logical questions concerned with the logic of validation:

1. *Viability:* Is it reasonable that the words of the text could mean what the interpretation suggests?
2. *Probability:* Is it the *most* reasonable interpretive construction?

These two questions structure the broad framework for the procedure. It is recognized, of course, that the answers to these questions are related to the evidence available. Since we are not omniscient, the evidence may be limited or may seem equally divided so that a clear probability does not emerge. In such cases the interpreter must settle for a less than morally certain position, as we discussed in chapter 13. However, the broad procedure in validation develops from these questions.

STEP 1

All incompatible interpretations of the literature are examined for viability.

Incompatible interpretations are conflicting or unrelated constructions or understandings of the textual meanings. While every interpretation is different in some respect, the differences among them arise for various reasons. These reasons need to be enumerated before

the incompatibility among interpretations can be classified. There are two classifications: (1) an incompatibility due to the meaning, and (2) an incompatibility due to the explanation of the meaning. The difference between these two is between the art and task of understanding, and the art and task of explaining.[2]

The first kind of incompatibility features the signs in the text that must first be construed or understood by an interpreter. These incompatibilities are real. The other kind of incompatibility is based on explanation; the meaning that the interpreter understands must be explained to new audiences. Thus, while different generations may share a common understanding of a text, the interpreter is nevertheless faced with the task of *reinterpreting* the great works of the past in terms his own age can perceive. Hirsch explains:

A translation or paraphrase tries to render the meaning in new terms; an explanation tries to point to the meaning in new terms. That is why the interpretation, like translation, is an art, for the interpreter has to find means of conveying to the uninitiated, in terms familiar to them, those presuppositions and meanings which are equivalent to those presuppositions and meanings in the original meaning.[3]

Differences in explanation are not necessarily incompatible, since they are seen in vocabulary differences, distinct strategies of communication such as explaining the meaning in a story or in an analysis, and recognizable differences due to the audiences addressed. These differences may be present even though the meaning construed or understood is the same. And these differences do not constitute incompatibility in understanding.

---

[2] J. A. Ernesti, *Elements of Interpretation* (Andover, Mass.: Andover Theological Seminary, 1837), cited by Schleiermacher. Chapter 1, section 4 originates the distinction between the *subtilitas intelligendi* and the *subtilitas explicandi.*

[3] Hirsch, *Validity in Interpretation,* 136.

Incompatible interpretations alter our understanding. They do not merely deepen the understanding or take a distinct point of view, but they present a sense of conflict or of unrelatedness with our previous understanding. This sense of incompatibility challenges our original understanding such that both or all conceptions of the meaning cannot be accurate. This incompatibility requires separate consideration in the process of evaluation. Different interpretations may be complementary or supplementary, but compatible. However, incompatible interpretations represent either conflicting or unrelated meanings.

This distinction between "different but comparable" and "different and incomparable" is rather abstract, and therefore an illustration may be helpful to clarify. Consider the meaning of the word *football*.

"Football" can be used in several senses. Some are compatible although different; others are incompatible. "Football" in reference to the American or Canadian game has different meanings. That is, although there are differences between the two games, they do not change the games. There is a difference in style and in certain rules, yes, but the games are not incompatible.

An incompatible sense for the term "football" is found in comparing the American game to the British game. To a sports fan the incompatibility is self-evident: no team in the National Football League drafts English schoolboys who are talented football players (with the possible exception of a placekicker). "Soccer" (English football) is not American football. This incompatibility is evident from a comparison of the component elements of each game:

Ball: English is round;
American and Canadian are oblong.

Strategy: English is to kick and head the ball;
American and Canadian is to run, pass, and kick the ball.

Goal: English is a netted cage;
American and Canadian is the end of the playing field with two upright posts.

Analogous to the interpretation of a word like "football," the difference and incompatibility of the interpretations of Bible books can be seen in the unfolding of the component implications of the meaning as a whole that are *in conflict.*

Another variety of incompatible interpretation occurs in the twentieth-century interpretations of the United States Constitution. Many Americans believe that the right to abortion is not implied in the constitutional provision of a person's right to privacy; instead, the Constitution intends to promote lawful activity in private rather than unrestricted behavior. Any instance of illegal behavior such as the taking of human life *is unrelated to* or *conflicts with* a citizen's right to privacy. Therefore judging between differences and incompatibilities of interpretations rests on identifying conflicting or unrelated meanings advanced as involved in the interpretation of a text. These component meanings are related to and supportive of larger interpretations of the whole text.

An interpretation stands or falls as a whole. As soon as the judge begins to pick and choose elements from several hypotheses, he simply introduces new, eclectic hypotheses, which in turn stand to fall as wholes. Belief in the possibilities of mere eclecticism is based on a failure to understand that every interpretation necessarily refers to a whole meaning.[4]

This does not mean that an inaccurate interpretation of the whole may not be brilliant in the interpretation of some particular implication in the text. Incompatible interpretations may share common interpretations of some implications. That shared interpretation of one implication does not make the interpretations compatible. Rather, each interpretation of a text's meaning must be judged in the interpretation of the whole text to which it is related.

However, many disregard the unity of a text's meanings to pursue interpretation eclectically. Eclecticism in interpretation is particularly common in biblical exegesis. In this approach one particular may be interpreted in terms of a theological hypothesis, another from a grammatical or historical hypothesis, while still another particular may be interpreted from a contextual hypothesis. The evaluation of an eclectic interpretation demands the weighing of each hypothesis and interpretation. In an eclectic interpretation, the task of validation does not admit to comparative weighing of the one interpretation of the meanings in the whole text.

And yet, the most reliable segment of the author's meaning on which to judge an interpretation is the literary whole of the full written text. Robert LaBreche writes, "As the quantity and diversity of any body of evidence grows, it becomes less likely that an erroneous interpretation can adequately explain it. Therefore, there are generally fewer possible interpretations of a whole context."[5] Since there is a greater body of evidence by which to test them, the interpretations of a whole text can be evaluated more reliably than interpretations of a single *crux interpretum* taken alone.

To illustrate this crucial distinction we will compare ten distinct interpretations of John 15:1–17, a passage that has abundantly yielded incompatible interpretations. Inasmuch as possible, the commentators' very words will be quoted. The type of meaning expressed in the subject and the complement— that is, the message—will be used to compare the interpretations of the passage as a whole.

C. K. Barrett: "Only in Christ can Christians live."[6] Barrett writes that John's "major interest is in the life of the church in the question of who are and who are not true disciples of Jesus."[7] Evidences of life mark the true and the false. There is no distinction between position and practice.

Rudolf Bultmann: "Faith and love form a unity; i.e., that the faith, of which it can be said, *kathos hagapasa humas* (even as I loved you) is authentic only when it leads to *agapan allalous* (loving one another)."[8] So existence of life and practice of life are identical.

Frederick Louis Godet: "He transports Himself in thought to the epoch when the earthly and purely internal reunion shall be consummated through His spiritual return. The glorified Christ has returned and lives in His own. They are united in Him, and, through him, among themselves. Under His impulse

---

[4] Ibid., 172.

[5] Robert LaBreche, "A Guideline for Recognizing Valid Interpretation of Scripture" (Unpublished research project, Dallas Theological Seminary, n.d.), 17.

[6] C. K. Barrett, *The Gospel According to John* (London: SPCK, 1955), 303.

[7] Ibid.

[8] Rudolf Bultmann, *The Gospel of John* (Philadelphia: Westminster, 1971), 529.

they work all together, like the members of one and the same body, in the Father's work. Such is the new position with a view to which He now gives them the necessary directions, warnings, and encouragement."[9]

In other words, union with Christ bears a duty that displays a demonstrable consequence. This consequence distinguishes between the apparent and the real.

Henry Alford: Vital union with Jesus rests on both the Father and the branches. "This verse [v. 6] is a most important testimony against supralapsarian error, showing that *falling from grace is possible,* and pointing out the steps of the fall."[10] The vital union can be severed by the disobedient branch.

F. B. Meyer: "Christ is the *Vine* in relation to His *believing ones* (the branches), whose organic connection with Him is the constant, fruitful, and most inward fellowship of life."[11]

John Calvin: "The heart of this comparison is that by nature we are barren and dry save insofar as we have been engrafted into Christ and draw a new and extraneous power from Him."[12] Providential grace distinguishes those rooted and those without root by their fruit.

Leon Morris: "Fruitfulness . . . is the result, not of human achievement but of abiding in Christ,"[13] ensured by the Father's pruning. The emphasis on fruitbearing sees pruning restored to ensure that this takes place.

C. H. Dodd: The mutual indwelling of the resurrected Christ in the disciple.[14]

Raymond E. Brown: "The basic meaning of the vine is quite clear. Just as Jesus is the source of living water and is the bread from heaven that gives life, so is he the life-giving vine."[15] The issue is to have life; "one must remain in Jesus as a branch remains on a vine in order to have life."[16]

Elliott Johnson: A fruitful union is the product of a continued working relationship in Christ.

These ten distinct interpretations can be grouped into three incompatible interpretations—that is, they understand the passage in conflicting senses.

a. An essential living union necessarily bears fruit under the Father's care. Fruit is presented as a test of the essential union with Christ, and fruitbearing as necessarily related meanings by definition. If you are united, you must bear fruit, by definition. (Interpretations 1, 2, 3, 5, 6, 8, and perhaps 9)

b. An essential living union is dependent on both the Father and the branch. This proposition has a distinct complement. No longer does fruit define the union. Instead fruitfulness is controlled by both the Father in judgment or the

---

[9] Frederick Louis Godet, *Commentary on the Gospel of John,* vol. 2 (1885; reprint, Grand Rapids: Zondervan, 1969), 292.

[10] Henry Alford, *The Greek New Testament,* vol. 1 (Chicago: Moody Press, 1958), 591.

[11] F. B. Meyer, *Expositions of John: Love to the Uttermost,* Commentary of the New Testament (London: Morgan & Scott, 1899), 240.

[12] John Calvin, *St. John, Part 2,* Calvin's New Testament Commentaries, vol. 5, trans. T. H. L. Parker (Grand Rapids: Eerdmans, 1961), 93.

[13] Leon Morris, *The Gospel According to John* (Grand Rapids: Eerdmans, 1971), 668.

[14] C. H. Dodd, *The Interpretation of the Fourth Gospel* (Cambridge: Cambridge University Press, 1953).

[15] Raymond E. Brown, *The Gospel According to John,* vol. 2 (Garden City, N.Y.: Doubleday, 1970), 672.

[16] Ibid.

branch in separating himself in disobedience. (Interpretations 4, perhaps 9)

c. A fruitful union is dependent on the Father's care and the branch's abiding. This proposition has a narrower subject, but shares the complement with the second view. It is incompatible because it is possible to have a fruitless but genuine union. (Interpretations 7 and 10)

In view of the ambiguity inherent in the figure of the vine and the branches, all these interpretations are *viable.* But they are not all compatible. The three groupings are incompatible, and thus the evidence needs to be weighed to determine the most probable interpretation. This brings us to Step 2.

STEP 2

The interpretations that are found to be viable are tested for probability.

As previously established, relevant or *admissible evidence* must define the type or class of meaning and increase our knowledge of that type of meaning. In our test case we will consider the evidence that focuses on the type of meaning interpreted in the subject and the complement. There are three disparate interpretations that in actuality involve combinations of two distinct subjects and two distinct predicates:

Subject: (1) a living union, or (2) a fruit-bearing union.

Complement: (1) depends necessarily on the Father's care, or (2) depends on the Father's care and the branch's abiding.

The procedure involves collecting the evidence defining and enriching our knowledge of the subject and the complement.

Subject

1. The occasion for the vine-branches discourse. A look at the reason for introducing the monologue provides some evidence for understanding the *union.*

a. Geographical occasions: Several commentators suggest that an environmental occasion caused the discussion to arise: vineyards on the way to Gethsemane, or the carved vine on the great doors of the temple, or a vine trained about the window of the guest-chamber. Alford regards all as fanciful.[17] These suggestions clearly appear to be without textual evidence and are inadequate reasons in themselves to account for the extended discourse that follows.

b. Situational occasions: Barrett regards the discourse (chaps. 15–17) to be an alternative "last discourse" to chapter 14 and suggests that it followed directly upon the narrative of the Last Supper. "Such a connection would confirm the view of symbolism which . . . is at least in part eucharistic."[18] Bultmann regards the discourse as a commentary of 13:34 and following, in the sense that it goes more deeply into the grounds of the command of love, already briefly defined by *kathos hagapasa humas* ("as I loved you").[19] However, both commentators fail to give evidence for the connection or for the intervening material in John 14.

C. H. Dodd presents a unified portrayal of discourses in view of the final supper (13:1–4). The discourses have a twofold intention:

First, to interpret the death and resurrection of Jesus as the eschatological event in the fullest sense, and in doing so to reinterpret the eschatological beliefs of the early church; and secondly, to set forth the nature of the new life into which

---

[17] Alford, *The Greek New Testament,* 1:590.
[18] Barrett, *The Gospel According to John,* 303.
[19] Bultmann, *The Gospel of John,* 529.

the disciples (and all Christians) are brought through Christ's death and resurrection.[20]

In a similar argument, Godet focuses on contextual and situational evidence.

Jesus had just promised to His own, in ch. xiv., the twofold reunion, heavenly and earthly, in which the separation should issue, the thought of which was now so greatly troubling them. In ch. xv, He transports Himself in thought to the epoch when the earthly and purely internal reunion shall be consummated through His spiritual return. The glorified Christ has returned and lives in His own.[21]

The discussion of the vine flows naturally from the issues already raised in the context. The choice of the "vine and branches" image needs no other occasion than that it aptly communicates the issues needing to be examined, as Dodd and Godet suggest. Still, there appears to be an implicit contrast between the image in reference to Israel's role in the Old Testament and the image in reference to Christ's new role. Although the occasion does not eliminate a discussion of the living union of a departed Christ (which he had already discussed in numerous ways: birth, bread, water, etc.), it favors a discussion about the new aspect in the functioning of this union in view of Jesus' impending departure and extended absence. The natural question raised by his announcement of his departure focuses on what will the disciples do in order to continue to grow in Jesus' life. This narrower and more immediately appropriate subject is introduced on this occasion to spur the fruitfulness of Jesus' union with His disciples. He replaces the nation as the source of life, and his disciples are the godly remnant.

2. *Features of the image of the vine and branches.* The central concern in consideration of the subject involves the features of the *union* addressed by the image. Three questions seem to be at issue:

a. *What is the point of the vine symbolism?* Brown recognizes three perspectives within which the vine symbolism is interpreted: Gnostic and Mandean sources, Old Testament and Jewish writings, or Oriental myth of the tree of life. He approves of Borig's work: "He finds the Old Testament and Jewish background for the Johannine symbolism far more plausible than any of the others."[22] The Old Testament prophets and hymnists commonly symbolize Israel as God's vine planted in the land (Ps. 80:8ff.; Isa. 5:1–7; 27:2–6; 14:8; Jer. 6:9 and 5:10; 12:10–11; Ezek. 15:1–6; 17:5–10; 19:10–14; Hos. 10:1). The Lord adopted the symbolism in the gospel literature (Mark 12:1–11 and parallels citing Isa. 5:1–7; Matt. 20:1–16; 21:28–32; Luke 13:6–9).

The value of the vine is commonly seen in its *fruitfulness* (Ps. 80:12; Isa. 5:3, 5, 7: fruit is justice, righteousness; 27:6; Hos. 10:1; Ezek. 17:8; 19:10). It is not the value of its wood (Ezek. 15:1–6). No value is placed on its providing shade or rest under its branches. Its beauty is found in its production.

Judgment comes in stripping away branches (Jer. 5:10) because she violated her terms of relationship (5:1–9).

In John, "the vine . . . ceases to represent Israel and becomes a Christological definition applied to Jesus Himself. . . . Jesus is all that the vine truly symbolizes."[23] The true vine is "not only, 'the vine by which prophecy is fulfilled:' not only, 'the vine in which the organism and qualities of the vine

---

[20] Dodd, *The Interpretation of the Fourth Gospel,* 399.
[21] Godet, *Commentary on the Gospel of John,* 2:292.
[22] Brown, *The Gospel According to John,* 2:669.
[23] Barrett, *The Gospel According to John,* 303.

are most nobly realized,' but, as in ch. 1:9, the true, i.e., the original or archetypal.''[24] It is interesting that Brown acknowledges the prophetic origin of the figure, but then puzzles over a changed sense in John's usage. An ''objection to attempts to find an Old Testament background for the Johannine vine and branches is that none of the Old Testament vine passages stress the vine as the source of life for the branches, the point that is capital in John.''[25]

While it is possible for Jesus to alter the point in the symbolism, he adopted the image with other elements parallel (Father is husbandman, concern for fruit, vine growing on earth). In addition, Jesus does not give a clue to his altering the symbolism he adopts. He merely identifies himself as the genuine vine. It implies that the vine of the Old Testament had proven to be unfruitful and thus judged (Mark 12:1–11). The central point in the symbol remains ''fruitfulness,'' but the change in the symbol introduces a new source of fruitfulness. Jesus fulfills all that Israel was promised to be. Israel was to look to YHWH as its source of life, and so does Jesus, who has such an identity with YHWH that he is also the source of life.

b. *Who are the branches?* The parable itself identifies the original branches with the eleven disciples: ''you are the branches'' (15:4). ''There is a mutual indwelling of the Father, Son, and disciple. The historical foundation of this relation is in the call of Christ (*exelexoman,* v. 16), and its outcome is the mutual love of Christians for one another (v. 13).''[26] So when

discussing the unfruitful branches, Calvin writes:

> It may be asked whether anyone engrafted in Christ can be fruitless. I reply that *many are reckoned by men's opinions* to be in the vine who in fact have no root in the vine. Thus, in the prophets the Lord calls the *people of Israel His vine* because by outward profession they had the name of the church.[27]

Calvin reasons on the basis that branches are represented by mere profession, supported on the basis that Israel's national profession is analogous to individuals professing relationship. Godet offers a related option:

> He is thinking of the future of His Church; He *sees beforehand those professors of the gospel,* who, while being outwardly united to Him, will nevertheless live inwardly separated from Him, whether in consequence of a decree which will prevent them from being truly converted, or as the effect of their neglecting the sacrifice even to the uttermost their own life, and to renew daily their union with Him.[28]

Godet sees the sense of ''you'' in reference to the eleven to mean only outward union, in which class there will be future ones who, unlike the eleven, have no inward union. Meyer offers another option when he says that unfruitful branches refer to the ''*lip-Christians* and those who say Lord! Lord!''[29]

The distinction in these interpretations between the elect branches and the nonelect branches depends on the interpretation of the symbolism used in the description of the unfruitful branches. The images of ''breaking from the vine'' (15:2) or ''nonabiding'' (v. 6) introduce traits of meaning that

---

[24] Alford, *The Greek New Testament,* 1:590.
[25] Brown, *The Gospel According to John,* 2:671.
[26] Barrett, *The Gospel According to John,* 304.
[27] Calvin, *St. John, Part 2,* 94.
[28] Godet, *Commentary on the Gospel of John,* 2:294.
[29] Meyer, *Expositions of John,* 240.

these interpreters judge incompatible with traits common to the class of the elect. Each chooses a class of meaning that will both include the branch in one sense and exclude it in another as incompatible because of departure.

Calvin chooses the prophetic reference to the class of national Israel as the vine, which included unfruitful branches (Jer. 5:10) that are stripped away. The Old Testament figure also included branches bearing worthless fruit (Isa. 5:2, 4) that are subject to judgment. Subsequent revelation (Rom. 9:6) also made it clear that not all Israel (national) are true Israel (spiritual). This makes a clear distinction between national election and individual election that Calvin does not make. Godet distinguishes between those who profess belief and those who profess and do believe the class of outward display, from which false teachers are excluded (Matt. 7:15–23). In each case, however, the class of meanings is defined outside the context of John 15 and therefore has questionable application to that chapter. Is this the type of meaning to which Jesus refers? There is no textual evidence to indicate that Jesus intended to portray professors or claimants as branches.

c. *What is the extent of the union?* In the natural figure, a living union is broader than a fruitful union. Although every fruitful branch is living, not every living branch is fruitful. There are seasons of the year when branches are not fruitful. Diseased branches may be alive but unfruitful. But a dead branch is not fruitful.

Yet the text of the discourse specifies the union more carefully than simply equating the vine-branch and the Lord-disciple. "The relation of Jesus and his disciples keeps breaking through the figurative language; and indeed some language is more appropriate to this relationship than it is to viticulture."[30] Branches have no choice in abiding. "The branch cannot sever itself from the vine."[31] This choice of union, however, is consistently related to fruitbearing (15:4–6). Such a choice is absolutely essential to bearing fruit, for "apart from me you can do nothing" (v. 5). There is a logical and necessary choice of relationship here. Every fruitbearing branch abides, and every abiding branch bears fruit. Thus the subject is narrowed to refer to fruitbearing unions.

Interpreters who attempt to establish a living union do so consistently by adopting a broader context. "The vine is a tree of life. Just as one can speak of *hudor zon* and of *artos* and *phos tas zoas,* so one can speak of *ha ampegos tas zoas.*"[32] Bultmann even concedes that the issue in John 15 is not the same issue of the choice to receive the life: "The discourse raises the question of decision only indirectly, because it is delivered to the circle of those who have already decided."[33] Other attempts to establish a living union from the connection to the Eucharist are unnatural. Brown concedes, "The image of eating the fruit of the vine is different from that of John, but the vine is presented as giving life."[34] But the life is given in the narrowed category of fruitbearing (vv. 4–6).

Thus again, the conclusion follows that the interpretation of a living union is not established although appeal is made to broader classes of meaning drawn from the broader context. As

---

[30] Brown, *The Gospel According to John,* 2:668.
[31] Alford, *The Greek New Testament,* 1:591.
[32] Bultmann, *The Gospel of John,* 530.
[33] Ibid., 531.
[34] Brown, *The Gospel According to John,* 2:671–72.

Leon Morris concludes, "The allegory of the vine brings before us the importance of fruitfulness in the Christian life and the truth that this is the result, not the human achievement, but of abiding in Christ."[35] This is the clear contextual type of meaning. So the subject of John 15:1–17 is not (1) a living union, but rather (2) a fruitbearing union.

Complement

The two distinct predicates stated earlier for the subject (union) are that it (1) depends necessarily on the Father's care, and (2) depends on the Father's care and the branch's abiding. The essential difference between these complements involves the relationship between the Father's care and the branch's abiding. The first complement affirms that the relationship between life and fruitbearing is necessary and dependent on the Father alone and thus fruit defines life. Calvin argues that blessing arises solely from the Father as expressed in his conception of "special grace":

Almost everyone is ashamed to deny that all the good he has comes from God. But then they imagine that a universal grace has been given them, as if it had been implanted in them naturally. But Christ insists chiefly on this, that the vital sap flows from Himself alone. It follows that man's nature of the vine is unfruitful and destitute of all good. For no man has the nature of the vine until he is implanted in Him. But this is given by special grace to the elect alone. So the Father is the first Author of all blessings, patting us with His hand. But the beginning of life is in Christ, in that we begin to take root in Him.[36]

But how does Calvin interpret the specific commands in this passage in view of special grace? What is the role of the branches' abiding? Calvin comments,

He again *exhorts them* to be diligent and careful in keeping the grace with which they were endowed. For *the security of the flesh* can never be stirred up enough. And indeed, Christ's only purpose is to keep us as a hen keeps her chicks under her wings, *lest we should be carried away by our carelessness and fly to our destruction.* Therefore, *to prove that He did not begin the work of our salvation only to interrupt it in mid-course,* He promises that His Spirit *will always be efficacious* in us *so long as we do not prevent Him.* "Abide in me, for I am prepared to abide in you," He says. And again, "He that abideth in me, the same beareth much fruit." With these words He declares that all who have a living root in Him are fruitful branches.[37]

Thus efficacious grace is the only factor on which fruitfulness depends. But it is an efficacious grace that excludes the means of the abiding branch. While he writes of the "believer preventing" the effects of grace, he describes unfruitful branches as unbelieving branches. "But it may be asked whether anyone engrafted in Christ can be fruitless. I reply that many are reckoned by men's opinions to be in the vine who in fact have not root in the vine."[38] So whatever the branch prevents, it is never complete. Fruit will necessarily appear because of the Father's care. As part of that care are warnings to take away the unfruitful: "Christ is arousing anxiety."[39] "For the security of the flesh can never be stirred up enough."[40] "He again draws attention to the punishment of ingratitude and so arouses and stimu-

---

[35] Morris, *The Gospel According to John*, 668.
[36] Calvin, *St. John, Part 2*, 94.
[37] Ibid., 95.
[38] Ibid., 94.
[39] Ibid.
[40] Ibid., 95.

lates them to perseverance. This last is indeed a gift from God, but the exhortation to fear is not unnecessary, for our rioting flesh can uproot us."[41] In Calvin's exposition, fruit is the necessary product of the Father's care, but abiding is necessary to prevent the flesh from rioting.

The question that arises is whether this does justice to the textual statements on "abiding" (KJV). Do the statements "abide in me . . . except ye abide in me," "he that abideth in me," "if a man abide not in me" (15:4–6) imply more than "preventing rioting"? Is there no positive initiative of "staying or remaining close" and "my words abide in you, ye shall ask what ye will" (v. 7)? Does not abiding involve all—scriptural meditation, prayer, dealing with sin, and obedience?

For this reason, the second complement affirms that the union depends on the Father and the branches. While the union depends on both the Father and the branches, even the metaphor makes it clear that this dependency is not equal or identical.

Alford combines the first subject with the second complement. For him, the message affirms that the living union depends on the Father's care and the branch's abiding. Then, in commenting on the removal of nonabiding and thus unfruitful branches, he writes:

This verse is a most important testimony against supra-lapsarian error, showing us that *falling from grace is possible,* and pointing out the steps of the fall. Observe this is *not said of the unfruitful branch,* which the Father *takes away* (in judgment): But of one *who will not abide* in Christ, becomes separated from Him.[42]

Thus Alford argues that within the scope of the believer's responsibility is the possibility to "fall from grace" and to lose one's union in life with God. However, based on the analogy of faith this contradicts the teaching of John's gospel on the security of the believer and the formulated doctrine of predestination. In John's gospel, the unqualified promise of the gift of eternal life implies that eternal life is an unconditional and thus permanent possession (1:11–12; 3:17; 4:14; 6:35; 7:37–39; 8:12). In addition, it conflicts with Jesus' own earlier teaching that the Father and the Son alone are responsible for the permanence of the living union and relationship: "I give them eternal life, and they shall never perish; no one can snatch them out of my hand [not even the branch]. My Father, who has given them to me, is greater than all; no one can snatch them out of my Father's hand" (John 10:28–30).

In a broader perspective, "falling from grace" violates the theological doctrine of predestination. "It received its first full and positive exposition at the hand of Augustine, who made divine grace the only ground of man's salvation . . . identifying predestination with God's broad providential control over all things."[43] Such gracious providential control conflicts with any concept of falling from grace.

The third option—combining the second subject with the second complement—avoids these difficulties with the contextual and theological data. It is that a fruitful union depends on the Father's care and the branch's abiding. The responsibility for abiding acknowledges the positive force of the commands. However as the discourse makes clear, abiding in no way earns or merits fruit or causes fruit to appear in a sufficient sense. Abiding is a necessary

---

[41] Ibid.

[42] Alford, *The Greek New Testament,* 1:591–92.

[43] Loraine Boettner, "Predestination," in *Baker's Dictionary of Theology* (Grand Rapids: Baker, 1960), 415.

response, but the necessity is not adequate in itself. The vine is the source and sufficient cause of fruitfulness.

In addition, the responsibility to abide is in no sense diminished by the providential role of the Father in fruitbearing. This fact was recognized in the balance stated in the Westminster Confession of Faith:

> God from all eternity did, by the most wise and holy counsel of his own will, freely and unchangeably ordain whatsoever comes to pass: yet so, as thereby neither is God the author of sin, nor is violence offered to the will of the creatures, nor is *the liberty or contingency of second causes taken away,* but rather established.[44]

Within this broad theological role of providence, the Father uses the choice to abide and the teaching of Christ to accomplish his purposes. Within those purposes, the branch is responsible to abide and so holds a responsibility for the Father's necessary pruning and removal of fruitless branches. The removal of the branch is a temporal judgment upon the nonabiding believer, who no longer shares a fruitful union.

Having determined that at least ten viable interpretations exist for John 15:1–17, and then having determined which one is the most probable interpretation, we are left with the task of specifying the level of certainty (the probability) that can be attached to this conclusion.

STEP 3

The weight of the evidence for viable interpretations determines the level of certainty.

Three incompatible interpretations of the message have been considered. They are in conflict with one another in the understanding of portions of the

passage. Even where the wording of the complement is identical, the sense is different because the subject and the knowledge of the class of meanings are different. The messages:

(1) A living union depends on the Father's care to bear fruit.

(2) A living union depends on the Father's care and the branch's abiding.

(3) A fruitbearing union depends on the Father's care and the branch's abiding.

We will weigh these data according to the three principles of probability.

1. Defining the message. The weight of textual data is strongest in support of the narrow message and the weight of the contextual data is stronger than any other source of data in defining the message.

a. Consideration of the subject "union." The subject concerns the union between the disciple on earth and the ascended Lord. The question concerns whether the textual data support with greater weight a living or a fruitful union. Clearly the vine is introduced as the "source of life" that fits equally either living or fruitful union. A life-giving source is necessary to both life in the branch and fruitbearing through the branch.

Fruit or fruitbearing is mentioned eight times in context. As a factor in defining the union, fruit is a more weighty evidence for the narrower fruitful union than for the broader living union. Fruit is an associated and occasional trait of life, but a necessary and diagnostic trait of fruitbearing. Thus the subject of a fruitbearing union is best supported by these two considerations in the textual data.

b. Consideration of the complement "depend on." The narrowest comple-

---

[44] Ibid., 416 (emphasis mine).

ment is "depends on the Father's care" to bear fruit. The other statement adds "the branches abiding." In its narrowness, however, the first complement does not easily include some of the textual data: "abide in me" (15:4, KJV), "he that abideth in me" (v. 5), "if a man abide not in me" (v. 6), "if ye abide in me" (v. 7). All these references to human response go beyond a negative sense of preventing fruit. Does the sense of "being diligent and careful in keeping the grace with which they were endowed" (Calvin) share in the sense and force of "abiding," or are those statements of text better accounted for in "the branches abiding?" The responsibility in the type meaning "abide" better accounts for the branches' activity of "my words abide in you" and "ye shall ask what ye will" (15:7).

To establish the narrower type, extra textual ideas of "irresistible grace" are introduced to explain fruitbearing. Thus in the complement the weight of the textual data supports the broader type of meaning, since the narrower type of meaning needs extra textual data to expand the narrower statement to include all the text's data.

2. Broadening our knowledge of the class of meaning. The weight of primarily extra textual data is introduced to support the conceptions drawn from the text. This example will be limited simply to illustrate the process.

a. Image of the vine. As the earlier discussion made clear, the image of the vine is clarified in the Old Testament, and the point of the image is consistently the fruitfulness or product of the vine. Israel is in no sense the source of life; she is a vine to bear fruit for her owner, YHWH.

b. Responsibility of the farmer and the branch. The development of the allegory clarifies only to a limited extent in specifying a branch's responsibility. In reality branches do not have responsibility for choices. The farmer prunes, the branch abides. It is dangerous to seek further information by extending the analogy by inferences beyond the expressed statements of Christ.

Therefore any further clarification of the type of mutual responsibility is normally discussed in the theological discussions of this class of meanings based on the analogy of faith. At the risk of oversimplification, we suggest that three different theological contexts have been construed:

(1) A strict Calvinistic position posits total and exclusive responsibility with God as a defining component of sovereignty. That total responsibility operates in irresistible grace in the lives of the elect to bring them to faith and bear fruit. Human responsibility does not rest in a realm of choice but on the fact that a holy God holds the person righteously responsible.

(2) A moderated Calvinistic position posits full creational and providential responsibility in the sovereign God. God's creation of man in his image means that a shared personal responsibility is exercised positively in the efficacious grace of God, in which the branch responds as God enables and in which the branch bears fruit as God expresses life. Human responsibility ultimately rests in the received realm of choice as a creature under God's creation. That shared responsibility is exercised negatively within the permissive will of God. Such a realm of creaturely choice does not limit God's sovereignty, but instead facilitates it.

(3) An Arminian position posits that a sovereign God distinguishes responsibility between God and his creatures. In prevenient grace, fallen creatures are enabled to choose, and the choice of life and fruit rests with the creature. Thus a believer can choose not to believe and thereby lose his life. Such a distinction in responsibility properly circumscribes God's sovereignty.

3. Identifying the unknown. In identifying the unknown, we attempt to clarify where additional study will contribute to increased certainty.

a. Mystery in the relationship between the farmer and the branch remains in each position.

(1) The strict Calvinistic position is logically consistent from the standpoint of total sovereignty. The unknown involves the moral responsibility and accountability of a creature. As a consequence, this alters the perceived sense of the commands in that they lose their positive force in the irresistibility of sovereign grace. For the force of the command is present as a warning lest the irresistible grace be rejected. The bottom line in this position is the right of a sovereign God with his creation extended through the logic of noncontradiction. However, this view appears to threaten the existence of human freedom.

(2) In the moderate Calvinistic position, the mystery resides in a full responsibility of God and the shared responsibility with creatures. The independence between God and man, who are related in creation, is obviously a mystery. It bears the same character of mystery of which G. K. Chesterton wrote:

The real trouble with this world of ours is not that it is an unreasonable world, nor even that it is a reasonable one. The commonest kind of trouble is that it is nearly reasonable, but not quite. Life is not an illogicality; yet it is a trap for logicians.[45] It looks just a little more mathematical and regular than it is; its exactitude is obvious, but its inexactitude is hidden; its wildness lies in wait. . . .

Everywhere in things there is this element of the quiet and incalculable. It escapes the rationalists, but it never escapes till the last moment.[46]

So it is with the interdependence of a morally sovereign God and a morally responsible man. It would seem—if God is sovereign, without any limit, and morally rules man's life in righteousness—that man is devoid of moral responsibility. Yet the text presents the branch with moral responsibility and accountability. The textual statement rather than the law of noncontradiction must be the bottom line in the interpretation of the particulars in the Bible, with the limits of knowledge resting in the limits of revelation.

(3) In the Arminian position, the mystery resides in the divided realm of divine responsibility. If God is sovereign, how can he divide his responsibility with his creatures and remain sovereign? The divided realm of moral responsibility involves decisions made by God and man—decisions of the same kind and influence. The bottom line is the right of human moral freedom and choice. But with this construction, serious questions are raised about the meaning of God's sovereignty.

So the choice of an interpretive option does not eliminate mystery. At issue is the choice of a bottom line on which the unknown rests. Is that bottom line the logical axiom of noncontradiction (options 1 and 3 starting from different points of view) or the clear direct statements of Scripture that are not contradictory but admit to mystery in their harmonization (option 2).

b. Unknown meanings rest also on

---

[45] Merrill C. Tenney, "The Gospel of John," in *Expositor's Bible Commentary,* ed. Frank E. Gaebelein, vol. 9 (Grand Rapids: Zondervan, 1981), 152. In view of this contextual and theological consistency, it seems unnecessary for Tenney to postulate concerning the branch removed from the vine: "possibly it could be a reference to Judas Iscariot." Judas Iscariot was never cleansed (John 13:10–11). Judas had left the group of disciples before Jesus told the discourse (13:30 and 15:1).

[46] G. K. Chesterton, *Orthodoxy* (Garden City, N.Y.: Image Books, 1959), 81.

the imprecision of the allegory. The nature of judgment—"he cuts off" (15:2), "such branches are picked up, thrown into the fire and burned" (v. 6)—and the distinction between the nonfruitful (v. 2) and the nonabiding (v. 6) are left vague. Again, the clarification of these unknowns awaits either specification in better understanding of the literary genre or further specification of the theology dealing with the same kinds of meaning.

The Nature of the Moral Interpretive Judgment

In legal judgments, there are two broad categories of the weight of evidence, as we saw earlier: (1) the preponderance of contextual evidence, and (2) the lack of "reasonable doubt." In our case study from John 15:1–17, the preponderance of contextual evidence favors the "fruitful union" message; the presence of mystery in the subject matter of the revelation limits biblical interpretation from a moral certainty beyond reasonable doubt.

A moral certainty beyond reasonable doubt must rest on a shared epistemological base. Is the epistemological base found in "thus says the Lord" or in the law of noncontradiction? Does the law of noncontradiction or reasonable thought serve to reason consistently beyond the statement to logical conclusions? Or, does the law of noncontradiction serve reasonable thought within the statements of revelation?

Two issues are at stake: the presupposition of an epistemological base, and the moral judgment based on the weight of evidence. The literal tradition consistently takes its stand on a biblical base; the statements of Scripture stand firm in spite of the presence of mystery. On this epistemological base, the literal tradition recognizes the valid application of the law of noncontradiction within the statements of Scripture. The nature of valid interpretation then rests within the parameters of the evidence marshaled for support of a given interpretive construction.

The task of validation uses many teachers reasoning in favor of an interpretive message. It will involve the history of interpretation as recorded in the commentary tradition; no single interpreter will accomplish the task. But a climate of vigorous discussion provides a healthy environment for believers to reach moral certainty. Although the task of validation is largely one for scholars to weigh, the product is needed by all believers.

CONCLUSION

In this chapter on the principle of validation, we have arrived at the heart of literal hermeneutics, for that principle focuses attention on the very nature of hermeneutics.

The Literal Hermeneutic

1. A literal hermeneutic is not primarily a method, although it does involve methodicalness. No group of principles applied according to some method will automatically bring understanding. Yet certain issues have appeared and reappeared that imply a methodicalness in the task of interpretation. As these issues are enumerated, the interpreter acquires a methodological self-consciousness to clarify the various viable interpretations. This self-consciousness gives direction in the midst of the various pressing issues of immediate textual questions.

In *Truth and Method,* Hans-Georg Gadamer has provided a pointed critique of our generation's preoccupation with method. Method is the tool and agent of a basic philosophical worldview of the interpreter; it is useful as a servant, but should never be elevated to the prominence of an ultimate master.

2. *A literal hermeneutic involves a philosophy of textual interpretation.* It has been commonly associated with a biblical worldview in which the biblical text is the basis of the meaning. It assumes that the interpreter can and must step out of his modern preunderstandings and begin to share the preunderstandings of the biblical world in order to discover the face value of the meaning.

This biblical world is not to be regarded as ancient in the sense of being outmoded, but rather in being old. The message as expressed is primarily a message of theological content, and it is addressed to an audience in terms of their relationship to God. This message is expressed and must be comprehended in the ministry of grace in the Holy Spirit, but the meanings generated through the Holy Spirit are not directly detectable through feeling, nor are they validated because one seeks the Holy Spirit. Instead, the truth taught by the Holy Spirit corresponds to the textual meanings expressed by the same Spirit through the human authors of Scripture. Therefore in its essence a literal hermeneutic is a strategy of validation of the meanings understood as taught by the Spirit, with the meaning expressed by the Spirit in the textual expressions directly.

3. *A literal hermeneutic is primarily a norm for judging the validity of a proposed interpretation.* But it is a norm of validation that seeks to make a judgment based on a general norm; the "literal sense" or "normal or simple sense" has been demonstrated in practice to be probably accurate. It represents a probability judgment reached on the basis of issues and factors taken in general.

One weakness of such a general norm is that it has greater probable validity with some genres of literature than with others. Thus it has been common to encourage more careful research to enhance our knowledge of a literary genre and thus increase our ability to apply the general norm of literal interpretation. The presence of a figurative sense in hymnic or prophetic literature, for example, is far more frequent than it is in legal or epistolary literature. This sensitivity to the individual application of validation judgments is certainly an important advance.

However, the basis of this textbook is the contention that any general norm of validation is impossible to establish its relevance in any specific case of interpretation. So the interpreter must settle for the general norm as probably relating to a specific interpretation. As the task of interpretation proceeds, that probable meaning is then treated as the actual meaning in the consideration of other unknown interpretations. The product of interpretation, therefore, is more than a house of cards in which the validity of subsequent interpretations rests on probability judgments whose probable accuracy is not considered.

The text contends that the probable accuracy of a textual construct must weigh the influence of its relation to the probable accuracy of the text as a whole. In this strategy, viability in interpretation is reached in the application of general norms. But it is reached in the probable accuracy of a particular interpretation based on the weight of evidence supporting the interpretation. Such a validation is intrinsic to that text in the context of that book.

Validation

1. *The task of intrinsic validation* may be summarized as involving two central issues:

a. *Distinguishing viable and incompatible interpretations.*

b. *Weighing the evidence in support of each incompatible interpretation.* The interpretation is compared in the statement of the message. There are three principles in the testing process:

(1) The better the interpreter knows the subject and complement based on the weight of internal textual evidence, the higher the probability that he knows the book.

(2) The better the interpreter knows the class of books or motifs with the same literary genre or the class of subjects (theology) based on the weight of textual and extratextual evidence, the higher the probability that he knows the book.

(3) The better the interpreter can identify what remains unknown, based on the data at hand, the higher the probability that he knows the book.

2. The process of intrinsic validation may be summarized in two stages:

a. Validation of various incompatible interpretations within the history of doctrinal tradition. The initial step in validation considers the history of the interpretations of the *crux interpretum.* These interpretations must be grouped into categories of viable but incompatible interpretations. Such incompatibility involves either conflicting or unrelated diagnostic traits of the type of meaning of the whole textual unit. These incompatible interpretations will in turn often generate conflicting or unrelated implications in the construct, and they cannot all be true. Some judgment of validation is needed to judge between them.

An initial aspect of this validation is to relate each interpretation to the doctrinal tradition of the interpreter. Each interpreter brings doctrinal preunderstandings to the study and interpretation of the biblical text. The relation of each interpretation of textual meaning must first be compared with the doctrinal tradition of the interpreter. Confirmation by a doctrinal tradition does not prove that an interpretation is true, but it does add the support of that tradition.

Departure from a doctrinal tradition raises caution and even skepticism toward adopting that interpretation. Yet the foundation, the bottom line, remains that textual meanings must control the conscience of the evangelical interpreter in his relation to God and to the revealed truth of the Scripture. So an ultimate stage of validation must follow in which a textual validation is considered within the commentary tradition.

b. Validation of various incompatible interpretation within a commentary tradition. The validation of a commentary interpretation involves both the claim to know and the weight of evidence used to support the claim to know the book or interpretation of the passage.

(1) The claim to know involves at least two distinct strategies:

(a¹) I know because I know the diagnostic meanings as expressed in the text;

(b¹) I know because I know other books of the same kind of literature or because I know what the tradition has said about the same subject (doctrinal teaching).

Since the claim to know what defines the meaning of the book cannot be denied by a claim to know other books, it follows that the task of validation must focus on the claim of what defines the meaning of the book. Yet a claim to know other books that are compatible in meaning might well support our claim to know a book, or it may hinder our claim to know. So the second claim must be considered to prevent a provincial or naïve consideration of the meaning of one book alone.

In addition, our claim to know a book or passage interpretation is specified and clarified by identifying the limits of our knowledge. Knowing this limit of knowledge does not strengthen our claim to know, but it does contribute to related issues in the discussion of the interpretation of the book or passage.

(2) The weight of evidence in support of an interpretation involves validating the claim to know from—

(a[1]) Textual evidence, which may have a role in defining the meaning of the book or passage;

(b[1]) Extratextual evidence, which may have a role in supporting or challenging the claim to know, although it can never define textual meanings.

Two kinds of support may be claimed from textual evidence. *Independent* evidence is claimed in the unique support of only one interpretation. The weight of such independent evidence is difficult to compare unless it falls decidedly in favor of one interpretation over the others. *Shared evidence* is claimed in support of more than one interpretation. The weight of such evidence falls in favor of the narrower construction of the diagnostic trait of the type of meaning. Extratextual evidence may not be weighed in support of diagnostic traits of the textual meaning.

Extratextual evidence may include sources that are related to the textual meaning. The first consideration is whether these other sources do in fact correspond with the textual meanings. Does the subject or literary structure of the other source correspond to the textual subject or literary structure? The second consideration is the weight of the evidence.

Judgment of Certainty

The total process of validation aims toward arriving at a judgment of certainty. Several general conclusions about certainty follow from the task of validation:

1. Without the support of doctrinal certainty, an interpreter would be wise to suspend judgment on the interpretation of a given passage.

2. With the support of doctrinal harmony, an interpreter must weigh the evidence in support of incompatible claims, to judge whether the weight is sufficient to remove reasonable doubt. If the evidence is sufficient, then the interpretation has moral certainty. Otherwise, one may have to settle for a practical certainty.

Glossary

Allegorical interpretation: Interpretation of a piece of literature as though it were an allegory in which the corresponding set of meanings are recognized.

Allegory: A narrative in which the people, things, and happenings refer to another set of meanings. It is a literary device in which one thing is described under the image of another.

Antonym: A word or expression that is opposite in meaning to another word or expression. (Sad/happy, tall/short, good/bad)

Archetype: An image, plot, motif, or character type that recurs throughout literature and whose meaning is readily if not universally understood.

Associated implication or trait: Any of the component meanings of a word, construction, or literary unit that are commonly present in the use of it, but which do not define the meaning as used.

Base meaning: The meaning of a word that is generally understood when the word is given with no context; also called the "central" or "unmarked" or even literal meaning.

Compatible interpretations: The relationship between two interpretations in which the diagnostic implications are seen to be different, but not contradictory in interpretation of the text or unrelated to the text.

Complement: A diagnostic implication of a type of meaning in a literary unit as a whole. The implication specifies the judgment or predication that the author makes about the subject as interpreted in the message of composition.

Component meaning: That submeaning of a whole, meaning, trait of the type of meaning, or implication of the intended meaning that is understood by analysis or exegesis. It may be a component meaning of a word, construction, or literary unit as a whole.

Connotation: An idea or implication suggested by or associated with the use of a word or construction in addition to the denotation. ("Liberal" can denote a number of things, but for conservatives in any field it usually has a negative connotation, and vice versa.)

Construction: An element in the textual composition with a distinct meaning such as a word, phrase, clause, sentence, or paragraph.

Context: The very complex and undifferentiated set of factors relevant to the understanding of the textual meaning. It begins with the parts of a sentence, paragraph, or discourse immediately next to or surrounding a specified unknown word or passage. It expands to include the entire physical, psychological, cultural, and historical milieu in which the utterance occurs. These factors will be treated as the type of a meaning of a textual unit.

Convention: A generally agreed-upon use and practice of social life in which customary usage or method of expression shares the meanings intended. It denotes a casual rather than natural or logical association between sign and meaning.

Crux interpretum: A passage whose meaning has remained unknown in the viewpoint of many interpreters.

Cultural context: The part of the context that includes the ideas, customs, skills, and arts of a given people in a given period in which the communication takes place; the specific consideration of nonlinguistic circumstances of the communication although language is one of the skills of a given people.

Deduction: The reasoning from a known principle to discern the contribution toward an understanding of an unknown but related textual component, from a premise to a logical and necessary conclusion about the textual meaning.

Defining implication or trait: Any of the components of meaning that are necessary to set the limits of meaning in a word or phrase of a language system in its base sense.

Denotation: The direct relation between words and constructions and persons, things, places, properties, processes, and activities external to the language.

Design: The group of diagnostic traits of textual composition that describe the boundaries of its meaning due to the means and manner of composition: the author's address of the audience, the structural features of composition, and the conventional use of language.

Different interpretations: The relationship between two interpretations in which there are distinct but compatible diagnostic implications. (A football is different from a soccer ball.)

Disparate interpretations: The relationship between two interpretations in which the diagnostic implications are either contradictory or unrelated in relation to the text so that the two interpretations are distinct and not both true.

Discourse: A piece of linguistic material displaying structural and semantic unity, coherence, and completeness and conveying a message; also called "text" or "textual unit."

Figurative (meaning, expression): Representing one concept in terms of another that may be thought of as analogous with it; the figure is not a synonym, but is expressed through an associated trait that becomes diagnostic. ("I am the Door.")

Focus: The center of attention in a discourse or a portion of a discourse.

Genre: A kind or type of literature with distinctive features, including rules or procedures, conventions and language usage, that influence the composition and expression of meaning.

Grammar: The part of the structure of language that deals with forms and structure of words (morphology), with their customary arrangement in phrases and sentences (syntax). This is usually distinguished from language sounds (phonology) and the study of meanings of constructions (semantics).

Hermeneutics: The science and art of textual interpretation toward the end of reaching validity in interpretation; as a science it develops and uses principles of viable interpretation, and as an art it develops a strategy for methodical study of the Bible in the use of the principles.

Historical context: The part of the context that includes the author, the original audience, the occasion for writing, and the people, places, and issues about which the author speaks.

Homonym: A word with the same pronunciation and/or spelling as another, but with an unrelated meaning.

Hyperbole: A figurative expression in which exaggeration is used for effect and is not meant to be taken in a direct, base sense.

Implication: The submeaning that is a component of the meaning considered as a whole, the trait that is related to the type of meaning, the component that is unfolded from the intended meaning; thus not distinguishing unstated or unsaid from stated or explicit component meanings.

Incompatible interpretations: The relationship between two interpretations in which the diagnostic implications are either contradictory or unrelated so that the two interpretations cannot both be true or in agreement.

Intend: To mean; with the added distinction between what is meant based on what is written in context from what could possibly be meant based on the language alone.

Inductive: The reasoning from particular facts or individual cases of meaning to discern the meaning of a unit as a whole.

Interpretation: The task of both understanding and relating (applying) a textual meaning communicated; in addition, the communication of that meaning in terms that a modern audience will comprehend.

Irony: A verbal method of humorous or subtly sarcastic expression in which the intended meaning of words is the direct opposite of their base or usual sense. *Dramatic irony* occurs when the reader knows more about what is happening than do some of the characters in the story; *irony of situation* occurs when the situation is the opposite of what might be expected or appropriate.

Language: A system of vocal sounds, words, and the ways of combining them that share meanings to a common speech community.

Linguistics: The science of language, including phonology, morphology, syntax, and semantics. General linguistics is usually subdivided into "descriptive," "historical," "comparative," and "geographical" linguistics.

Literal meaning: (1) The interpretation that bases the sense of the passage and the references to history on the actual textual clues; this interpretation allows for figures of speech textually recognized ("literal interpretation"); (2) the sense of the word as commonly or ordinarily meant, the base sense with a direct rather than figurative reference ("literal sense").

Literary criticism: The study and evaluation of imaginative writings describing the structure of different genres, considering themes, mood, tone, plot motifs, image patterns, vocabulary, conventions, etc.

Literary design: See *Design.*

Literary genre: See *Genre.*

Metaphor: A figure of speech containing an unstated comparison, in which a word or phrase ordinarily and primarily used to refer to one thing is applied to another, thereby communicating a new perspective in the new reference.

Morpheme: The smallest grammatical piece of language. Some words, especially particles, comprise only one morpheme. Others comprise several morphemes (un-shak-able). Morphemes are often classified as stems and affixes.

Personification: A figurative expression in which human attributes are attached to an animal, an object, an abstract quality or idea, or God.

Preunderstanding: The aspect of the task of interpretation that describes what the reader-interpreter brings to the task of interpretation; a shared knowledge of the language and of the ancient world, shared cultural values, and presuppositions, etc.

Polysemy: The condition of a word or construction having several or many meanings.

Polyvalent text: The designation of a textual unit as supporting two or more incompatible meanings.

Referential meaning: Any of the components of the textual meaning intending to direct attention to a person, thing, or event, a word or construction used to denote.

Satire: A literary work in which vices, follies, stupidities, abuses, etc., are exposed to ridicule and contempt.

Semantics: The branch of linguistic study concerned with contextual meaning, considering both the development and change in meanings, the comparison and contrast of the meaning of constructions.

Semantic field or domain: A definable area of cultural experience (1) covered by a set of related words, or (2) covered by one word with a range of different uses; the defining features of the field are represented by the diagnostic implications shared in common by the set of words, or the defining features of the field of one word are represented by the sum of the compatible implications.

Sense meaning: Any of the components of the textual meaning, considering only the textual signs and not considering a particular historical reference.

Sign: Any linguistic unit such as a word, letter, or construction that is held to signify or stand for people, places, ideas, or functions of language.

Simile: A figure of speech in which one is likened to a dissimilar thing by the use of "like" or "as." ("He is like a tree planted by streams of water.")

Subject: A diagnostic implication of a literary unit; it identifies what the author intends to speak about in the whole literary composition.

Supplementary implication or trait: A component of meaning that is necessary to that word or phrase in the language system without setting the limits of the meaning as a definition.

Synonym: A word having the same or nearly the same meaning in one or more senses as another word in the same language system. (Good = favorable/beneficial/proper/honest/worthy)

Symbol: Something that stands for or represents another thing; especially an object used to represent something abstract. A morpheme sign is a symbol within a language system that is more clearly limited in what it stands for.

Taxonomy: A set of meanings that reflects a system of classification of experience. The system is structured from the most general meaning to the subordinate, most particular meanings. In the set of meanings "biblical books," the most general is theological themes and the most particular is message.

Text: See *Discourse*.

Theological themes: The diagnostic implication of a book that identifies the shared content in each book of the canon: (1) what does the book say about God? (2) what does the book say about the purpose of God in what he says and does in history? (3) what does the book say about the administration of these purposes among the elect people of God?

Trait: That which distinguishes and defines a distinct type of meaning; the components of meaning that are necessary to diagnose the type as a whole or are necessarily associated with the presence of this type.

Type: The general structure, plan, style, and content characterizing and distinguishing the members of a class or kind of textual composition. The type of biblical textual meaning is characterized by three diagnostic traits: theological theme, literary design, and message.

Understand: That aspect of the task of interpretation of textual meaning in which one construes the type of meaning expressed in the text.

Valid interpretation: A well-grounded interpretation based on the consideration of hermeneutical principles and weighing of the text evidence in support of one's conclusions. As such it is able to withstand the criticism of other viable interpretations by demonstrating the probable weight of support of the evidence.

Viable interpretation: An interpretation that is workable in having support from the text. It is likely to have a real chance of being a valid interpretation.

Index of Persons

Subject Index

Scripture Index

Numbers in italics indicate places where a passage is analyzed in the text to some degree.